CENTURY
FAMILY
LEGAL GUIDE

by
JOSEPH W. MIERZWA, J.D.

ProSe Associates, Inc.
Highlands Ranch, Colorado

This book is designed to provide you with accurate information about the law so that you can deal more effectively with the legal situations that concern you. However, your own situation may be different from the ones described in this book. In addition, laws are subject to change and varying interpretations. As a result, this book is sold with the understanding that neither the author nor the publisher is engaged in rendering specific legal or other professional services to any individual.

Some of the material in this book appeared in different form in "Home Lawyer" (copyright 1991, OverDrive Systems, Inc.), and is used with permission.

Published by:
ProSe Associates, Inc.
P.O. Box 4333
Highlands Ranch, Colorado 80126

Printed in the USA

10 9 8 7 6 5 4 3 2 1

Library of Congress Catalog Card Number: 93-86934
ISBN: 0-9637285-0-4

INTRODUCTION

In earlier, simpler times, laws themselves were far simpler than they are today. As American society becomes more complex, the laws that govern our relationships with each other continue to become more complex as well. For most Americans, the law is a complicated and sometimes contradictory set of rules made by people in faraway places, and written in ways that make them nearly impossible to understand without a legal education.

In fact, while many laws are extremely difficult for even experienced lawyers and judges to interpret, the basic principles of most laws are relatively straightforward. In general, American laws are intended to provide order, to help protect our rights to life and property, and to keep any one group from becoming too powerful at the expense of another. While there's plenty of room for disagreement about how well our laws fulfill this intended purpose, most of us would agree that the rights we enjoy and the legal responsibilities we must bear are far preferable to those experienced in other parts of the world.

Unfortunately, some lawyers and legal scholars seem to enjoy making even the simplest of laws difficult to understand. These lawyers fill their writings and conversations with mysterious Latin and Old French terms, odd words left over from medieval English, and other "mumbo-jumbo." Some of these lawyers use this incomprehensible language simply because they spend most of their time talking to other lawyers who already "speak their language," and forget that people from other walks of life may not understand what they're saying. Others indulge in this "legalese" in order to cloak the law in a veil of mystery that only they can penetrate on your behalf (for a fee, of course).

And a big part of the problem is that few law schools spend much time teaching students how to communicate with their clients effectively.

The 21st Century Family Legal Guide was written to help explain not only what the law says, but also to help readers understand that the best tool in any kind of legal dispute is common sense. We believe that the best way to use the legal system is to be educated about what the law is, how the law works, and the methods for staying out of (or at least minimizing) conflict before it blossoms into an expensive and time consuming lawsuit.

While this book is not designed as a do-it-yourself guide, it has been written to help you keep legal fees to a minimum by giving you information you can use to ask the right questions when you do need a lawyer's help. It will even tell you how to find the right lawyer when you need one. And it will direct you to the some of the best do-it-yourself books and software that can help you handle legal tasks on your own if you decide to do so.

We've divided *The 21st Century Family Legal Guide* into eighteen chapters. Each chapter discusses a particular area of the law and the way it affects your everyday life. If you know the general area of the law you're interested in learning more about, turn to the appropriate chapter as listed in the Table of Contents. If you're not sure where to find the discussion of a particular subject, check the Index at the end of the book.

Obviously, it's impossible for any one book, no matter how comprehensive, to answer every question you may have about the law. Laws vary from state to state and from city to city, and new laws are being made by state legislatures and courts every day. Add the thousands of pages of federal laws and regulations that are enacted each year, and there's no way for anyone to know everything there is to know about the law. The information in *The 21st Century Family Legal Guide* is based on general principles of law and the law in the majority of states. But before you take any action based on the statements made in this book, be sure to check the law in your state, city or county, or the latest version of the federal law involved in your situation. Your county courthouse's law library is a valuable resource not just to lawyers but to the general public as well. If you live in or near your state capital, you can find even more resources available at your state Supreme Court library. If you live in or near a city where a law school is located, the law school library is also an excellent resource.

ProSe Associates, Inc. is the publisher of *The 21st Century Family Legal Guide*. Our company's goal is to provide up-to-date and useful information about topics of interest to businesses and consumers in plain English. We welcome your comments and suggestions for future editions of *The 21st Century Family Legal Guide*. You can write to us at:

ProSe Associates, Inc.
Department FLG
P.O. Box 433
Highlands Ranch, CO 80126

CONTENTS

The ProSe Letter

Because the law can change so rapidly in ways that affect your family, your home, your job, and your business, you need a way to keep abreast of the latest developments taking place in the courts and legislatures.

That's why you need a subscription to the *ProSe Letter.* Four times a year, the *ProSe Letter* brings you the latest news about the law and its impact on your life. You'll find out about the latest federal legislation, court decisions, and trends in state laws and regulations. Written in easy-to-understand language (but respectful of your intelligence), the *ProSe Letter* helps you make sense of the law. And that can save you time and money.

An annual subscription to the *ProSe Letter* is regularly $16. However, readers of *The 21st Century Family Legal Guide* can receive a full year of the *ProSe Letter* for only $12. Or if you prefer, you can obtain a sample copy for only $5, which we will credit toward a subscription.

To subscribe, or to receive your sample copy, send your check or money order (no cash, please) along with your name and address to:

The ProSe Letter
Dept 21-C
P.O. Box 4333
Highlands Ranch, Colorado 80126

The ProSe Letter comes with a 30-day money back guarantee. If for any reason you wish to cancel your subscription, simply let us know within 30 days, and we'll promptly refund your annual subscription fee.

CHAPTER ONE
YOUR RIGHTS AND FREEDOMS

In this chapter, we will look at the sources of your rights as a citizen or resident alien of the United States, and we will discuss some of the most cherished rights Americans possess, such as the right to free speech and religion, the right to bear arms, and the right to privacy.

None of the rights possessed by Americans is absolute. The need for order in society sometimes requires that the rights of the individual give way to the greater right to peace, health, and safety in the community. As a result, the rights Americans take for granted have been limited (some would say eroded) over the course of our nation's history. In some cases, your rights may even be restricted or suspended, and we'll look at those situations as well.

WHERE YOUR RIGHTS COME FROM

Essentially, the rights Americans enjoy are derived from four sources; the U. S. Constitution, state constitutions, federal laws, and state laws.

The first and most important source of your rights is the U.S. Constitution, which sets out the powers of the federal government. More specifically, the source of your individual rights is contained in the first ten amendments to the Constitution, referred to as the Bill of Rights.

The Bill of Rights was created and ratified at the same time as the Constitution, and was originally intended to limit the intrusiveness of the federal government into the lives of the people. It's important to remember that the United States came about as the result of a revolution against the tyranny of the British government. The last thing many of the revolutionaries who fought the British wanted to do was to substitute one all-powerful government with another.

While the Bill of Rights was created to protect Americans from federal tyranny, initially it had no effect on their relationships with the governments of the states in which they lived. That was a matter covered by the constitutions of the states themselves, which serve as the second source of Americans' rights. But while the terms of these constitutions were generally similar, they were not identical. As a result, some states extended greater protection to those who lived within their boundaries than were afforded to those who resided elsewhere.

It was only after the Civil War and the passage of the Thirteenth and Fourteenth Amendments to the U.S. Constitution that the protections contained in the Bill of Rights against federal government intrusion into the lives of Americans was extended to protect Americans from the intrusion of state governments as well.

The Fourteenth Amendment stated that "all persons born in or naturalized in the United States, and subject to the jurisdiction thereof, are citizens of the United States and of the State wherein they reside." As a result of this declaration, and the Amendment's other statements that all U.S. citizens are entitled to due process and the equal protection of the law, individuals were able to petition the federal government for assistance when the individual rights guaranteed by the Bill of Rights were violated by the government of the state in which they resided.

As a result of the Fourteenth Amendment, state constitutions cannot be more restrictive in the rights they grant than the U.S. Constitution. However, there is nothing that restricts the states from affording protections to their citizens that go beyond those guaranteed by the U.S. Constitution. So, for example, a state may not permit or authorize discrimination on the basis of religion in its state constitution, since this discrimination is prohibited by the federal Constitution. On the other hand, a state may enact a provision in its constitution extending protection to homosexuals, even though the U.S. Constitution does not prohibit discrimination on the basis of sexual orientation.

Over the years, court decisions have expanded the protections granted by the U.S. and state constitutions to protect not only American citizens, but anyone residing legally in the United States. And in recent years, some courts have interpreted the U.S. and state constitutions as protecting the rights of those aliens who are here without the government's permission.

A variety of federal and state statutes also grant rights to Americans. Two of the most important of these laws are the federal Civil Rights Acts of 1964 and 1968, which guaranteed equality to all people, regardless of race, color, religion, or national origin in the use of public accommodations such as restaurants and hotels, in housing, and granted equal opportunities in employment and education. The rights of women to equal employment and educational opportunities were granted by these acts, and others.

More recently, the Americans with Disabilities Act (ADA) granted added legal protection from discrimination to people who suffer from (or who are perceived to suffer from) disabilities. The list of disabilities covered by the ADA is lengthy, and the accommodations that employers, the government, and the owners of businesses and buildings must meet are extensive. Although the ADA requires "reasonable accommodation" that doesn't create an "undue hardship" on employers and business operators, the definition of these terms is vague at best, and will ultimately be defined through the multitude of lawsuits brought by the disabled in the attempt to enforce the rights granted to them under the ADA.

In fact, it may be appropriate to say that the rights guaranteed to Americans are only those rights granted to them by the courts in their interpretation of the constitutions and the laws that are their source. To a great extent, the language of the U.S. Constitution and the Bill of Rights was intentionally vague, so that its usefulness would outlive the time in which it was created. Since then, statutes enacted at both the federal and state level have also been subject to varying interpretations.

Once a court such as a state court of appeals or the U.S. Supreme Court has issued a decision, other courts will follow the "precedent" established in deciding later cases which have similar facts. In this way, the law achieves a measure of stability, and the public can have some sense of what outcome to expect in the future.

But while precedents are important and stabilizing, they are not eternal. So while a court decision that was reached many years ago may have influence on a court today, it may no longer be decisive. A good example of how precedents change over time concerns the decisions reached by the U.S. Supreme Court in the years before the Civil War. At an earlier time in our history, the Court ruled that slaves were not to be counted as people. If precedents such as this could never be overturned, blacks might still be prohibited from voting, holding public office, or attending public schools.

However, the movement from refusing to recognize the humanity of slaves to their full recognition as citizens of the United States did not occur overnight. It was through a series of decisions, each one modifying and building on the precedents before it, that brought us to the current state in which black Americans have the same rights as all other Americans.

Courts use a variety of techniques in order to resolve disputes about what a law says and what it may mean. Some judges give great deference to the "plain language" of the law. Others review the circumstances surrounding the enactment of the law and the records of the legislative hearings in trying to arrive at the law's meaning. As we examine the rights Americans consider most precious, we will see how the courts interpret these laws and the rights they grant in response to changing social pressures and their own views of how justice is best served.

YOUR RIGHT TO SPEAK AND PUBLISH

The First Amendment to the U.S. Constitution states that "Congress shall make no law . . . abridging the freedom of speech, or of the press . . ." Many state constitutions contain similar or even identical provisions.

While the language of the First Amendment seems pretty clear on its face, the limitations placed on speech and the press in this country are extensive. For example, you may not engage in speech that is defamatory, or which urges others to commit crimes. You may not urge a specific plan which would lead to the violent overthrow of the government, either when speaking or publishing. You may not publish materials which are obscene or lewd, although deciding what kinds of materials fall into this category is never an easy task.

If you work for the government, your right to speak and publish freely is also limited. If you have access to top secret or classified information, the government may prohibit you from revealing that information to others in order to protect the public safety.

If you are a teacher, you may not make statements that disrupt the operation of the school in which you work. For example, a teacher who taught his students that blacks were genetically inferior to whites could be prohibited from making such statements, or even fired if he refused to refrain from making them.

If you run a business or practice a profession, your right to speak freely is limited. While there's no law requiring individuals to tell the truth (unless they are under oath) businesses can't make false claims about the products they sell or the services they provide. Professionals, such as doctors, lawyers, and dentists may be restricted in the types of claims they make and the way in which they make them. For example, many states prohibit lawyers from using client testimonials or hiring actors to portray clients in their television advertisements.

Want to have your own radio or television station, where you will be free to broadcast your views about the world to the public? You'll have to be licensed by the Federal Communications Commission, and your background will be investigated to be sure that allowing you to own a station will be in the best interests of the public. If you don't devote a certain amount of programming to alternative viewpoints, or if members of the public complain that your programming is offensive, you may lose that license after you obtain it. And if one of your announcers uses offensive language or discusses "adult" topics during times when children may be listening, you could be fined by the FCC.

On the other hand, the guarantees of free speech and press contained in the Constitution have been expanded to some other kinds of expression, often referred to as "symbolic speech." If you want to paint a picture of the mayor of a major American city dressed only in ladies' undergarments, you are free to do so. If you want to use the American flag as a rug for people to walk on in order to see your work of art, or burn the same flag in an act of political protest, courts have ruled that your right to do so is protected by the First Amendment.

All of which goes to show that it can be difficult to determine in advance the kinds of speech to which the courts will extend constitutional protection. In 1992, for example, the U.S. Supreme Court overturned the conviction of a young man who had burned a cross on the lawn of a black family. In doing so, it held that a city ordinance that prohibited hateful speech or expression directed at someone because of their race, gender, religion, or national origin was unconstitutional.

FREEDOM OF RELIGION

In addition to the guarantee of free speech and a free press contained in the First Amendment, the Amendment also declares that "Congress shall make no law respecting an establishment of religion, or prohibiting the free exercise thereof."

As with the other provisions of the Bill of Rights, this simple sentence has been the subject of intense debate over the history of our nation. Much of that debate has been conducted in the past fifty years or so, as the courts have struggled to prevent an excessive entanglement between religion and the state.

For example, in 1948 the U.S. Supreme Court ruled that allowing children to attend "released time" programs in a public school building violated the First Amendment. A released time program is one in which children are allowed to leave public school classes early in order to receive religious instruction. The Court held that by allowing such classes to be conducted in the public school building, the government was allowing publicly funded facilities to be used for the teaching of specific religious doctrine. In addition, allowing these classes to be taught in public schools gave assistance to the religions using the facilities, since the law compelled public school attendance. Because children are motivated to a great extent by peer pressure, the children receiving religious instruction would exert influence over those who didn't, depriving them of their right to form their own religious beliefs (or their right to have no religious beliefs at all.)

And yet for almost one hundred fifty years, the courts had permitted schools to require student prayer. It wasn't until the early 1960s that the U.S. Supreme Court held that requiring students to pray or to study the Bible in public schools violated the First Amendment.

Since then, school prayer has been one of the most often contested issues before the Supreme Court. In most of these decisions, the Court has continued to develop the wall between religion and the state. While the earliest decisions prohibited praying out loud, later decisions prohibited even moments of silent prayer and meditation. Invocations at public school graduation ceremonies have also been banned, on the grounds that they have the effect of advancing religion and promoting excessive entanglement between church and state.

The courts have also limited the applicability of the First Amendment to the practice of religion. While the Court has wisely noted that it's impossible to punish a person for what they believe, the practice of religion can be punished. So although some religious groups believe in bigamy, the Supreme Court has ruled that laws which prohibit bigamy do not violate these groups' First Amendment rights, since the need to maintain order in society was more important than the rights of an individual to practice his religion.

Similarly, court decisions have prohibited the practice of snake handling in order to protect the safety of the public (including the church's members) and have outlawed the use of illegal drugs such as peyote in religious ceremonies. And in some cases, the courts have ordered that blood transfusions be given to members of religions that forbid their members from receiving them, on the grounds that the state's interest in preserving life is more important than the right of the individual or the church to practice its faith.

In 1993, however, several Supreme Court rulings seemed to suggest that the Court was re-examining the results of some of its earlier decisions. In one case, the Supreme Court ruled that if a school provides its facilities to other groups during off hours, it must also make those facilities available to religious groups as well. In another, it overturned an ordinance in Hialeah, Florida, which prohibited ritual animal sacrifice, on the grounds that the prohibition violated the rights of the followers of the Santeria religion by keeping them from practicing their religion, which requires animal sacrifices.

And in yet another decision, the Court held that allowing a public employee to serve as the sign-language interpreter for a deaf child attending a religious school did not violate the constitution's requirement of separation of church and state, even though the public employee would spend at least part of his time translating religious teachings.

Many people question how the courts can place so many restrictions on the interaction of religion and the government. They point to the fact that our currency carries the motto "In God We Trust," that our Pledge of Allegiance refers to the United States as "one Nation, under God," and that each meeting of the Congress begins with an invocation.

Legal scholars and the courts routinely answer these concerns by making a distinction between the acknowledgment of God and the recognition of a particular religious belief. They also claim that a distinction can be made between the prayers conducted in Congress and those held in schools, since the former are conducted for and in the presence of adults, and the latter are held in the presence of children, who are particularly swayed by the influence of teachers and classmates. A congressional representative who chooses not to participate in prayers, the reasoning goes, is less likely to feel the disapproval of his peers than a school age child who refuses to participate in classroom prayers.

While to many this distinction seems to be an exceedingly fine one, it will undoubtedly continue to guide the courts in future decisions. One of the questions yet to be decided will concern whether or not tax revenues can be used to pay for vouchers that would allow parents to send their children to religious private schools rather than public schools. A multitude of other questions, many as yet unknown, will also be raised as the courts struggle with the issues of religion and government.

THE RIGHT OF ASSEMBLY

The First Amendment covers more than the freedom of speech, press and religion. It also states that "Congress shall make no law abridging . . . the right of the people peaceably to assemble, and to petition the government for a redress of grievances."

As we've already seen in regard to the other rights set forth in the First Amendment, the right to assemble freely is not without its limitations. For example, cities can require groups that want to hold parades or rallies to obtain permits. But the standards they use in granting these permits must be applied equally to all applicants. Any ordinance that allowed some groups to hold rallies and parades but refused that right to others would violate the constitutional rights of the group that was refused a permit.

Suppose, for example, that a neo-Nazi group wanted to hold a parade to celebrate the birthday of Adolf Hitler. A city that allowed other groups to parade and hold rallies to celebrate the birth of Martin Luther King, Jr. could not prohibit such a gathering, even though most members of the public would find such a parade offensive.

However, suppose a group wanted to assemble for the purpose of urging its members to march on and burn down the state capitol. Because such a group presents a clear and present danger to the safety of the public and the order of society, not only could the government refuse to allow such a gathering to take place, it could even arrest those attending such an event for unlawful assembly and conspiracy to commit a crime.

THE RIGHT TO BEAR ARMS

According to the language of the Second Amendment of the U.S. Constitution, "A well regulated militia, being necessary to the security of a free State, the right of the people to keep and bear arms, shall not be infringed." Over the past twenty-five years, the meaning of this sentence, which contains only twenty-seven words, has been the subject of increasingly angry debate.

For many legal scholars, the most important part of the Second Amendment is contained in the first half of the sentence.

They hold that those who wrote and approved the Constitution and the Bill of Rights were not as concerned with the individual's right to gun ownership as they were with the need to keep firearms available for the defense of the country from its enemies.

Others emphasize the second half of the statement, and claim that the intent of the Second Amendment is to preserve the rights of the individual to own guns from intrusion by the government, and to keep the government's own power under check. They note that the reason for the success of the American Revolution, conducted against what at the time was considered the legitimate government of the American colonies, was that individual citizens owned arms. Therefore, they argue, the Constitutional protection afforded to gun ownership is not directed so much at putting guns at the disposal of the government as it is to remind the government that its authority lies with the people, whose use of arms led to the ouster of the British, and who could rise up again to overthrow any other illegitimate form of government.

Depending on which side of the argument your own beliefs most closely coincide with, gun ownership in America is either the subject of too little regulation, or too much. What's undeniable, however, is that the courts have ruled that the government has the right to impose reasonable regulations concerning the possession and ownership of guns. And it seems likely that additional forms of gun control will be enacted in the future.

For example, you can be legally required to register any firearms you own, and you can be prohibited from owning certain kinds of weapons, such as automatic assault rifles and machine guns. A number of states require a waiting period between the time when you apply to purchase a gun and the time you receive it, so that it may investigate your background (and also to give you time to reconsider your purchase if you've made it with less than honest intentions for the gun's use). In addition, late in 1993 Congress passed and the President signed the so-called "Brady Bill," mandating a nationwide five day waiting period for handgun purchases, and even more stringent gun control laws are now under consideration by Congress.

Many laws restrict the way you use a gun after you obtain it. You cannot carry a concealed gun or other kinds of dangerous weapons on your person, although you may be able to obtain a permit to do so if your life has been threatened, or if your job or profession makes you a likely target for criminals. However, police departments are growing increasingly reluctant to issue such permits, and obtaining one has become virtually impossible in some parts of the country.

Critics of increasing the level of government regulation of gun ownership point out that most criminals are not deterred by gun control laws. Most criminals obtain their weapons by stealing them, or by purchasing them from others who have stolen them. These critics agree with the popular bumper sticker that states "When Guns Are Outlawed, Only Outlaws Will Have Guns." They believe that more important than restricting gun ownership is requiring the courts to impose stiff prison sentences on criminals who are convicted of using a gun during the course of committing a crime. And they claim that a criminal is less likely to invade the home or business of someone who may have a gun available for self-defense.

Supporters of increased gun control legislation argue that the number of crimes of passion committed by people with easy access to firearms would be significantly lower if it were more difficult for them to get their hands on those firearms in the first place. They also claim that the number of accidental deaths and injuries due to the misuse of firearms could be reduced by making guns harder to obtain. And they argue that, with fewer guns in our homes and businesses, there would be less chance of these legally obtained weapons falling into the hands of burglars and other criminals.

When it comes to the question of gun control, there is no easy answer. By understanding the issues involved in the debate, each individual can decide which solutions seem the most likely to help reduce the problem of violent crime.

THE RIGHT TO PRIVACY

The rights to speak and publish freely, to assemble, to be free of government intrusion into matters of religion, and the right to bear arms are all clearly granted in the Bill of Rights. The right to privacy, to be free from intrusion into one's private affairs, is not specifically mentioned in the Bill of Rights.

Nonetheless, the right to privacy has been recognized by the courts as being among those protected by the Constitution. The right to privacy is derived from several of the Amendments which make up the Bill of Rights, including the Third Amendment (which protects you from having soldiers placed in your home by the government), the Fourth Amendment (protecting against unreasonable searches and seizures) and the Fifth Amendment (which protects you from being forced to incriminate yourself). In addition, the Ninth Amendment states that just because a right is not specifically mentioned elsewhere in the Bill of Rights, the omission doesn't mean that it is to be denied to the people. This "catch-all provision" of the Ninth Amendment has also been used to protect the right to privacy.

What exactly does the "right to privacy" entail? In addition to keeping the police and other government officials from snooping into your personal affairs without prior authorization from the courts or from Congress, the right to privacy prevents the enforcement of laws that unreasonably interfere with your ability to make decisions about the way you live your own life.

For example, the use of contraceptives, even by married couples, was once prohibited by state laws, and similar laws made it a crime for anyone to give advice on how to avoid pregnancy. In 1965, the U.S. Supreme Court ruled that such laws were an unconstitutional violation of the right to privacy which married couples are legally entitled to possess. Seven years later, the Court extended this right of privacy to all individuals, whether married or unmarried.

In 1973, the Court held in the case of *Roe v. Wade* that the right to privacy entitled a woman to decide for herself whether or not to obtain an abortion. While the government may make reasonable regulations about abortion in order to protect health and life, any outright ban on a woman's right to obtain an abortion was prohibited.

While this principle continues in force today, subsequent Supreme Court decisions have tended to permit additional restrictions on the right to an abortion. For example, a state may impose a brief waiting period between the time a woman makes an inquiry about an abortion and the time when she receives it. And the state may require minors to notify their parents before receiving an abortion and obtain the consent of one parent to the procedure, although it must also provide an alternative method by which the minor can obtain court approval for the procedure in lieu of parental consent.

On the other hand, the Supreme Court has also held that the state can enact laws which make certain kinds of sex acts, such as oral or anal sex, illegal even when they take place in private between consenting adults, since the government has an important interest in encouraging traditional values.

In order to strengthen your right to privacy when the law requires you to reveal certain information to government agencies such as the Internal Revenue Service or the Social Security Administration, Congress passed the Privacy Act of 1974.

Under this Act, an agency collecting information on individuals may use that information only for the purpose for which it was collected. For example, if the Social Security Administration obtains information from you regarding your sources of income, it cannot turn that information over to the IRS for use in a prosecution against you for tax evasion. The Privacy Act also gives you the right to know what information a government agency has in its files about you, to obtain copies of that information, and to correct mistakes or add essential details that explain the government file's contents. Most states have also enacted laws similar to the federal Privacy Act.

Another law, the federal Right to Financial Privacy Act, is designed to help you keep your records at banks, savings and loans, and other financial institutions protected from secret, unwarranted government intrusion. Under this Act, your financial records cannot be revealed to a government agency without your consent or a court order and subpoena issued to collect information pertaining to a legitimate investigation based on the belief that a law has been broken and your financial records will provide necessary evidence.

The federal Family Educational Rights and Privacy Act of 1974 was enacted to give parents and adult students the right to examine the records kept by schools, and to challenge alleged errors and make corrections. Under this Act, parents have the right to know about any requests made by anyone to see the records, including the name of the person or institution making the request and the reason for it.

Once a child reaches the age of 18 or enrolls in a post-secondary institution, these rights become exclusive to the child, and parents are no longer allowed to see the records without the child's consent. Students may permit colleges and potential employers to see and evaluate their records, but they cannot be required to do so.

Your right to privacy helps to prevent unreasonable government intrusion into your personal life. But it also prevents other individuals from invading your privacy as well. For example, you can file a lawsuit against individuals who invade your privacy by tapping your telephone, opening your mail, or who otherwise eavesdrop on you without legal authorization or your consent. And you can bring legal action against those who damage your reputation through libel or slander, or who disclose to the public the private events of your life in a manner designed to injure your good name.

You can also file a lawsuit against someone who portrays you in a false light and damages your reputation. For example, suppose your picture is taken as you walk out of your local bank with a large package under your arm. The picture is then published by your local newspaper, along with the caption "Not All Bank Robbers Use Guns." While your name is never mentioned in the article, you could claim that using your picture to illustrate the article suggests to the public that you are a bank robber. If you can show that the newspaper created this image intentionally, or even through its carelessness, you would be entitled to damages to repay you for the injury caused to your reputation.

YOUR RIGHTS IN A CRIMINAL INVESTIGATION

The Bill of Rights and the constitutions of the individual states also provide important safeguards when you are suspected of a crime. The Fourth Amendment protects individuals against unreasonable searches and seizures, and requires law enforcement officials to obtain warrants based on probable cause and which describe the places to be searched and the items or persons being sought.

The Fifth Amendment protects an accused person from being forced to testify against himself, and prohibits double jeopardy (being tried by the same government more than once for the same crime). It also guarantees the right to a trial by jury for most serious crimes, including those in which the death penalty may be administered.

The Sixth Amendment guarantees that a person accused of a crime will be informed of the charges against him, and receive a speedy trial on those charges. The Sixth Amendment also guarantees that a person charged with a crime will be able to subpoena witnesses to testify on his behalf, to have the right to confront and cross-examine the witnesses against him, and have the right to legal counsel.

The Eighth Amendment prohibits excessive bail and excessive fines, and forbids "cruel and unusual" punishment. But what the courts consider to constitute cruel and unusual punishment has changed dramatically over the past two hundred years. In the 1780s, "cruel and unusual" punishment included being beheaded or burned at the stake. Today, some convicted criminals have successfully raised the argument that being housed with other convicts who smoke constitutes "cruel and unusual" punishment for nonsmokers, since their health is jeopardized by secondhand smoke.

For a more complete discussion of your rights when you are charged with a crime, please see Chapter Seventeen, "Crime and Punishment."

YOUR RIGHT TO TRAVEL

Americans like to travel, and most of us take our right to move about the country freely and to relocate from one place to another for granted. In the former Soviet Union and the People's Republic of China, as well as in other countries, however, residents have not been accorded this same freedom to travel. In these countries, a person who wants to move from one area of the country to the other may be required to obtain a permit from the government before being allowed to do so, and there is no guarantee that such a permit would even be granted.

Americans also have the right to travel outside the country, and to be allowed back in upon their return from a foreign nation. Again, the situation is different in some other countries, where the government restricts or prohibits its citizens' right to leave the country.

As we've already seen, however, no right is absolute, and even the right to travel may be subject to government restrictions under certain circumstances. For example, the government can prohibit your travel to enemy nations during time of war, or to countries with which we have no diplomatic ties, such as Libya or Iraq, since it cannot intervene to protect your safety in these countries.

If you have been charged with a crime and have been freed on bail pending your trial, the court can order you to remain in the state unless you receive its permission to travel elsewhere. And if there is some concern that you would flee the country in order to avoid prosecution, you may be required to surrender your passport to the court to prevent you from leaving the United States.

Similarly, if you have been released on parole or probation after being convicted of a crime, you may be required to report your whereabouts to the court or to a parole or probation officer on a regular basis, and you may need advance permission in order to move out of the court's jurisdiction. This restriction can be imposed by the court without being a violation of your constitutional rights, since the need to safeguard the public exceeds your individual right to travel freely.

YOUR RIGHT TO OWN PROPERTY

Under provisions of both the federal Constitution and the constitutions of the individual states, your right to buy, own, and sell both real property and personal property is legally protected. The government is prohibited from taking your property without at least giving you a chance to be heard by a court in order to oppose the government's attempt.

Your property can be taken away from you under some circumstances. If the government believes that the best use of your property is a public one, it can condemn your property under its power of "eminent domain," but it must compensate you for the value of the property. If you are accused or convicted of a crime, or if a crime takes place on property you own, the government may file a forfeiture claim, and if that claim is successful, you may be deprived of your property without compensation. And if you fail to pay your property taxes, your property may be sold to satisfy the debt owed to the government. You'll find more about the ways you can lose your property in Chapter Four, "Your Home," and Chapter Seventeen, "Crime and Punishment."

YOUR RIGHT TO DEFEND YOURSELF

You have a legal right to use reasonable force to defend yourself from physical assaults by others, and to prevent others from stealing your property or attacking other persons. And even when it turns out that you weren't in jeopardy of a physical attack against yourself, you still have the right to defend yourself if you reasonably believed you were in danger.

For example, suppose you are walking to your car in a poorly lighted downtown parking lot in a less than savory part of the city. As you approach your car, you pass a group of youths hanging around another vehicle. Suddenly, you hear a loud shout directly behind you and a hand presses hard against your back. You turn around and strike your "assailant" only to discover that the person you struck had not actually attacked you, but had been pushed into you by another member of the group as a prank. Because of your reasonable belief that you were being attacked, you would not be guilty of battery for striking him.

In some cases, you are even entitled to use deadly force to protect yourself and others, but only when you reasonably believe that you or the person you are coming to the defense of are in danger of being killed or seriously injured. So while it's legally permissible to shoot and kill an assailant who attacks you with a knife or some other dangerous weapon, shooting someone who merely makes a threatening gesture or throws a punch is not. Nor is using deadly force against someone who is threatening your property but not your life. You cannot, for example, shoot or stab someone who is stealing property or money from your store, or burglarizing your home.

In a few states, unless you are in your own home or in some other situation where you cannot escape, your right to self-defense is further restricted. In these states, you must first make a reasonable attempt to retreat from your assailant before using deadly force to defend yourself.

Finally, when it comes to defending your property, most states require that you warn the other person before using any force, unless doing so would put your personal safety in jeopardy. And while it's acceptable to use physical force to stop a burglar from leaving your home, or to capture him as he climbs out the window with your belongings, the right to defend your property doesn't permit you to enter the burglar's home and reclaim the items stolen from you. To get your property returned, you must notify the police, and rely on their assistance in getting your property back.

CHAPTER TWO
MARRIAGE, DIVORCE, AND FAMILY LAW

Not so many years ago, the law considered a man's wife and children as little more than his property, and he was free to treat them accordingly. Few areas of the law have undergone as much change in the past half century as the area known as family law, and few areas of the law affect so many people.

In this chapter, we'll look at the legal issues surrounding getting married and getting divorced, raising a family, and the continuing responsibilities and rights divorced parents have in regard to their children. We'll discuss some of the ways laws affect alternative family arrangements and relationships that fall outside the traditional concept of what constitutes a marriage. We'll also look at how the law affects your elderly parents and your relationship with them, as well as ways in which you can help protect them from trouble when they become ill or incapable of handling their own affairs.

MARRIAGE

The word "marriage" describes both the contract entered into between husband and wife and the relationship created by that contract. Like any contract, the marriage contract can be broken. But because of society's interest in promoting marriage, the government must approve the ending of a marital relationship.

Although most of us view the concept of marriage differently than our grandparents, most of the elements of a legal marriage remain the same. For example, if you're already married to someone, you cannot legally marry another person until your first marriage ends, either through annulment, by divorce, or by the death of your spouse.

Similarly, at present the law in every state only recognizes marriages between an unmarried male and an unmarried female. If you want to "marry" a person of the same sex, the law does not recognize that relationship as a marriage. Almost all of us know or have heard of gay or lesbian couples living in a "family" relationship. But the law doesn't extend the rights of a married couple to these arrangements. So, for example, a gay man's right to inherit from his companion isn't protected by law, and he can't receive his partner's government or pension benefits.

In at least one state, however, this may be changing in the near future. The Hawaii Supreme Court has ruled that under the state constitution, which prohibits discrimination based on sexual orientation, the government must show a compelling reason for continuing the ban on same-sex marriages. This test is extremely difficult to meet, since it requires the state to show that the prohibition on these marriages is essential to protect the public safety, health, and welfare, and that the government has no less intrusive method of doing so than an outright ban.

By the year 1995, it's conceivable that same-sex marriages may be permitted in Hawaii. And if they are, the federal Constitution's requirement that states give "full faith and credit" to the public acts of another state may make it possible for homosexuals to marry in Hawaii and then have those marriages treated as valid in every other state.

Our society still claims to place a great deal of importance on traditional marriage as an institution that promotes and upholds society's values, and so many laws still exist with the purpose of promoting and encouraging marriage as an institution. For example, every state has laws prohibiting marriages between men and women who are closely related. Marriages between parent and child, grandparent and grandchild, brother and sister, uncle or aunt and niece or nephew are forbidden everywhere, and many states prohibit marriages between first cousins. A few states still forbid marriages of habitual criminals, alcoholics and drug addicts, and the mentally incompetent.

Each state sets a minimum age at which a person may marry. In most states, men may marry at eighteen, and women at age sixteen. A number of states will let a couple marry earlier if they obtain parental consent for the marriage. In several states, a boy as young as fourteen and a girl as young as twelve may marry if they have parental approval.

There are only two legally recognized ways to marry. The first is through a wedding ceremony performed by a person authorized by the state to perform weddings, and witnessed by at least one or two other people.

While every state recognizes the validity of such ceremonial marriages, only fourteen states and the District of Columbia recognize common-law marriages. To enter into a valid common-law marriage, the couple must enter into a mutual promise to be married, and present themselves to the community as husband and wife from the time the promise is made. As with a ceremonial marriage, a common-law marriage can only be ended by annulment, a divorce, or the death of a spouse.

PRENUPTIAL AGREEMENTS

Until recently, marriage relationships were governed by the expectations of society and the agreement of the husband and wife to abide by their marriage vows. Today, traditional roles are changing, and women who a few decades ago would have been expected to stay home and raise a family are working outside the home to supplement the family's income. Where not so long ago a couple stayed married until "death do they part, " today more and more individuals are entering second, third and fourth marriages.

As a result, many couples contemplating marriage, especially those who are entering into a second or subsequent marriage, are creating prenuptial agreements (also called "antenuptial agreements") that carefully describe the rights and responsibilities of each partner in the relationship.

Prenuptial agreements can set out the rules for virtually every aspect of a marriage, from dividing responsibilities for housework, to deciding the way in which household bills and expenses will be paid, to setting out the number of children a couple will have, when they will have them, and who will be primarily responsible for their care.

One of the most important justifications for having a prenuptial agreement is to provide for the inheritance rights of children from a previous marriage. Without a prenuptial agreement, a current spouse will be entitled to receive some property from a spouse's estate under what are known as "elective share" laws, even if the spouse leaves nothing by will. A prenuptial agreement can allow each partner to make provisions for the distribution of property without having to worry that the surviving spouse will renege on an oral promise to take a reduced share, or even nothing at all of the deceased spouse's property.

With a valid prenuptial agreement, each spouse can waive the right to inherit from the other's estate. As long as the agreement is voluntary, and each of them has sufficient knowledge of the extent of the other's property, a written prenuptial agreement of this type will be legally enforceable. However, if one spouse fails to disclose assets, and the other spouse's decision to sign a prenuptial agreement is not a well-informed one, a court will not enforce the agreement.

Courts can also refuse to enforce agreements which they feel promote divorce. For example, a prenuptial agreement in which the husband offers a large financial settlement to his wife on the condition that she not contest a divorce would probably be rejected as unenforceable in most states.

If you're thinking about making a prenuptial agreement, you should be sure to discuss doing so well in advance of your impending marriage date. Each party must have adequate time to decide what he or she wants included in the agreement, and there has to be adequate time for each party to seek independent assistance from an attorney before signing the agreement.

You don't necessarily need a lawyer to draw up a prenuptial agreement, but if you decide to get legal help, never use a single attorney to represent both of you in creating it. Doing so makes it easier for one party to later claim that his or her interests weren't adequately protected. And you should never try to "spring" a prenuptial agreement on your prospective spouse just before the wedding. Even if he or she signs the agreement, its validity could be contested later on the basis of fraud, duress, or undue influence.

In most states, only you and your prospective spouse need to sign the agreement in order to make it valid. In a few states, however, the law requires you to sign the document in front of witnesses. Even if the law in your state doesn't have this requirement, it's a good idea to have the document witnessed and notarized, since doing so will also help to guard against later claims of fraud or duress.

LIVING TOGETHER WHEN YOU'RE NOT MARRIED

As we've already seen, the law extends extra protections to people who comply with the requirements for a legal marriage. These extra protections haven't slowed the increase in the number of people who choose to live in relationships other than those authorized and recognized by law. According to some estimates, more than four million people in the United States now are living together in a relationship other than a legally recognized marriage.

Many of these people see marriage as an unnecessary complication of their living arrangement, one that replaces loving care with legal obligations. However, not being married can give rise to more problems than these people might suspect. For while the law has ways of protecting the rights of the legally married, it doesn't always provide the same safeguards to couples living in nontraditional relationships.

For example, if a spouse dies without a last will and testament, the law protects the surviving spouse by providing an alternative in the form of intestate succession. Under the laws of intestate succession, a surviving spouse in a legal marriage is entitled to receive some or all of the deceased spouse's estate. But if a life partner who is not a legally recognized spouse dies without a will, the law makes no provision for the survivor, even though the relationship may have lasted longer than most marriages. Similarly, the law safeguards an unsuspecting spouse from being disinherited through the "elective share" we discussed earlier. But no such protection is granted when one partner in a non-marital relationship decides to leave all of his estate to someone other than the other partner.

One way in which some of these problems can be overcome is by creating a document known as a cohabitation agreement. Similar in many ways to a prenuptial agreement, this "living together" agreement can be used to describe how property accumulated during the relationship will be divided if the relationship ends, how housework and other responsibilities will be divided, and how bills and expenses will be paid.

With a cohabitation agreement, an unmarried couple can delineate the rights and responsibilities of their relationship in a manner that's legally enforceable. However, it's never a good idea to include provisions describing the sexual rights and duties of each partner in a cohabitation agreement. Some courts may not enforce an agreement in which one partner agrees to have sexual relations with the other in return for other considerations, since this could be interpreted as furthering prostitution.

Although the rights and responsibilities of unmarried people are usually left for them to define, the same isn't true when the relationship results in a child. Unwed parents have the same legal duties of raising a child as their married counterparts have, with the same responsibilities for providing for the child's health, education, and welfare.

If the relationship ends, the non-custodial parent is legally and morally obligated to financially support his or her child until the child is recognized by the law as an adult. Similarly, the parent who retains custody of the child is required to allow reasonable visitation rights, unless there is a question of physical or mental abuse. All the legal procedures available to a divorced person to help enforce these rights are also available to an unmarried parent, regardless of the nature of the relationship that created the child.

Depending on where you live, an unmarried couple may be entitled to other legal protection as well. Today, the laws in many states and cities across the U.S. afford special protections to couples who live in homosexual or heterosexual relationships outside of marriage. In at least 28 cities or counties, these couples are permitted to register themselves as "domestic partners." In some cases, this registration makes each partner eligible for benefits from the other partner's workplace, such as family or medical leave. Other communities make it illegal for some landlords to discriminate against tenants on the basis of sexual orientation, with the result that homosexual couples find it easier to live together openly.

On the other hand, some communities and states have acted to limit the legal protection afforded to homosexuals on the basis of their sexual orientation. In 1992, Colorado voters passed an amendment to the state constitution prohibiting laws that gave homosexuals protection on the basis of their homosexuality. This amendment has yet to be enforced, however, as gay rights' groups were able to obtain an injunction blocking it from being used. The state of Colorado has expressed its intention to pursue the matter to the U.S. Supreme Court, which until now has never granted protected status to homosexuals in the same way it has extended protections to women, as well as to racial, religious, or ethnic minorities.

ADOPTION

Adoption is the legal process by which the law permits the creation of a parent-child relationship which did not previously exist. When you adopt a child, the law recognizes the child as the equivalent of your own biological offspring. The adopted child has the same rights of inheritance as a biological child, and adoptive parents have the same duty to provide financial support for an adopted child as they have for biological children.

Most adoptions take place in one of two ways. The most common way to adopt a child is through an adoption agency operated or licensed by the state. The second way, private adoptions arranged by an attorney, are becoming an increasingly important adoption method.

In a private adoption, the birth mother will usually know more about the prospective adoptive parents than she would in an agency situation, and may even meet with them in person to discuss the way in which she wants her child raised. The adoptive parents may agree to provide for the natural mother's medical expenses and living expenses during the pregnancy, as well as to pay the legal fees and costs associated with the adoption. However, state laws often prohibit any other kinds of payments to the natural mother, and making such payments can render the adoption illegal.

Qualifications for adoptive parents are set by the laws of your state, and some variations exist from state to state. Generally, however, all states consider such factors as the age of the adoptive parents, as well as their financial situation and personal stability. Although at one time it was virtually impossible for a single person to adopt a child, today more and more children are placed with single parents. And while homosexual couples were almost always excluded from consideration as adoptive parents, the modern trend in many states is to give these couples equal consideration.

Most state adoption agencies discourage the placement of black or mixed race children with Caucasian adoptive parents, since the current belief of social scientists is that such children will be denied the opportunity to learn about their cultural heritage, and will suffer from a confused sense of cultural identity.

Of course, the consent of the child's natural parents is required, unless the state has terminated their parental rights. And if the child is old enough, (usually around twelve years of age), the state will require that he or she consent to the adoption as well. In most states, it's even possible for one adult to adopt another, a process that has sometimes been used in order to provide inheritance rights to a longtime friend or companion when it would have been difficult to do so otherwise.

The issue of consent is an important one, and an individual or couple which is considering adopting a child needs to be well informed about the rights of the birth parents to withdraw consent to the adoption. In some states, the birth parent has the right to change her mind about giving her child up for adoption for as long as six months. If she withdraws her consent during this period, the courts will almost invariably return the child to her, unless it can be shown that she is unfit to be a parent. And if the birth mother can convince a court that her consent to the adoption resulted from fraud or undue influence, the right to withdraw that consent can continue for far longer.

Similarly, it's important to take every possible step to identify the child's natural father and obtain his consent to the adoption as well. In several cases, birth mothers have intentionally misrepresented the identity of the fathers of the children they have put up for adoption, or indicated that they did not know the father's identity. When the biological fathers learned of these deceptions, they have been successful in obtaining the return of the children from their adoptive parents.

Although at one time a great deal of secrecy surrounded adoption records, a number of states have made it easier for adopted children to learn about their natural parents. In some states, an adopted child can gain access to non-identifying information about a biological parent, such as medical histories. In other states, information about the biological parents' identities can be released to an adult adopted child, but only if the biological parent consents in advance. Your county law librarian can refer you to sources of information about the specific laws in your state.

Adopting a child can be an expensive and time-consuming process, and failing to follow the appropriate procedures to the letter can result in heartache for just about everyone involved. If you are considering offering your child for adoption, or if you're considering becoming an adoptive parent, you should consult with an attorney experienced in the field for a thorough consultation about the adoption laws of your state.

GETTING DIVORCED

A divorce is a judgment by a court that ends a marriage and redefines the relationship of the former husband and wife. In some cases, where the couple has been married for a short period of time and where there are no children, the relationship will simply end, and the parties will go their own way. But when the marriage has been of longer duration, when there are questions and conflicts about how to distribute property acquired during the marriage, and especially when there are minor children to support, the end of the marriage doesn't mean the end of all contact between the former husband and wife. In fact, if the children are very young, a relationship between ex-spouses can continue for many years after a divorce is granted.

Until the 1970s, the law made it extremely difficult to end a marriage. Divorces were granted only when one spouse or the other was guilty of what's known as "marital misconduct," such as physical cruelty, abandonment or adultery. As a result, obtaining a divorce was an embarrassing and traumatic experience, and many couples remained in loveless marriages out of fear of the scandal that would result from making the accusations necessary to obtain a divorce.

While no one would suggest that divorce today is an easy or inconsequential experience, states have changed their divorce laws significantly during the past quarter century in ways that tend to lessen the trauma of divorce. Today, every state and the District of Columbia have enacted what are known as "no-fault" divorce laws.

These laws no longer require proof of marital misconduct by one spouse or the other. Now, in order to obtain a no-fault divorce, a court must find that a couple's marriage is irretrievably broken, that the couple is incompatible, or that it suffers from irreconcilable differences. In some states, a divorce may be granted by showing that the couple have lived apart for a specified period of time.

Although these no-fault divorce laws no longer require that the spouse seeking the divorce show misconduct by the other spouse, in about two-thirds of the states a petition for divorce may still be based on grounds of misconduct. In these states, courts can consider a spouse's misconduct when deciding issues such as child custody, visitation and alimony payments.

No-fault divorce is sometimes confused with uncontested divorce, but the two are not the same. In an uncontested divorce husband and wife have no disagreement about ending the marriage, and agree with each other about how to divide marital property, who will pay spousal and child support (and how much), and the issues of child custody and visitation. In a no-fault divorce, any or all of these issues could be a source of conflict between the parties which must be decided through negotiation or the imposition of a decision by the court.

Although the exact procedures for obtaining a divorce vary somewhat from state to state, the basic steps in obtaining a divorce are essentially the same just about everywhere. To begin the divorce proceeding, a petition is filed by one of the spouses requesting that a divorce be granted. Not surprisingly, the spouse who files the petition is referred to as "the petitioner." The petition states the grounds on which the divorce is sought. It may ask the court to award a specified amount of alimony (also called spousal support, or maintenance). If there are children, the petition may include a proposed custody and visitation arrangement. It must also state why this particular court has jurisdiction over the divorce.

A court's jurisdiction is its legal authority to hear a particular case. In divorce proceedings, jurisdiction is primarily based on the state and county in which one or both of the spouses reside. Most states require that you be a resident of the state for a specified period of time before filing the petition.

The court will then issue a summons and a copy of the petition to the other spouse (called "the respondent"), which serves as notice that the divorce petition has been filed and gives the respondent a chance to answer the petition. Failing to file an answer will allow the divorce to proceed uncontested.

If both spouses agree about all the issues surrounding their divorce, they can file a copy of their separation agreement at this point to expedite the divorce process. By filing the answer and the separation agreement, the respondent agrees to accept the court's jurisdiction, and asks the court to approve the settlement and grant the divorce. If the court finds that the settlement is acceptable, it will grant a divorce.

If areas of disagreement still exist, the next step after the respondent's answer is a process called discovery. In this step, each side in the divorce assembles evidence regarding the issue or issues in debate. This can be a relatively informal process, or one which takes the form of interrogatories, depositions, and subpoenas, as each side tries to make the best case for its position. After discovery, settlement negotiations will be held in an attempt to arrive at an agreement acceptable to both husband and wife.

If an agreement is reached, a court hearing is held. The settlement is reviewed, and if the court finds it to be fair, the divorce will be granted. If there's no agreement, the court will conduct a trial on the disputed issues and decide the outcome under the guidelines of state law. Ultimately, the divorce will be granted. The court will issue a final decree, or judgment of divorce, and in some states a divorce certificate will be filed with a state agency, such as the Office of Vital Records. At this point, the marriage is officially ended.

ALIMONY

Although most of us are familiar with the term alimony, "spousal support" and "maintenance" are the two terms replacing the word alimony in modern usage. Like most of the laws surrounding divorce, the laws about spousal support have changed a great deal in the past quarter century.

At one time, alimony was often the sole means of support for a divorced woman. The wife of 30 years ago may have spent her whole adult life as a homemaker and mother, and had few if any marketable job skills. Alimony payments were intended to allow a divorced woman to live in a style similar to what she'd enjoyed during her marriage.

Modern theories on spousal support take a different approach. Today, spousal support is considered to be "rehabilitative" — that is, it's intended to provide the divorced spouse with a financial cushion until he or she can become self-supporting. In most cases, spousal support may be awarded for anywhere from a few years to a decade, although for some people who have been married for many years and who never worked outside the home during marriage, a longer period of spousal support may sometimes be awarded.

On the other hand, if a couple divorces after only a few years of marriage, or if each spouse is working and self-sufficient, a court may decide not to award any spousal support at all. In fact, only about 20 percent of divorce decrees include an award of spousal support.

DIVIDING MARITAL PROPERTY

At one time, the majority of states held that property belonged to the spouse whose name was shown on the title document. Title to real estate, automobiles and other valuable property was often held by the husband in his name alone, even if the wife had contributed financially to its purchase. As a result, a divorced woman was often left with little or nothing in the way of property to call her own.

Today, the majority of states follow a practice known as equitable distribution in deciding how to divide marital property. Under this practice, courts consider the contribution of each spouse in acquiring the property. Under equitable distribution, a spouse's contribution as a homemaker and primary child care provider is considered in the same way as income from a job, or other assets used to acquire property during the marriage.

Nine states, known as community property states, consider all the property acquired during the marriage as owned equally by both husband and wife. These states are Arizona, California, Idaho, Louisiana, Nevada, New Mexico, Texas, Washington and Wisconsin.

A few of these states also class some property as quasi-community property. Basically, this is property acquired during the marriage, but in a non-community property state, by a couple who then moves to a state that follows the community property rule. The property is then treated as community property. This rule obviously was of greater importance before most states adopted the equitable distribution system.

In both equitable distribution and community property states, some property falls outside the category of marital property. Property a person inherits is considered separate property, as is property obtained as a gift or which belonged to a spouse before the marriage took place.

CHILD SUPPORT

Courts and legislatures on both the state and federal level have tried to address the problems involved in determining fair and adequate child support and enforcing support orders. The sad fact remains, however, that child support is too often neglected or evaded entirely by the parent who's supposed to pay it.

If you are the parent of a minor child, whether by birth or through adoption, you have a legal obligation to provide financially for that child's shelter, food, clothing, education and medical care. No matter how bitter or unpleasant a divorce may be, no matter how disagreeable an ex-spouse becomes, even when visitation is unfairly withheld, your obligation to provide for your child continues until that child becomes a legal adult.

Federal law now requires each state to establish guidelines for calculating child support. The purpose of these guidelines is to eliminate unfair or arbitrary awards of support. In most states, the guidelines are fairly well defined, and take into account the incomes of each parent and the number of children to be provided for. The parent who receives physical custody of the child usually contributes a smaller share financially, because of the extra expenses associated with having custody.

Unfortunately, arriving at an award of child support is one thing; enforcing that award is another problem entirely. According to U. S. Census Bureau statistics, only about 26 percent of parents who have a court order for child support actually receive all the money they are supposed to get. One in three children who are entitled to support get nothing at all from the non-custodial parent.

In an effort to combat this problem, every state has now passed the Uniform Reciprocal Enforcement of Support Act, or its successor, the Revised Uniform Reciprocal Enforcement of Support Act. These laws were designed to make collection of support from an out-of-state parent an easier task. They permit a parent who has been awarded child support in one state to collect it from a parent who lives out of state by using the court system itself. The court in the state when the support was awarded contacts the court in the state where the non-paying parent lives. That court then orders the parent to make the support payments.

While these laws seem to be of great value, they don't always work as planned. First, the parent with custody has to know where the other parent is living, which in itself isn't always easy to do. Second, even if the parent is found, the court in the state where he lives may modify the amount to be paid, and may be inclined to do so if the parent claims to be out of work or down on his luck. And finally, given the number of other cases the courts have to deal with, these cases tend to get relegated to the bottom of the pile.

There are other methods available for collecting unpaid child support. Various state laws permit support payments to be withheld from a parent's paycheck, and by 1994 every state must have procedures in place for this kind of withholding. The IRS can withhold a delinquent parent's income tax refund and take other steps such as seizing property, and state revenue departments can also seize tax refunds to satisfy unpaid child support obligations. A parent who refuses to make court ordered child support payments can also be subject to charges of contempt of court and can also face criminal prosecution.

CHILD CUSTODY AND VISITATION

Child custody can take one of several forms. Sole custody gives one parent physical custody of the child as well as legal custody, the right to decide how the child is to be raised. Sole custody has traditionally been the most common custody arrangement in the United States.

In the past dozen years, however, a number of states have expressed a preference for awarding joint legal custody. In a joint custody arrangement, both parents theoretically share in making decisions about how the child is raised. In most joint custody arrangements, sole physical custody is given to one parent so that the child can enjoy a relatively stable home environment. However, joint physical custody, in which the child lives for alternating periods with each parent, has also been awarded. Many experts feel that this arrangement can be more difficult for the child, and such arrangements are rare.

Joint custody arrangements require the cooperation of both parents in making decisions about issues such as schools, religion and outside activities. If the divorce is bitter and there is a great deal of conflict between the parents, however, a sole custody arrangement is probably preferable. In fact, some states still look with disfavor on joint custody arrangements, or prohibit them entirely, because they feel that parents who cannot live together probably will have a difficult time in agreeing on how to raise their children.

Whatever form custody takes, state laws require that the arrangements be in the best interests of the child. At one time, courts almost universally awarded sole custody to the mother, believing that the child's mother was the best person to raise the child. Today, courts are supposed to consider which parent has been the more active participant in raising the child when deciding on granting custody. Even so, the vast majority of children remain with their mothers after divorce.

A parent who does not receive physical custody is entitled to reasonable periodic visitation with his or her child, which usually takes place in the non-custodial parent's home. However, if there is a reasonable and provable fear that the parent may harm the child, or has been guilty of abuse in the past, the court can either require supervised visitation or deny it entirely.

The vast amount of media attention provided to the issue of child abuse, particularly sexual abuse, has led to a marked increase in the number of charges of abuse hurled by one parent against another during divorce proceedings. Because such accusations must be treated seriously by a court in deciding issues of custody and visitation, even clearly unfounded claims of abuse must be investigated. As a result, divorce and custody proceedings can drag on for months longer than necessary, with the parent accused of child abuse prohibited from visits with his children, or allowed to visit them under supervision by a social worker or some other person authorized by the court. In a number of cases, unfounded allegations of abuse have been used as a tool to injure the reputation of one spouse, or as a way to extort additional support money.

No one would argue that a child abuser should be afforded the same custody or visitation rights as other parents. However, no parent who has not abused his or her child should ever be silent in the face of such accusations. If you have been wrongfully accused of child abuse, there are several organizations which can provide you with support, advice, and in some cases, even legal assistance. One such organization with chapters in many parts of the country is VOCAL (Victims of Child Abuse Laws). Your attorney can help put you in contact with this group or other similar groups in your area.

Although it may seem unfair to require a parent to pay support when the parent who has custody denies visitation, in the eyes of the law the issues of visitation and child support are not connected. As the courts see it, failing to allow visitation may penalize the parent, but the failure to pay support penalizes the child. As a result, even if visitation is denied by the custodial parent, child support payments must still be made as ordered.

Rather than withholding payment of court ordered child support in retaliation for being denied visitation, the non-custodial parent must petition the court to enforce visitation rights awarded at the time of the divorce.

WHEN CHILDREN ARE OUT OF CONTROL

Not so many years ago, a "juvenile delinquent" was a minor who smoked, used tough language, and (if he was a really hard case) shoplifted or took the neighbors' cars for a joyride. Today, many juvenile offenders are more likely to be in trouble for rape, armed assault, robbery, or even murder.

Parents have a responsibility to control their children to the best of their abilities. But societal changes in the past thirty years have led to increased numbers of teenage pregnancies, single parent families, child abuse, and the collapse of the nuclear family as the principal device for achieving and maintaining order in the community.

Unfortunately, the law generally hasn't kept up with some of these changes. Courts continue to hold that children who are out of control (called "incorrigible children") need to be rehabilitated and returned to their families, even when these families are unable or unwilling to provide guidance or discipline. State statutes limit the financial liability a parent must bear when a child damages the property of another, or causes injuries.

We live in a world in which the concept of children as innocents is no longer completely valid. Gang activities often involve children as young as nine or ten, because gang leaders know that the law will allow these youngsters to return to the street without suffering any great consequences for their actions. Sexual assaults have been carried out by boys as young as eight years old.

The law in most states provides for the removal of children who are out of control from the custody of their parents. However, most courts will remove a child from his home only after trying every other avenue of discipline, and in some cases, trying all of them time and time again. But even in states that enforce these laws, the situations in which the children are placed is often little better than what they've already experienced. An incorrigible child may find himself in a group home or youth detention center, surrounded by other troubled kids who spend the bulk of their day watching television, getting into fights or even learning about new ways to break the law. For some young people, time spent in a detention center actually becomes a badge of honor, a tribute to their own "badness."

This is one area where the law currently gives more weight to treating offenders with kid gloves rather than acting to protect the safety of the general public. Our nation's children will be best served when they have reasonable expectations placed upon them, not just by the law, but by their parents as well, and when they understand that the legal consequences of failing to meet society's expectations will be serious, prompt and consistent. Without the involvement of responsible parents, however, the law cannot even hope to deal with the growing number of children who are out of control.

GRANDPARENT VISITATION

One of the saddest consequences of divorce occurs when loving grandparents are denied the opportunity to visit with their grandchildren. Today, grandparent visitation laws permit grandparents to petition for a court order allowing them visitation privileges when a divorce or separation takes place.

If grandparents win a court order of visitation rights, they can seek a contempt of court citation against a parent who continues to deny them those rights. On the other hand, an order requiring grandparent visitation, like any court order, can be appealed to a higher court if an argument can be made that it was erroneous, or not in the best interests of the grandchild.

To win a court order of grandparent visitation, you usually must show that you have played an integral part in your grandchild's life and that it is not in the child's best interest to be kept away from you. If you have only seen your grandchild occasionally, or you have been only peripherally involved in his or her life, however, you may have a difficult time winning a visitation order.

If you are awarded visitation privileges, they will usually continue until the child becomes an adult, or until the court determines that visitation is no longer in the grandchild's best interest. And if your grandchild is adopted by someone other than a stepparent, visitation rights may also be terminated.

A court order permitting grandparent visitation doesn't mean that the grandchild's parent will be prohibited from moving out of state, although it may contain provisions for modifying visitation rights when an out-of-state move takes place. For example, a court which had ordered visitation for one weekend each month could modify the order and require the parent to allow the grandchildren to visit during summer vacation or over the Christmas holidays.

Although not long ago it appeared as if the battle for grandparents' visitation rights had been won, a new wrinkle was introduced during the summer of 1993, when the Tennessee Supreme Court found that state's law regarding grandparents' visitation unconstitutional. The court held that the parents' right to privacy granted under the Tennessee Constitution protected them from outside interference in the way they raised their children. It ruled that courts could not substitute their judgment about what was in the best interests of a child unless the child's parents were found to be unfit. So if a child's parents wanted to keep that child from visiting with his or her grandparents, the court could not order visitation without violating the parents' privacy rights. Legal experts expect that the Tennessee Supreme Court's decision will bring about new challenges to similar laws in other states.

THE AGING OF AMERICA

America's population continues to grow older. By the year 2030, the number of people over the age of 60 will have increased by more than 50 percent. As a result, many people now find themselves in the position of having to care for an aging parent at the same time they are trying to raise their children. Although in general there is no legal requirement that an adult child care for an elderly parent, many people feel at least a moral obligation to provide for those who brought them into the world and cared for them during their younger years.

While most elderly Americans continue to lead active and healthy lives, some will inevitably fall victim to the illnesses and infirmities associated with growing old, such as Alzheimer's

Disease, which take their toll on the ability of an elderly person to live independently.

If you're faced with the problem of helping an elderly parent manage his or her affairs, the law provides several avenues of assistance.

If your parent is having problems with managing his or her financial matters but is otherwise able to care for himself, you may file a petition in state court asking it to establish a conservatorship for your parent's property, If your parent is unable to manage his other affairs as well, you may petition for a guardianship, which gives the guardian full control over all the decisions surrounding a person's life.

Even if your parent consents to the naming of a guardian, a court hearing will still be required. If your parent disputes the establishment of a conservatorship or guardianship, he or she is entitled to be represented by an attorney, to present evidence, and to testify about his ability to continue managing his own affairs. If the court decides a custodianship or guardianship is necessary, it will then appoint a person who it believes will act in the best interest of your parent. In some cases, that may be someone other than you.

A guardian or conservator can be required to post a bond to ensure the court that he or she will act responsibly in managing the elderly person's property and personal affairs.

Because a guardianship deprives the ward of many important rights necessary for independent living, it should be used only in cases where it is absolutely necessary. An older person can arrange to have a friend or family member write checks and make sure that bills are paid on time by executing a power of attorney. A power of attorney is a document in which one person (called the principal) authorizes another person (called the attorney-in-fact) to act on his behalf.

This document allows one person to give another person the authority to act on his or her behalf in the management of personal affairs. With a durable power of attorney, the attorney-in-fact can pay bills, manage a business, conduct real estate transactions, or perform any function that the principal authorizes. A durable power of attorney will remain in effect even if the person who makes it later becomes incompetent or incapacitated.

Another option is a so-called "springing" power of attorney, which only becomes effective when a specified event takes place, such as the incapacity of the person who authorizes it. In any case, a power of attorney can only be created while the principal is legally competent. If your elderly parent is presently incapable of managing his or her affairs, it's already too late to have a power of attorney created.

NURSING HOMES

Today's working families are often faced with the realization that there's no one family member who can stay home and care for an elderly parent. In some cases, a family member may suffer from a debilitating disease which requires constant nursing care. One of the options available to these families is a nursing home, also referred to as a long-term care facility.

Federal and state laws set standards that the various types of nursing homes must meet. A license to operate a nursing home will not be issued by the state regulatory agency unless the facility has complied with minimum standards set out in state law. The agency responsible for monitoring nursing homes may vary, but in most states the responsibility belongs to the Department of Health.

Of course, just because a nursing home meets minimum government standards doesn't mean it's right for your parent. Most of us would prefer to have our elderly relatives living in a facility that goes far beyond the minimum. That's why you should be sure to check out any nursing home personally. You'll want to be sure that your parent is getting high quality care, and government regulators just aren't equipped to do much more than enforce the minimum standards necessary to protect residents health and safety.

Nursing homes can be very expensive, with annual charges at some homes in excess of $70,000. When asking about the monthly charge for care, be sure to find out what services are included in that charge. The nursing home staff should tell you what services require additional payment, whether you must give the nursing home a deposit and what procedure must be followed to obtain a return of that deposit.

Another important question is whether the nursing home is certified under Medicare or Medicaid. Medicare will only pay for skilled nursing home care if it occurs within 30 days of a hospital stay. The full cost of such nursing home care is paid by Medicare for the first 20 days. For stays that last over 20 days, Medicare will only pay a percentage of costs up to 100 days. After 100 days the resident is entirely responsible for the cost.

Medicaid will pay for care in both skilled and intermediate care facilities. If the facility accepts Medicaid as payment, you cannot be billed for any costs that are included in that Medicaid reimbursement. You are entitled to keep a portion of each month's income as a personal needs allowance. For a further discussion of Medicaid, Medicare, and other government programs, be sure to read Chapter Thirteen, "Your Government Benefits."

NURSING HOME ALTERNATIVES

As nursing home care grows more expensive, a number of alternative living arrangements for seniors have begun to develop.

One such alternative is a so-called "assisted living" facility. In these facilities, the residents have their own fully equipped apartments, as well as a group dining facility where they can take some of their meals with other residents. These facilities usually have some kinds of organized activities designed to ensure that residents get out for shopping trips, concerts, and other cultural events. They provide assistance for older persons who may need help with dressing and bathing, and they usually have professional nursing staff or emergency medical personnel on duty around the clock. The cost of living in one of these facilities averages about two-thirds of what nursing home care costs, and gives the resident a greater sense of privacy, freedom, and autonomy than nursing home residents have.

Even less expensive are senior communities, sometimes referred to as congregate living facilities. These have many of the features of an assisted living facility, but are designed for older persons who are in good health and have less need of medical assistance. As a result, a congregate living facility may not have trained personnel on duty on a 24-hour a day basis.

Unlike nursing homes, these facilities are generally less regulated by government agencies, so you'll need to take extra care if your elderly parent is considering living in one of these communities. Be sure to visit the facility at least several times at varying times of the day, and ask if you may have a meal in the group dining facility. Observe the interaction between residents and staff members, and don't be afraid to ask questions of those already living there. Listen closely to their answers; enthusiastic responses about the quality of the facility are generally a good sign.

ABUSE OF THE ELDERLY

Abuse of the elderly is as unthinkable and as horrifying as the abuse of children, and by some accounts seems to be growing just about as quickly. According to some studies, each year more than 1.5 million adults over the age of 60 are the victims of abuse or neglect each year. About two-thirds of these cases involve abuse by a younger person who depends on the victim for support.

There are laws in most states designed to protect the elderly from abuse. At least forty-four states have enacted mandatory reporting laws which require health care workers and other professionals to report suspected cases of abuse. Some states have laws which provide for fines and prison sentences for persons who convicted of neglecting an elderly person in their care. In many states, an older person can obtain a court order of protection which prohibits the abuser from having physical contact with the elderly person.

For more information about the rights of the elderly, you may want to contact your county law library or your state's department on aging. A list of these offices follows at the end of this chapter. You can also obtain a referral to lawyers in your area who specialize in issues effecting the elderly by contacting:

The National Academy of Elder Law Attorneys
1730 East River Road, Suite 107
Tucson, Arizona 85718

Additionally, there are some programs providing free or low cost legal services to the elderly which have been established and funded through the federal law known as the Older Americans Act. These services are often provided through your community's legal aid society.

STATE AGENCIES ON AGING

Alabama
Commission on Aging
770 Washington Avenue
Montgomery, AL 36130
(205) 242-5743
toll free in state: (800) 243-5463

Alaska
Older Alaskans Commission
P.O. Box C
Juneau, AK 99811-0209
(907) 465-3250

Arizona
Aging and Adult Administration
1400 West Washington
Phoenix, AZ 85007
(602) 542-4446

Arkansas
Office of Aging and Adult Services
Department of Human Services
P.O. Box 1437
Little Rock, AR 72203
(501) 682-2441

California
California Department of Aging
1600 K Street
Sacramento, CA 95814
(916) 322-5290

Colorado
Aging and Adult Services Division
Department of Social Services
1575 Sherman Street
Denver, CO 80203-1714
(303) 866-3851

Connecticut
Department on Aging
175 Main Street
Hartford, CT 06106
(203) 566-3238
toll free in state: (800) 443-9946

Delaware
Department of Health and Social Services
Division of Aging
1901 N. DuPont Highway
New Castle, DE 19720
(302) 421-6791
toll free in state: (800) 223-9074

District of Columbia
D.C. Office on Aging
1424 K Street, NW
Washington, DC 20005
(202) 724-5626

Florida
Aging and Adult Services
1317 Winewood Boulevard
Tallahassee, FL 32301
(904) 488-8922

Georgia
Office of Aging
878 Peachtree Street, NE
Atlanta, GA 30309
(404) 894-5333

Hawaii
Executive Office on Aging
Office of the Governor
335 Merchant Street
Honolulu, HI 96813
(808) 586-0100

Idaho
Idaho Office on Aging
Statehouse
Boise, ID 83720
(208) 334-3833

Illinois
Department on Aging
421 East Capitol Avenue
Springfield, IL 62701
(217) 785-2870
toll free nationwide: (800) 252-8966

Indiana
Aging Division
Department of Human Services
P.O. Box 7083
Indianapolis, IN 46207-7083
(317) 232-7020
toll free in state: (800) 622-4972

Iowa
Department of Elder Affairs
914 Grand Avenue
Des Moines, IA 50319
(515) 281-5187
toll free in state: (800) 532-3213

Kansas
Department on Aging
Docking State Office Building
915 Southwest Harrison Street
Topeka, KS 66612-1500
(913) 296-4986
toll free in state: (800) 432-3535

Kentucky
Division for Aging Services
275 East Main Street
Frankfort, KY 40621
(502) 564-6930
toll free in state: (800) 372-2991

Louisiana
Office of Elderly Affairs
P.O. Box 80374
Baton Rouge, LA 70806
(504) 925-1700

Maine
Bureau of Elder and Adult Services
Statehouse
Station 11

August, ME 04333-0011
(207) 626-5335

Maryland
Office on Aging
301 West Preston Street
Baltimore, MD 21201
(301) 225-1100
toll free in state: (800) 243-3425

Massachusetts
Executive Office of Elder Affairs
38 Chauncy Street
Boston, MA 02111
(617) 727-7750

Michigan
Office of Services to the Aging
P.O. Box 30026
Lansing, MI 48909
(517) 373-8230

Minnesota
Minnesota Board on Aging
444 Lafayette Road
St. Paul, MN 55155-3843
(612) 296-2770
toll free in state: (800) 652-9747

Mississippi
Division of Aging and Adult Services
421 West Pascagoula Street
Jackson, MS 39203-3524
(601) 949-2070
toll free in state: (800) 222-7622

Missouri
Division of Aging
Department of Social Services
P.O. Box 1337
Jefferson City, MO 65102-1337
(314) 751-3082
toll free in state: (800) 392-0210

Montana
The Governor's Office on Aging
State Capitol Building
Capitol Station
Helena, MT 59620
(406) 444-3111
toll free in state: (800) 332-2272

Nebraska
Nebraska Department on Aging
301 Centennial Mall South
P.O. Box 95044
Lincoln, NE 68509
(402) 471-2306

Nevada
Division of Aging Services
Department of Human Resources
340 North 11th Street
Las Vegas, NV 89101
(702) 486-3545

New Hampshire
Division of Elderly and Adult Services
6 Hazen Drive
Concord, NH 03301-6501
(603) 271-4680
toll free in state: (800) 351-1888

New Jersey
Division on Aging
Department of Community Affairs
South Broad and Front Streets
CN 807
Trenton, NJ 08625-0807
(609) 292-4833
toll free in state: (800) 792-8820

New Mexico
State Agency on Aging
224 E. Palace Avenue
Santa Fe, NM 87501
(505) 827-7640
toll free in state: (800) 432-2080

New York
New York State Office for the Aging
Agency Building 2
Albany, NY 12223
(518) 474-4425
toll free in state: (800) 342-9871

North Carolina
Division of Aging
Department of Human Resources
693 Palmer Drive
Raleigh, NC 27603
(919) 733-3983
toll free in state: (800) 662-7030

North Dakota
Aging Services
Department of Human Services
600 East Boulevard
Bismarck, ND 58505
(701) 224-2577
toll free in state: (800) 472-2622

Ohio
Ohio Department of Aging
50 West Broad Street
Columbus, OH 43266-0501
(614) 466-5500

Oklahoma
Aging Services Division
Department of Human Services
P.O. Box 25352
Oklahoma City, OK 73125
(405) 521-2327

Oregon
Senior and Disabled Services Division
Department of Human Resources
313 Public Service Building
Salem, OR 97310
(503) 378-4728
toll free in state: (800) 232-3020

Pennsylvania
Department of Aging
231 State Street
Harrisburg, PA 17101-1195
(717) 783-1550

Rhode Island
Department of Elderly Affairs
160 Pine Street
Providence, RI 02903-3708
(401) 277-2858
toll free in state: (800) 322-2880

South Carolina
Commission on Aging
400 Arbor Lake Drive
Columbia, SC 29223
(803) 735-0210

South Dakota
Office of Adult Services and Aging
700 North Illinois Street
Pierre, SD 57501
(605) 773-3656

Tennessee
Commission on Aging
706 Church Street
Nashville, TN 37243-0860
(615) 741-2056

Texas
Texas Department on Aging
P.O. Box 12786
Capitol Station
Austin, TX 78741
(512) 444-2727
toll free in state: (800) 252-9240

Utah
Division of Aging and Adult Services
Department of Social Service
P.O. Box 45500
Salt Lake City, UT 84145
(801) 538-3910

Vermont
Department of Aging and Disabilities
103 South Main Street
Waterbury, VT 05676
(802) 241-2400

Virginia
Department for the Aging
700 East Franklin Street
Richmond, VA 23219-2327
(804) 225-2271
toll free in state: (800) 552-4464

Washington
Aging and Adult Services Administration
Department of Social and Health Services
OB-44A
Olympia, WA 98504
(206) 586-3768
toll free in state: (800) 422-3263

West Virginia
Commission on Aging
State Capitol
Charleston, WV 25305
(304) 348-3317
toll free in state: (800) 642-3671

Wisconsin
Bureau of Aging
Division of Community Services
217 South Hamilton Street
Madison, WI 53707
(608) 266-2536

Wyoming
Commission on Aging
Hathaway Building
Cheyenne, WY 82002-0710
(307) 777-7986
toll free in state: (800) 442-2766

CHAPTER THREE
LANDLORDS AND TENANTS

For many Americans, a rented apartment or house is their first "home away from home." Millions of Americans, either out of choice or necessity, will live in rented homes for all their lives. Other thousands of Americans act as landlords, leasing one or more units to renters. In this chapter, we'll take a look at the legal rights and responsibilities of both landlords and tenants, and discuss some of the legal issues that surround the landlord-tenant relationship.

Before we begin, however, it's important to remember that landlord-tenant relationships are generally a matter of state and local laws, and can vary pretty widely from one place to another. If you have specific questions about the exact provisions of the law in your area, a good resource to know about is your local department of housing. In many communities, this department can provide pamphlets that outline the local laws governing landlord-tenant issues.

In most larger cities, there are tenants' rights organizations that can provide assistance when you have a problem with a landlord, and landlords' organizations to provide assistance to property owners and managers. And your state or local bar association's lawyer referral service can help you obtain low cost legal advice and assistance, including help in drafting residential leases and (if necessary) handling evictions. By following the advice in this chapter, however, you should be able to avoid many of the most common problems that occur when you are either a landlord or a tenant.

FINDING GOOD TENANTS

When you decide to become a landlord, there are a number of steps which you will need to take to locate good tenants, protect your property from excessive damage, and minimize conflict and problems with your tenants.

First, you will need to decide what kind of tenant you are looking for, how much rent you want to charge, and how other kinds of expenses (such as utilities, trash removal, and heating oil) will be apportioned. Will you expect the tenant to bear these costs, or will you provide some or all of these services at your own expense? Will you accept renters who have pets, or do you want to prohibit them entirely?

While you can't engage in illegal discrimination as a landlord, that doesn't mean you can't exercise some discretion in selecting the tenants who will live in your property. If, for example, you have a small one bedroom home available to rent, you can certainly limit the number of people who will live there. If you are a single woman renting a room in your home, you generally have the right to refuse to rent to a man.

However, state and federal equal housing laws generally prohibit you from turning down families with children, and from discriminating on the basis of race, sex, religion, national origin, or disability. And in some communities, you cannot discriminate on the basis of a prospective tenant's sexual orientation or marital status. Your community housing department can fill you in on the exact details of the laws in your area, and you can usually find this information in the state statutes and local ordinances which are available at most public libraries, or at the county courthouse's law library. For information about federal equal housing laws, contact the U.S. Department of Housing and Urban Development (HUD). You can find the number for the HUD office in your area in the U.S. Government listings of your telephone directory.

The most important issue for any landlord is collecting the agreed upon rental payments on time. While there's no way to absolutely guarantee that a tenant won't turn out to be a deadbeat, there are some things you can do to minimize this possibility.

You should require any prospective tenant to complete a rental application. You can find preprinted application forms at many stationery and office supply stores. A good application form will ask for the following information:

- The applicant's name
- The applicant's current address and length of time there
- The applicant's previous address and length of time there
- The applicant's employer and length of time on the job
- The applicant's previous employer and length of time on the job
- The applicant's gross monthly income
- Credit and banking references
- Employment and personal references
- Whether the applicant has any pets, and if so, what kind and size
- The name and previous address of any co-applicant, or anyone else who will live in your property
- For co-applicants, all of the information requested of the applicant

In addition, the form should include a statement that authorizes you to verify all of the information provided, including checking references and obtaining a credit report. You should be sure to have the applicant and co-applicant sign the application form.

Once you have the completed application in hand, follow up on any applicants who meet your preliminary criteria, and eliminate those who don't. For example, if you are renting a house you own for $800 per month and the applicant only has $1200 per month in income, you probably don't need to inquire any further.

For the applicants who pass the first screening, contact employment and personal references, and obtain a credit report from one of the major credit reporting agencies, such as TRW, TransUnion, or Equifax. You can get these reports directly by paying an annual fee and a fee for each report directly to the credit bureau. If you belong to a landlord's association, it may have arranged a discount for its members, so check there first before going directly to the credit bureau.

Contact the applicant's current and previous landlords for information about what kind of tenant the applicant has been. One good question to ask is whether or not the landlord would rent to this applicant again. Don't be surprised if you don't obtain much information through this process, however, since landlords are increasingly wary about the potential for a lawsuit if they make unflattering remarks about a tenant. Ultimately, you'll still need to exercise your own judgment about any applicant. But the more information you can gather, the better informed your decision will be.

As a landlord, you have a right to expect that your tenants will pay their rent on time and in the amount agreed upon. You also have a right to expect your tenants to use the home you've rented to them in a reasonable manner. It's not usually considered reasonable to use a home as an oil-change center, for example, unless you specifically permit a business use in your rental agreement.

You should also expect your tenants to treat appliances, plumbing, and the residence itself with reasonable care, and to report any damage or other problems as soon as they're discovered, so you can fix them promptly.

Tenants who abuse the property you've rented to them, or who fail to pay the rent on time, or who breach their lease in other ways can be evicted, but the eviction process can be slow and require added expense for the landlord. (We'll discuss evictions in more detail later in this chapter.)

The best way to assure yourself that your expectations of your tenants will be met is to carefully screen and select the tenants to whom you rent and to clearly state the tenants' responsibilities in your rental agreement.

THE RENTAL AGREEMENT

Once you've decided on a tenant, you will want to use a rental agreement, or lease, to formalize your relationship. While it's possible to proceed without a written agreement if your tenant will be occupying your property on a month-to-month basis, a written lease is the only way to be sure that both you and the tenant have a clear understanding of the terms and conditions governing your relationship.

You can have a lawyer prepare a lease for you to use, or you can obtain a standard preprinted lease at many stationery and office supply stores. If you belong to a landlords' organization, it will usually have a standardized lease that complies with state and local laws for its members' use. In general, you'll want a lease to include:

- A description of the unit to be rented
- The dates that the lease begins and ends
- The names of all the parties to the lease
- The amount of rent and when it is due
- The amount of any security deposit or other deposits
- A prohibition against pets, or a description of those permitted
- A statement prohibiting or regulating the tenant's right to sublet
- A clause allocating responsibility for utilities and other expenses
- The address to which any notices required by law can be sent
- A requirement that any changes to the lease also be made in writing
- A description of how the lease is terminated or renewed
- The other obligations of landlord and tenant

The lease should be signed at the end by everyone who will be obligated by the lease terms. That means the landlord, the tenant, and any co-tenants.

A lease is a contract, and like all contracts it can be amended and modified for different situations. If you are using a preprinted lease, you can delete certain provisions by lining through them and initialing the change (the tenant must also initial changes to be bound by them). If you want to add a term or condition, most preprinted leases provide a blank space where you can make your addition.

SECURITY DEPOSITS

The lease should clearly set out the requirements for the tenant's security deposit. A security deposit is almost always a good idea when you rent an apartment or residence. This deposit is designed to ensure that the tenant lives up to the promises made in the lease agreement. If the tenant breaks the lease or causes excessive damage to the rental unit, the landlord can use the deposit to offset the additional costs that result.

It's important to note that the security deposit is not intended to serve as a substitute for rent. Many tenants think that they can skip their last month's rent payment and have the landlord use the security deposit as compensation. In fact, some state laws actually prohibit a landlord from applying a security deposit toward unpaid rent.

State laws that regulate security deposits in residential rental agreements vary so widely that it's impossible to describe them all in detail here. In general, however, these laws regulate the maximum amount that can be charged as a security deposit, and they can also restrict the landlord's use of the deposit. For example, most states require that security deposits be placed in escrow, and some states require the landlord to place the deposit in an interest bearing bank account, and pay the interest to the tenant. When the tenant moves out, the landlord is required to either return the deposit within a specified period of time (such as 30 days) or notify the tenant in writing why all or some of the deposit is being withheld. The landlord may be legally required to provide the former tenant with an itemized list of the damage claimed.

If a former tenant disputes the damage claim, a trip to court may be required to settle the matter. In many states, small claims court will be the court with jurisdiction over a security deposit dispute. If the court finds that the landlord was not justified in keeping the deposit, some states can require the landlord to pay a sum equal to two or three times the actual amount of the deposit.

Besides a security deposit, some landlords also charge a non-refundable cleaning deposit. This deposit is used to cover the cost of painting, carpet cleaning and other expenses the landlord will incur when the tenant leaves. If the landlord accepts pets, a pet deposit may also be required to cover the expense of removing pet stains and odors from the rental unit when the tenant moves out.

SAFETY AND SECURITY

Landlords are legally responsible for keeping common areas, such as hallways and the grounds in an apartment complex reasonably safe, clear of debris, and well lighted. They must provide adequate door and window locks to prevent strangers from entering your rental property, and in some states they have to provide smoke detectors and fire extinguishers to help protect you from fire.

Landlords are also responsible for ensuring that their employees don't present a danger to tenants. That means they have to take reasonable precautions, such as conducting background checks, when they hire maintenance people, janitors, or anyone else who may have access to your residence.

Landlords aren't insurers, however, and so tenants need to purchase renters' insurance to protect their personal belongings from damage, destruction or loss due to fire, burglary, or some other cause. (A renters' policy doesn't cover the building itself, but only its contents.) It also provides liability protection in case someone sues you because of an injury they suffer in an area of the rental property that's under your control, or because of your negligence. Renters' insurance is relatively inexpensive, as insurance goes, and in most parts of the country you can purchase an adequate policy for $100 or thereabouts. Before you do, however, be sure to read Chapter Ten, "Your Insurance," for advice about selecting the right insurance company.

HOW TO BE A SMART TENANT

Until now, our discussion has focused on landlord-tenant relationships primarily from the landlord's point of view. As a potential tenant, there are some steps you can take before you sign a lease to minimize potential problems with your landlord.

Once you're accepted by a landlord as a potential tenant, you should be sure to ask for a chance to inspect your new home before you actually sign a lease. This is especially important if you've only seen a model unit in a large apartment complex, since the model will certainly have been far better maintained and decorated than the unit you'll actually be renting.

During this inspection, which should be conducted with the landlord or the landlord's representative present, document any problems or damage you discover, and ask the landlord to fix them before you take possession of the premises. If you can't get the landlord to agree to do so before you sign the lease, you should have the defects noted in an attachment to your lease, as well as a provision for when they will be fixed. If the landlord fails to honor this provision, you will have evidence of the breach and stand a better chance with the courts if you move out and the landlord sues you for doing so, as well as evidence that the damage existed before you moved in and wasn't caused by you.

If the landlord simply refuses to make written provision for fixing damage or repairing defective appliances and the like, you should reconsider whether or not this is the kind of place you want to live in. Don't rely on oral promises that "everything will be taken care of." If the landlord intends to honor his promise, he won't mind putting it in writing.

If the place you're considering is in very poor condition, or if the grounds are badly maintained, you may want to think twice about renting it, no matter what promises the landlord agrees to make in writing about repairs. A landlord who's willing to show a poorly maintained property may not be someone you can rely on to perform the necessary repairs and maintenance, no matter how favorable a rental agreement you negotiate.

Most states have what are known as "implied warranty of habitability" laws. Generally, these laws require a landlord to provide a residence that's suitable for occupancy by humans and free of conditions that pose a threat to the life, health, or safety of occupants.

Unfortunately, the interpretation of "habitability" from one state to another is extremely inconsistent. In some states, courts may interpret this warranty as requiring a landlord to maintain air conditioning, elevators, appliances and other conveniences in good working order. In other states, landlords can just about meet their legal obligations by merely providing heat, water, and a roof.

In those states which don't imply a warranty of habitability, landlords are only required to provide what's called for in the lease. So if the roof's caving in and your lease doesn't require the landlord to maintain the premises and make repairs, you could end up literally sleeping under the stars and still be required to pay rent. You can find out about the laws in your state by contacting your local housing department, tenants' rights organization, or the consumer affairs division of the state attorney general's office.

The law in every state entitles you to a reasonable expectation of privacy in your own home, even if you're a renter. In most cases, this means you don't have to allow your landlord unlimited access to the premises. However, you may be required to allow your landlord to enter to make repairs, or to show the property to a prospective tenant if you're not renewing your rental agreement. Your lease should require that your landlord give you reasonable advance notice of the need to enter your rental unit, except in case of an emergency, such as a fire or to fix a burst water pipe.

TO SUBLET, OR NOT TO SUBLET

To borrow from Shakespeare's *Hamlet*, "that is the question." But before we can try to answer it, it may be helpful to define a few terms.

A sublease involves a transfer of something less than all of the interest a tenant has in his lease. In contrast, an assignment is the transfer of all the tenant's rights and responsibilities contained in the entire lease to another person. To illustrate the difference, let's look at two examples.

Wendy has a one-year lease on her apartment in Chicago. Two months into the lease, her employer asks her to take a temporary six month transfer to San Francisco to rescue a failing division of the company. Wendy wants to keep her apartment in Chicago to return to when the assignment on the West Coast is finished, so she may try to sublease it to another for the six months she is away. The subtenant gets less than the entire remainder of the lease.

On the other hand, Wendy's neighbor Jim, who works for the same company, is given a promotion and a permanent transfer to San Francisco. However, he also has ten months remaining on his lease. If Jim finds someone to assume the rest of the lease period, he will assign his lease to the new tenant.

There are some other differences as well. When you sublease to another, you in effect become the subtenant's landlord. However, your own obligations to your landlord are not ended with the sublease. If the subtenant doesn't pay the rent, you are still required to do so. If the subtenant damages the property, you are responsible for the damages.

With an assignment, the landlord can sue the new tenant directly for damages or for late rent. But in most cases, the landlord also retains his right to sue you as well. So if you have money and the tenant to whom the lease was assigned doesn't, guess which one of you the landlord will decide to pursue in court?

In most cases, landlords prefer not to permit a tenant to sublease or assign their lease at all. In others, a landlord may allow a tenant to sublet or assign the lease, but only with the landlord's advance written permission and approval of the subtenant. But even when your lease contains this kind of provision, the landlord can usually refuse to accept any proposed subtenant without explanation. The way to be sure that the landlord won't be unreasonable is to include a provision in your lease stating that the landlord will not be unreasonable in withholding his approval of a subtenant.

If you are going to assign or sublet your lease, you will want to be just as careful about the person to whom you sublet as your landlord was in approving you. That means taking applications, checking credit, work, and personal references, and contacting previous landlords for recommendations. And you'll also want to have a written agreement with the subtenant that outlines your mutual rights and responsibilities, including when and how you can recover the property if the subtenant fails to pay rent or otherwise breaches the agreement.

As you can see, answering the question "to sublet or not to sublet," isn't an easy one, whether you are a landlord or a tenant. Doing so requires using some sound judgment and common sense, along with a knowledge of your legal rights.

WHEN YOU HAVE A COMPLAINT

It's January and temperatures are well below freezing, but your landlord hasn't made the necessary repairs on your furnace. Or the refrigerator the landlord provided doesn't work properly, with the result that your food is spoiling and ice cream turns to soup within hours after you bring it home from the store. Or the deadbolt lock on the front door is broken and the door can't be secured properly, depriving you of sleep and worrying you about the safety of your family and property.

In these and other situations where you need to make a complaint to your landlord, your best first step is to simply call him on the telephone. Most landlords want to keep their tenants happy, since it's much easier and far cheaper to keep a good tenant than to find a new one.

If your landlord doesn't take action to resolve your complaint, your next step is to notify him in writing of the problem. Your letter should be clear and concise, but not threatening. In your own words, tell the landlord the problem you have and the actions you want him to take, and set out a reasonable time limit, such as ten days or so, for his response.

If the problem still isn't attended to, you'll want to send another, more strongly worded letter. This time, send the letter by certified mail, return receipt requested. If the problem involves a dangerous condition on the property, such as a missing stair rail or a problem with wiring, send a copy of the letter to the local housing department. Always keep copies of any letters you send, and maintain a log of telephone calls you make in regard to a problem with your landlord.

If problems continue unabated, your next step depends on both your own disposition and the law in your area. In some states, the law allows a tenant to pay for necessary repairs and deduct the cost from the next month's rent payment. In others, you may be able to move out of the apartment and end your rent obligation by claiming that the landlord's failure to make necessary repairs amounted to what the law calls "constructive eviction." In either case, you will need to notify the landlord in advance of any actions you take, and give him one last chance in which to make the repairs you require.

Unfortunately, many tenants, especially older ones, suffer inadequate maintenance silently. In most cases, they do so out of fear of "making a scene" or because they are afraid the landlord will evict them from their homes. But in most communities, the law is on your side, and a landlord can't engage in retaliatory eviction if you report a code violation to the authorities, or if you complain about inadequate maintenance and repairs.

As a tenant, you have a right to expect that your landlord will live up to the terms of your lease and the provisions of the law. Knuckling under to a bad landlord makes things worse, not only for you but for the community at large, since poorly maintained properties have a negative effect on surrounding properties in the neighborhood.

BREAKING YOUR LEASE

People often wonder whether or not they can break their lease. The answer is yes. A lease is a contract, and thousands of contracts are broken every day. The better question to ask is what the consequences will be if you break your lease.

In general, if you break your lease your landlord has a right to go to court to seek enforcement of the lease. If he wins, the court can order you to continue to pay rent, even if you live somewhere else. You may also be required to pay your landlord's court costs and attorney fees.

However, your landlord has a responsibility to mitigate, or lessen, the damages he suffers. That generally means that he can't just let the property stand vacant and expect you to pay the rent. He must advertise the property and make it available to others. Once he leases the property to another, your legal responsibilities end.

But keep in mind that the landlord has a right to recover the costs associated with finding a new tenant from you. And your landlord isn't required to rent the property to the first warm body that comes along, although he can't be unreasonable in rejecting prospective tenants. If the rental market is slow, it may be months before a suitable new tenant is located, so you can still be obligated for rent during that whole period of time.

If you think you may need to break a lease because of a possible job transfer, it's best to let your landlord know about this as soon as possible, even before you sign your lease. Some landlords will allow you to lease for a shorter period of time, while others may allow you to break the lease by giving advance notice of 30 or 60 days. Your landlord may also agree to let you out of your lease early in return for a penalty payment. If the landlord won't agree to these concessions, however, you may have to explore other alternatives, such as subletting the property, or pay the price for leaving before your lease expires.

Of course, it may be possible to break a lease without suffering any penalty when the landlord fails to provide adequate maintenance and the property becomes unsafe or unfit for humans to live in. In these cases, tenants may argue that the landlord's neglect amounts to "constructive eviction," claiming that the landlord has deprived them of the benefit of their bargain. Things have to be extremely bad before this argument will succeed, however. Just because the property is unpleasant to live in, or because you've suffered an inconvenience, such as a stove that the landlord keeps having to fix, isn't enough to support a claim of constructive eviction.

DISCRIMINATION

If you are turned down for a rental, or if your landlord refuses to renew your lease, the landlord must not have based his decision on illegal grounds. Under federal law, a landlord cannot refuse to rent to a potential tenant because of the tenant's race, national origin, sex religion, or disability. In many situations, a landlord is also prohibited from discriminating against families with children. And as we've already seen, state and local laws may prohibit discrimination against other kinds of individuals.

If you suspect you have been the victim of illegal discrimination in applying for or renting a home, you can contact your community's fair housing agency or human rights commission. You can also obtain advice about federal anti-discrimination laws from the Fair Housing and Equal Opportunity Office of the U.S. Department of Housing and Urban Development. You should not wait too long to file a complaint, since federal law requires that you do so within 180 days of the alleged discriminatory act.

You may also want to consider filing a lawsuit against the landlord you believe is guilty of illegal discrimination. If successful, you can collect actual damages (such as the additional amount you had to spend for rent elsewhere), punitive damages up to $1,000, and ask the court for reiumbusement of court costs and reasonable attorney fees.

EVICTIONS

If ever there was a "no-win" proposition, it's eviction. For the tenant, an eviction can be a matter of enormous embarrassment. An eviction can cause severe damage to your credit record, and serves as a source of stress, anxiety, and even fear. For the landlord, an eviction means loss of income, as well as court costs, legal fees and the added expenses of finding a new tenant.

Like other legal matters, the process for carrying out an eviction differs from state to state. Generally, however, the process requires several steps.

First, the tenant must be in breach of some serious term of the rental agreement. In most cases, that means failing to pay the rent on time and in the required amount.

Second, the landlord must notify the tenant in writing of the breach and give the tenant an opportunity to cure, or correct the breach. If the tenant takes the steps necessary to get back in compliance with the lease's terms, he has the right to continue his tenancy.

If the tenant remains in breach, the next step a landlord must take is to file suit and serve the tenant with a summons and complaint. In most situations, that means having the sheriff or some other party deliver the summons to the person or persons occupying the rental property in person. In some situations, it may be possible to serve the summons and complaint by mail, but doing so usually takes longer and helps to drag out the proceedings.

A court hearing is then held to determine who is entitled to possession of the property. At this hearing, a tenant has the right to raise any defenses he may have to the eviction. If, for example, the landlord claims that the rent hasn't been paid, the tenant can prove that it was paid with a canceled check or a rent receipt. The tenant might also bring proof that the rent money was applied to making repairs that the landlord refused to make, if that's permitted by state law.

If, however, the court finds in favor of the landlord, the tenant will be required to move out, usually within a few days. If the tenant still refuses to leave the rental property, the landlord can't physically do anything to remove the tenant, but must contact the county sheriff or other local law enforcement officials and have them conduct the eviction.

As we've already noted, state and local laws and ordinances are meant to keep landlords from taking the law into their own hands when they want to evict a tenant. Unfortunately, that doesn't always prevent ill informed or downright rotten landlords from doing things the law says they can't do. Here are just a few of the illegal practices landlords have been known to engage in.

- Waiting until the tenant leaves for work and changing door locks
- Turning off utilities, such as water and electricity
- Playing loud music or making loud noises in an attempt to force the tenant out of the property
- Removing the tenant's belongings and placing them in the street
- Physically threatening the safety of the tenant, the tenant's family, or even the tenant's pets

If you are a landlord thinking of using one of these techniques as a way to force your tenants off the property, think again. In addition to the criminal charges you may face for some of these actions, state laws provide penalties for landlords who engage in unlawful eviction attempts. You could be severely fined, and end up facing a civil lawsuit by the tenant as well.

If you are a landlord faced with the possibility of evicting a tenant, or a tenant concerned about the eviction process, you will want to contact an attorney, or a self-help group such as a tenants' or landlords' association about the specifics of the eviction laws in your community.

In addition, some communities have established informal dispute resolution programs designed to hear landlord-tenant disputes before they reach the point where court action becomes necessary. Your community housing authority can tell you if there's a service available in your area. It may be possible to avoid the eviction process altogether through the use of these services.

CHAPTER FOUR
BUYING, SELLING, AND OWNING A HOME

In this chapter, we look at the most expensive and one of the most emotional investments the majority of us will ever make. Whether it's a farmhouse in the country, a house in a suburban subdivision, a condominium on the beach or a share in a cooperative apartment building, the law controls the ways in which real estate is bought and sold. It also regulates the ways you can use your property once you own it, and sets out a variety of rights and responsibilities for home owners. In some cases, the law even allows the government to take your property from you. We'll discuss how this can take place, and what your rights are if the government decides it needs your property for a public purpose.

If you're a renter, or if you're thinking about becoming a landlord, you'll want to look at Chapter Three, "Landlords and Tenants" for information about the way the law affects you.

TYPES OF HOMES YOU CAN BUY

You've been living the life of an apartment dweller for too long, and now you're ready to take the plunge into home ownership. You know that owning a home is generally a good investment, and that the interest you pay on your home mortgage is one of the few big tax deductions left for the average person. Before you begin the search for your dream home, there are some things you ought to know.

Basically, there are three kinds of homes available for sale or purchase. A single family home sits on a parcel of land separate from the homes around it. You own both the land and the lot upon which it is built. You alone are responsible for the upkeep and maintenance of your property.

A condominium is one unit in a building or complex of other units or buildings. As a condominium owner, you receive title to your own unit, but you don't have any individual ownership rights to the ground upon which the complex or building is constructed. This so-called "common area," which may also include halls, parking facilities and the surrounding gardens and paths is usually owned by the condominium developer or the association that manages the complex, and the cost of maintenance and improvement of these areas is shared jointly by all the owners of units in the complex.

A cooperative is a kind of corporation that owns property which has been divided into various apartments. When you "buy into" a cooperative, you become one of its shareholders, but you don't actually purchase any real estate, not even the unit you live in. The cooperative itself owns the property, and you obtain what's called a "proprietary lease" from the cooperative. To become a shareholder in the cooperative you have to be voted in by the other shareholders. You get a voice in deciding how the cooperative is run, and who else gets to buy shares in the cooperative, by voting as a shareholder at cooperative meetings. Finally, when it comes time to sell your shares, the purchaser usually must also be approved by a majority of the other cooperative members.

USING A REAL ESTATE BROKER

Whichever kind of home you decide is right for you, the chances are that you will use the services of a real estate broker to help you in your search and to guide you through the buying process. While it's possible to buy a home directly from a seller without using a broker's services, real estate brokers can provide a valuable service, especially to a first time home buyer.

For example, a good real estate broker will be familiar with all the properties for sale in the area you want to purchase in and in the price range you can afford. He may even be able to recommend other communities in the area which would suit your purposes but which you might not have considered on your own. Real estate brokers can provide information about taxes, schools and community services in the area of your choice, and they can provide guidance about financing your home purchase. If you are moving to a community in a new state, they can give valuable information about obtaining business and professional licenses, paying utility deposits, and may even be able to arrange discounts on moving company services.

However, unless you sign what's known as a buyer's brokerage agreement, it's important to remember that a real estate broker is considered by the law to be the agent of the seller, and has a legal obligation to get the best possible price for the seller's property. That means that you should be somewhat cautious about revealing too much information to the broker about your feelings about a particular property.

If, for example, you tell the broker that you love a particular house and would be willing to pay the asking price for it, you may find it impossible to make an offer below the asking price and have that accepted by the seller. A real estate broker is legally required to present all written offers to the seller, but he also has a duty to the seller to tell him if your offer is the best one you'll make. If the broker knows you are willing to go higher to get the house, he can't encourage the seller to accept your lower offer. If he did, the seller could sue him later for the difference between what you paid and what you were willing to pay. And since a broker's commission is typically a percentage of the sale price, it's against his own interests to suggest the lower price as well. So it's best to play it close to the vest if you are using the services of a real estate broker who works for the seller.

If you are selling a home, you don't need a real estate broker to do so. But unless you are willing to advertise the home yourself, conduct tours, qualify buyers, and arrange for the real estate contracts and closing, a broker's services can be a good investment. In most cases, brokers charge a commission to the seller of from five percent to seven percent of the sale price of the property. However, some real estate brokers are now charging much lower commissions if you are willing to share some of the responsibility for selling your home, such as conducting open houses for prospective buyers. Some real estate brokers have even begun to charge a flat fee for the services they provide. And although some brokers would prefer that you not know it, real estate commissions are always negotiable. So if you live in a market where there's a lot of demand for houses you should be able to bargain for a lower commission.

When you use a real estate broker to sell your house, you will sign what's known as a listing agreement, which gives the broker the authority to find a buyer and receive his commission. There are several kinds of listing agreements that real estate brokers use.

The listing agreement you are most likely to be presented by a broker is the "exclusive right to sell" agreement. With this agreement, you promise the broker that he will receive a commission if the house is sold by anyone during the term of the agreement. Under an exclusive right to sell agreement, you have to pay the broker's commission even if you sell the home yourself. It's easy to see why this is the listing agreement brokers favor the most.

A better agreement, at least from the seller's point of view, is the exclusive agency agreement. With this kind of agreement, you only pay the broker's commission if the sale results from his efforts. If you sell your house to your nephew or to someone else you find on your own without any input or assistance from the real estate broker, you owe him no commission.

An open listing agreement not only gives you the right to sell your house yourself, but it also gives you the right to list the house with other brokers as well. You only pay a commission to the broker who actually finds the buyer. Open listings are not looked upon favorably by most real estate brokers, and it's unlikely you'll convince a broker to go for this kind of agreement.

In any case, you should try to avoid signing a listing agreement that lasts for more than 90 days. Most brokers will try to convince you to sign a six month agreement, and in sluggish markets they may even ask for a one year agreement. The problem with such long agreements is that they don't provide adequate motivation for the real estate broker to sell your home quickly. It's better to sign an agreement for a shorter term. If you think the broker is making a good faith effort to sell your property, you can always renew the agreement. That way, if you think the broker isn't trying hard enough to find you buyers, you aren't stuck for a long period.

While it's possible to cancel a brokerage agreement on the grounds that the broker isn't making a reasonable effort to market your property, your definition of "reasonable" may be different from the broker's, or a court's definition. Many lawsuits have been filed by brokers against homeowners who tried to get out of a too-lengthy listing agreement, and many of those lawsuits have been successful. Better to limit your relationship with any one broker to the shortest time period possible.

You'll also want to negotiate a provision in your listing agreement stating that no commission is earned by the broker until the sale of your property actually closes. In some cases, a defect in the title to the home made it impossible for the buyer to complete the purchase. In other cases, the seller changed his mind after the contracts were signed and refused to complete the deal with the buyer.

In many of these cases, the broker who arranged the sale was able to collect the commission he would have earned if the sale had been completed, because the listing agreement stated that the commission was earned when the broker found a buyer who was ready, willing, and able to make the purchase. While it's not likely that a broker will agree to a provision that deprives him of your commission if you simply change your mind about the sale, you shouldn't have to agree to pay the commission if the sale isn't completed through no fault of your own.

THE HOME BUYING PROCESS

Once you've found the home you want to buy, you'll make what's commonly known as an offer to purchase. This is a written document stating the price you're willing to pay for the property, as well as any contingencies, or conditions, you want to include. Some common contingencies are that the offer is subject to a satisfactory termite inspection and radon test, the buyer's ability to obtain financing, and the buyer's ability to sell his or her current home. The buyer attaches a check for an amount of money (usually from $100 to $500) that shows the sincerity of the offer and delivers it to the seller. The offer gives the seller a time limit of a up to a few days to consider the offer. If the seller doesn't accept the offer within this time limit, it expires, and the buyer's check is returned to him.

The seller has the choice of accepting the offer, rejecting it, or making a counteroffer. For example, a seller's counteroffer to a buyer's offer of $100,000 for the house in question might be $110,000, rather than the $120,000 the house was listed at. The buyer then has the choice of accepting or rejecting the counteroffer or making another counteroffer. (In this example, perhaps by raising the price to $115,000.) This step may be repeated several times in the process of arriving at a final agreement.

Once an agreement is reached, buyer and seller will execute what's known as a binder. The binder is a document that locks in the agreed upon price and keeps the seller from selling the property to anyone else. It's also accompanied by an earnest money deposit, which serves as the seller's consideration for taking the house off the market.

The binder is not the final contract for the transfer of ownership of the property. Most binders contain a provision that requires the parties to sign a contract for sale within a specified period of time, or cancel the agreement. If the contract isn't drawn up on schedule, the buyer is entitled to the return of his earnest money deposit.

After the binder is signed, the actual real estate purchase contract is drawn up. In this contract, all of the details of the sale are included, as well as the contingencies that must be met before the sale is completed. For example, if the buyer requires a termite inspection, the contract should provide that the seller will make any necessary repairs revealed by the inspection up to a specified dollar amount. If the damage exceeds this amount, the buyer may have the option of making the extra repairs or backing out of the contract.

The contract should also contain a clause requiring that the earnest money deposit be placed in an escrow account. With an escrow account, the earnest money isn't delivered to the seller until all the provisions of the contract are met and the escrow holder (usually a bank) receives notice that the deal is complete and the money can be released. Never give an earnest money deposit directly to the seller, since you may have to file suit to get it returned if your deal goes sour.

While the real estate purchase contract is used to set out the terms of the sale, the deed is the document that actually transfers ownership of the property. Your contract will specify the kind of deed you'll receive. The best kind of deed from a buyer's point of view is what's known as a "full covenant and warranty" deed. When you receive this kind of deed, the seller promises that there are no encumbrances or defects in the title to his property other than the ones he discloses in the deed. An "encumbrance" may be an easement that gives someone else the right to use a part of the property, or zoning regulations or a covenant in the seller's deed that restricts the way in which the property can be used by its owner. A "defect" may be a forged deed that was given at some time in the past by a previous seller who didn't actually have the right to sell the property. If it later turns out that there are any defects or encumbrances which the seller didn't know about or failed to disclose, the buyer can file suit for any damages that he suffers as a result of the defect.

A deed "with covenant's against the grantor's acts" states that the seller hasn't done anything to cause a defect or encumbrance other than what he has already disclosed, but it releases him from liability for defects caused by a former owner that are unknown to him at the time of the sale.

A "quitclaim" deed provides no warranties at all. It doesn't even promise that the seller actually has any interest in the property he's selling. It merely states that if he does have an interest in it, he's transferring that interest to you. Accepting a quitclaim deed can be risky, and you probably should get some professional legal advice before you agree to do so.

Your real estate purchase contract will also include a clause about title insurance. Title insurance is designed to protect the buyer, as well as the mortgage lender on the property, from losses that result from any known or unknown defects in the title you receive from the seller. As the buyer, you'll probably be required to purchase a lender's title insurance policy to protect the mortgage company or bank from losing its interest in the property. But you'll also want to obtain an owner's policy to protect your own interest in the property from a potential claim that your title is defective.

Typically, a title insurance policy is purchased by paying a one-time fee equal to around one percent of the purchase price of the property. In some parts of the country, the buyer pays for this policy, while in other parts of the country, the seller provides it, but in any case it's an item that can be negotiated between buyer and seller.

What kinds of title "defects" will a title insurance policy protect you from? As we've already mentioned, a forged deed can create a real problem if someone who would have a claim to the property shows up in the future. Another problem that can arise occurs when you purchase a home from the person whose name appears on the deed to the property as the sole owner. Unknown to you, however, the seller is married at the time the sale takes place. Even though the deed to the house is in his name alone, the seller's spouse may be legally entitled to a share of the house, especially if its located in a community property state. Years later, that spouse could raise a challenge to your ownership of the property.

Title insurance protects you from this kind of claim, but it usually protects you only up to the limits of the purchase price of the property. So if you purchase a home for $100,000, your protection extends to that amount. If the house appreciates in value over the years, and is worth $300,000 at the time the claim is made, your protection is still only $100,000. Be sure to read the terms of your policy carefully so that you understand any limitations on the coverage it provides.

GETTING A MORTGAGE

Nearly everyone who buys a home finances the purchase by obtaining a mortgage. Generally, mortgages fall into one of two categories; fixed rate or adjustable rate mortgages. However, in recent years a number of other kinds of mortgages have become available, which we will also discuss.

With a fixed rate mortgage (also called a "conventional" mortgage), you repay the lender in equal monthly installments of principal and interest over a specified period. Most fixed rate mortgages are for 15 or 30 years, but there are some 20 year mortgages, and a few lenders even offer 40 year repayment periods. Keep in mind that the longer the life of the loan, the smaller your monthly payment will be, but you will end up paying much more in total. The shorter the term of the loan, the higher the monthly payment, but you'll have paid less interest overall by the end of the loan.

An adjustable rate mortgage, (also called an "ARM") has a variable interest rate which changes on a regular schedule set by your lender. In most cases, an ARM's interest rate can be changed annually, although some lenders offer six month, three year, and five year ARMs as well. Unlike a conventional mortgage, which sets out the monthly repayment for the life of the loan, the payment schedule of an ARM fluctuates with changes in market interest rates. When interest rates go up, your payment will increase; when they decrease, so does your payment.

Generally, the initial interest rate for an ARM is two or three percentage points lower than for a fixed rate mortgage. You get this lower rate in return for assuming the risk that interest rates will rise and that you will end up paying more in the future. In the late 1980s and early 1990s however, as interest rates declined, home owners with ARMs actually saw their payments drop, in some cases pretty significantly. For these buyers, the ARM allowed them to save additional thousands of dollars on the purchase of their homes.

Even when interest rates rise, most ARMs limit the amount of any annual increase, and place a lifetime cap on the total increase in interest you can be charged. But be careful, because some ARMs provide for what's known as "negative amortization." What this means is that if interest rates rise by four percent and the annual cap on your ARM is two percent, the additional two percent increase is added to the balance of your loan as principal.

A few years of negative amortization and you can end up owing a fairly big balance at what you thought was the end of your loan. That may mean making a lump sum payment to the lender, or even obtaining a new mortgage loan. It's best to avoid ARMs that contain negative amortization provisions, no matter how attractive the initial interest rate may be.

Lenders use a number of methods to calculate changes in the interest rates of an ARM. Most financial experts suggest you try to get an ARM that links changes in interest to the rate paid on one year U.S. Treasury securities. ARMs linked to this index seem to average a lower total cost than those tied to other kinds of indexes.

Other kinds of mortgages that combine the features of fixed rate and adjustable rate mortgages are also available. A Graduated Payment Mortgage (GPM) starts out with a relatively small initial payment, which increases each year for a five or ten year period. At the end of this period, you continue to pay a fixed payment with no further increases until the mortgage balance is paid off.

With a so-called "7-23 mortgage" you pay a fixed interest rate for the first seven years of the loan. At the end of the seven year period, there's a one-time adjustment to the interest rate, which you then pay for the remaining 23 years of the loan.

No matter what kind of mortgage you decide on, you'll have to complete a mortgage application provided by your lender. In most cases, this is a standard form designed by the Federal National Mortgage Association (FNMA), popularly referred to as Fannie Mae. The FNMA buys mortgages and then issues securities to investors which are backed by the mortgages, so it wants to be sure that lenders get detailed financial information about borrowers before making a lending decision.

To complete the application form, you'll need to provide detailed information about your current employment and income, as well as your past employment history. If you're self-employed, plan on providing copies of income tax returns and profit and loss statements covering the last three years of your self-employment. You'll be asked about your credit history, including your outstanding credit card debts, student loans, and other obligations, such as alimony and child support. You'll be asked whether there are any unpaid liens or court judgments against you or your property, and whether you've ever declared bankruptcy.

You will also need to disclose how much you have for a down payment, and show where the down payment will come from. If you plan on borrowing some of the down payment from family members, be warned that doing so could disqualify you from receiving a mortgage. This is one case where receiving money as a gift really works in your favor, although the person making the gift will probably need to complete a form acknowledging that the money is a gift and not a loan.

Mortgage lenders are allowed to charge an upfront application fee which usually amounts to several hundred dollars, as well as what's called a loan origination fee, typically one percent of the amount you've applied to borrow. You will also be expected to pay for a credit report, which can run another $100 or so, but this fee is usually paid at closing.

If your application is approved, you will receive what is known as a loan commitment letter. This letter will tell you how much the lender will agree to let you borrow, and at what interest rate. It will also contain an expiration date, so if you don't follow through on the purchase within the period of time allotted, you may have to requalify. You should also receive a preliminary Truth-in-Lending Statement, setting out all the costs associated with the loan and the total amount you will pay over the life of the loan. Keep in mind that this is an estimate only and could change if you need to borrow more or if interest rates change; the exact amounts will be provided at closing.

Most lenders will require at least a 10 percent down payment before they will offer to make a loan. And even then you may be required to purchase private mortgage insurance to guarantee payment of your loan if your down payment is less than 20 percent. However, there are several government sponsored programs designed to help you obtain a mortgage when you have little money for a down payment.

The Federal Housing Administration (FHA) insures lenders for up to 95 percent of the value of a home, so with an FHA guaranteed loan you need only make a five percent down payment. And qualified veterans can obtain a guarantee from the Department of Veterans Affairs which will allow them to buy a home worth as much as $144,000 with no down payment at all. Your mortgage lender can provide details and applications for either of these programs.

Obtaining a mortgage is a time consuming and stress inducing process, but on the positive side, mortgage interest is still deductible on your federal income tax return, up to

$1 million. And if you obtained your mortgage before October of 1987, even this cap doesn't apply.

CLOSING THE SALE

Once a mortgage is obtained and all the other contingencies in the real estate purchase contract are satisfied, ownership of the home will be transferred at what's commonly referred to as a closing. In some areas of the country, both buyer and seller attend the closing, while in other communities each side meets separately with an employee of the lender or title company to complete the deal.

At the closing, all the final financial details of the purchase will be taken care of. The buyer will give his check for the down payment, and the lender will provide a check for the balance of the purchase price.

The buyer will also be required to pay additional expenses, known as "closing costs," or "settlement costs." In most cases, these costs represent a significant amount of money above and beyond the down payment. These costs typically include the cost of obtaining a credit report, a survey and a property appraisal, the title insurance premium, as well as recording fees and attorney fees if a lawyer's services were used. You'll also have to pay the premium for a homeowners' insurance policy before the lender will hand over its check, since it wants to make sure there will be money to pay off the mortgage or rebuild the property in case of a fire or other damage.

If the seller has paid all his taxes for the year, he's entitled to repayment of the portion that covers the time the new buyer will own the house. So, for example, if the annual real estate taxes of $2,000 were paid on January 1, and the house is sold on October 1, the buyer must reimburse the seller $500. And the seller is also entitled to a refund for any utility payments he made that actually cover the time you own the house.

Under federal law, when you apply for a home mortgage, your lender must provide you with a good faith estimate of the closing costs you'll encounter within three days of receiving your application. It must also give you a copy of the booklet entitled "You and Settlement Costs" at the same time. And it must give you a copy of the actual closing statement at least one day in advance of the closing, so you'll know exactly how much money you will need to bring to the table to close the sale. In most cases, you will be expected to bring a certified check to pay for these expenses.

As the closing continues, the title insurance policy will be presented for inspection and compared to the description of the property in the deed provided by the seller, to be sure that all known defects and encumbrances are accounted for, and to be certain that the property covered by the policy is the same as that described in the deed.

The buyer will also have a chance to examine the deed, as will the lender, to assure themselves that everything is in order. If the buyer and lender are satisfied that the deed is correct, the seller will sign the deed over to the buyer. Remember that if the seller is married, the spouse should also sign the deed, even if he or she isn't named as an owner of the property, in order to prevent possible future claims to the property.

If the home being sold is one that's newly constructed, the seller will provide a "certificate of occupancy." This document is issued by the local building inspectors, and declares that the building conforms to all local codes in effect at the time it was built. The seller will also provide any warranties for the foundation or other elements of the home at this time.

Once everyone is satisfied that all the documents are in order, the seller gets his money (minus any money he owes to his own mortgage lender) and the buyer gets the keys to the property. But before moving in, there's one more step that needs to take place to protect the buyer's interest in the property.

RECORDING THE DEED

Once the closing is complete, the buyer or a representative of the lender will have the deed recorded at the county recorder's office in the county where the property is located. Having the deed recorded immediately is essential, since recording is what provides notice to the world that you are the new owner of the property. If you fail to record the deed, it's possible that a crooked seller could actually sell the property to someone else after you. If that buyer records his deed before you record your own, the second buyer is considered the legal owner of the property, even if you can prove you received your deed first. Happily, such occurrences aren't common, but they have happened from time to time. Be sure to have your deed recorded as soon as possible and preserve your rights to the property. Otherwise, you may have to sue the seller in order to get your money back — and a seller who's willing to sell a piece of property twice is probably going to be very hard to find and serve with a lawsuit.

WILL YOU NEED A LAWYER?

Whether or not you need a lawyer's assistance in buying or selling a house remains a source of debate. However, in most cases you can take all the steps necessary to make an offer, negotiate a contract, and close the sale without the help of an attorney. This is especially true when you buy a new home from a reputable builder, or when you use the services of a real estate broker. In fact, real estate brokers are considered to be engaged in "the limited practice of law" when they write contracts and conduct closings.

If you're not using a broker, or if you have concerns about any of the steps involved in the home buying process, a good real estate lawyer can be a tremendous help, especially when you're dealing with surveys, titles, and closing documents. In some communities, real estate lawyers are charging less than $200 to review documents and attend closings. That's a small price to pay when you consider that you could run the risk of losing some or all of so large an investment.

OWNING A HOME

When you become a homeowner, you take on a number of legal responsibilities. In addition, the law places a number of restrictions on the uses to which you can put your property.

Zoning laws have been enacted in almost every county in the nation, and are designed to preserve the character of your community and set guidelines for orderly growth. Generally, zoning laws limit the use of property to one of several categories. In an area zoned for single family residential use, only single family homes may be built. In an area zoned for multiple family residential use, apartment buildings and condominiums are also permitted.

Commercial zoning means that businesses such as shops and offices may be built and operated lawfully within the area. Industrial zoning permits the operation of manufacturing facilities. And mixed-use zoning may allow some or all of the above uses for property within the zoned area.

Zoning regulations are made and enforced at the local level, either by the county or the municipality in which the property is located. Violating zoning ordinances is usually punishable by a fine, and you can be required to put a halt to the activity that's in violation of the ordinance. For example, if you are operating a beauty shop out of your home in violation of the zoning ordinances in your community, the zoning board can obtain a court order requiring you to close the shop.

In some cases, it's possible to get what's known as a variance, or exception, to the local zoning ordinances, that can allow you to use or expand your property in ways that might not ordinarily be permitted. For example, many urban communities have what are known as "set-back" requirements, that require you to keep the outer walls of your residence a specified number of feet away from the road, and from the property of your neighbors. If you want to add an addition that would bring your home in violation of the setback requirements, you would have to obtain a variance from the local zoning board before beginning construction. If you started the construction without doing so and it was later discovered that you had violated the zoning laws, you could be required to remove the addition at your own expense, an unpleasant and expensive prospect at best.

The procedure for obtaining a variance varies from one locale to another, so you should contact your local zoning board for specific information about the application process in your community.

If you want to build an addition or a deck, install an inground spa, or give your home a major revamping, getting clearance from the zoning authority is only the first step. You'll also need to call the local building department and obtain a building permit before you begin. The building department is the agency responsible for setting standards for the kinds of materials you must use and the construction procedures that must be followed in order to help protect homeowners and the public from the consequences of substandard work. The building department will review and approve your plans, inspect the work as it's done, and finally approve the project at its completion. You'll be required to pay a fee for this government service.

If you live in a subdivision, chances are you will also need to obtain the approval of your local homeowners' association before you can proceed with any significant remodeling or renovation of your property. In most of these communities, your deed will contain what are known as "covenants, conditions, and restrictions," or CCRs. These CCRs are an agreement between you and the homeowners association, or between you and your neighbors. Generally, they restrict the ways in which you can use or alter your property, or require you to obtain approval from the homeowners' association before you proceed.

For example, CCRs can prevent you from using your front lawn as a junkyard, which hardly anyone would consider to be an unreasonable restriction in a residential area. But CCRs can also require you to paint your house a certain color, use specified materials if your roof, sidewalk or driveway needs repair, limit the kinds of plants and trees you can use in landscaping, and prohibit you from putting a television antenna or satellite dish on your property.

It's a very good idea to be sure to find out about the covenants in an area where you are considering buying a home before you make an offer to purchase. That way, you can decide if the covenants are too restrictive for your tastes.

If you decide to purchase a condominium or a share in a cooperative rather than a single family home, you'll also be subject to the rules of the condominium association or the cooperative's bylaws. Again, it's best to review these documents before you decide to purchase a home in one of these communities.

You will also have to pay regular maintenance fees or dues to the condominium association or cooperative corporation to pay for the upkeep and improvement of the building grounds and amenities, such as swimming pools and recreational facilities.

As a homeowner, you're also responsible for ensuring that your property is maintained in a safe condition. If you're a single family home owner, that means making sure the sidewalks and driveways are kept reasonably free of debris and cleared of snow and ice after a storm. If you know that there's a dangerous condition on the property, such as a loose stair rail or a rotting step, you must repair the dangerous property as soon as possible, but in the interim you should also be sure to warn people who come onto your property about the problem. If you don't, and they are injured, you can be held liable.

You have an additional responsibility to protect children from anything on your property that presents a danger to them but which could cause them harm. Under the "attractive nuisance" doctrine, you can be held liable if, for example, you have a swimming pool or hot tub in your yard that's unfenced or otherwise unprotected, and a child falls in and drowns or slips and injures himself. Simply putting up a "no trespassing" sign isn't enough, since the law assumes that young children aren't mature enough to recognize the consequences of their actions, even when they are trespassers. A high fence with a locked gate and a heavy cover over the water's surface when not in use are your best protection. But no matter how carefully you take precautions to protect children and adults, you'll want to purchase homeowners insurance to protect you in case an accident does occur on your property.

HOMEOWNERS INSURANCE

Homeowners insurance not only protects you from potential liability claims when someone else is injured on your property. It also helps to protect your own property from damage or destruction. A comprehensive homeowners policy provides protection against potential losses from perils such as fire and smoke, theft, vandalism, burglary, bursting pipes, and wind and storm damage.

Most homeowners policies exclude coverage for earthquake damage, although in states such as California this coverage can be purchased in addition to the standard coverage. Most policies also exclude flood coverage, but in some parts of the country it's possible to obtain flood insurance through the federal Flood insurance Program. Your insurance agent or your state's department of insurance can provide additional information about this program.

Homeowners policies come in a variety of forms, but the best kind of policy to buy is the most comprehensive policy you can afford. You should buy a policy that covers at least 80 percent of the value of your property if you own a single family home, and 100 percent of your property if you live in a condominium or cooperative.

You only need 80 percent coverage for a single family home because at least twenty percent of the value of your property is in the land, which won't need to be rebuilt if your house is completely destroyed. You need 100 percent coverage for a condominium, however, because since you don't own the land on which it's built, it won't be calculated into the replacement cost.

You should also buy a policy that will pay the replacement cost of your personal property, up to the policy's limits. That means buying a policy that will, for example, buy you a new television set if your old one is stolen or destroyed. If you purchase a policy that pays the "fair market value" for your losses, you won't get a new television. Instead, the policy will reimburse you for the depreciated value of the television. So if your television was five years old when it was destroyed, the insurer will give you enough money to buy a five year old television.

Your policy should provide coverage for additional living expenses that you might incur if your home is damaged or destroyed and you have to find temporary living quarters elsewhere. This coverage should pay for hotel accomodations or a temporary apartment, as well as meal expenses you have to pay while living out of your home.

You should also consider buying a policy that provides automatic inflation coverage. With this coverage, the limits of your policy (and your premium) are adjusted annually to reflect the increase in the value of your home and property. However, be sure to review the proposed increases when you receive your policy renewal notice each year. Some insurers raise these values far more quickly than circumstances warrant, and being overinsured just means that you are paying for coverage you don't really need, and which you can't collect on if you do suffer a loss.

Finally, you'll want to be sure you have a substantial amount of liability coverage in your policy. Most homeowners policies offer a minimum of $100,000 of liability protection. In most cases however, you should consider purchasing additional liability coverage, since you could face a potentially much larger claim if someone is injured while on your property.

An umbrella policy provides large amounts of liability coverage above the limits of your homeowners policy, but you need to buy the homeowners policy first, since an umbrella policy only pays for damages when they exceed the primary coverage in your homeowners policy. You can usually buy an umbrella policy with a million dollars of liability coverage for around $200 or so. If you have a lot of assets to protect, an umbrella policy may be worth considering. But for most people, buying the highest amount of coverage you can get in a homeowners policy is probably enough.

For information about how to pick an insurance company and the problems and pitfalls associated with filing an insurance claim, be sure to read Chapter Ten, "Your Insurance."

Whichever company you pick, there are a number of things you can do to lower the cost of your homeowners insurance. Increasing your deductible (the amount you have to pay before the insurance policy reimburses you for losses), and installing deadbolt locks, burglar alarms, fire extinguishers and smoke detectors can reduce your annual premiums as much as 15 percent or more, depending on the insurance company.

PROPERTY TAXES

As a homeowner, you'll be required to pay property taxes on your home. In many cases, these taxes are collected on a monthly basis by your mortgage lender, which holds them in an escrow account and advances them to the tax authority on your behalf as they become due.

It's a good idea to keep an eye on how much your lender collects for taxes each month. If the amount is much more than necessary to meet your tax obligations, you should consider asking your lender to recalculate the amount collected. In most cases, the money the lender collects earns interest for the lender, but not for you, so some lenders have tried to collect as much as possible in order to get more in interest and improve their own bottom line. Generally, the amount a lender collects for your tax account shouldn't be much more than the actual amount you will owe for taxes, although it's reasonable for a lender to collect a small amount over the expected tax bill to account for a change in valuation or the amount you're assessed. However, if the lender consistently collects more than an additional 10 percent or so, it's time to express your concern. If the lender won't make a voluntary adjustment, the consumer affairs section of your state attorney general's office may be able to help. In some states, the law limits the excess a lender can charge for a tax account.

The amount of property tax you'll have to pay is generally based on the local taxing authority's assessment of the value of your property. In most cases, this value is arrived at by comparing your property to others in the community that are comparable in size, age and condition. In most communities, you'll receive a notice of the assessed value of your home each year from the taxing authority.

If your assessment increases dramatically, or if you think it's inaccurate or otherwise unfair, you have the right to challenge the assessment. Your assessment notice will usually provide the exact details for appealing the assessment, but generally you have to give written notice of your intention to appeal the assessment within a specified time period, such as 30 days. If you miss the cutoff date, you can lose the right to an appeal.

In order to get a reduction in the assessed value of your property, you'll have to provide evidence that the assessment is wrong. In some cases, doing so isn't very complicated. For example, if the assessment shows that your house contains 2,000 square feet of living space when it actually only contains 1,500, all you may have to do is provide details of the actual square footage to the assessors. In other cases, however, challenging an assessment may require obtaining an independent appraisal from a professional appraiser, or obtaining information about recent sales of similar properties in the community where you live.

For the most part, you don't need the help of a lawyer to challenge a property tax assessment. Nor do you need to hire one of the many companies that claim they can reduce your property taxes for you. A number of these companies have sprung up in recent years, and most of them charge half of the amount you save in taxes as their fee for representing you before the local tax authorities. But since the procedures for representing yourself are relatively straightforward, you can probably handle the early stages of an appeal on your own. If you do, however, and you don't obtain the result you want, a lawyer's help may be worthwhile in pursuing any further appeals, since the procedures become more complicated at this stage.

HOME REPAIRS AND IMPROVEMENTS

If you own an older home, or even one that's relatively new, you may decide that you want to make some renovations to increase your enjoyment and the home's value. As we've already seen, you'll need the approval of your local government and perhaps that of your homeowners' association before you begin. If you're doing the work yourself, good for you. If you're like most of us, however, you will probably hire someone to do any major remodeling or other significant home improvements.

Unfortunately, the home improvement industry is one that has more than its share of unqualified, slipshod, and downright crooked practitioners. To protect yourself from these bad apples, you should take a few important precautions.

First, you need to get estimates from a number of possible contractors. Don't just hire the company with the biggest ad in the Yellow Pages — ask friends, neighbors, and business associates for their recommendations. Checking with the officer who makes home improvement loans at your bank can also be a good way to get recommendations, as can asking local real estate brokers.

When you interview potential contractors, ask them for written estimates, and for the names of other satisfied customers for whom they have recently done work that's similar to the project you want them to do for you. (Getting a recommendation from someone who had a garage built isn't any indication that the contractor can handle remodeling your bathroom.)

Contact the contractor's references, and ask if it's possible for you to actually see the finished job. Don't be afraid to tell the contractor that you are getting estimates from others; it may help you get a better price.

In the estimate, you should expect the contractor to be as specific as possible about the materials to be used. If you want a specific brand of whirlpool tub installed in your new master bathroom, for example, have the brand name noted in the estimate. You also want to know if the contractor's employees will do the work, or if subcontractors will be hired to perform some or all of the work. And be sure to find out what kinds of warranties the contractor gives on materials and workmanship. Finally, check with the local office of the Better Business Bureau to find out if there have been any complaints about the contractor, and how those complaints were resolved.

When you have made your decision about which contractor to hire, it's time to sign a contract. Your contract should be as specific as possible, even more specific than the estimate.

First, if you are dealing with a corporation, or an individual using a fictitious business name, this should be noted in the contract, along with the name and address of the person to whom you can send notice of any breach or default. If things go sour and your contractor doesn't live up to his promises, you will need this information in order to file a lawsuit.

Architectural drawings or plans being used in the project should be attached to and made a part of the contract. The contract should set out a scheduled date on which the work will begin, and a date on which it will be finished. By including a clause that states that "time is of the essence in the performance of this contract" the contractor is put on notice that you expect him to finish the work on time. If you can, include a clause that provides a financial penalty if the contractor misses the completion date by more than a few days.

Your contract should also include the schedule by which you will make payments. Never pay a contractor the full amount of the job in advance, since by doing so you lose any leverage you may have to get the job finished. The final payment to the contractor should be contingent on the completion of the job to your satisfaction, including cleaning up left over materials and fixing any minor problems that remain when the job is done.

You'll also need a provision that requires the contractor to provide you with "lien waivers" from subcontractors and suppliers the contractor uses. In most states, if you pay the general contractor but the contractor fails to pay suppliers and subcontractors, they can place a mechanic's lien against your property.

Depending on the provisions of your state's lien laws, you could be required to pay them yourself, which means paying twice for the same job! A contract provision that requires the contractor to provide lien waivers before you make your final payment can help provide additional protection.

The contract should require the contractor to obtain all the necessary permits and inspections necessary to do the job, and to provide you with copies. The contractor should also be required to provide proof of workers' compensation and liability insurance, and the contract should also contain an agreement by the contractor to indemnify you from any claims or damages that may arise in the course of the work done on your property.

The contract should also include a clause that the relationship the contractor has to you is that of an independent contractor and not that of an employee. Under federal law, you are responsible for paying Social Security taxes and withholding income taxes from the wages of employees, which you don't want to do in this situation.

Whatever warranties the contractor makes in regard to materials or workmanship should also be included in the contract, as well as how long those warranties will last. However, keep in mind that warranties issued by contractors are only as good as the contractors themselves. A "lifetime warranty" doesn't do you much good if the contractor goes out of business.

Finally, be sure the contract includes a provision that requires any changes in plans, materials, or workmanship be made in writing and signed by both you and the contractor.

Never use the services of a contractor who won't give you a written contract, and never sign a contract until you've conducted a thorough investigation of the contractor's reputation in the community. Be especially wary of contractors who show up at your door claiming that they have materials left over from another job in the neighborhood, and offering to fix your roof or repave your driveway for a bargain price "but only if you can pay us right away." This con game has been used to scam thousands of homeowners in all parts of the country out of millions of dollars.

By using caution and a bit of common sense, you can save yourself money, time, and a great deal of aggravation when making home improvements and repairs.

HOW YOU CAN LOSE YOUR HOME

When you own your own home, there are a number of steps you will want to take to make sure you don't lose the property. The first and probably most obvious is to be sure that you make your mortgage payments on time. If you don't, your lender may have the right to foreclose on your mortgage.

In general, foreclosure proceedings follow the same pattern no matter where you live. Your lender must give you notice that you are in default on your mortgage, and give you an opportunity to bring your payments up to date within a specified period of time. If you don't, the lender then goes to court and obtains an order of foreclosure. This order gives the lender the right to sell your property to the highest bidder.

If the property sells for less than the amount you owe, the lender can go to court again to seek what's known as a deficiency judgment for the balance. With a deficiency judgment, the lender can garnish your wages or attach your personal property in order to collect the balance owed on the mortgage. On the other hand, if the property sells for more than the amount you owe, you get the balance, minus the lender's attorney fees, court costs, and other costs associated with the foreclosure sale.

In every state, you have the right to redeem the property right up until the time of sale by making all the back payments you owe, plus an extra amount for interest and costs. In some states, you can even redeem your property after the sale. To do so, you must make all the legally required payments within a time period specified by state law.

If you are falling behind on your mortgage payments, one of the best things you can do is let your lender know about your problems as soon as possible. You may be able to refinance your loan, or make payments of interest only until your financial circumstances turn around.

In some instances, you can protect your credit record by offering your lender what's known as a deed in lieu of foreclosure. With a "deed in lieu" you agree to hand over your interest in the property to the lender. While you lose the property, you keep a foreclosure off your credit record, which can make it easier for you to obtain another mortgage in the future.

In any situation where foreclosure is a possibility, you should definitely consider getting the assistance of a lawyer. State laws on foreclosure vary widely, and the willingness of a lender to pursue foreclosure proceedings depends on a variety of factors, such as the state of the local economy and the time it takes to resell a foreclosed property. A lawyer with experience in this area may be able to negotiate a deal with your lender that you wouldn't be able to get on your own. And at the very least, a good lawyer can give you advice about the alternatives that may be available, including bankruptcy.

Foreclosure is one way you can lose your property, but there are a number of other situations in which the loss of ownership can take place. As we've already seen, if a contractor or subcontractor supplies materials or services to improve your property, it may be entitled to a mechanic's lien against the property. If the debt goes unpaid, it's possible that the contractor could force a sale of your property in order to obtain its money.

Failing to pay property taxes can lead to a tax sale of your home. In some states, the government doesn't even have to give you notice that it plans to sell your home for back taxes, so it's essential that you stay on top of the situation. If your taxes are collected by your mortgage lender, you should get a statement from the lender showing when the taxes were paid. If you own your home outright, be sure to make the payments to the tax authority on time and in the correct amount.

As with foreclosure sales, some states allow a property owner to redeem the property sold at a tax sale even after the sale has occurred. And as with a foreclosure, a lawyer can be an important source of advice and assistance if your ownership of your home is threatened by a tax sale.

Your home ownership can also be placed in jeopardy when you fail to pay your income taxes, or when a creditor obtains a court judgment against you. In either case, your home could be sold to satisfy the amount you owe, although your home lender will have first priority to the proceeds of a sale to satisfy a court judgment. In the case of the failure to pay taxes, however, the government gets priority to any sale proceeds.

Although it doesn't happen often, you can also lose owner-ship of your property, or at least a part of it, through what's legally referred to as "adverse possession." If someone other than you uses or occupies your property without your permis-sion, and you don't take any actions to stop him, after a period of time specified by state law you could lose your right to claim that property as your own.

Most commonly, adverse possession comes into play when a neighbor erects a fence on your side of a property line. If you don't take action to stop this encroachment on your property, and a sufficient amount of time passes, the property on which he's encroached could actually become his instead of yours. In most states, many years have to pass before your neighbor could claim the property as his own, but even so, it pays to know where your property lines are and to protect them diligently.

CONDEMNATION AND FORFEITURE

One of the most cherished myths in American society is the belief that the right to private ownership of property is greater than the government's right to interfere with that ownership. Many people believe that if they mind their business, pay their mortgage payments and keep their taxes up to date, no one can take their property from them.

Nothing could be further from the truth. At every level, the government has the right to take your property away from you for public use, under the power of eminent domain. Under this governmental power, the interests of society as a whole are considered to be more important than the rights of the indi-vidual. If the best use of your property is a public one, as determined by the government, then you can be deprived of your property (even when you don't want to give it up) through what are known as condemnation proceedings.

Condemnation isn't the same as confiscation, however, and you must be compensated for the property by the government entity that takes it from you. In addition, the government is usually prohibited from taking any more than the minimum amount of your property necessary to serve the public purpose. But ultimately, if the government wants your property, and unless you can show that the condemnation of your property is clearly in violation of the law, the government will almost certainly get what it wants at the price it wants to pay. Again, if you receive a condemnation notice from a government agency, get in touch with an experienced lawyer immediately.

Finally, there's yet another way that you can lose the ownership of your home. In some states, if your home is found to be the site of criminal activity, the government may confiscate it under what are known as civil forfeiture laws. Depending on the forfeiture laws in your state and the way the courts have interpreted those laws, you could actually use your home even if you were unaware that the criminal activity was taking place.

For example, in one case an elderly man lost his home after his grandson was arrested for distributing illegal drugs from the property. And in some cases, the state doesn't even have to obtain a conviction in order to obtain the forfeiture of your home. At the risk of sounding like a broken record, contact a lawyer immediately in the event you are faced with a forfeiture of your property to law enforcement authorities.

CHAPTER FIVE
YOUR CAR

The average sticker price of a new car is now well past the $13,000 mark, so it pays to be well informed before you make your next car purchase. In this chapter, we will look at the advantages and disadvantages to buying versus leasing and make some comparisons between purchasing a new vehicle and one that is pre-owned.

Cars and drivers are also the subject of many areas of the law, from licensing to liability. To help you understand how the law affects you as a driver and automobile owner, we will also take a look at warranties and repairs, licensing and insurance requirements, drunk driving laws, and what you should do if you are ever involved in an automobile accident or receive a ticket.

BUYING A NEW CAR

Owning and operating a motor vehicle is an expensive proposition. In addition to the price of the automobile itself, insurance, financing, and the cost of fuel and maintenance makes owning an automobile much more expensive that most people realize.

Depreciation also contributes to the expense of owning a new automobile. Most automobiles begin to lose value the minute they are titled, with some cars losing as much as 25 percent of their value during the first year. So while that expensive luxury model you have been considering may seem like a good idea now, after a few years you may find yourself "upside down," that is, owing more on the car than you could get if you tried to sell it.

Lenders generally insist that your monthly payment for a new car not exceed 15 percent of your monthly after-tax income. In order to meet this figure, many automobile dealers and lenders now offer payment plans that stretch on for five or even six years.

As with most major purchases, it is important to shop around for the best financing available. If you are considering purchasing a particular model of automobile, your bank, savings and loan, or credit union can probably provide valuable information about auto loans before you begin the negotiating process. At many financial institutions, you can even pre-qualify for your loan. The lender tells you exactly how much it would be willing to lend you for a particular model of car you're considering. Knowing exactly how much you can afford to spend can help you avoid being talked into a more expensive model.

One recent development in the auto industry is the increase in so-called "one-price" dealerships. At these dealerships, you don't have to go through the song and dance negotiations utilized by traditional dealers. Instead, the dealership gives you a fixed price for the make and model of car you want to purchase. While this may seem like a much less stressful way to buy a car, studies have shown that in most cases the dealers who use this system actually make more on each sale than dealers who negotiate a price with their customers. Even so, some customers are willing to pay a higher price in order to avoid having to haggle with a salesperson and a sales manager.

If you purchase your car from a traditional dealer that negotiates on price, it's important to remember that no matter how friendly your salesman appears, his income depends on obtaining the best possible price for the vehicle you want to purchase. While the salesperson may claim to be working to obtain the best possible price on your behalf, he is an employee of the auto dealership. By being a well-informed consumer, you can avoid paying more than necessary for the car you want, while allowing the dealer to make a fair profit on the sale.

Because automobile dealers negotiate car sales on a daily basis, you need to be armed with as much information as possible before beginning to deal for your new car. Several publications, including *Edmund's New Car Prices,* the *Kelly Blue Book,* and *Consumer Reports* can provide information about base car prices, as well as the dealer's cost for options such as power steering, sun roofs, air conditioning, and premium sound systems. *Consumer Reports* is also a good source of information about the reliability and safety of various models of automobiles, as well as recalls and service bulletins (notices sent to new car dealer service departments about common problems with a particular model).

Although most new car dealers operate ethically and honestly, there are still some dealers who bend the truth and the law in order to squeeze the last dollar out of a new car buyer. One of the most common tricks still used by these dealers is the "bait-and switch." The dealer advertises a great deal on a car you're interested in buying. You hurry down to the dealer's lot, only to be told that the advertised car isn't available. However, the dealer does have a similar car on the lot available at the same price, although it has fewer options than the unit that was advertised, or it has one with identical equipment at a price that's higher than the one in the ad.

Dealers use the bait-and-switch because they know their trained salespeople can talk most customers into a car they really want, once they get them on the lot. Honest dealers who advertise a price will indicate the inventory number of the car featured in the advertisement.If you think you've been subjected to an illegal bait-and-switch, leave the lot immediately and file a complaint with your state's automobile dealer licensing department.

A similar tactic takes place when a salesperson shows you a car and quotes you a very attractive price. You sit down in the salesperson's office and write up an offer, which the salesperson then takes to his manager for approval. When he returns, the sales manager has raised the price significantly over what the salesperson originally indicated the price would be. It seems, the salesperson explains, that he had mistaken the car you want to purchase for a less expensive unit. Of course, the salesperson reminds you, even though the price is higher, he knows that you really want this car, and once you finance the purchase you'll only be paying ten or twenty dollars more per month. So why not go ahead and make yourself happy by agreeing to the higher price?

If you really want to make yourself happy, turn down this offer and tell the salesperson you want the car for the price you were originally quoted. In nearly every case, the sales manager will authorize a lower price, although it may not be as low as the salesperson's quote. If you're still not satisfied, stick to your guns. Get up and walk out of the showroom. If you've done your research, you will know what price the dealer needs to get to make a fair profit.

Believe it or not, some dealers have used really outrageous tactics to keep customers from leaving their showrooms. If they've taken your car for a test drive in order to figure its trade in value, they may tell you that the keys to your car have been misplaced. You're kept sitting in the salesperson's office while he continues to wear down your resistance and get you to sign a sales contract. To avoid this situation, keep a spare set of keys in your pocket. In at least one case, a dealer told a customer that it had already sold his car to someone who had seen it in the parking lot, and so he would have to buy the new car they had been dealing on. No dealer can sell your car until you have signed over your ownership to it, and if you ever hear a story like this, get up, go to the nearest phone and call the police. You'll be surprised how quickly your own car will be returned.

Once you have come to an agreement on price, don't sign anything until all the promises the salesperson and sales manager have made are in writing on the contract. If the salesperson agreed to upgrade the standard AM-FM radio to a CD player, for example, make sure that this is included in the purchase agreement. Be sure that the contract includes the car's correct VIN, or Vehicle Identification Number, which is stamped on a metal plate inside the car's windshield on the driver's side. (If you are ordering a car from the manufacturer, however, this number won't be provided until the car is delivered.) Your contract should also include a list of the car's standard equipment and any options, as well as the size of the engine. You might be surprised to find out that the six-cylinder engine the salesperson told you was standard in the car is really an extra cost option.

If you haven't obtained financing from your bank, savings and loan or credit union, you may be tempted to consider dealer financing. At one time, dealer financing was more costly than what you could obtain elsewhere, but today many manufacturers offer financing at very low interest rates. In some cases, you may be offered the choice of a low interest loan or a cash rebate. If you have your own financing already lined up, the rebate will usually be the better choice.

No matter what, don't take the car off the dealer's lot until you have completed all the paperwork and are absolutely sure you have been approved for financing. Most automobile purchase agreements contain a clause known as a bailment provision. This provision says that if you aren't approved for your loan and the purchase falls through, the dealer can charge you a daily fee and a mileage fee for the time you have the car in your possession. This fee may be as much as $60 per day and 60 cents per mile, and even more for some models. If you take the car off the lot on Friday, drive it 300 miles over the weekend and then learn on Monday afternoon that your loan application was turned down, you could end up owing $420 for what amounts to a weekend rental. While you or the dealer may be able to find another source of financing, it's bound to be more expensive than the deal you thought you had, either because you will have to pay a higher interest rate or make an additional down payment, or both.

BUYING OR SELLING A USED CAR

Because cars lose much of their value in the first year or two of ownership, a used car can represent a significant savings over one purchased fresh from the new car lot. On the other hand, you could be buying someone else's problems.

If you are considering making a used car purchase, you will want to do some basic research in advance. Once you have decided upon a particular model of used car, check *Consumer Reports* to determine if the car you are considering has a history of mechanical or safety problems. You will also want to obtain information about used car prices from publications such as *Edmund's Used Car Prices* or the *Kelly Blue Book,* both of which are generally available at your local public library.

Whether you buy your used car from a dealer or from a private individual, there are some steps you should take to be sure that the car you are considering is mechanically sound and reasonably priced. You will want to take your prospective purchase for a thorough test drive, checking for any obvious problems with handling, engine function, and braking. Be sure to inspect the car carefully both inside and out for flaws in the paint or mismatched paint colors that may indicate that the car has been in an accident. For a fee of $100 or so, you can have an independent mechanic inspect the car for problems and provide you with an estimate of the cost of any repairs that will need to be made. The cost of these inspections is minimal when compared to the potential cost of undiscovered mechanical problems. If you decide to take this step, try to find a mechanic who only does diagnostic inspections. Otherwise, the mechanic may try to convince you to have him do repairs that could later turn out to have been unnecessary.

If you buy a used car from a dealer, federal law requires the dealer to place a sticker in the car's window stating whether any warranties are given with the car. If the dealer offers a warranty, the sticker must disclose whether the warranty is "full" or "limited," and how long the warranty will last. If the warranty is a limited warranty, the sticker must disclose what percentage of the costs of parts and labor the dealer will pay.

Keep in mind that most used cars are sold "as is" and the seller usually makes no warranties about the car's condition. However, most states impose a so-called "implied warranty of merchantability" on cars sold by used car dealers, which means that the car is reasonably safe to operate under normal conditions. Other than that, unless the dealer makes a specific promise in writing to make repairs, you are on your own. In some states, even this implied warranty can be disclaimed if the dealer makes a conspicuous statement on your contract that it's doing so. And the implied warranty of merchantability doesn't apply in any state to a private party who sells you his car. So if a used car you purchase from your next door neighbor breaks down five minutes after you have closed the sale, you will usually be stuck with the cost of repairs, unless you can show that the seller committed fraud by intentionally misrepresenting the car's condition.

When you purchase a used car from either a dealer or a private individual, federal law requires that the seller give you an odometer statement. This statement will indicate one of three things:

- That the mileage shown on the odometer is the car's true mileage
- That the odometer has "turned" and the mileage shown is lower than the true mileage of the car
- That for one reason or another, such as because the odometer had to be replaced, the odometer mileage isn't accurate.

Even though intentionally tampering with an odometer is a crime under federal law and the law in most states, there are still plenty of unscrupulous sellers who do just that. In order to protect yourself, have a mechanic inspect the car for wear and tear that exceeds what would be reasonable for a car with the mileage shown on the odometer, such as a brake pedal cover that's worn smooth, or excess engine wear.

Some used car dealers offer financing, and even advertise that they will finance anyone, regardless of past or current credit problems. In most cases, this is a very expensive way to finance a car, since the car itself is often priced much higher than its true market value. Add in the high interest rates the dealer will charge and your total monthly payment can escalate quickly. Miss a payment, and the dealer can repossess your car and sell it again, charging you for any difference between the amount you promised to pay and the amount he receives from a subsequent buyer.

WARRANTIES AND SERVICE CONTRACTS

All new cars sold in the United States come with written manufacturer's warranties, as well as implied warranties provided for by state law. Under the federal Magnuson-Moss Act, automobile warranties must be in legible type and in language that the ordinary person can understand.

A manufacturer's warranty must indicate what parts of the automobile are covered, which parts are not covered, and the manner in which warranty claims can be made. At a minimum, most automobile manufacturers offer full warranty coverage for

12 months or 12,000 miles, whichever comes first. During this period, the manufacturer agrees to make any needed repairs that are the result of defects in materials or workmanship. The manufacturer is not required to replace items which wear out as the result of normal use, such as brake pads or windshield wiper blades. Tires are warranted separately by their manufacturer.

In addition to the basic warranty, most automobile manufacturers also provide extended warranties for the car's power train. Generally, the power train is defined as the car's engine, transmission, and front, rear, or four-wheel drive systems. Some of these warranties may last up to seven years or 70,000 miles, but they may also require the car owner to pay a deductible for each repair made. You can ask for a copy of the auto manufacturer's warranty before you make your purchase. Be sure you understand all of its terms, and don't rely on the oral promises of a salesman that are in contradiction of the written warranty.

Many auto dealers now offer a variety of extended service plans, under which a new or used car purchaser can protect against major repair bills beyond the life of the manufacturer's warranty. Basically, these plans require the purchaser to pay several hundred dollars for coverage, and also to bear the cost of a deductible amount each time a repair is made. Before purchasing one of these extended service plans, you should know that many of them contain a great number of exclusions which in effect make them nearly worthless. For example, most service contracts exclude coverage for damage due to "owner abuse." Some service contract companies use this provision to exclude just about any claim made, and the burden of proving that the defect was not the result of abuse is on you. And a service contract purchased from a dealership may become worthless if the dealership should go out of business, unless it is backed by an automobile manufacturer or a major insurance company.

LEASING A CAR

With automobile prices rising and interest paid on consumer loans no longer deductible from your federal income tax, more and more consumers are turning to leasing their automobiles rather than purchasing them.

Most automobile dealerships offer today what is known as a "closed end" or "walk-away" lease. Under this kind of agreement, you agree to lease your automobile for a specified period of time with a maximum amount of mileage permitted. At the end of the lease, you have the option of purchasing the car or returning it to the dealer. Your lease payment is based upon the company's prediction of the value of the automobile at the end of the lease period. If the automobile is damaged beyond ordinary wear and tear while in your possession, or if you exceed the specified number of miles, additional charges will be collected from you at the end of the lease.

If you decide to lease a car, be sure that your lease agreement specifies whether you or the company will be responsible for regular maintenance and repairs. Although most leases require very little upfront money, some dealers now want several thousand dollars as a "capital reduction" fee at the outset of the lease. In essence, this is the dealer's way of keeping monthly payments attractive, and a low monthly payment is what attracts many consumers to leasing in the first place. But let's look at what a large capital reduction fee does to that payment.

Suppose a dealer advertises a $250 lease payment for 48 months on a car with a sticker price of $17,000. If there's no capital reduction payment due at the beginning of the lease, you can drive the car for four years for $12,000. But suppose the dealer also wants a capital reduction payment of $2,000. Now you're spending $14,000 for the same four year period, which translates into a monthly payment of over $291. And if you want to buy the car at the end of the lease, you will end up paying thousands of additional dollars to do so, dollars you may have to finance at a relatively high cost, since lenders charge higher interest rates on older cars.

Finally, you should also keep in mind that you are not the owner of an automobile you lease. As a result, lemon law protection which state laws provide to car purchasers may not be available to you.

LEMON LAWS

Under current state and federal laws, a consumer who buys a car that turns out to be a lemon has many more rights than he would have had in the not-too-distant past. While the details of these consumer protection statutes (known as "lemon laws") differ somewhat from state to state, they all have some elements in common.

Generally, to qualify for lemon law protection, you will have to prove three things: 1) that during the car's warranty period, you reported a malfunction to the manufacturer or its authorized representative, such as the dealership where you bought the car; 2) that the malfunction was serious and severely impaired the car's usefulness and value; and 3) that the dealer or manufacturer was unable to repair the malfunction after a specified number of attempts (three in some states, four in others), or that the car was out of use for 30 days during the warranty period while repairs were being attempted.

In most states, before you can file a suit under the lemon law statutes, you are required to have participated in a mediation or arbitration program in an attempt to reach an out-of-court settlement.Participation in these programs is free to the consumer, but the effectiveness of the programs varies considerably. Some programs, such as AutoCAP, the Ford Consumer Appeals Board (FCAP) and the Chrysler Customer Arbitration Board (CCAB) are "dealer sponsored" which means they are financed by the auto industry itself. In some cases, these programs tend to unduly favor the auto manufacturer over the consumer. Other programs, such as the American Arbitration Association (AAA) and AUTOSOLVE operate more independently, and consumers may have a better chance of receiving a favorable outcome when their claims are heard by these panels.

If you have a complaint about your car which you haven't been able to resolve directly with your dealer's service department, you will need to take advantage of the program your car's manufacturer participates in. You can usually find this information in the owner's manual or warranty that came with the car, or simply by asking the dealer. Write or call the program's office to get information about the procedures necessary to file a claim for mediation or arbitration.

Under most dispute resolution programs, an arbitrator's decision is binding on the manufacturer, but not on the consumer. So if you are dissatisfied with the decision of the arbitrator, your next step will be to file suit against the manufacturer. If your lawsuit is successful, the manufacturer can be ordered to provide you with a replacement vehicle or a refund of the amount you paid for the car, minus a reasonable deduction for the actual use you got from the vehicle.

AUTO REPAIRS

Accidents happen, and even the best built and best maintained cars need repairs from time to time. While having your car worked on is inconvenient at best, there are far too many rip-off artists who prey on the ignorance of car owners to charge for unnecessary repairs, or who charge far more than they should for repairs you do need.

Sadly, the days of the corner garage staffed by mechanics who lived in the neighborhood and who depended on the loyalty of their customers for their success are just about gone. With them went much of the personal service and commitment to doing the job right which ensured that loyalty. Today when you need your car repaired, you're more likely to take it to a dealership, to a repair facility run by a large national retailer such as Montgomery Ward or Sears, or one of the increasing number of shops that specialize in a few areas of car repair and maintenance, such as 15-minute oil changes, brakes and tires, or mufflers.

No matter where you go to get your car serviced, (and it doesn't matter which type of service facility you use, since all of them have their fair share of con artists and mechanics who are poorly trained or just plain incompetent), there are some steps you can take to protect yourself from overcharges and poor service.

Your first step is to do some research. Ask your friends, coworkers and neighbors for the names of the service facilities they use, as well as the ones they avoid. Once you've gathered some names, check with the local office of the Better Business Bureau to find out about any complaints it has on file about the service facilities, and how those complaints were resolved. If you're still concerned, you might also check with your state's consumer protection office.

Of course, if you find yourself stranded on the highway or in a strange town, you won't have the time to do this kind of research. And some service stations and repair shops situated along interstate highways and main tourist routes have been known to take advantage of drivers from out of town. Attendants at these stations have been known to puncture tires and radiators, put Alka-Seltzer tablets in batteries to make them foam, and use other gimmicks to force or frighten out of town motorists into having repairs made that weren't needed before the motorist stopped for gas. It pays to know enough about how your car works so that you can check its oil and tire pressure yourself at the self-service pumps so you can avoid this kind of rip-off.

However, if you do need help in an emergency, you can protect yourself to some extent if you belong to a motor club, such as the American Automobile Association (AAA) or one that's sponsored by one of the oil companies, such as Texaco or Amoco. These clubs usually do at least a cursory screening of the repair shops they work with, so it's unlikely you'll run into an out-and-out thief if you use the club to arrange for emergency service. And whether repairs are made locally or when you are away from home, use a credit card to pay for the services, since you may be able to dispute the bill and have charges for unnecessary or shoddy work removed from your credit card statement.

Once you have decided where to have repairs done, be sure to get everything in writing beforehand. If you are having major work done, get a written estimate detailing what the mechanic is going to do, the cost of parts for doing it, and the labor charges you'll be expected to pay. In some states, a mechanic may be entitled to vary his final charges from the written estimate by a specified amount, such as $100 or 10 percent, without having to get further authorization from you to proceed.

Find out what warranty for parts and labor the shop provides, and get it in writing. Don't rely on a mechanic's oral statements; if the shop plans to stand behind its work, it should be willing to commit itself to a written warranty.

Unless repairs are being made at no cost to you under the terms of your warranty, always insist on having the defective parts a mechanic takes out of your car returned to you. In many states, the law requires a work order to have a box for you to check indicating you want your old parts returned, but if there isn't one on your work order, write "Shop to Return Parts to Customer" on the face of the order before you sign it. This way, if you think the mechanic replaced a part that didn't need replacement, you can take the part to another mechanic or auto supply dealer to have it tested. And if it does turn out that the part was replaced unnecessarily, you'll have evidence in case you have to file suit to get your money back.

Never sign a blank work order, or one that's vague about what work is going to be done. A work order that says something like "Fix Front End" gives the mechanic a lot of leeway in determining what to do and what to charge.

AUTOMOBILE INSURANCE

State laws require car owners to purchase minimum amounts of liability insurance to cover bodily injury and property damage caused by you or someone authorized by you to drive your car.

Despite what state laws say, the unfortunate fact of the matter is that many drivers simply neglect or refuse to purchase the required insurance coverage. And if they purchase the minimum coverage required by law, it may not be enough to pay for damages caused in a serious accident. As a result, in addition to liability insurance, you should also consider buying uninsured or underinsured motorist's coverage. In the event that you are involved in an accident with an uninsured motorist, or one whose coverage is inadequate, your company will provide payment for any injury or damages you suffer as a result of their negligence.

NO-FAULT INSURANCE

More than half the states have enacted laws providing for so-called "no-fault" automobile insurance. While the details of these laws vary from state to state, no-fault statutes generally allow a driver who is injured or who suffers property damage in an automobile accident to collect payment from his own insurance company, up to a specified limit, regardless of who caused the accident. Under no-fault coverage, the driver himself may have been responsible for the accident, but is still entitled to receive payment up to the limits of no-fault coverage.

If the damages suffered by a driver who wasn't at fault exceed the limits of no-fault coverage, he can then file a claim against the negligent driver to recover the additional amount. The negligent driver's insurer would then either pay the claim, attempt to settle for a reduced amount, or defend its customer in the event of a lawsuit.

COLLISION AND COMPREHENSIVE

In addition to liability insurance coverage, you may also consider purchasing collision insurance. This coverage pays for damage for your car up to the automobile's cash value. For example, if you drive a car which is five years old and are involved in an accident, your insurance will pay only the "book value" of the car, or the repair cost, whichever is lower.

Comprehensive insurance coverage protects your automobile against theft, fire, flood, and glass breakage. However, comprehensive insurance coverage does not extend to collision damage, engine problems or other mechanical difficulties, or normal wear and tear to the vehicle.

While both collision and comprehensive coverage may be valuable during the early years of car ownership (and are usually required by the lender who provides your car loan), the rapid depreciation of most automobiles may make these coverages less valuable as time goes on. If your car is paid for and more than five years old, you may want to consider dropping these coverages from your insurance policy.

If you do have collision and comprehensive coverage, check to be sure that the policy doesn't require you to accept so-called "after market" parts manufactured by companies other than the one that built your car. In many cases, these parts are nowhere near as durable or sturdy as those made by the car's manufacturer, but insurance companies want you to use them because they are usually much cheaper. Some insurance companies have tried to force consumers to pay the difference if they insisted on

OEM (original equipment manufacturer) parts. Unless your policy specifically requires you to accept the cheaper replacements, don't let yourself be talked into it by a claims adjuster or your insurance salesperson.

HOLDING DOWN INSURANCE COSTS

Automobile insurance rates for identical coverage can vary significantly from company to company. If you are a good driver, with no accidents or tickets in the last three to five years, many insurance companies will offer you reduced rates for insurance coverage. And automobile insurers offer a wide array of discounts for a variety of reasons. For example, if you drive your car less than 10 thousand miles per year, you will pay less than someone who drives 20 thousand miles a year. If you live in a rural or suburban area, your rates are likely to be lower than if you live in the city where there's more traffic and higher theft and vandalism rates.

Young drivers usually pay more than older drivers for the same coverage. However, if your son or daughter has completed an approved driver training course, or maintains good grades (usually at least a B average) he or she could be eligible for a discount.

If your car is equipped with an airbag or motorized seatbelts, or if you've installed a car alarm or other anti-theft device, you may also be entitled to receive a discount. You could also get a reduced premium if you purchase your auto insurance from the same company that provides your homeowner, health or life insurance policy, or if you insure more than one car with the same company.

Finally, you may want to consider raising your deductibles (the amount you pay out of your own pocket) as one way to lower your automobile insurance costs. For example, if you raise your collision deductible from $200 to $500, the cost of that coverage could drop 20 percent or more.

It's a good idea to check with your insurance agent from time to time to make sure you are receiving every discount you are entitled to, since many agents won't volunteer this information. Remember that insurance agents generally receive a percentage of the amount you pay for coverage as their commission, so getting you the cheapest coverage takes money out of the agent's pocket. As with other consumer purchases, it pays to shop around for the best deal possible, so don't hesitate to compare the cost of identical coverage from other insurers with that offered by your current insurance company.

YOUR DRIVER'S LICENSE

Even though the United States Constitution guarantees your right to travel freely, it doesn't give you the right to drive a car or operate a motor vehicle. Driving is considered a privilege, not a right, and the government has a right to set standards to determine who can drive legally.

In most states, you must be at least 16 years of age in order to get a driver's license, and you will have to pass a variety of tests and pay a license fee. Tests can include a written examination, a practical test of your driving ability, and a cursory vision test. If you pass all of these, and if you haven't had your license suspended or revoked elsewhere, you will receive a driver's license.

Even then, your license may contain certain restrictions. For example, unless you take additional tests (and pay extra fees), you may be prohibited from operating a commercial vehicle, any vehicle over a specified weight, or a motorcycle. If your vision is poor, you may be required to wear eyeglasses or contact lenses while driving. And if you are elderly or have a previous record of tickets or accidents, you may be required to submit to retesting more frequently than other drivers.

AUTOMOBILE ACCIDENTS

If you are involved in an automobile accident while you are driving, there are several steps you must take in order to protect yourself from resulting legal problems.

The first rule to remember is, whatever else you do after an accident, don't leave the scene without stopping. Penalties for "hit-and-run" are severe.

The second rule is to forget rule one if you are bumped from behind on a deserted road. In recent years, a growing number of motorists have been assaulted, robbed and raped after getting out of their cars in these circumstances. If you are alone on an empty stretch of road or on a deserted city street, especially if it's late at night, don't get out of the car. Instead, drive to the nearest police station and report the accident there. If you can't get to a police station or you don't know where to find it, head for the nearest place where there are other people around, like an all night restaurant or service station. Honk your horn and flash your lights; someone who plans on hurting you won't want that much attention called to him.

If you're in a heavily travelled area and there are other people around, get your vehicle out of the flow of traffic so you don't run the risk of further damage or injury. Get medical assistance for anyone who may have been injured in the accident. If a victim is unconscious or complains of neck or back pains, it is best not to move them, but you should give whatever first aid you can and stop serious bleeding until trained emergency medical personnel arrive.

Be sure to obtain the following information from any other driver involved in the accident: the driver's license number; the year and make of other cars involved in the accident; the names, addresses, and telephone numbers of all drivers, passengers and other witnesses to the accident; and, if the driver is not the owner of the vehicle, the owner's name, address and telephone number.

Be sure to file a police report for any accident which involves physical injury or death, or any property damage. If the police come to the scene of the accident, the police officer's name and badge number, as well as the location of the police station where you can obtain a copy of the accident report.

Notify your insurance agent about the accident. You may also wish to consult with an attorney in regard to any claims you may have against the other driver or drivers.

Don't make any rash statements about who was at fault in the accident. Even if you feel that the accident was your fault, there may be circumstances of which you are unaware which will lessen your responsibility. Admitting guilt at the scene of the accident to the others involved or to witnesses or the police may jeopardize your legal rights later on.

Similarly, if you are approached by the other driver's insurance company with a quick offer to settle your claim, be very cautious about accepting such an offer. Some serious injuries may not become apparent until weeks or even months after the accident has occurred, and settling your claim too quickly may make it difficult to collect for those injuries later on. Get the advice of an experienced attorney if you have any questions or concerns about your rights and responsibilities after an automobile accident.

TRAFFIC TICKETS

It's the rare driver who goes a lifetime without getting a traffic or parking ticket. And while it's tempting to ignore a parking ticket fluttering under your windshield wiper, or tear up that speeding ticket the officer handed you, doing so is a bad idea. There's nothing quite like getting pulled over on your way to work or on an outing with your family for making an illegal turn or running a stop sign and being handcuffed and arrested for ignoring a previous ticket. And more than a few drivers have been dismayed to return to their parked cars only to find that the car has a "boot" on its wheel, a device that prevents it from being driven away.

If you think you've received a ticket you didn't deserve, it's useless to argue with the officer who issued it, and doing so may even work against you when it comes time for your day in court, since police officers usually have a much greater recall of uncooperative motorists than those who just take the ticket and go on their way. If you want to fight a ticket, the proper place to do so is in traffic court. The ticket will indicate the time and place where you can appear to contest it.

While it can be frustrating and time consuming to go to traffic court, and you may be tempted to simply pay the fine and be done with the matter, there are some times when fighting a traffic ticket makes sense. Speeding and traffic tickets can lead to increased insurance rates, and repeated offenses can lead to the suspension or loss of your driver's license. So if you got a parking ticket while you were legally parked, or if you can show that the police officer who issued the ticket made a mistake, you should seriously consider going to court.

In most cases, you don't need a lawyer's help to fight a traffic ticket. Although the procedures may vary a bit from court to court, generally you simply appear in court on the day scheduled and wait for your case to be called. The traffic court judge will ask for your plea, at which point you say "Not Guilty."

The court will then ask the prosecuting attorney to present his case, which will usually consist entirely of the testimony of the officer who wrote the ticket. The attorney will ask the officer to identify himself, give an account of the events leading up to the ticket and identify you as the driver to whom the ticket was issued. You then get a chance to cross-examine the officer, and present any evidence you may have in your defense, such as your own testimony and the testimony of other witnesses. The prosecutor gets to cross-examine you and your witnesses, and that's about it. The judge then renders his decision.

While it's not necessary to get a fresh haircut and wear your Sunday best to traffic court, being neatly dressed and treating the judge, the police officer and the prosecuting attorney with courtesy won't hurt your case. And if you spend a little time preparing your case before you get to court, rehearsing your questions and organizing your thoughts, you can present your case more clearly and more importantly, more quickly. Traffic court judges have crowded courtroom schedules, and they tend to appreciate brevity and clarity.

In some cases, simply showing up to contest the ticket may be enough to lead to a dismissal. In order to proceed with its case, the government will almost always need the testimony of the officer who wrote the ticket. Occasionally, because of a scheduling conflict, the officer won't be in court when he's supposed to be. If he's not there, you can ask the court to dismiss your case for lack of prosecution.

Finally, if the offense you've been charged with is a serious one, you may want to at least talk to an attorney beforehand, and you might even want to have one represent you if you are facing suspension or loss of your license, or if you think being found guilty will cause a big jump in your insurance rates. While there are plenty of times when a lawyer's help isn't necessary, it may be a false economy to save a few hundred dollars in legal fees only to pay that and more in increased insurance rates and added inconvenience.

DRIVING UNDER THE INFLUENCE (DUI)

Getting any kind of ticket is frustrating, but getting arrested and charged with driving under the influence of alcohol or drugs is just about as bad as it gets, short of being charged with vehicular homicide. Each year, nearly 1.5 million Americans are charged with driving while intoxicated. But this is just the tip of the iceberg. Some experts estimate that in any given time and place, one in 50 drivers on the road is legally intoxicated. In 1992, more than 25,000 Americans died and more than a million were injured in accidents involving drunk drivers.

In most states, a blood alcohol content of .10 percent is the threshold for finding a driver legally intoxicated. Statistics show that drivers who equal or exceed the .10 percent figure are more than six times more likely than sober drivers to be involved in an automobile accident. As a result, several states have lowered the threshold requirement to .07 percent or less.

For most people, it doesn't take a great deal of alcohol to reach these blood alcohol levels. For a person who weighs 180 pounds, three or more drinks of hard liquor in a one hour period can cause a blood alcohol concentration in excess of .10 percent. And while some people believe that drinking beer or wine poses less danger of intoxication, the amount of alcohol in a 12 ounce bottle of beer or a 6 ounce glass of wine is equal to that in a 1½ ounce drink of hard liquor.

Because of the ongoing danger presented by drunk drivers, many states have set up road block programs that allow police officers to briefly stop drivers to determine if they are driving while intoxicated. If a police officer suspects that a driver stopped at one of these "sobriety checkpoints" is driving under the influence of alcohol, he or she may be required to submit to a roadside sobriety test, and to provide a breath or blood sample to measure blood alcohol concentrations.

Although the United States Supreme Court has ruled that such roadblocks do not violate a driver's federal constitutional rights, state courts have arrived at varying conclusions when they have been challenged for violating rights granted under state constitutions. Some state courts have held that sobriety checkpoints do violate a driver's right not to be subject to unreasonable searches and seizures, while others have taken the opposite view.

In most states, under a legal doctrine known as "implied consent" the law considers you to have agreed to submit to blood alcohol testing when you obtained your driver's license. Refusing to submit to a blood alcohol test can lead to an automatic suspension or revocation of your driver's license. And in most states, you do not have a right to consult with an attorney before taking such a test.

Penalties for driving while intoxicated are severe, and are becoming more so all the time. In some states, a first offender who is found guilty of driving under the influence of alcohol can be sentenced to as much as 90 days in the county jail, fined up to $500, and have his driver's license suspended for up to two years. A second offense can lead to a year in jail and a fine of $1,000. Third and subsequent offenses can bring as much as a five-year prison term.

If you are ever charged with driving under the influence of alcohol or driving while intoxicated, it is important that you get help from an attorney as soon as possible. This is   time when you don't want to try to do-it-yourself. You can   in the name of an attorney experienced in this area of the   from your state bar association's referral service.

CHAPTER SIX
YOUR JOB OR BUSINESS

Whether you work for someone else or own your own business, the law affects your career in many ways. In this chapter, we will look at some of the legal issues surrounding business ownership. On the employees' side of the picture, we'll look at hiring and employment practices, including your rights under state and federal anti-discrimination laws. We'll examine the problem of sexual harassment in the workplace, and discuss some of the important legal issues you may encounter as either an employer or employee in regard to layoffs, firings, and unemployment compensation. Finally, we'll discuss the current state of worker compensation laws.

OWNING YOUR OWN BUSINESS

At one time or another, almost everyone thinks about starting a business and being his own boss. And each year, hundreds of thousands of Americans take the plunge and actually start their own businesses. Whether you are thinking about beginning part-time while you keep your present job, or risking everything on a full time venture, there are some important legal issues you should consider carefully before you begin.

First, you need to decide which legal form your business will take. Most new businesses begin as a sole proprietorship. According to the federal Small Business Administration, about four out of five new businesses operate as sole proprietorships.

A sole proprietorship is owned entirely by one person, although the owner may have others working for him as employees. A sole proprietorship's chief advantage is the relative ease with which it can be started. About all you have to do is obtain the appropriate licenses and permits from your local government and you can begin. Recordkeeping is usually much simpler with a sole proprietorship than with other kinds of business organizations, and filing tax returns is far simpler than for a partnership or corporation.

On the negative side, if you operate a business as a sole proprietorship, the law considers the business to be nothing more than an extension of you, the owner. If a product you manufacture causes injury to a user, you can be held personally liable for the damages the user suffers. If you fall behind on payments to suppliers and lenders to your business, they can attach your personal assets, such as your car and home, in order to assure themselves of payment. And if your business fails, you will be personally liable for paying off the business' debts, even if it means filing for personal bankruptcy.

The second most common form of business organization is the corporation. Although most people identify the corporation with giant companies like General Motors and IBM, the majority of corporations are small, with only a few stockholders. In many cases, one person owns all the stock in a corporation.

The law considers a corporation a separate legal entity which has the right to enter into contracts, to own personal property and real estate, and to sue and be sued. As a result, the stockholders of a corporation assume no personal liability for the debts of the business. Their risk is limited to the amount of their investment in the firm. This limitation on personal liability is one of the chief benefits of using the corporate form for your business. Another advantage of a corporation include a stockholder's ability to sell his interest in the company without first obtaining the approval of other stockholders. And unlike sole proprietorships or (as we'll see in a moment) partnerships, a corporation can continue to exist indefinitely regardless of whether investors or owners quit, die, or declare bankruptcy.

In some cases, however, establishing your business as a corporation provides less protection than you might think. For example, many lenders and suppliers to small corporations will require what's known as a "personal guaranty" — the promise of a shareholder in the corporation to be personally responsible for the corporation's debt if it defaults. And if the corporation is run in a way that makes it impossible to distinguish between its activities and those of its shareholders, a court can "pierce the corporate veil" and impose personal liability on the corporation's stockholders.

For example, the laws in most states require corporations to hold an annual meeting and keep minutes of the decisions made by the corporation's board of directors. A corporation that fails to meet this legal requirement could be found to have forfeited its corporate status, and the owners of the corporation could be held personally responsible for the actions taken by the corporation.

There are some major disadvantages to organizing your business as a corporation. One of these is the extra paperwork necessary. Another disadvantage is the possibility that the corporation's profits will be subject to double taxation. Because a corporation has the status of an "artificial person" it must pay taxes on its profits. And when the stockholders receive some of those profits in the form of dividends, they are taxed again as income to the stockholder.

To avoid this double taxation, many small corporations operate as "S Corporations." Under the federal Internal Revenue Code, a corporation which elects to operate as an S Corporation pays no income taxes on its profits. Instead, profits are paid by the shareholders of the corporation on their personal returns.

Not every corporation can qualify for this special tax treatment. To obtain IRS approval as an S Corporation, the corporation must be corporation organized under the laws of one of the states, and not a foreign corporation. It must have no more than 35 shareholders, none of whom are non-resident aliens. In addition, only individuals, estates, or trusts can own stock in the corporation. Finally, the corporation can issue only one class of stock. (For a discussion of classes of stock, see Chapter 8, "Your Money.")

To become an S Corporation, the company must file Form 2553 with the Internal Revenue Service. S Corporation status can continue indefinitely, provided all the above conditions continue to be met. However, S Corporation status ends automatically as soon as any one of these conditions changes in a way that disqualifies the corporation from S Corporation treatment. For example, if another corporation bought stock in the S Corporation, the S Corporation status would terminate, since only individuals, trusts, and estates can own S Corporation stock.

A partnership is a contractual relationship in which two or more persons carry on a business, sharing the potential for financial loss as well as the potential for earning a profit. While it's possible to begin a partnership without having any kind of formal, written agreement between the partners, doing so is a very bad idea. In a partnership, the actions of one of the partners is legally binding on all the other partners in the business. If you don't have a written agreement which sets out the limits to what each partner can do, you could be faced with paying off debts incurred without your knowledge or approval by one of your partners.

By having a written partnership agreement, you can set out the duties and rights of each of the partners. With a written agreement, you can also provide for the way in which the partnership's profits will be split, how a partner can sell or transfer his interest in the partnership to another, and what will happen to the partnership's assets if the partners decide to end the business.

Partnerships fall into one of two sub-categories. In a general partnership, each partner has the authority to enter into contracts and carry on all the business of the partnership, and each partner may be forced to assume full financial liability for the debts of the partnership.

In a limited partnership, there is at least one general partner who is responsible for the management of the partnership's business activities. The other partners, called limited partners, take no role in management, but act merely as investors. As a result, the limited partners are not exposed to financial liability beyond the amount they have invested in the partnership. Most states have adopted the Uniform Limited Partnership Act to regulate the way limited partnerships operate. For example, the Act limits the kind of investment a limited partner can make to cash or property; personal services cannot be considered as an investment in the partnership. Most states require limited partnerships to disclose the nature of the partnership to the public, such as by using the letters "LTD" after the business name.

A partnership is considered a separate entity by the Internal Revenue Service, and is required to file an annual tax return. But the partnership doesn't pay taxes; each partner reports his share of the partnership's profits on his individual tax return.

A major disadvantage to using a partnership as a form of business is the lack of flexibility in its makeup. For example, if one of the partners dies, the existing partnership ends, even though the business itself may carry on. When it does, the law considers the business to be a new partnership between the heirs of the deceased partner and the surviving partners.

Another problem can occur when a partner leaves the partnership without providing adequate notice to the partnership's creditors. In some situations, the former partner has been held liable for the partnership's debts long after leaving the business, when the creditor could show that he extended the credit based on his belief that the former partner was still a member of the partnership.

In some states, it's now possible to operate your business through another legal entity known as a limited liability company, or LLC. Limited liability companies have been described as combining some of the advantages of a corporation and a partnership without the disadvantages of these two more traditional forms of business. Tax advantages enjoyed by partnerships and the limited personal liability associated with corporations are combined when a limited liability company is established. Although the LLC laws adopted across the country vary to some extent from state to state, there are general features common to all of these statutes.

For example, each LLC law provides that individual owners will not be personally liable for debts or obligations of the company. An LLC is a separate legal entity that can sue and be sued and purchase and own property. Similar to corporate requirements, "articles of organization" must be filed with the secretary of state and a registered agent must be designated within the state to receive legal notices and accept service of summons. At least two members must initially be involved in forming an

LLC, with "member" being defined to include individuals, general or limited partnerships and corporations.

While an LLC shares the corporate trait of a limit on personal liability, it differs from a corporation because there is no opportunity to freely transfer an interest in an LLC. All the remaining members of the LLC have to agree to any transfer of a membership interest unless the transfer only involves the right to receive profits or the return of contributions to the business.

Unlike corporations, which can exist indefinitely, a limited liability company cannot exist for more than thirty years. During that time, however, the death, withdrawal, expulsion or bankruptcy of one member does not necessarily represent the end of the LLC, as it would with a partnership. If all of the remaining members agree, the LLC can continue, and in a few states the law allows the business to continue with the consent of fewer than all the remaining members.

In a few states, there are some restrictions on the types of business that can be conducted as limited liability companies. For example, several states prohibit banks or insurance companies from being operated as limited liability companies.

GETTING LICENSES AND PERMITS

Just about every state, county, and municipality has licensing requirements which you must meet before you can begin operating your business. Although these requirements will vary somewhat from one locality to another, here's an overview of some of the kinds of licenses and permits you may be required to obtain.

In most states, the first step in operating a business is obtaining a business permit or license. The requirements for obtaining a license depend to a large extent on the kind of business you intend to operate. If you are opening a retail shop, you will need a retail business permit. If you are starting a restaurant, you'll need a business license and a permit from the local board of health. If you are opening a liquor store, you'll need a license from the governmental body that regulates liquor stores, such as the state Department of Revenue.

Depending on the nature of your business, you may be required to answer a number of questions about your background, and law enforcement authorities may conduct an investigation as well. For example, if you want to open a liquor store or a restaurant that will serve alcoholic beverages, you can be asked about any criminal convictions in your background, and you may be refused a license if your previous history convinces the licensing authority that you don't have the requisite moral character to be allowed to serve alcohol. Similar investigations may be conducted before you can open a child care or elder care facility. If your application for a license of this type is denied, you can appeal the decision. The procedure for filing an appeal will vary from one place to another, but you can obtain specific information about how to proceed with an appeal by contacting the licensing body. In most states, the licensing authority must provide you with this information when it notifies you that it has rejected your application.

In most states, operating a business without first obtaining the appropriate license is considered a misdemeanor, and may be punished by a fine or (in rare cases) imprisonment for up to a year in jail. If you are buying a business from its previous owner, you must obtain a new license — you can't operate on the license of the former owner.

If your business sells goods or services subject to state or local sales taxes, you will need to obtain a sales tax permit. You can obtain the application for a sales tax permit from your state's department of revenue. In some states, you may be required to make a deposit with the department of revenue to cover a portion of the amount of taxes you estimate you will owe during the tax year. Other states may require that you post a performance bond; if you fail to pay taxes on time, the state can collect on the bond to ensure that it receives the money you owe.

If you operate your business under a name other than your own, you will probably have to file a "fictitious business name" registration form with your state or local government. For example, if you operate your partnership under the name "Quality Partners," you must register the name so that the public will know who is actually operating the business. However, if your last name is Smith and your partner's name is Jones, and you call your auto repair business "Smith and Jones Auto Repairs" you may not need to file a fictitious business name statement, since the public has notice of who the partners are. Your county clerk can tell you what forms you need to file in your state to register a fictitious business name. Usually, you'll be required to make the filing within 30 days of when you begin conducting business under the fictitious name. You may be required to place a notice in your local newspaper informing the public of the name the business will use and the names of the business owners, and in some states you are required to renew the filing every few years.

HOME BASED BUSINESSES

Special rules usually apply to a business which you intend to run from your home. Many communities have strict regulations regarding the kinds of businesses that can be operated in a residential area. While you may not have any trouble if you want to run a word processing or desktop publishing business out of a spare room, the situation may be different if you plan on using your garage as a warehouse, if you will be hiring employees, or if you intend to have clients visiting you during the day.

Before you begin a home based business, you should check with your community zoning commission to learn about any restrictions on the kind of business you can operate and the ways in which you can operate it. You should also take a look at the deed to your home. It may contain covenants, or promises, which limit your home business beyond what the zoning laws require. If you operate a home business in violation of these covenants, other property owners may file suit against you to stop your business and to compensate them for damages which result from your business operations, such as a reduction in the value of their own property.

Operating a home based business still entitles you to deduct a portion of home expenses such as mortgage interest, utilities and insurance from your federal income tax. But you must keep very good records, and you must use your home office as your exclusive place of business. If you have a business office outside the home, you can't take a deduction for home office use in regard to the same business. In 1993, the U.S. Supreme Court sided with the Internal Revenue Service in interpreting the allowable deduction for a home business very narrowly. For the most current information, contact the IRS at 1-800-TAX-FORM and ask for Publication 587, "Business Use of Your Home."

INDEPENDENT CONTRACTORS

Once your business begins to grow, you'll probably want to consider using independent contractors, or hiring employees. An independent contractor is defined as someone who pursues a trade, occupation or business independent from that of the person who employs him. If the employer only has the right to control the result of the work done and not the time, means or methods used to do it, then the work is probably done by an independent contractor and not an employee.

For example, suppose you hire Jed's Delivery Service to deliver packages to your customers. If Jed uses his own car, does the job at the time he chooses, and doesn't have to report in to tell you where he is and what he's doing during the day, he's probably an independent contractor. But if you provide the delivery vehicle, require Jed to show up at a particular time each day, and to check in when he's finished his deliveries, he's probably an employee.

There are a number of reasons why it's important to correctly distinguish independent contractors from employees. First, an independent contractor is responsible for paying his own income taxes. A company that uses an independent contractor isn't required to withhold taxes for Social Security and income taxes. A company that uses an independent contractor's services doesn't have to pay for workers compensation and unemployment insurance coverage for the contractor, as it would for an employee. And an independent contractor isn't eligible for employee benefit plans that an employer may offer. Finally, anti-discrimination laws that apply to the way employees are recruited, hired, and fired don't always apply when a company selects an independent contractor to provide services.

Some employers try to stretch the definition of an independent contractor to cover workers who are actually employees. If this practice is discovered by the state or federal Department of Labor, the employer can be held liable for overtime and back wages owed to the misclassified worker. Additionally, the IRS can assess back taxes and penalties against an employer that tries to avoid making Social Security contributions and income tax withholding by classifying employees as independent contractors.

RECRUITING AND INTERVIEWING JOB APPLICANTS

Federal and state laws prohibit most employers from discriminating among employees and job applicants on the basis of race, national origin, religion, sex, or disability. The federal Age Discrimination in Employment Act protects workers 40 years of age and older from being discriminated against by employers. In addition to these protections, some state laws also prohibit discrimination on the basis of marital status or sexual orientation.

Generally, the federal anti-discrimination laws apply to employers with 15 or more workers, but state laws often apply to much smaller companies. These laws limit the kinds of questions an employer may ask of a job applicant, and generally permit employers to seek only the information that will help them determine an applicant's ability to do the job for which he applied.

As an employer, you should avoid asking questions pertaining to a job applicant's personal life. For example, you should not ask any questions about the applicant's marital status or plans for marriage, the applicant's age or date of birth, or whether the applicant's spouse will approve of the applicant working for your organization.

You should also avoid asking about the kind of work an applicant's spouse may be engaged in, and you should not ask about the number of children an applicant has or any plans the applicant has for starting a family, or if the applicant has elderly parents to whom he provides care. Other questions that should also be avoided would involve the applicant's place of birth, national origin, religious and political affiliations.

If a potential employer asks you any of these questions on a job application or during a job interview, you have a couple of choices in regard to offering a response.

First, you may simply refuse to answer the offending questions. However, if you refuse to answer, you may want to remind the interviewer that questions of this nature are prohibited by law unless they are somehow relevant to the job application process. In some very limited situations, employers can practice what would otherwise be illegal discrimination when it is based on what's known as a "bona fide occupational qualification," or BFOQ. An example of a BFOQ is a requirement that applicant's for the director of a church sponsored summer camp be a member of the sponsoring church's religion. In most cases, however, the interviewer will be hard-pressed to provide a legitimate reason for asking an applicant to provide this type of information.

If you like, you may decide to answer the questions even though they are legally prohibited. In this case, if you do not receive a job offer and you can show that your answers were used to eliminate you from consideration, you may be able to file a discrimination complaint against the prospective employer.

If you're an employer, by this time you may be wondering what kinds of questions you can ask a job applicant. Generally, you're on safe ground asking the following questions:

- The applicant's name and any other names he or she worked under
- The applicant's address
- If the applicant is a U.S. citizen (but not if the applicant is a naturalized citizen, since this could lead to charges of discrimination on the basis of national origin)
- If the applicant is eligible to work in the U.S.
- If the applicant has ever been convicted of a crime (but not if he's ever been arrested)
- The applicant's educational background, provided that it's relevant to the job being applied for
- The applicant's job history, including the names and addresses of former employers, the kinds of jobs previously held, the terms of previous employment, wages earned, and the reasons for leaving previous jobs
- Personal or employer references

Note that while it's perfectly legal to ask for references from previous employers, you can't contact previous employers without getting the applicant's permission to do so. And because of concerns about being sued for defamation or violating a former employee's right to privacy, getting a meaningful reference from a past employer is becoming increasingly difficult. In most cases, references will be limited to providing information about when the applicant worked for the previous employer, the job or jobs he held while employed there, and how much money the applicant was earning at the time he left.

TESTING JOB APPLICANTS

What if you intend to test applicants to determine if they're qualified to do a particular job? The law allows you to administer pre-employment tests that measure an applicant's skills and knowledge, provided that the test is relevant to the job applied for, and provided that you administer it to all applicants and under similar conditions. But even this last requirement is changing. Some rejected job applicants have filed suit under the Americans with Disabilities Act, claiming that they suffer from learning disabilities and charging that they were illegally discriminated against because they weren't given extra time to take a pre-employment test. Blind applicants may need to have tests provided in something other than written form (such as braille), and deaf applicants may need to have translators provided to assist them in the test taking process.

Other kinds of tests, such as those designed to provide a "personality profile" of a prospective employee, are highly suspect, not only because they are often used to discriminate against minority applicants, but because the results of these tests are often meaningless. It's best to avoid this kind of testing entirely.

At one time, many employers required prospective employees to submit to polygraph, or lie-detector tests. However, a federal law, the Employee Polygraph Protection Act, now prohibits most employers from requiring a job applicant to submit to this type of testing. In fact, this law not only prohibits employers from requiring the test, it even prohibits employers from merely requesting job applicants take a polygraph test in most situations. (The Employee Polygraph Protection Act doesn't apply to government employees, FBI contractors, some security positions, and employees of drug companies whose jobs will put them in contact with controlled substances.)

As an employer, you probably can require that a job applicant take a drug or alcohol test as a condition of getting the job, but only if you notify applicants in advance that passing a drug test is a condition of employment, and only if you have already made an offer of employment to the applicant. Alcohol and drug urinalysis tests must be conducted by a government certified laboratory, and the applicant must be able to give his sample without being observed by the employer or any agent of the employer (including a lab technician). If the applicant tests positive, the result must be confirmed by a second, independent test, and the results of any positive test must be kept confidential.

Finally, employers may not require applicants to take a physical examination until after an offer of employment has been made. The employer must require all applicants who have been offered employment to submit to a physical; they can't pick and choose. But the applicant can't be denied employment on the basis of the results of a physical exam, unless health is a bona fide qualification for performing the job. Under the Americans with Disabilities Act, an employer with 15 or more employees must make "reasonable accommodations" for disabled applicants that will allow them to perform the job for which they were hired, and provided it doesn't create an "undue burden" on the employer.

GETTING PAID

Under federal law, the minimum wage in the United States in 1993 was $4.25 per hour. But not every worker is covered by this law. For example, managers, executives, and workers who are paid on a commission basis aren't covered by the federal minimum wage law, and neither are babysitters or newspaper delivery people. And if you work in a field where you would be expected to earn tips (such as when you work as a waiter or taxi driver) your employer only has to pay you one half the minimum wage, provided you don't have to pool your tips with those received by others working for the same employer. The assumption behind this rule is that you will receive at least enough in tips to meet or exceed the minimum wage. If you've ever worked for tips, however, you know how flawed this assumption can sometimes be. And if your employer provides housing, meals, or transportation to and from work for your convenience, and you voluntarily accept, the employer can also credit the "reasonable costs" of providing these benefits to the minimum wage.

Most states have their own minimum wage laws, which generally match the federal standard. In some states, however, the minimum wage is higher than that established by federal law, and in those states you usually must be paid according to the state standards rather than the federal ones.

If you work more than 40 hours in a week, under federal law you are entitled to receive overtime pay at 1½ times your regular hourly rate, unless your job is considered exempt from the provisions of the Fair Labor Standards Act (FLSA). Among others, commissioned salespeople, drivers, farm workers, and executive, administrative, and professional employees aren't covered by the FLSA.

As with minimum wage laws, the provisions of state overtime laws are generally similar to those enacted by the federal government. In a few states, however, you are entitled to overtime if you work more than a specified number of hours in the work day, rather than in the work week. For example, in California most employers must pay overtime to workers who put in more than 8 hours in a day. In Florida, manual laborers who work more than 10 hours in a day must be paid at the overtime rate.If you work in a state with more restrictive laws than those enacted on the federal level, and your job isn't exempted from federal coverage, you get the benefit of the federal laws more liberal rules.

Although there's no federal law that sets out the requirements on how often you must be paid, all but a few states have passed laws covering the frequency with which employers must pay their workers. In most states, you must be paid at least once a month, while in others you must be paid twice a month, and a few require weekly payment of wages.

One problem often encountered by both employer and employee concerns the area of wage garnishment. If a worker is sued successfully, the winning party can ask the court to order a garnishment of the worker's wages. The employer must then withhold a portion of the worker's wages and pay that portion to the winner of the lawsuit.

Under federal law, a worker generally must be allowed to keep either 30 times the minimum wage, or 75 percent of disposable earnings, whichever is greater. If the garnishment is for child support payments, however, more of your pay may be withheld, depending on how far behind you are on support payments, and whether you have another spouse or child to support.

Garnishments, especially multiple garnishments, can be a headache for employers, who have to figure out how much to withhold and the priority of conflicting claims. At one time, having your wages garnished even once could lead to losing your job. Under current federal law, you can't be fired when your wages are garnished for a single debt. If you have multiple garnishments, the federal statutes don't protect you from being fired, although some state laws prohibit firings in this situation as well.

The rules on when you must receive your final paycheck vary depending on whether you leave your job voluntarily or are fired, and they also vary from state to state. In some states, an employer who fails to pay you within the time limit specified by law can be subject to a financial penalty equal to a percentage of the amount owed, or attorney fees needed to collect the unpaid wages, or some combination of both.

Your state department of labor can provide you with information about the specific laws in your state regarding garnishments, the frequency with which you must be paid, state minimum wage laws and rules for overtime pay. You'll find a list of these departments and their addresses and telephone numbers at the end of this chapter.

EMPLOYEE BENEFITS

With a few exceptions, employers are not required to provide fringe benefits such as paid sick days, paid personal leave days, group health insurance or life insurance, or retirement plans. By law, most employers are only required to provide two kinds of employee benefits. An employer must provide adequate workers' compensation coverage in the event an employee should suffer a work-related injury. And, since 1993, many employers are now required by federal law to provide up to 12 weeks of unpaid leave each year to most workers when the worker or a member of the worker's immediate family is ill, or when a new baby is born or adopted. State family leave laws may apply to your situation as well.

If an employer chooses to provide additional employee benefits, such as insurance and pension plans, federal and state laws generally require that they be offered on an equal basis to all full-time employees. However, some other kinds of fringe benefits, such as expense accounts, company cars, and mileage reimbursement, when they're offered at all, need only be offered to those employees whose positions require them to travel or entertain business clients.

Keep in mind that state and federal laws which prohibit discrimination in hiring also prohibit discrimination in the area of employee benefits. No benefits may be offered which discriminate among employees on the basis of age, sex, disability, religion, race, or national origin.

Part-time workers may not be eligible for the same types of benefits offered by an employer to full-time workers. However, many employers now offer part-time employees the opportunity to participate in a limited benefit program. If you are a part-time employee, you should contact your employer's personnel office for information regarding any benefits you might be eligible to receive.

UNIONS AND THE RIGHT TO WORK

In the early part of the nineteenth century, workers who attempted to organize a union could be charged with criminal conspiracy. As recently as the early years of the twentieth century, union leaders were arrested when they organized work stoppages and picket lines. It wasn't until the 1930s that federal laws began to protect the rights of workers to organize unions and keep their jobs when they became union members.

Today, a number of federal laws govern the relationships between employers and labor unions. The Labor Management Relations Act, also known as the Taft-Hartley Act, is the most important of these laws.

Under the Taft-Hartley Act, employees have the legal right to organize or join a union, take part in strikes and peaceful picketing, and bargain collectively through their elected union representatives. An employer who tries to interfere with these rights, such as by firing a worker who is a union organizer, or who refuses to engage in good faith bargaining with the employees' authorized representatives, is guilty of an unfair labor practice.

Employers can take some actions without being guilty of an unfair labor practice. For example, they can prohibit a worker from distributing union literature during working hours, and keep off duty workers and organizers who are not employees from entering the premises, but only if the policy is applied evenhandedly and doesn't unfairly single out union activity. That means the employer must prohibit the distribution of all literature, not just that related to union activities, and must keep representatives of other organizations besides a labor union out of the premises.

An employer can't prevent you from talking with other employees about union activities when you are off duty, even when you are in the company lunchroom or in other nonworking parts of the employer's facility. But it doesn't have to let you use the company's facilities for union meetings, unless it allows other organizations to use them.

If your union goes on strike, the employer has the legal right to hire replacement workers so it can keep its business operating. Depending on the reason for the strike, it may not be required to rehire striking workers once the strike is over. (This last provision may change in the near future — the Clinton Administration has proposed rules that would require employers to rehire striking workers under just about any circumstances.)

Another important federal law, the Labor-Management Reporting and Disclosure Act, also known as the Landrum-Griffin Act, protects workers not from the misdeeds of their employers, but from the acts of unions themselves. Under Landrum-Griffin, union members must be given the right to speak at union meetings, and assemble to discuss, criticize and even oppose the positions taken by union leaders without fear of reprisal. Union members are guaranteed the right to nominate candidates, campaign in union elections, and vote for the union's leadership. The union must file their financial statements, constitutions, by-laws and other organizational documents with the federal government.

Federal law allows the individual states to pass what are known as right-to-work laws. In some states, an employee can be required to pay union dues when hired to work at a company that has a collective bargaining agreement with a recognized union, even if the employee doesn't want to become a union member (and federal law prohibits unions and employers from forcing an employee to join a union as a condition of employment). The logic behind this requirement is that since the employee benefits from the union's collective bargaining strategy, it would be unfair to allow him to avoid the assessment of dues imposed on union members.

In a right-to-work state, an employee cannot be forced to pay dues to the union. And even in states without right-to-work laws, an employee doesn't have to contribute to the union's political activities. That portion of the employee's dues must be refunded if the employee requests the refund.

Federal labor laws are extremely complex, and it's impossible to summarize them thoroughly in only a few paragraphs. If you want more detailed information about these laws, contact the U.S. Department of Labor in Washington, D.C. About two-thirds of the state have enacted right-to-work laws, and your state's department of labor can be of assistance in providing information about the status of right-to-work legislation in your state.

SEXUAL HARASSMENT

Of all the legal issues that surround the workplace, probably none has received as much attention in the past decade as that of sexual harassment, and none has been the source of so much anger and conflict between the accuser and the accused.

Some kinds of sexual harassment are obvious to anyone. An employer who conditions a raise, promotion, or even continued employment on the basis of sexual favors from the employee is clearly guilty of sexual harassment. An employer who pinches, fondles, or makes crude sexual remarks about an employee, or in front of employees, is also guilty of sexual harassment.

Other kinds of harassment, however, are not always so readily apparent. An employer who makes a remark about an employee's personal appearance may be guilty of sexual harassment, or he may not. Much depends on the context of the comment, and whether or not it was part of a pattern of behavior on the employer's part. Under federal guidelines, sexual harassment occurs whenever the actions of an employer, fellow employees, or even the customers of the employer act in a way that creates a "hostile working environment." If a co-worker contributes to the hostile working environment with nude calendars in his workspace, or by making repeated requests for a date, the employer has a responsibility to put a stop to those actions. In a relatively recent case, a Las Vegas casino was found guilty of sexual harassment because its customers made unwelcome comments to a female blackjack dealer and looked at her in a way that made her feel uncomfortable. The casino's liability was based on its refusal to take immediate actions against the offending customers after the dealer complained about their behavior.

Today, it's an unwise business owner who engages in any form of sexual harassment, and every business owner should make it clear to employees and supervisors that sexual harassment will not be tolerated. A sound company policy would encourage employees to bring complaints of sexual harassment to the attention of management without fear of reprisals. If the harassment is caused by the employee's supervisor, alternative notification procedures should be set out clearly.

The company should investigate harassment charges quickly, but thoroughly. In one case, a major oil company fired an executive accused of sexual harassment in an anonymous letter. The company's internal investigation was based on rumors about the executive, but made no attempt to evaluate the credibility of the persons interviewed. As a result, the executive was awarded a half million dollars in damages when he filed suit for wrongful discharge.

Finally, a sound company policy will clearly set out the disciplinary actions that can be taken against those found guilty of harassment, which could include requiring the offender to attend sensitivity training, suspension, or even dismissal.

Although courts have held that the purpose of laws prohibiting sexual harassment is not to desexualize the workplace, the best course any employer can take is to actively discourage any behavior that could be construed even remotely as harassment. While they can't control what employees do outside the workplace, employers need to do everything they can to discourage sexual conduct, flirtation, coarse language, and objectionable behavior at work.

Finally, it's important to remember that sexual harassment doesn't necessarily apply only to offensive conduct by males toward females. Successful claims have been brought by males harassed by females, and same-sex harassment claims have also been successful.

MAKING A DISCRIMINATION OR HARASSMENT COMPLAINT

As we have already seen, a multitude of federal and state laws prohibit discrimination on the basis of race, national origin, religion, sex, age, or disability, as well as sexual harassment.

If you believe you have been illegally discriminated against by an employer, or if you are the victim of sexual harassment, you should contact the federal Equal Employment Opportunity Commission (EEOC) office in your area for information about filing a complaint. If your employer has less than 15 employees, the EEOC generally does not have jurisdiction to investigate your complaint, or require the employer to remedy the problem. State laws, however, do cover most small employers, and you should contact your state's Department of Labor for information about procedures for filing a complaint.

If you decide to file a complaint with the EEOC, you must make your charges within 180 days of the discriminatory act about which you are complaining. If you wait any longer (even one day) the EEOC will not help you or investigate your complaint. If you live in a state that has its own agency to investigate complaints of unlawful job discrimination, the EEOC will do nothing for 60 days, in order to give the state agency time to review and resolve the complaint. That means you should file a complaint with the state agency at the same time you notify the EEOC. In some cases, the 180 day filing requirement can be extended to 300 days if you complain to a state agency, but it's best not to take chances on missing the deadline for bringing your complaint to the EEOC.

Generally, you must make your complaint in writing, signed and sworn to before a notary public or some other official authorized to administer oaths. You should mail your complaint by registered mail, return receipt requested, although you can sometimes file a complaint in person at the EEOC office in your area. Your complaint has to be specific enough to allow the EEOC to figure out whether or not you've alleged a violation of the anti-discrimination laws. It should include the dates and times of the alleged discriminatory acts, and the names of the persons who committed them.

Within ten days of receiving your complaint, the EEOC must notify the employer that you have filed a charge against it. The employer has the right to contest your charges, and the EEOC has the right to inspect the employer's records, interview other employees and question witnesses to the alleged discrimination, and bring a lawsuit against the employer.

By law, the EEOC has 180 days to try to negotiate a settlement between an employer who has illegally discriminated and the employee discriminated against. If it can't reach a settlement that's acceptable to both parties, the EEOC can either file suit on your behalf, or issue what's known as a "right-to-sue" letter, which gives you an additional 90 days in which to file a lawsuit on your own. Generally, you still have the right to file suit under state civil rights laws even if the EEOC doesn't provide a right-to-sue letter, or if you miss the 90 day deadline, although you must comply with the statute of limitations provided for by state law.

While you have the right to be represented by an attorney in any EEOC proceedings, you'll generally have to pay for that representation out of your own pocket. In a few cases, (such as a complaint brought under the Americans with Disabilities Act) the court can appoint a lawyer to represent you in a lawsuit if you can't afford to hire your own attorney, but such appointments are pretty rare.

Up until a few years ago, an employee who brought a lawsuit charging intentional job discrimination was generally limited to receiving reinstatement and back pay. Since 1991, however, an employee who proves a claim of intentional illegal discrimination is also entitled to seek punitive damages, although the amount that can be awarded is limited by the number of employees who work for the lawbreaking employer. For example, if an employer has more than 15 but fewer than 100 employees, the maximum amount of punitive damages that can be awarded is $50,000. And no matter how large the employer is, the maximum allowable award in any case is $300,000.

UNEMPLOYMENT COMPENSATION

The laws that determine when a worker is entitled to unemployment compensation vary from state to state, and trying to define and explain all the variations is impossible in a book like this one. However, we can describe some of the basic rules regarding eligibility for unemployment pay, and how the amount you will receive is determined.

In trying to define when you are entitled to unemployment compensation, it's probably easiest to describe the situations when you aren't entitled to receive it. Generally, you won't be eligible for unemployment benefits when:

- You quit your job
- You are terminated for violating your employer's rules or engaging in misconduct
- You are out of work due to a labor dispute, such as a strike

However, there are exceptions that may entitle you to unemployment pay even in these circumstances.

For example, if you quit your job because your employer failed to keep a promise to you about training or a promotion, some states will allow you to collect unemployment benefits. Other states have permitted employees to obtain unemployment benefits when the employer made a significant change in the worker's job responsibilities, hours, or working conditions without first consulting the worker and obtaining his agreement to the change.

Similarly, in some cases employees who were fired for being late to work, or for breaking other employer rules, were held to be entitled to receive unemployment benefits, even though being late was against the employer's rules. In deciding whether a firing for "cause" is justified, state unemployment agencies and the courts look at how reasonable the rule is that the employee broke, as well as how reasonable the employer's actions were in firing the employee for breaking the rule.

As for "labor disputes," whether or not you are entitled to unemployment benefits may depend on why the dispute took place. If you're locked out by your employer, some states would allow you to receive compensation, but would deny compensation if you were on strike. Other states might allow you to collect even if you were on strike, if the strike was brought on by an unfair labor practice of your employer, such as violating the terms of its contract with your union.

In any case, it's always worth taking the time to apply for unemployment compensation whenever you are fired or laid off, or when your employer made it clear that he'd like you to quit. You'll want to file your claim immediately, since it may take several weeks between the time you file and the time you receive your first check. To file an unemployment claim, you'll usually need to visit the state unemployment agency in your area (in Colorado, however, you can apply over the telephone).

You'll be asked to provide the name and address of your previous employer, as well as those of other companies you worked for during the past few years. You'll also be asked why you left your job.

The unemployment agency will send a notice of your claim to your last employer, which gets a chance to tell the agency in writing why you were dismissed and challenge your claim. Many employers routinely challenge unemployment claims, because the rates they pay for unemployment insurance depend to a great extent on the number of claims filed by former employees. Even if the employer files a challenge, you are entitled to receive benefits until the employer's appeal is heard.

After the unemployment agency gets the employer's response, it makes a determination as to whether or not you are eligible for benefits. If you are denied benefits, you can appeal the agency's decision, although your benefit payment may be suspended pending the outcome of the appeal. If you are awarded benefits, the employer can appeal that decision, although your benefit payments will continue during the appeals process. In either case, the appeal must be filed within the time limits set out on the notice sent by the unemployment agency (usually ten days or so).

In most states, the initial appeals hearing is relatively informal. A referee or administrative law judge (called an "ALJ") will hear evidence from you and from the employer and decide whether or not the initial determination about whether to pay or deny benefits was correct. In some cases, the employer won't even bother to send a representative, although it may provide a written statement for the ALJ's consideration.

The ALJ will make a ruling within a few days of the hearing, and whichever side loses can appeal that decision as well. At this point, the procedures become more strict and complicated, and you may want to consult with or even hire an attorney to provide assistance if you want to appeal. If you're the worker, you might want to contact the community legal aid office, which can sometimes provide low cost or even free services in an unemployment compensation appeal. If you're the employer, you don't have this option available to you, but you may be able to get some advice and assistance from a professional or trade association to which you belong.

If you are ultimately awarded unemployment benefits, the amount you'll receive will be determined by a complicated formula that takes into account the amount of money you earned during the past year (called the "base period"), as well as income you have available from other sources, such as a part-time job with another employer. If you have dependents, that often gets added into the calculation as well. Generally, your weekly benefit will be between 25 percent and 50 percent of the maximum weekly pay you received during the base period, although most states put a cap of $250 to $300 per week on this amount. Unemployment compensation is considered income by the Internal Revenue Service, and you must report it on your Form 1040 when you file your income taxes.

You can usually continue to collect benefits for up to 26 weeks, and even longer in some cases. While you receive benefits, you are expected to actively look for work and accept a suitable job when one if offered. A "suitable job" is one for which your training, education and experience qualifies you. You don't have to take the first job offer that comes along, if, for example, your last job was working as a manager at IBM and the offer you receive is with a lawn mowing service. But the longer you remain unemployed, the more likely it is that the unemployment agency will begin to urge you to consider work outside your previous field.

MASS LAYOFFS AND PLANT CLOSINGS

In most cases, employers can decide to stop operating their businesses without providing any advance notice to their employees. However, a federal law, the Worker Adjustment and Retraining Notification Act (WARN), requires employers with 100 or more full-time employees to give at least 60 days notice if a full or partial shutdown of an employment facility, such as a manufacturing plant, will cause 50 or more full-time employees to lose their jobs. Notice must also be given of temporary closings expected to affect the same number of employees for six months or more, as well as layoffs that will reduce the workforce by one-third for 30 days or more.

Other workforce reductions can also require advance notification under the federal law, and some states have enacted similar laws as well. An employer who violates the federal law can be fined up to $500 a day, and can be required to provide back pay and benefits to employees for each of the 60 days they did not receive notice.

WORKERS COMPENSATION

State laws require most, but not all, employers to provide workers' compensation coverage for their employees. For example, some states exclude coverage for household workers and farm laborers, and a number of states exempt companies with only one or two employees from the requirement to provide workers' compensation coverage.

Workers compensation is essentially a system of no-fault insurance. Under workers compensation, an employee who is injured on the job is compensated for that injury without having to prove that his employer was negligent. In return, the employer gets the assurance of knowing that it won't be hit with a big lawsuit when a worker is injured. To cover the cost of workers compensation coverage, the employer passes that cost along to its customers in the form of higher prices.

Under most workers compensation laws, an employee is entitled to benefits when injured in the course of employment (while the employee is on the job) and when the injury arises out of the employment (something foreseeable given the nature of the job).

For example, suppose you are employed as a warehouse worker, whose job is to move pallets of grocery items from the loading dock to specified places in the warehouse with a forklift. If you are injured while working your regular shift when a pallet tips over and crashes down on your head, you've been injured in the course of your employment, and your injury arose out of the course of your employment.

Unfortunately, situations that can lead to a workers compensation claim aren't always so clear. Suppose that instead of being injured while on the job, you injure yourself in the company parking lot as you return from lunch. Depending on the state in which you live, a workers compensation claim based on this scenario could either be denied or accepted.

Or suppose you are at work, driving your forklift, when another employee who dislikes you decides to intentionally crash his forklift into yours. Whether or not you'll receive workers compensation may depend on whether the dislike was due to some work-related issue, such as a dispute over a promotion, or whether it was based on a more personal matter, such as his belief that you've been having an affair with his wife.

The modern trend in workers compensation cases is to interpret workers compensation laws in the light most favorable to the employee. As a result, injuries which only a few years ago were deemed ineligible for workers compensation are now more likely to be declared compensable. However, most jurisdictions still disqualify workers when their injuries are the result of their own misconduct, such as when they intentionally disobey their employers' safety rules. And a number of states reject claims by workers who were intoxicated or under the influence of drugs at the time the injury occurred.

If you are injured on the job, or suffer an injury which you believe is work related, you should notify your supervisor about it immediately. If you fail to notify your employer within the time limits set out by state law, you may have even a legitimate claim denied. And in some states the law requires notice within a few days, or as soon as possible, so it's best to act quickly.

Your employer will be required to submit a notice of your claim to the state industrial safety department, and you will need to file a workers compensation claim with the state workers compensation board. While the time limit for notifying the board often isn't as stringent as that for notifying your employer, the sooner you file the sooner you can begin to receive benefits.

Your claim will be examined, and if it's found to be valid, you may be compensated for the cost of medical treatment, as well as amounts paid for items such as crutches and prescription medication. You will also be entitled to receive disability benefits which are designed to reimburse you for earnings lost due to your injury.

Because the premiums employers pay for workers compensation insurance depends to a great extent on the number of claims filed by employees, an employer may contest your claim. It can require you to submit to a medical examination by a physician of its choice, but you also have the right to an exam by a doctor of your own choosing. A hearing will be held by a workers compensation referee to determine whether or not your claim is valid. Either you or your employer has the right to appeal from an unfavorable decision.

Workers compensation appeals can be tricky, and you may want to get some professional legal help if your initial claim is denied. In a few states, the state itself provides legal assistance to a worker whose claim has been denied. In most states, however, you'll either need to contact the local legal aid office, or hire a private attorney to assist you. Many workers compensation lawyers will take your case on a contingent fee basis, and those fees are usually limited by state law. You'll find a list of state bar associations which offer referral services at the end of Chapter Seventeen, "Your Lawyer."

Because workers compensation laws are supposed to provide adequately for injured workers while limiting an employer's liability for work-related injuries, most states do not allow an employee to file a lawsuit against their employer if workers compensation is available. In a few states, however, the law will allow a worker to bring a lawsuit if the injury is a result of the employer concealing dangerous working conditions or deliberately violating legally established safety guidelines.

In a number of states, workers have the choice of accepting workers compensation coverage, or "opting out" of the system. A worker who opts out and is then injured in the workplace has to file a lawsuit to recover for injuries, lost wages, and medical expenses. Of course, a worker can't wait until he suffers an injury before opting out, but must decide early on in his employment about whether or not to participate in the workers compensation system.

Unlike unemployment benefits, which are considered taxable income by the Internal Revenue Service, workers compensation benefits are not taxable. Workers compensation benefits are not limited by other kinds of private insurance which may cover you, such as a long-term disability policy. But federal Social Security disability benefits are reduced during the period you are eligible for workers' compensation.

Finally, just about everything we've said about workers compensation law may be subject to substantial change in the not too distant future. The Clinton administration's health insurance policy proposals may include eliminating state workers compensation entirely and combining it with a national health insurance program. However, it's unlikely that any change will take place without lengthy Congressional debate and delay, a long transition period, and plenty of public notice.

STATE LABOR DEPARTMENTS
For information about the laws governing employers and employees in your state, contact your state department of labor at the address and telephone number listed here.

Alabama
Labor Department
64 North Union Street, Room 651
Montgomery, AL 36130
(205) 242-3460

Alaska
Labor Department
P.O. Box 1149
Juneau, AK 99802
(907) 465-2700

Arizona
Labor Division
800 West Washington Street
Phoenix, AZ 85007
(602) 542-4515

Arkansas
Labor Department
10421 West Markham Street
Little Rock, AK 72205
(501) 682-4500

California
Industrial Relations Dept.
P.O. Box 603
San Francisco, CA 94101
(415) 737-2600

Colorado
Labor and Employment Department
600 Grant Street, Suite 900
Denver, CO 80203-3528
(303) 837-3801

Connecticut
Labor Department
200 Folly Brook Boulevard
Wethersfield, CT 06109
(203) 566-4384

Delaware
Labor Department
820 North French Street
Wilmington, DE 19801
(302) 571-2710

District of Columbia
Human Rights Office
2000 - 14th Street, N.W.
Washington, DC 20009
(202) 939-8740

Florida
Labor and Employment Security Department
2590 Executive Center Circle East
Tallahassee, FL 32399-2152
(904) 488-4398

Georgia
Labor Department
148 International Boulevard
Atlanta, GA 30303
(404) 656-3011

Hawaii
Labor and Industrial Relations Department
830 Punchbowl Street
Honolulu, HI 96813
(808) 548-3150

Idaho
Labor and Industrial Services Department
Statehouse Mail
Boise, ID 83720
(208) 334-3950

Illinois
Labor Department
310 South Michigan, 10th Floor
Chicago, IL 60604
(312) 793-2800

Indiana
Labor Department
100 North Senate Avenue, Room 1013
Indianapolis, IN 46204
(317) 232-2378

Iowa
Human Rights Department
Lucas State Office Building
Des Moines, IA 50319
(515) 281-5960

Kansas
Civil Rights Commission
Landon State Office Building
No. 851, South
Topeka, KS 66612-1258
(913) 296-3206

Kentucky
Labor Cabinet
127 Building
U.S. Highway 127 South
Frankfort, KY 40601
(502) 564-3070

Louisiana
Labor Department
P.O. Box 94094
Baton Rouge, LA 70804-9094
(504) 342-3011

Maine
Labor Department
20 Union Street
P.O. Box 309
Augusta, ME 04332-0309
(207) 289-3788

Maryland
Licensing and Regulation Department
Labor and Industry Division
501 St. Paul Place
Baltimore, MD 21202
(301) 333-4179

Massachusetts
Labor Executive Office
1 Ashburton Place, Room 2112
Boston, MA 02108
(617) 727-6573

Michigan
Labor Department
611 West Ottawa Street
Box 30015
Lansing, MI 48909
(517) 373-9600

Minnesota
Labor and Industry Department
443 Lafayette Road
St. Paul, MN 55155
(612) 296-2342

Mississippi
Employment Security Commission
P.O. Box 1699
Jackson, MS 39215-1699
(601) 359-1031

Missouri
Labor and Industrial Relations Department
421 East Dunklin Street
Jefferson City, MO 65101
(314) 751-4091

Montana
Labor and Industry Department
P.O. Box 1728
Helena, MT 59624
(406) 444-3555

Nebraska
Labor Department
P.O. Box 94600
Lincoln, NE 68509
(402) 475-8451

Nevada
Labor Commission
505 East King Street, Room 602
Carson City, NV 89710
(702) 885-4850

New Hampshire
Labor Department
19 Pillsbury Street
Concord, NH 03301
(603) 271-3171

New Jersey
Labor Department
John Fitch Plaza, CN 110
Trenton, NJ 08625
(609) 292-2323

New Mexico
Labor Department
1596 Pacheco Street
Santa Fe, NM 87501
(505) 827-6838

New York
Labor Department
State Campus, Building 12
Albany, NY 12240
(518) 457-2741

North Carolina
Labor Department
4 West Edenton Street
Raleigh, NC 27601
(919) 733-7166

North Dakota
Labor Department
600 East Boulevard Avenue
Bismarck, ND 58505
(701) 224-2661

Ohio
Civil Rights Commission
220 Parsons Avenue
Columbus, OH 43266-0543
(614) 466-2785

Oklahoma
Labor Department
4001 Lincoln Boulevard
Oklahoma City, OK 73105
(405) 528-1500

Oregon
Labor and Industries Bureau
1400 S.W. 5th Avenue, Suite 409
Portland, OR 97201
(503) 229-5737

Pennsylvania
Labor and Industry Department
Labor and Industry Building
Harrisburg, PA 17120
(717) 787-3756

Rhode Island
Labor Department
220 Elmwood Avenue
Providence, RI 02907
(401) 457-1800

South Carolina
Labor Department
P.O. Box 11329
Columbia, SC 29211-1329
(803) 734-9594

South Dakota
Labor Department
700 Governors Drive
Pierre, SD 57501
(605) 773-3101

Tennessee
Labor Department
501 Union Building
Nashville, TN 37219
(615) 741-2582

Texas
Employment Commission
101 East 15th Street
Austin, TX 78778
(512) 463-2800

Utah
Commerce Department
P.O. Box 45802
Salt Lake City, UT 84145-0801
(801) 530-6701

Vermont
Labor and Industry Department
State Office Building
120 State Street
Montpelier, VT 05602
(802) 828-2286

Virginia
Economic Development
Labor and Industry Department
205 North 4th Street
Box 12064
Richmond, VA 23241
(804) 786-2377

Washington
Labor and Industries Department
General Administration Building
HC-101
Olympia, WA 98504
(206) 753-6307

West Virginia
Commerce, Labor, and Environment Department
Labor Division
1800 Washington Street East
Charleston, WV 25305
(304) 348-7890

Wisconsin
Industry Labor and Human Relations Department
P.O. Box 7946
Madison, WI 53707
(608) 266-7552

Wyoming
Labor and Statistics Department
122 West 25th Street, 2nd Floor East
Cheyenne, WY 82002
(307) 777-7261

CHAPTER SEVEN
YOUR CONSUMER RIGHTS

Not so many years ago, the law's interest in protecting consumers from sleazy merchants and defective products was pretty much summed up by the Latin phrase "caveat emptor," which means "let the buyer beware." The assumption was that consumers had the opportunity to examine goods before they bought them. If they weren't satisfied with their quality, or if they were concerned about price, they were always free to go elsewhere.

Today, the assumption that consumers have all the necessary skills to decide if a product is defective or simply not up to standards is less true than it was in the past. Advances in technology and science make it impossible for the ordinary person to know whether or not an item will be defective before making a purchase, or if it will do the things the manufacturer claims it will do.

As an example, look at the growth of computer technology in just the last few years. Many of us count on our computers to help us run our businesses, manage our home finances, and provide entertainment for our children. But very few of us know enough about computers to be able to tell at first glance whether or not a computer will perform as its manufacturer promises.

It wasn't until the 1960s that the state and federal governments began to show a real interest in providing increased protection to consumers. Since then, the consumer protection movement has grown dramatically, so much that many manufacturers and merchants now grumble that our laws are tilted too far in favor of consumers.

And yet despite all the consumer protection laws that have been passed in the last three decades, thousands of consumers are still victimized each year. In this chapter, we'll examine your legal rights as a consumer. But we'll also look at some common sense approaches to help you avoid swindlers and con artists masquerading as legitimate businesses. We'll also show you how to avoid a bad deal, and minimize your risks when dealing with businesses by mail or over the telephone, as well as how to find help in the event you do fall prey to a consumer problem.

In addition to the information contained in this chapter, you will also find discussions of some typical consumer problems elsewhere in this book. For example, you will find information about home improvements and repairs in Chapter 4, "Your Home," while automobile purchases and repairs are discussed in Chapter 5, "Your Car." Credit and collection matters are discussed in detail in Chapter 8, "Your Credit."

CONSUMER CONTRACTS

As a consumer, you enter into dozens of different contracts each and every week. For example, when you buy your breakfast at the local diner on your way to work, you've made a contract. In return for the bacon, eggs and coffee, you agree to pay the restaurant the price of the meal. Most of these contracts are carried off without a hitch; you pay for what you get, and you get what you pay for. And when the price involved is relatively small, any problems that do arise are usually easy to deal with. The merchant gives you a refund of the purchase price, or a new item, or you simply resolve to take your business elsewhere in the future.

Sometimes, however, serious problems can occur, especially when more significant amounts of money are involved. Some merchants are less than cooperative in working with their customers to resolve any problems, no matter what amount of money is involved. And in some cases merchants are downright deceptive in the way they advertise and the quality of what they deliver.

To help you avoid some of these more unpleasant situations, it's important to clear up some of the more popular misconceptions about consumer transactions.

First, always remember that in most cases, an oral contract is just as enforceable as a written one. While it's true that laws require some kinds of contracts to be in writing (such as those for the sale of real estate, or when the goods being purchased exceed a certain value, such as $500), other kinds of contracts are equally enforceable whether they are written or not.

The problem with oral contracts isn't that they are unenforceable, but that they are so much more difficult to prove than a written agreement. For example, if you make an oral agreement with your neighborhood handyman to waterproof your redwood deck and he fails to complete the job in the way you thought you had agreed upon, how can you prove what the terms of the agreement were? Essentially, you will have to go to court and tell your story to a judge. The handyman will have his own story to tell, one which may be far different from yours, but which may be equally credible and convincing.

But if your agreement is in writing and signed by both you and the handyman, and the handyman fails to live up to the terms you set out in writing, it's much easier to convince a court that the agreement has been breached and that you are entitled to damages, payment of the money necessary to make the job right.

Another common myth related to consumer contracts is that consumers have the legal right to return goods for any reason at all. While it's true that many manufacturers and retailers have very liberal returns policies, in most states there is no law that requires merchants or manufacturers to accept returns unless the goods sold prove defective. So before you buy, it's important to know exactly what the merchant's returns policy is, and to be sure that the item you want to purchase is the right one for you if that policy is less than generous.

Another popular misconception involves the "cooling-off" period that lets consumers back out of certain kinds of consumer transactions. Just about any lawyer who has ever worked with consumers has had a client who believed that the law allowed him to change his mind about a purchase even after he signed a sales contract. For some reason, many consumers believe that this is especially true when they are purchasing a car.

As a matter of fact, the Federal Trade Commission does have a rule that calls for a three day cooling-off period. But that rule only applies to very specific kinds of consumer contracts. In order to qualify, the contract must be for an amount greater than $25. It must have been made in your home or at another location that's not the seller's ordinary place of business, such as at an exhibit hall or in a hotel room or restaurant.

But if you enter the sales contract at the seller's place of business, or if the sale was begun at the seller's place of business and merely concluded in your home, the FTC rule doesn't apply. Similarly, if the sale is made by telephone, or if the contract is for items like real estate, securities, or insurance, the contract isn't covered by the Federal Trade Commission rule. Unless you live in a state that has its own laws providing cooling-off periods for other kinds of sales, such as for health club contracts, dance lessons, or sales made over the telephone, your contract becomes a legally binding document the moment you sign it.

So what's a consumer to do? First, don't allow yourself to be pressured by a salesperson into signing a contract with which you're not completely comfortable. While it may be hard to resist an offer that's "good today only," chances are it will be much harder to live with the terms of an agreement that obligates you to make payments you can't afford, or purchase merchandise you don't really want. And you may be surprised at how often you can get a deal that's not much different from the "today only" offer a day or two (or even weeks) later.

Never sign any contract that contains terms you don't completely understand. You may not want to rely on the seller's explanation of these terms, either, since a salesperson has a vested interest in getting your signature on the dotted line. If you need objective advice about what a contract term means, many lawyers will review a sales contract and explain its terms for a very modest fee.

You should never sign any contract that isn't completely filled out, or which contain terms that are different from what you thought you were agreeing to, since most sales contracts contain a paragraph which invalidates any previous agreement or understanding between you and the seller. If you've been promised something by the salesperson that doesn't appear in the written contract, have that promise added in writing to the agreement.

If you're financing your purchase, be sure the contract spells out the sale amount, your down payment, and the amount you are financing. The contract should also disclose the interest rate and annual percentage rate you'll pay, the number of payments you will make, and the total amount you will have paid when the contract is completed. And you should also have the right to pay off the balance of your purchase at any time without incurring a penalty.

Once you have signed a sales contract, be sure you receive a copy that's signed by the salesperson or other authorized company personnel. Keep the copy of the contract in a safe place, along with warranties and other information about the product or service you've purchased.

If the sale is one that's covered by the FTC Three-Day Rule, the salesperson is legally obligated to inform you of your right to cancel at the time of the sale. In addition, you should be given two copies of a cancellation form. In order to cancel, you simply sign and date the form and mail it to the company before midnight of the third day after the date on your contract. Although it's not required by law, it's a good idea to send the notice by certified mail, return receipt requested, so you will have proof of when you mailed it and when the company actually received it.

After receiving your cancellation notice, the company must cancel and return any contracts you signed within 10 business days. If you gave the seller any goods as a trade-in (such as your old vacuum cleaner), the goods must be returned to you along with any money you paid within this same 10 business day period.

If the seller left the goods you purchased with you, it must pick them up within 20 days of the date you canceled your contract, or make arrangements for you to return them at its expense. If the seller fails to make the pickup or arrangements for return that are agreeable to you, you are legally permitted to dispose of the goods as you wish.

This doesn't mean, however, that you can do anything to make it impossible for the seller to obtain the goods from you. For example, if you agree to be home at a specified time and then don't answer the door when the seller or his representative come to collect the goods, you forfeit your rights under the Three-Day rule, and you can be held to the original terms of your agreement. Similarly, if you accepted merchandise in good condition but return it in damaged condition, you can be held to the terms of your original contract.

TELEMARKETING SALES

The past decade has seen an explosion in the number of products and services being offered for sale by telephone. In their own defense, telemarketers claim that they provide consumers with valuable product information, allow consumers to make informed buying decisions, and are less intrusive than an in-person sales presentation.

Telemarketing's detractors point to calls that come at every hour of the day and night, rude and/or uninformed telephone solicitors, and the use of computerized telemarketing messages that cannot be disconnected by hanging up the phone. And while they acknowledge that recently enacted state and federal laws designed to clamp down on telemarketing abuse and fraud are a step in the right direction, they rightly note that tracking down a crooked telemarketer is still a difficult task for law enforcement officials.

While there are some less than honest businesses using telemarketing to sell their products and services, the fact remains that many reputable companies also use telemarketing to sell their products. If you receive a telemarketing call, how can you minimize the risks involved in making a purchase over the phone?

First, don't hesitate to ask the telemarketer questions about the product or service being offered. If the salesperson can't or won't answer your questions to your satisfaction (and many of them won't be able to, since they work from scripts and have little knowledge about the products they sell), ask for written information to be mailed to you. If the telemarketer refuses to provide this information, hang up the phone. A legitimate company that's concerned about satisfying its customers wants you to be well informed about what you're buying before you buy it.

Be especially cautious when dealing with telephone callers who claim to be conducting a "survey" that suddenly turns into a sales pitch for magazine subscriptions. In many cases, these subscriptions turn out to be more expensive than the price you'd pay on the newsstand, and you find yourself with a three to five year subscription to publications you have little or no interest in receiving.

Never give your credit card number to a telephone salesperson or anyone you're unfamiliar with. Many unwary shoppers have found big charges rung up on their accounts as a result of giving this information to an unscrupulous telephone caller. And never give your checking account number to a telephone solicitor. A dishonest solicitor can use that information to create what's known as a demand draft, allowing him to withdraw money from your account. While you will eventually get your money back from the bank if a fraudulent draft is used to withdraw funds from your account, you can be faced with the embarrassment and hassle of bounced checks and the time you will have to take to get the matter straightened out.

Avoid purchasing investments of any kind from an unsolicited telephone caller, especially those that promise extravagant returns. Dozens of fraudulent "boiler room" operations are being conducted at any given time, offering unwary consumers the chance to "invest" in gold, or platinum, or oil wells, or whatever else the boiler room operator thinks will be most tempting to consumers looking for a quick killing and a big return on their dollars. The boiler room salesperson is an expert at describing the big payoff awaiting you "if you send your money in today." And he's also an expert at refusing to take no for an answer. Some boiler room salespeople will call a potential victim repeatedly over a period of several days, claiming that the potential investment has already gone up in price, and giving the "investor" one more chance to get in on the boom before it's too late.

While it may seem like a cliche, offers that seem too good to be true usually are, and thousands of consumers all across the country have seen their life savings dwindle or even disappear in bogus investments sold by telephone.In fact, some consumers have even gone into debt, borrowing money to invest in these fraudulent schemes.

A reputable investment firm will be happy to provide written material about its programs, fees and sales commissions, and give you ample time to consult with independent advisors to help you reach a decision before making an investment.

You should also be wary of telephone solicitations made on behalf of charitable organizations, since some con artists masquerade as charities in order to separate you from your money. A telephone solicitor who contacts you on behalf of a charity should be willing to answer the following questions:

- *What is the exact name of your charity and where is your office located?* A local office of a nationally recognized charity is preferable, but listen carefully to the charity's name, since some con artists use names similar to those of authentic organizations.

- *Are you a volunteer or a paid solicitor?* Charities that use paid solicitors often receive less than ten cents on the dollar after expenses and salaries are paid, so your next question to a paid solicitor should be —

- *How much of my donation will actually go to the charity, and how much will go to pay expenses?*

- *Will you send me written information about your organization, including a budget and financial statement?* A reputable charity will have no problem honoring this request.

Be wary of solicitors that offer to send someone to your home to pick up your contribution, since con artists are interested in getting your money in their pockets as soon as possible, before you have the time to check out their stories. A legitimate charity will have no quarrel with sending you a pledge card and allowing you to make your contribution by mail.

Although the federal government and many states prosecute telephone swindlers, their task is greatly complicated by the anonymity of the telephone salesperson and solicitor, the reluctance of embarrassed consumers to admit to being swindled, and the mobility of crooked telephone sales operations, which may set up shop in one state this week and move to another state the next.

If you think you've been the victim of a telephone sales scam, or if you have concerns about any solicitation's legitimacy, contact your local police or the district attorney's office. And remember that if you're concerned about doing business with anyone who's made an unsolicited telemarketing call to your home or business, your best defense is to hang up the phone.

BUYING BY MAIL

Mail order is big business in America, and with good reason. It's convenient, private, offers consumers access to products that may not be available locally, and in many (but not all) cases can cost less than shopping at a retail store.

Unfortunately, as in any field, there are some mail order merchants more interested in taking your money for nothing than in providing quality goods at a fair price. If you're thinking of making a mail order purchase, here are some steps you can take to protect yourself and your hard earned money.

First, try to do business with reputable and established mail order merchants. While a new company can be every bit as honest and reliable as an older one, many new businesses fail in the first few years of their existence. If a company's been around for awhile, it may be a somewhat better risk than one that's brand new. References from friends who have been satisfied with a company's products and service can be very helpful. You can also check with the Better Business Bureau in your area to see if there are any records of complaints about the company.

Once you're satisfied that you want to do business with a particular company, be sure to keep copies of orders you place and any other correspondence you send. If you're enclosing payment with your order, use a check, money order, or a credit card, but never send cash through the mail. If you use a credit card and the item is not as it was represented, or if it never arrives at all, you may be able to have your credit card issuer erase the charge from your account. You'll find more information on these "chargebacks" in Chapter 8, "Your Credit."

When you place your order by mail, federal law requires that the company must fill it within 30 days, or notify you in writing about when delivery will be made, unless it already stated a different time period for delivery in the advertisement to which you responded. If delivery can't be made within 30 days or as otherwise promised, you have the right to cancel the transaction and have your payment refunded.

If you buy through the mail from one company, chances are you'll soon be receiving lots of advertisements from other mail order merchants. That's because many mail order companies augment their income by selling their customers' names to other companies. To get your name removed from these lists, you can contact the company directly, or write to:

The Direct Marketing Association
Mail Preference Service
6 East 43rd Street
New York, NY 10017

and ask for a removal form. When you complete and return this form to the Direct Marketing Association (DMA), your name will be removed from the mailing lists of companies who are members of the association. Although this will result in a greatly reduced number of sales pieces in your mailbox, not all mail order companies are members of the DMA, however, so you can still expect to continue to receive some mail order solicitations.

If you are concerned about receiving mail order sales materials for adult oriented or sexually explicit products, there's another step you can take. Contact your local post office and ask to have your name placed on the list of those who do not want to receive sexually oriented ads. Fill out and return the form provided to you by the post office, and be sure to include the names of everyone in your household who does not wish to receive these advertisements. Any company that mails sexually oriented ads to you after your name is added to the post office's list is in violation of federal law.

Under federal law, if a company mails you goods which you didn't order, you are allowed to keep those goods without paying for them. If you receive unordered merchandise, you may consider such items to be a gift from the sender. In some cases, however, con artists may try to convince you to pay for unordered merchandise, and may even threaten to turn your account over to a collection agency, or file a lawsuit against you.

If you are sure that you did not order the merchandise, report such tactics to your local postmaster, who will forward your complaint to the Postal Inspection Service for investigation. Companies that use such tactics are subject to serious penalties.

DOOR-TO-DOOR SALES

For a variety of reasons, the door-to-door salesperson isn't encountered as often today as in the past. Telemarketing and mail order catalogues, along with the more recent cable television shopping channels, have all helped to reduce the ranks of door-to-door salespeople. Justified concerns about opening our doors to strangers have also cut the door-to-door salespersons' numbers. And in many communities, local ordinances restrict or even prohibit door-to-door salespeople from plying their trade.

Some companies, however, still rely heavily on door-to-door consumer sales as their chief source of income. In the event that a salesperson shows up at your door with an enticing offer of a product you actually want, here are some precautions you should take.

First, be cautious about dealing with anyone who won't tell you his or her name, or the name of the company they represent. If you've never heard of the company, or if for any reason you feel uncomfortable about letting the salesperson into your home or continuing your conversation, politely, but firmly, close and lock your door. Door-to-door salespeople are used to rejection, and you need not be concerned about hurting their feelings with a polite "no, thank you."

If you have an interest in the salesperson's product but don't want to let him or her into your home, see if you can make an appointment to meet the salesperson at the company's office, or try to arrange for the salesperson to return when you can have someone you trust in the house with you. In the meantime, you may want to call the salesperson's company to confirm his or her identity. You may also want to check with the Better Business Bureau and your state's office of consumer protection for any complaints they may have on record about the company or its sales practices.

While we're on the subject of unannounced visitors at your door, you should exercise the same precautions about allowing anyone who claims to be a city inspector, utility company worker or government employee into your home. Any legitimate employee of one of these organizations will be happy to provide you with identification, and will wait while you verify his identity with his employer. In some communities around the country, older persons and women home alone with their children have been victimized by bogus government inspectors. If you have any doubt whatsoever about the identity of someone who comes to your home and asks for entry, close and lock the door and call the police.

DEFECTIVE PRODUCTS

While there is no law which requires a company to provide a written warranty on its goods, federal and state laws extend special protection to consumers who purchase goods which prove to be defective. All goods sold to consumers carry what is known as an implied warranty of merchantability. In plain English, this means that if you buy a product for a particular purpose, it must be able to do what it was intended to do. For example, if you buy a coffee maker, the product should be able to make coffee. If it won't, you are entitled to return it to the merchant who sold it to you and exchange it for one that works as promised.

And while no law requires a manufacturer to provide a written warranty, most manufacturers do, chiefly as a way to build consumer confidence in the quality of the goods that they sell.

Under the federal Magnuson-Moss Warranty Act, all written warranties of limited duration for products valued at $15 or more and sold to consumers must contain certain information, and that information must be expressed in clear, concise and everyday language. The precise nature and duration of the warranty must be stated at the top of the warranty document. For example, a warranty that promises to replace or repair any defect for a year after purchase at no expense to the consumer must be titled "Full One-Year Warranty," while one that pays for parts but not for labor required to make the repairs must be headed "Limited One-Year Warranty."

The Magnuson-Moss Warranty Act includes a number of other specific requirements that must be met by a company providing a written warranty. Among these requirements:

- If the product costs more than $15, a copy of the warranty must be included with the product, and a copy must also be available at the retail store for you to read before you make your purchase.
- If the warranty is a full warranty, it must be transferable during its duration, unless the warranty clearly states otherwise. For example, a full warranty "for as long as you own your refrigerator" is not transferable; but a "full five-year warranty" must be transferred along with the product it covers if the original purchaser sells or gives the item to someone else. Magnuson-Moss doesn't require that a limited warranty be transferable, but if it isn't, the manufacturer must clearly state that it isn't in the warranty papers.
- The warranty must provide instructions on how and where to obtain repairs or service. If the warranty is a full warranty, shipping or mailing costs for repairs must be covered by the manufacturer. If the warranty is a limited warranty, however, the consumer may legally be required to bear these costs.
- If you make a claim under your warranty while it is in force and that complaint is not satisfied by the time the warranty expires, your rights under the warranty in regard to the unsatisfied complaint remain in effect.

In addition to protecting consumers, Magnuson-Moss also gives manufacturers some specific legal rights in regard to the warranties they offer. For example, a company need not honor its warranty if the product has clearly been misused by the consumer. And the manufacturer can require you to use authorized repair facilities; a do-it-yourself repair or one made by an unauthorized service center can invalidate your warranty.

Many retailers have established policies of accepting returns of defective merchandise with no questions asked. If the merchandise was purchased by mail or phone, however, or if the retailer requires you to return the item to the manufacturer, then you'll need to write a letter to accompany your return.

When writing, be as specific as you can be about the nature of the product defect. It's not enough to say "this product doesn't work." Include enough information so that the product can be readily identified by the seller or manufacturer, such as its color, model number and serial number. If the product came with a warranty, you may want to include a photocopy, so the seller will know that you know what you're entitled to receive under its terms.

Always tell the seller what action you expect it to take in regard to your complaint, such as replacement, repair, or a refund of your money. But keep in mind that under the terms of your warranty, the seller may only be required to replace or repair the defective product. You will almost never get a refund unless you ask for it, however, so if a refund is what you want, don't hesitate to say so.

If you believe that a product's defect poses a potential safety hazard, you should contact the Consumer Product Safety Commission with information about the problem you encountered. This federal agency maintains offices in major cities around the United States. You can find the address and phone number in your telephone directory, or by calling the Federal Information Center number in your area. The Consumer Product Safety Commission investigates complaints about unsafe household products and recreational merchandise, and can order the recall of defective merchandise that poses a danger of injury to the public.

HOW TO MAKE AN EFFECTIVE CONSUMER COMPLAINT

Whenever you have a consumer complaint of any kind, it's important to bring it to the attention of the right people. Merchants are unable to correct problems with their products or service if they remain unaware of them, and most good merchants are happy to listen and respond to legitimate complaints. So whether it's a defective product, an inconsiderate or inattentive salesperson, or a product or service that simply doesn't live up to its advertisements, you'll be doing the seller a favor by letting it know about your problem.

In some cases, a telephone call may be all that's needed. Many companies now offer toll-free customer service telephone numbers, and the best of these companies give their customer service representatives the authority to make credits and refunds, provide replacement merchandise and take other actions to remedy your complaint without having to wait for a supervisor's approval.

If you make your complaint by telephone, be sure to record the day and time of your call, the name of the person to whom you speak, and the promised response from the company. If the telephone representative can't solve your problem right then, ask for a time frame in which you can expect action. If the response isn't delivered as promised, however, you'll need to follow up with a letter to the company.

When you write a letter of complaint, be as specific as possible about the problem you encountered and the response you expect. It's a good idea to enclose copies of sales agreements, warranties, and other relevant documents with your letter, but be sure to keep the originals of these documents along with a copy of your letter in a safe place, such as a fireproof box in your home.

You may want to direct your complaint to the President or Chief Executive Officer of the company, since doing so makes it likely that it will be answered more promptly and increases the chances that you'll be satisfied with the response you receive. You can get the name of the President or CEO by simply calling and asking the switchboard operator for that information. By sending your letter certified mail, return receipt requested, you will have proof that the letter was delivered in the event the company later claims it wasn't aware of your problem.

If your complaint is still ignored, or if you aren't satisfied with the response you receive, there are several other avenues you may want to explore in pursuing your complaint further. Every state has a Consumer Protection Office, usually administered by the office of the state Attorney General. You may want to contact this office with an account of your problem and the lack of response from the company. You'll find a list with the name and address of the attorney general's office in each state at the end of this chapter.

You should also file a complaint with the local office of the Better Business Bureau. In many communities, the Bureau will contact the company on your behalf in an effort to resolve the dispute. It will also keep a record of the complaint you've registered and the company's response for reference by other consumers.

If your complaint involves services rendered by a person licensed by a state agency, such as a lawyer, doctor, real estate agent, plumber, or contractor, you should contact the appropriate agency as well. Serious complaints can lead to the suspension or revocation of a state issued license.

One very good way to get your complaint dealt with by a company that has previously failed to do so is to take your story to the media. In most major cities, at least one television or radio station will have a reporter who investigates and reports on consumer problems. Many newspapers also have reporters who do the same kind of stories. Since most companies would prefer to avoid bad publicity, you may be able to get your problem resolved by a consumer reporter when other tactics have failed. And even if you don't, the company's lack of good customer service may be exposed to the public and serve as a warning to other consumers before they make the same mistake you did in dealing with the uncooperative company.

A number of federal agencies also record and investigate consumer complaints. The Federal Trade Commission investigates claims of false or deceptive advertising, as well as credit and lending practices. The Food and Drug Administration hears complaints about marketing of food products, drugs, vitamin supplements and medical devices. The Postal Inspector investigates claims of mail fraud, and the Consumer Product Safety Commission investigates claims of defective and unsafe household goods. You can obtain the address and telephone number of any of these agencies from your local telephone directory, or by calling the Federal Information Center number found in the U.S. government listings of your phone book.

In most cases, however, these government agencies do not intercede on behalf of individual consumers. If you can't obtain satisfaction through negotiations with a merchant or professional who you paid for a defective item or inadequate service, you will probably have to file a lawsuit. You can find out more about the steps in filing a civil suit in Chapter 16, "Your Day in Court."

CONSUMER SCAMS AND RIP-OFFS

While most merchants are honest people trying to earn an honest living, there are plenty of con artists and swindlers in the world masquerading as legitimate business people. Unfortunately, it's not always easy to tell which is which.

Trying to describe all the different swindles consumers are subjected to is a monumental task that's far beyond the scope of this book. Many of these con games have been run for years, although they may undergo subtle variations from time to time as con artists keep them modern. And new scams seem to spring up every day, as fast-buck artists and fly-by-night operators exercise their creativity in devising ways to separate you from your money.

To help yourself avoid being fleeced by a consumer scam, you may want to ask yourself the following questions before you invest any money in a product, service, or investment.

- *Is it reasonable for a company to sell the product I'm being promised at the advertised price?* Not too many years ago, thousands of consumers mailed away $5 for "precious emeralds" advertised as being worth much more in dozens of newspapers and magazines across the country. What they received was a poor quality emerald chip worth far less than the money they paid. Similar scams have been run for cookware sets that melted when used and electric trains that turned out to be tiny plastic battery operated models quite unlike what the advertisement led purchasers to believe they would receive. And the thousands of consumers who mailed in their checks for the "universal coathanger" received nothing more than a nail to hammer into the wall.

- *What do I know about the person or company making this offer?* Many con artists cook up elaborate backgrounds for themselves, and they may even use names that sound similar to those of legitimate companies. Some swindlers have been known to join churches and make a great show of their religious devotion in order to ingratiate themselves with other members of the congregation, then use the trust they've built to con them out of thousands of dollars through phony investment schemes. While the fellow offering to make you a millionaire may be making a legitimate offer, he could also be setting you up for a big financial loss. While doing a little investigating, such as by checking alleged college degrees, professional memberships and employment credentials, and even contacting your local police department may seem overly suspicious to you, there are hundreds, even thousands of consumers kicking themselves today for not doing exactly that.

•*If this deal is so terrific, why is it being offered to me?* Even though it may be hard on the ego, this is an especially good question to ask yourself when you are being offered the chance to make an overnight fortune in some mysterious investment. Unless you are already a megabucks investor, the really big money deals are made among those with far more capital to spare than most of us have. By the time they filter down to the general public, the fast money has already been made.

Oil and gas deals, commodities options, precious metals investments and collectible coins, stamps and antiques are some of the areas where many phony investment offers are made. By playing on your ego and making you believe you'll be investing in an area usually dominated by the rich and famous, and by trading on the reluctance many people have about admitting that they don't understand a complicated investment offer, thousands of boiler room con men have made themselves rich at the expense of consumers. Simply put, if the deal is so great, why is someone trying to sell it to you, a stranger, instead of keeping it to himself or sharing it with his friends?

For a thorough look at the way con artists take advantage of consumers, you may want to read *How Con Games Work*, written by M. Allen Henderson and published by Citadel Press. Your local bookstore or public library can help you find a copy.

In addition, the U.S. Government's Consumer Information Center publishes a variety of brochures and booklets on consumer topics, including information about how to recognize various swindles and scams. Many of these publications are free, and others are available for a very small charge. You can obtain a free catalog of publications that are currently available from the Consumer Information Center by writing to:

CATALOG
Consumer Information Center
Pueblo, Colorado 81009

Finally, remember that scam operators rely on their victims' gullibility and their later embarrassment at being fleeced to protect them from the law. If you've been victimized by a con artist, you'll do yourself and your neighbors a favor by reporting the problem to the police or other law enforcement authorities.

STATE ATTORNEY GENERAL OFFICES

Your state attorney general's office is a valuable resource when you have a complaint about a company's business practices. For information about filing consumer complaints, contact the office for your state.

Alabama
Attorney General
11 South Union Street
Montgomery, AL 36130
(205) 242-7300

Alaska
Law Department
Consumer Protection Division
1031 West 4th Street, Suite 110
Anchorage, AK 99501
(907) 276-3550

Arizona
Attorney General
1275 West Washington Street
Phoenix, AZ 85007
(602) 542-4266

Arkansas
Attorney General
200 Tower Building
4th and Center Street
Little Rock, AR 72201
(501) 682-2007

California
Justice Department
Attorney General
P.O. Box 944255
Sacramento, CA 94244-2550
(916) 324-5437

Colorado
Law Department
(Attorney General)
1525 Sherman Street, 3rd Floor
Denver, CO 80203
(303) 866-5005

Connecticut
Attorney General Office
55 Elm Street
Hartford, CT 06106
(203) 566-2026

Delaware
Justice Department
(Attorney General)
820 North French Street
Wilmington, DE 19801
(302) 571-3838

District of Columbia
Legal Counsel Office
District Building, Room 528
Washington, DC 20004
(202) 727-6952

Florida
Legal Affairs Department
(Attorney General)
The Capitol
Tallahassee, FL 32399-1050
(904) 487-1963

Georgia
Law Department
(Attorney General)
132 State Judicial Bldg.
Atlanta, GA 30334
(404) 656-4585

Hawaii
Attorney General
415 South Beretania Street
Room 405
Honolulu, HI 96813
(808) 548-4740

Idaho
Attorney General
Statehouse, Room 210
Boise, ID 83720
(208) 334-2400

Illinois
Attorney General
500 South Second
Springfield, IL 62706
(217) 782-1090

Indiana
Attorney General
219 State House
Indianapolis, IN 46204
(317) 232-6201

Iowa
Attorney General
Hoover State Office Bldg., 2nd Floor
Des Moines, IA 50319
(515) 281-8373

Kansas
Attorney General
Judicial Center, 2nd Floor
Topeka, KS 66612
(913) 296-2215

Kentucky
Attorney General
116 Capitol Building
Frankfort, KY 40601
(502) 564-7600

Louisiana
Justice Department
(Attorney General)
P.O. Box 94005
Baton Rouge, LA 70804
(504) 342-7013

Maine
Attorney General
State House Station 6
Augusta, ME 04333
(207) 289-3661

Maryland
Attorney General Office
7 North Calvert Street
Baltimore, MD 21202
(301) 576-6300

Massachusetts
Attorney General
1 Ashburton Place, Room 2010
Boston, MA 02108
(617) 727-2200

Michigan
Attorney General
525 West Ottawa Street
Law Building, 7th Floor
Lansing, MI 48913
(517) 373-1110

Minnesota
Attorney General
State Capitol
St. Paul, MN 55155
(612) 297-4272

Mississippi
Attorney General
P.O. Box 220
Jackson, MS 39205
(601) 359-3680

Missouri
Attorney General
P.O. Box 899
Jefferson City, MO 65102
(314) 751-3321

Montana
Justice Department
(Attorney General)
Justice Building
215 North Sanders
Helena, MT 59620
(406) 444-2026

Nebraska
Attorney General
2115 State Capitol Bldg.
Lincoln, NE 68509
(402) 471-2682

Nevada
Attorney General
Heroes Memorial Bldg.
Carson City, NV 89710
(702) 885-4170

New Hampshire
Attorney General
208 State House Annex
Concord, NH 03301-6526
(603) 271-3655

New Jersey
Law and Public Safety Department
(Attorney General)
Justice Complex
CN 080
Trenton, NJ 08625
(609) 292-4925

New Mexico
Attorney General
P.O. Drawer 1508
Santa FE, NM 87504-1508
(505) 827-6000

New York
Law Department
(Attorney General)
State Capitol, Room 221
Albany, NY 12224
(518) 474-7330

North Carolina
Justice Department
(Attorney General)
P.O. Box 629
Raleigh, NC 27602
(919) 733-3377

North Dakota
Attorney General
600 East Boulevard Avenue
Bismarck, ND 58505
(701) 224-2210

Ohio
Attorney General
30 East Broad Street
Columbus, OH 43215
(614) 466-4320

Oklahoma
Attorney General
112 State Capitol Bldg.
Oklahoma City, OK 73105
(405) 521-3921

Oregon
Justice Department
(Attorney General)
100 Justice Building
Salem, OR 97310
(503) 378-6002

Pennsylvania
Attorney General
Strawberry Square, 16th Floor
Harrisburg, PA 17120
(717) 787-3391

Rhode Island
Attorney General Department
72 Pine Street
Providence, RI 02903
(401) 274-4400

South Carolina
Attorney General
P.O. Box 11549
Columbia, SC 29211
(803) 734-3970

South Dakota
Attorney General
500 East Capitol
Pierre, SD 57501-5090
(605) 773-3215

Tennessee
Attorney General
450 James Robertson Parkway
Nashville, TN 37219
(615) 741-6474

Texas
Attorney General
P.O. Box 12548
Austin, TX 78711-2548
(512) 463-2191

Utah
Attorney General
236 State Capitol
Salt Lake City, UT 84114
(801) 538-1015

Vermont
Attorney General
109 State Street
Montpelier, VT 05602
(802) 828-3171

Virginia
Attorney General Office
101 North 8th Street
Richmond, VA 23219
(804) 786-2071

Washington
Attorney General
Highways Licenses Building
7th Floor, MS-PB71
Olympia, WA 98504
(206) 753-2550

West Virginia
Attorney General
State Capitol
26 East
Charleston, WV 25305
(304) 348-2021

Wisconsin
Justice Department
(Attorney General)
P.O. Box 7857
Madison, WI 53707-7857
(608) 266-1221

Wyoming
Attorney General
123 Capitol Building
Cheyenne, WY 82002
(307) 777-7841

CHAPTER EIGHT
YOUR CREDIT

America is a credit-based society. Consumer loans, credit cards, home mortgages, and other kinds of financing arrangements allow us to purchase goods and services which cost more than we have readily available in cash. In this chapter, we will look at the ways in which you can obtain credit, keep your credit record clean, and discuss steps you can take if your debts become a problem.

ESTABLISHING CREDIT

Trying to establish credit can be a real paradox; lenders want to examine your credit references to be sure you are reliable and can be counted on to repay your debts before they'll give you credit, but you can't get a credit record to examine until someone gives you a loan. Still, there are some steps you can take to begin building a credit record.

One often recommended method of obtaining a first-time loan is to establish a savings account with a bank, savings and loan or credit union in your area. You then ask this institution to provide you with a loan, and offer to let it hold the savings account as collateral. Today, many banks offer so-called "secured" MasterCard and Visa accounts which serve much the same purpose, but allow you to use your credit in stores, hotels and restaurants. These cards look exactly like other unsecured cards of the same type, so no one but you and the issuing bank need know that the card is secured by a bank account.

Once your loan or credit card application is approved, you make the regularly scheduled payments, perhaps even paying the loan off several months in advance. Your lender will then report you to the large credit reporting agencies such as TRW, Equifax and TransUnion as a reliable customer, and you will find it much easier to receive approval on future credit applications.

At one time, this was probably the best way for a young person just starting out to obtain credit. Today, however, using a savings account to secure credit is probably better left to those who have had previous credit problems, such as serious delinquencies or bankruptcy. For people without a credit record, getting credit isn't as tough as it used to be. If you are a full-time college student, for example, you can apply for a MasterCard or Visa from Citicorp without having to have a job or any other source of income. And Citicorp will consider giving one of its cards to other persons provided they have an annual income of at least $8,000, or less than $700 per month.

Another way to establish credit is through applying for a gasoline credit card or a card issued by one of the nation's larger department stores. Many of these companies have very lenient credit-granting policies, and you may find it easier to obtain credit from them than from a bank or other lending institution. Again, once you establish a record as someone who pays bills promptly, getting credit from other sources becomes a much easier task. In fact, after a little while you may find yourself receiving letters from credit card issuers telling you that you have been pre-approved to receive their cards.

Of course, not everyone who applies for credit is going to get it. You can be turned down for credit if you have no income, or very little income, if your job history is brief or erratic, or if your current debts (including lines of credit you have on current credit cards) are too large in relation to your income. For example, if you already have a couple of MasterCard and Visa accounts, you could be turned down for additional credit, even if you keep your current balance on each of the accounts low.

SELECTING A CREDIT CARD

Bank credit cards such as MasterCard or Visa provide consumers with what is known as a form of revolving credit. These credit cards allow consumers to borrow against a pre-established maximum credit line. As payments are made and the account balance reduced, the amount of principal repaid is automatically added back into the credit line.

Although bank credit cards may all look the same, they can vary widely in terms of interest rates and annual fees. If you decide to apply for a bank credit card, you should carefully read the Truth in Lending disclosures on the application in regard to the costs associated with a particular credit card.

While some bank credit card issuers still provide cards with no annual fee, other banks may charge as much as $75.00 annually to a credit card member. And interest rates may vary widely, from as little as 9.9 percent to 20 percent or more. Because personal credit card interest charges are no longer deductible on your federal income tax return, you should carefully consider applying for a card with a lower rate rather than holding and using a card which charges a higher rate of interest. Of course, the better your credit record, the easier it becomes to get a low interest card, since these cards are usually issued only to consumers with outstanding credit.

You should also compare the grace period provided by the various card issuers you are considering. Some card issuers offer a 25-day grace period, during which it charges no interest on your account. Others begin to charge interest from the day a purchase you make with your credit card is "posted" or received by the card issuer. With modern electronic communications, that's often the same day you use the card. Obviously, the longer the grace period, the better.

If you plan to use your card to obtain cash advances at a bank or through automatic teller machines, you need to know what charges you will incur by doing so. For example, some cards charge a minimum fee of 2 percent of the amount of the transaction, or $10, whichever is greater. And interest charges usually begin to accrue immediately, even if you normally have a grace period when you use the card to purchase merchandise or services.

Most credit card issuers now offer some kind of premium card, with higher credit lines, additional services and incentives such as rebates and rental car insurance, discounts on long distance telephone calls, even medical and legal referral services.

None of this is free, however, and these premium cards usually require an additional annual fee and may charge a slightly higher interest rate.

In many areas of the country, there has been a recent proliferation of so-called "shopper's cards," which allow consumers to make purchases from a catalog and finance those purchases on the company's own credit card. You may have received a solicitation in the mail, telling you that you've been pre-approved for one of these cards, which the mailing refers to as a "Gold Card," often with a very high credit limit of $5,000 or even more.

It's only after you agree to take the card, however, that you learn about the restrictions placed on its use. In most cases, you will find that the merchandise contained in the catalogs you are required to make your purchases from is priced much higher than what you would find in many retail or discount stores.

Because most of these shopper's cards require you to pay an initial fee and charge relatively high interest rates, you may end up spending significantly more for your purchases than you would if you had made them elsewhere. And because many of these operations are here today and gone tomorrow, you may end up holding a card which is of no value when the company closes its doors without warning.

While many people feel a sense of superiority when they pay for the items they purchase with cash or a check instead of a credit card, buyers who use a credit card often have more legal protection when they purchase defective or unsatisfactory merchandise than those who pay with cash.

Under federal law, you can withhold payment on a credit card purchase under the following circumstances:

- The amount of the purchase exceeds $50
- You have made a "good faith" attempt to resolve the problem with the merchant
- The transaction took place within your home state or within 100 miles of the state where you live, or you ordered the merchandise or services from a mail solicitation sent by or on behalf of the company that issued the credit card

Once you notify the credit card issuer that you are disputing the charge because of your dissatisfaction with the merchandise or services provided by the merchant, neither the merchant or the card issuer can report you as delinquent to a credit reporting agency until the dispute is settled or a court orders you to make payment.

CREDIT CARD BILLING ERRORS

Your credit card issuer will provide you with a statement for each month in which there is a balance owed on your account. If you believe a statement contains an error, such as a charge for an item you didn't order, the federal Fair Credit Billing Act protects you. Here's how this law works:

First, you must notify the creditor as soon as possible after you discover the suspected error, but no later than 60 days after you receive your statement. You must notify the creditor about the error in writing — a telephone call won't protect your rights.

Once the creditor receives your written notice of the problem, it has 30 days to acknowledge that it has received the billing error notice. Within 90 days of receiving your written notice, the creditor must either correct the billing error, or notify you that it has investigated your problem and either will not correct the alleged error or make only a partial correction, and explain the reasons for its decision. If the creditor exercises this option, you have the right to request any documentation which the creditor used to reach its decision.

While your claim is being investigated, you have the right to withhold payments relating to the disputed amount.If the creditor agrees that a mistake was made, it must credit your account for any amount which you paid due to the improper billing, along with any finance or late charges that were imposed.

If the creditor refuses to acknowledge the error after investigating your claim, it must allow you at least 10 days from the time it notifies you that it has rejected your claim in which to pay the disputed amount. If you still refuse to pay, the creditor can report you to a credit bureau as delinquent. But if you notify him in writing that your refusal to pay is based on your continued belief that the bill is incorrect, any report it makes to a credit bureau has to disclose that your refusal is based on a dispute about the bill's legitimacy.

IF YOUR CREDIT CARD IS LOST OR STOLEN

Federal law provides that you cannot be held liable for any unauthorized use of your credit card once you notify the card issuer that the card was lost or stolen. Even if the card is used before you notify the issuer, the maximum amount for which you can be held liable on any card is $50. And many card issuers don't even try to collect this amount.

Still, it's a good idea to keep a list of your credit card numbers and the telephone numbers of the card issuers in a safe place. If your card is lost or stolen, you should report it as soon as you discover the problem.

If you have a credit card or two, you probably have received a solicitation from a credit card protection service. For an annual fee (usually $24 or so) the service will notify all your credit card issuers on your behalf if your cards are stolen or misplaced. Some of these companies may provide an additional service or two, such as emergency medical referrals or a discount on locksmith services if you lock yourself out of your car. For the most part, you can easily do for yourself the services these companies provide and save the annual fee.

PERSONAL LOANS

Most banks and other financial institutions offer a variety of loans to consumers. Home mortgages and auto loans are probably the most commonly offered loans of this type. However, it's also possible to obtain loans for home improvements, remodeling, medical bills, college and technical school tuition, and other items consumers may need to finance.

As with credit card rates, loans offered by financial institutions can vary greatly in terms of interest rates and payment schedules.It pays to shop around among several institutions when applying for a personal loan. Keep in mind, however, that many financial institutions do charge a loan application fee, so find out first what that fee will be.

In some cases, a lender may require a co-signer (in legal terms, a guarantor), someone who agrees to assume responsibility for repaying the loan if the borrower fails to make the required payments. If you are ever asked to co-sign a loan for a friend or relative, you should carefully consider the responsibilities you will be assuming if you agree to do so. In many states, a lender may seek repayment in full from a co-signer upon a single late payment from the original borrower. You might also want to consider that the lender probably wouldn't require a co-signer if the borrower's credit record was a good one, so you may want to think long and hard before taking on the risk involved in co-signing a loan.

If you still decide to act as a co-signer, FTC regulations and the law in most states require the lender to provide you with a copy of the underlying loan agreement which you are agreeing to guarantee payment of, and a separate document which explains your rights and obligations as the co-signer. A lender who fails to provide you with these documents may be unable to obtain repayment from you if the borrower defaults.

CONSUMER CREDIT PROTECTION

A number of federal laws have been enacted in order to protect the rights of consumers in credit transactions. Probably the most important of these laws is the federal Truth-in-Lending Act. This law requires lenders to carefully state all of the terms of a loan agreement. Terms of the agreement which must be disclosed include the finance charge, the annual percentage rate, penalties for late payment, and other pertinent facts.

If a lender advertises any one of these elements, it must also disclose all of the other elements as well. For example, if the lender advertises a 6.9 percent interest rate for car loans, it must also tell you the length of the loan, the amount of down payment required, and provide information about the monthly payment on a typical loan. This requirement explains the small print you see at the bottom of your television screen when auto dealers or manufacturers advertise a special loan rate. Unfortunately, while the Act requires that the disclosures be made, it doesn't require the lender to make them very clearly.

A lender who fails to make the disclosures required under the Truth in Lending Act can be sued by the borrower.

Your bank, savings and loan, or credit union can provide you with additional information about the Truth in Lending Act.

The federal Equal Credit Opportunity Act (ECOA) prohibits lenders from asking borrowers for information about their race, religion or nationality. This law also requires lenders to consider sources of income such as Social Security, annuities, pension payments, and alimony or maintenance payments made to a divorced spouse. It also prohibits lenders from refusing to grant credit to a woman on the basis of her sex or her marital status. As a result, many women who were previously unable to obtain credit now are eligible to receive loans and credit cards.

The Fair Credit Reporting Act gives consumers the right to review information kept by the various credit reporting agencies. The law requires lenders to tell a rejected credit applicant why he or she was turned down. If the rejection was due to a negative credit bureau report, a consumer has the right to receive a copy of that information free of charge. The Act also gives consumers the right to know the names and addresses of anyone who has requested a credit report in the past six months, as well as the right to challenge information in the credit report that is inaccurate or incomplete.

You should check your credit record from time to time, especially before you decide to apply for a large amount of credit, such as a home mortgage. According to some studies, more than half of all the credit records on file with the largest credit bureaus contain one or more errors. Some of these errors are minor, but others may seriously affect your ability to obtain credit.

In 1992, TRW, one of the nation's largest credit reporting agencies, entered into an agreement with the Federal Trade Commission, under which it promised to provide any consumer who requests it one copy of his or her credit report each year at no charge. For exact information on how to get your free report, call TRW at the number listed under "Credit Reporting Agencies" in your local Yellow Pages.

Violations of the federal Truth in Lending Act and the Fair Credit Reporting Act are investigated by the Federal Trade Commission. You can contact this agency by writing to:

Federal Trade Commission
Bureau of Consumer Protection
Pennsylvania Avenue and Sixth Street NW
Washington, D.C. 20580
(202) 326-2222.

PAYMENT PROBLEMS

Unfortunately, as consumer credit has become easier to obtain, many people have found themselves over-extended and unable to make the payments required by their credit agreement. If you should ever find yourself in this unhappy situation, there are some steps you can take.

Your first step is to get in touch with your creditor as soon as you know you will be unable to make a scheduled payment. In many cases, the lender may be willing to let you make a smaller payment than what you originally agreed to, or re-arrange your payment schedule. This type of arrangement can also help to preserve your good credit record, since your creditor may decide not to report you as delinquent to the credit reporting agencies.

If you have already fallen behind on your scheduled payments, you will probably be contacted by the lender's collection department. At first you'll receive a gentle reminder, but if you still don't make the payments you agreed to, further communications will take on a much less accommodating tone. If you still can't pay, the creditor's next step will be to turn your account over to a collection agency or an attorney who specializes in collections.

DEALING WITH BILL COLLECTORS

Chances are, if you have ever had credit (and there are very few Americans who haven't) you've been late on a bill or two at some time in your life. After the recession of the early 1990s, hundreds of thousands of Americans have fallen behind on their payments for cars, furniture, credit card bills, and other consumer items.

If you're behind on your bills by more than a payment or two, sooner or later you can count on a call from a collection agency, asking you when you are going to pay up. Most of us dread dealing with collection agencies; there's a stigma attached to falling behind on payments. Unfortunately, bill collectors don't really care about the reason you are late with a payment, or that you have other creditors who also need to be paid. Bill collectors get paid a percentage of the amounts they collect. While a collector may make sympathetic noises, the bottom line is that he wants payment, and the sooner the better.

A number of state and federal laws have been enacted to protect consumers from threats and harassment by bill collectors. Unfortunately, most Americans don't know about these protections, a fact that many collectors take advantage of when they call or write. To protect yourself from these sleazy operators, you need to know how the law protects you.

FEDERAL LAWS THAT PROTECT YOU

The most important protection Americans receive from debt collectors is contained in the federal Fair Debt Collection Practices Act, or FDCPA, which was passed by Congress in 1978 and has since been amended several times. Under this law, you have a number of important rights you should know about.

First, the FDCPA applies to collection agencies and attorneys who are engaged in the collection of consumer debts owed to a creditor, but not to the creditor itself. The FDCPA also exempts government employees such as tax collectors from its provisions. What this means is that if you owe money to Jack's Friendly Furniture Mart and Jack or one of his employees calls to collect the debt, or if the state department of revenue calls about your back taxes, the FDCPA doesn't apply. While there's not much you can do about government bill collectors, state laws that regulate debt collection practices usually do prevent a private creditor from using harassing debt collection techniques. You can find out about the specific debt collection laws in your state by contacting your state Attorney General's office or Department of Consumer Protection. A list of these offices can be found at the end of Chapter Seven, "Your Consumer Rights."

The FDCPA sets limits on the tactics a debt collector can use when communicating with you about a debt it claims you owe. Unless you give a debt collector prior authorization to do so, he cannot communicate with you:

• At any unusual time or place, or a time or place which the collector should know is inconvenient for you. Specifically, the FDCPA prohibits debt collectors from contacting you before 8 o'clock in the morning, or after 9 o'clock in the evening.

- At your place of employment, provided that the collector knows or has reason to know that your employer prohibits you from receiving calls or personal visits at work.

- If the collector knows you are represented by an attorney in regard to the debt he's trying to collect, he may only communicate with your attorney, provided he can find out who your attorney is and your attorney responds to his letters or calls, or unless your attorney gives the collector permission to call you directly (and if he does, you need another attorney!).

The FDCPA also prohibits debt collectors from communicating with third parties, such as your spouse, your boss, or your neighbors about your alleged debt, although a collector may make a report to a credit bureau. However, a debt collector can communicate with other people who know you for information about where you can be found, if, for example, your address has changed. But if he does so, such as by calling your former neighbors, he is severely limited in what he can say to them. He cannot tell your neighbors he's trying to collect a debt, nor can he contact them more than once, unless they ask him to, or unless he believes they gave him the wrong information and now have access to the right information.

The FDCPA also limits the ways a collector can communicate with you (or with others) in writing. For example, a collection agency cannot send you a telegram or a letter with anything on the outside of the envelope that indicates the letter is from a collection agency. And the FDCPA prohibits a collection agency from sending you a postcard of any kind about your debt.

Under the FDCPA, a debt collector is prohibited from taking any actions that might be considered harassing, oppressive or abusive. Among other actions that are prohibited, a debt collector cannot:

- Use or threaten to use violence or other criminal means to harm you, your reputation, or your property
- Use obscene or profane language
- Publish lists of consumers who are alleged to refuse to pay

debts (except to credit bureaus and some other authorized
parties)

- Advertise the sale of a debt in order to coerce payment
- Cause a telephone to ring repeatedly, or engage in repeated
telephone conversations with the intention to abuse, an-
noy, or harass anyone at the called number
- Place telephone calls without meaningful disclosure of the
caller's identity. For example, a debt collector can't pretend
to be from a government agency or the police. In some
cases, debt collectors have been known to claim that they
were calling with news of an accident involving a family
member, or even a death in the family, in order to reach the
debtor.

Keep in mind that this is only a partial list of prohibited
activities and that other kinds of common tactics used by debt
collectors are also violations of the FDCPA. In one case, a debt
collector called a young mother about a debt she was alleged to
owe. During the course of the conversation, the collector made
snide references to the woman's jewelry and asked whether she
had a wedding ring, remarked that the woman "shouldn't have
children if she can't afford them," and used a false name to identify himself. All of this was found to be a violation of the FDCPA's
prohibitions against harassment, oppression and abuse.

Other abuses by debt collectors have had even more tragic
consequences. In the January, 1993 issue of the *American Bar
Association Journal,* an article tells of the case of a woman who
attempted suicide after a bill collector called her at her job and
threatened to have her arrested if she didn't make good on a
bounced check in the amount of $212.

One way in which debt collectors try to convince debtors to
make past due payments is by offering to take postdated checks.
A postdated check is one that you write today, but date for some
time in the future. "Of course," the collector tells you, "your
bank can't cash a check until the date on its face." If you are
expecting to receive money in the near future, you may be
tempted to go along with the collector's suggestion.

Don't give in to the temptation. Because checks are pro-
cessed electronically, there is nothing to stop the collector from
taking a postdated check and cashing it immediately. As a

result, you could end up with your checking account overdrawn, and bouncing other checks you've written. Guess what? That means overdraft and bounced check charges and (probably) calls from other collection agencies.

Under the FDCPA, a debt collector can't accept a check that's postdated by more than five days, unless he notifies you in writing than he plans to deposit it between three and ten business days before he does so. To see exactly what this means, suppose you give a bill collector your check on July 1, but dated July 4. The bill collector can deposit that check immediately.

But suppose you postdated the check to August 1. The bill collector is in violation of the FDCPA if he deposits that check without notifying you in writing at least three business days but no more than 10 business days before doing so. If he notifies you more than ten business days before August 1, he's also in violation of the FDCPA. In fact, not only is the bill collector in violation of the FDCPA by depositing a postdated check without giving you proper notice, he's also in violation merely by threatening to do so.

Other actions prohibited by the FDCPA include implying that the collector is vouched for or bonded by the U.S. or state government, or using a badge or uniform or anything that resembles a badge or uniform. A debt collector can't threaten or imply that your failure to pay a debt will result in your arrest or imprisonment, or the seizure, garnishment, attachment or sale of your property or wages unless taking such action is lawful and the debt collector or the creditor actually intends to take such action. Making an empty threat to take any of these actions whether they are legal or not is a violation of the FDCPA.

A DEBT COLLECTOR'S OBLIGATIONS

Not only does the FDCPA set out the kinds of tactics a debt collector is prohibited from using, it also requires him to do certain things in regard to notifying you about the debt you are alleged to owe. Either in its first communication with you, or within five days after first contacting you about a debt, a debt collector must send you a written notice that contains:

- The amount of the debt
- The name of the creditor to whom the debt is owed

- A statement that the debt will be assumed to be valid unless you send a letter disputing its validity in whole or part to the collector within 30 days of the notice
- A statement that if you do dispute the debt in writing within 30 days, the collector will obtain verification of the debt or a copy of any judgment obtained against you and mail the verification or judgment to you
- A statement that the collector will provide you with the name and address of the original creditor if different from the current creditor

If you request verification of the debt or the identity of the creditor during the 30 day period, or dispute the debt during that time, the collector is prohibited from taking any further actions or making any further contact with you to collect the debt. A sample letter from you to the collection agency in which you deny owing the debt would look like this:

June 1, 1994

XYZ Services Company
1313 Mockingbird Lane
Deadbeat, SD 81123

Gentlemen:

I have received your letter of May 27, 1994, indicating that you are collecting a debt on behalf of Applejack Appliances.

I hereby dispute this debt. Thank you for your attention to this matter.

Sincerely,

(Your Signature)

Your Name (Printed)
Your Address
Your City, State and Zip

You should send the letter by certified mail, return receipt requested, so you will have proof that it was mailed within the 30 day period and that it was received by the collection agency.

Proof is important, since the FDCPA lets collectors off the hook if their actions are the result of negligence on their part rather than intentional conduct. By showing that you complied with the terms of the law, you have a better chance of winning a case against a collection agency that violates the FDCPA.

This letter will probably result in the collector sending you verification of the debt it's trying to collect. Then again, it may not. Some debt collectors are perfectly willing to try to collect debts based entirely on the assurances of their clients that you owe money. They count on your fear of having your credit ruined, and hope that you'll be willing to settle for at least some partial payment just so they will go away. If you don't owe the debt, (and for that matter, even if you do owe it) don't let yourself be bullied by a debt collector. The law is on your side.

One very important provision of the FDCPA gives you complete protection from the letters, calls, and visits of debt collectors. Under this provision, a collection agency can't make any further contact with you at all about a debt it claims you owe once you notify it in writing that you want no further communication from it. It doesn't matter if you owe the debt or not. After you notify the debt collector to stop contacting you, it must do so, except to tell you that it's received your notification or that it will take some other specified action (such as filing a lawsuit) against you.

A letter telling a collection agency that you do not wish to be contacted by them would look something like this:

July 1, 1994

XYZ Services Company
1313 Mockingbird Lane
Deadbeat, SD 81123

Gentlemen:

This letter will serve as notice to you that I do not wish to receive any further contact from you or any of your employees in regard to alleged debts I may owe.

Your prompt attention to this matter is expected.

Sincerely,

(Your Signature)

Your Name (Printed)
Your Address
Your City, State and Zip

As with the letter denying that you owe a debt, it's best to mail this letter by certified mail, return receipt requested. If the collection agency fails to honor your request, you will have proof that the letter was received at the agency, and bolster your case that the collector's conduct in contacting you after it had your letter in its possession was an intentional violation of the FDCPA.

PENALTIES FOR VIOLATING THE FDCPA

No law has much effect unless it provides for penalties when violations occur. The FDCPA provides some significant punishment for debt collectors who are found guilty of violating its provisions.

First, a debt collector who violates the FDCPA is liable for any actual damages you suffer as a result of his illegal actions. Actual damages might include loss of income (for example, if your boss fired you because the collector contacted you at work after you told him not to) and other financial loss that you can show was directly caused by the debt collector's actions.

You may also be entitled to other damages, such as punitive damages, up to a maximum amount of $1,000. And a debt collector may be required to pay your court costs and reasonable attorney fees.

That last provision is an important one, since without it, many attorneys would be reluctant to get involved in helping you file suit against a collection agency that violates the FDCPA. What it means is that a lawyer who wins an FDCPA case is entitled to the prevailing hourly rate charged by attorneys in the community multiplied by the number of hours reasonably spent on the case. It doesn't matter if the debt collector was trying to collect $10 or $10,000.

And there's another important penalty in the FDCPA that may attract an attorney's attention and make him willing to help you. Under the FDCPA, it's possible to bring a class action suit against a debt collector who has a habit of using illegal collection practices. In a class action suit, people who are in similar situations are allowed to consolidate their individual rights to file a lawsuit into a single legal action.

Chances are, if a debt collector treats you in a way that violates the FDCPA, you are not alone. A successful class action suit brought under the FDCPA could cost a debt collector 1 percent of its net worth or $500,000, whichever is less, in addition to damages up to the $1,000 permitted in an individual lawsuit. And as in an individual lawsuit, the court may also award reasonable attorney fees, which can mount up quickly in a class action.

Even though the penalties for violating the FDCPA are clear, and even though the rewards for filing a successful suit can be significant, not many lawyers specialize in protecting consumers from the unscrupulous and illegal practices that many debt collectors still engage in. Your best bet is to find a lawyer who has experience in handling consumer protection cases. Letting him or her know that you are familiar with the FDCPA may help persuade him to take your case.

Some experts suggest that you check with a legal aid clinic for help, and that may be a good idea if your income is so low that you can't afford a private attorney. But legal aid offices are often swamped with other kinds of cases that seem (at least to the attorneys who work there) to be more important than yours.

One good source of legal help may be the referral service run by your state or local bar association. You can find the addresses and telephone numbers for these referral services at the end of Chapter 18, "Your Lawyer." In most cases, an initial meeting with a lawyer to discuss your case will be free or at very low cost, usually $25 or so.

You don't have to tolerate the abuse, harassment and offensive tactics used by debt collectors. By knowing your rights, you can fight back. Being in debt is never fun, and being behind on debts can be a real nightmare, even without having to deal with debt collectors. By making it clear you won't stand for abuse, you'll help not only yourself, but others as well.

BANKRUPTCY AND ITS ALTERNATIVES

At one time, filing for bankruptcy carried with it the stigma of failure. Persons who filed for protection through the bankruptcy courts were often characterized as "dead beats" who ran up big bills with no intention of ever repaying them.

In fact, however, most consumers who file for bankruptcy are honest, working people who have encountered a period of financial difficulty, such as large and unexpected medical bills, or a layoff from their job. In 1992, the most recent year for which statistics are available, nearly one million Americans filed for personal bankruptcy.

Before filing for bankruptcy, there are several options which you may want to consider. One alternative is the non-profit Consumer Credit Counseling Service. This organization, which has offices in every state, can often help the over-extended consumer arrange a modified payment plan with creditors. This allows the lender to receive the full amount owed and allows the consumer to preserve his or her credit rating. In addition, some attorneys can act as an intermediary between you and your creditors and arrange to have your payment schedule modified.

Don't fall prey to debt consolidators who offer you loans to pay off your current debts. Without a solid understanding of how to manage your credit, chances are you will simply make things worse by renewed borrowing on accounts you pay off with the debt consolidation loan. And be wary of companies that offer to "fix your credit file" or "approve loans to anyone" in return for an advance fee of several hundred dollars or more. These scams prey on the honest poor who want to avoid ruining their credit at any cost.

In the event that bankruptcy is ultimately the only solution to your financial problems, you will have several options to consider before you file. If you have a regular source of income, you may want to consider filing a Chapter 13 bankruptcy.

In Chapter 13 (also known as a "wage earner's plan"), the bankruptcy court supervises and administers a repayment program which allows you to pay off your debts over an extended period of time, and in some cases by reducing the amount owed to the creditor. In most Chapter 13 plans, your employer will send your paycheck directly to a trustee, who will then make payments to your creditors.

Although this plan is similar to non-bankruptcy arrangements that can be made by credit counselling services and attorneys, it has the added advantage of being binding upon your creditors. Once a Chapter 13 plan is instituted, none of the creditors you list on your bankruptcy petition can take any collection actions against you.

The other form of bankruptcy generally available to individuals is a liquidation or Chapter 7 bankruptcy. In a Chapter 7 proceeding, a court-appointed trustee takes title to all of your "non-exempt property" and sells it. The sale's proceeds are then divided among your creditors according to the priorities listed under federal bankruptcy law. Exempt property is the property you are allowed to keep when you file for bankruptcy, and varies somewhat from state to state.

Generally, exempt property includes your car (up to a certain value), clothing, some household furnishings and appliances, a limited amount of jewelry and personal effects, some of the equity in your home, the tools of your trade or profession (again, up to a specified value), welfare benefits, some of the cash or loan value of a life insurance policy, and pension benefits if earned as a public employee. Everything else is considered non-exempt.

Opinions differ as to whether or not you need the help of an attorney in order to file for bankruptcy. Essentially, filing for bankruptcy under Chapter 7 requires the completion of a series of forms which you can obtain from the clerk of the bankruptcy court. On the forms, you list your debts as well as your exempt and non-exempt property, and any property transactions you were involved in during the previous two years.

Once the forms are completed, you file them with the bankruptcy court. The court appoints a trustee who takes legal control of your non-exempt property and uses it to pay your creditors. There's a creditors' meeting, where the people to whom you owe money can challenge your filing. But if no exceptions to your bankruptcy filing are made (and they rarely are, unless creditors suspect fraud) the trustee sells your property, divides up whatever he can collect for it among the creditors and asks the court to schedule a final discharge hearing. At this hearing, the court discharges the debts listed on your filing, and sends you a notice of discharge. From start to finish, the whole process takes several months.

Keep in mind that not all debts can be discharged through bankruptcy. Debts for back alimony or overdue child support can't be discharged, nor can debts for taxes less than three years past due, or student loans that first became due less than seven years before the filing. Debts you owe as a result of fraud, theft or embezzlement can't be discharged, and neither can court-ordered restitution payments or judgments incurred because of a DUI conviction, or money you owe because of your willful actions that caused injury to another. And debts you incurred just prior to filing for bankruptcy won't be discharged either.

Secured debts, such as your home mortgage or a car loan, can be discharged in bankruptcy, but the lender is allowed to reclaim its collateral, unless you negotiate a new repayment agreement.

Because the procedure for filing a Chapter 7 bankruptcy is relatively straightforward, you can do most of the work yourself, and there are several good books available to help you in the process. One such book is entitled *How to File for Bankruptcy* (Nolo Press) which is available at most bookstores.

Filing a Chapter 13 bankruptcy is somewhat more complicated, since instead of having the court simply discharge your debts you set up a plan to repay your creditors over several years. While it's still possible to handle a Chapter 13 bankruptcy on your own, you might want to meet with a bankruptcy lawyer before doing so, at least to get a more comprehensive look at the process than this book can provide.

A lawyer's advice can also be helpful before you file any bankruptcy, since it may provide you with some other ideas for dealing with your creditors short of a bankruptcy filing, as well as deciding which kind of bankruptcy you should file if bankruptcy is your best option. Many lawyers who handle Chapter 13 bankruptcy proceedings will let you pay your legal fees over the same period of time as the repayment plan set up for your creditors.

CHAPTER NINE
YOUR MONEY AND INVESTMENTS

In this chapter, we will look at how state and federal laws help to protect your hard earned money, whether you deposit that money in a bank, savings and loan, or credit union, or invest it in stocks, bonds, or mutual funds. We'll also discuss the life insurance you need as well as the life insurance coverage you don't need to buy.

Our goal isn't to give you advice about how to invest, since that's way outside the realm of expertise of most attorneys (this one included). But we can show you some steps to take to protect yourself when you choose an investment advisor, and how the law helps you safeguard your money when you entrust it to another. And we can provide some valuable information about what to do when you think you have been treated unfairly by a financial institution or a brokerage firm.

BANKING YOUR MONEY

For most of us, the return we get on our money is important, but not as important as being assured of the return of our money. To help protect customers at financial institutions, the federal government provides insurance protection. If the bank, savings or loan or credit union where you deposit your money is protected by this insurance, you are entitled to receive all of your money back, provided your accounts don't exceed the limits of the insurance. (For convenience sake, we will use the term "bank" to describe any of the above institutions in this chapter, unless the information pertains specifically to a savings and loan or credit union.)

Depositors at banks and savings and loans are insured by the Federal Deposit Insurance Corporation, commonly referred to as the FDIC. Credit union members are insured by the National Credit Union Share Insurance Fund. To obtain federal insurance coverage, financial institutions are expected to meet certain minimum financial requirements and pay a fee for the insurance.

Currently, federal insurance protects depositors up to a maximum of $100,000. Contrary to what some people believe, note that the coverage is for a total of $100,000 per depositor, not $100,000 per account. If, for example, you have $10,000 in a checking account and another $100,000 on deposit in passbook savings and certificates of deposit at the same bank, your total protection is limited to $100,000, which means you may not get the additional $10,000 back if the bank should fail. Even if you opened the accounts at separate branches, it's all considered subject to the $100,000 limitation, since a branch can't fail unless the entire bank goes under.

There are some ways to have more than $100,000 on deposit at a single financial institution and have the entire amount receive complete federal insurance coverage. For example, a married couple could have $100,000 in separate accounts held in each spouse's name and an additional joint account with another $100,000. In this scenario, all $300,000 would be covered by federal deposit insurance. Trust accounts you set up for your spouse, a child or a grandchild are also covered up to $100,000, regardless of the amount you have deposited in other accounts at the same bank. But if you set up a trust for a parent or anyone other than a spouse, child, or grandchild, the trust account's balance is combined with your other accounts when determining FDIC coverage.

Beginning in December of 1993, the rules regarding coverage of IRA and Keogh accounts changed. Before the change, IRAs and Keoghs each were eligible for full coverage of up to $100,000. After the change, these accounts are now lumped together and entitled to a total of $100,000 in coverage. So if you have $80,000 in a Keogh and another $40,000 in an IRA at the same bank, after December of 1993 only $100,000 of the total will be covered by FDIC insurance, leaving you with a potential loss of $20,000 if the bank should fail.

For most people, $100,000 of federal deposit insurance is more than adequate. But if you do have more than $100,000, it's probably best to simply open another account at another federally insured bank in which to deposit the excess.

Unless you are willing to risk losing all your money, stay away from any financial institution that hasn't obtained federal deposit insurance coverage, even if it claims its depositors' funds are privately insured, or insured by a state government fund. One of the great tragedies of the 1980s and early 1990s was the failure of a number of institutions which lacked FDIC coverage. In some cases, depositors at these banks were left waiting for months and even years before receiving only a small amount of the money they had placed on deposit; in other cases, they received nothing at all. Although more and more financial institutions have joined the federal deposit insurance system, there are still some that haven't, usually because they can't qualify for coverage. To attract customers, these institutions usually advertise that they pay a much higher interest rate on accounts than you can get at a federally insured bank. Unless you can get proof that a bank has federal deposit insurance, our advice is to steer clear of it entirely. One final tip: mutual funds which you purchase through your bank are not considered bank accounts for the purpose of receiving FDIC coverage.

In some ways, choosing the institution in which you'll deposit your money depends as much on your personal needs as it does on such considerations as interest rates, fees, and the charges you will be assessed if you bounce a check. For some people, personal service is important; these customers like to know the tellers and managers by name, and they expect bank employees to know their names as well. For other people, all that matters is that deposits get credited on time, and that account statements show up when they are supposed to. These customers may not even use a local bank, but may bank by mail with an out-of-state bank if it pays slightly higher interest rates than local financial institutions.

Obviously, no one likes to be treated rudely, but some banks make a point of treating even long time customers as if they were potential criminals. They demand identification from people who have been coming to the same teller windows for years, respond rudely to inquiries about opening new accounts, and act as if the customer works for them rather than the other way around.

Unfortunately, there isn't much the law can do to prevent rude behavior, but you can do a lot. First, never accept rude or discourteous treatment from a bank employee without asking to speak to the manager. If you can't get the manager to deal with the problem, or if he seems no more courteous than the teller about whom you're complaining, you can make a statement simply by moving your accounts out of the bank and taking your business elsewhere.

You may not be able to do this all at once, especially if you have money in certificates of deposit that will incur a penalty if you cash them before their maturity. But you can refuse to re-new those certificates as they come due, and you can close checking and savings accounts anytime you want without penalty.

When you do change banks because of rude behavior, be sure to write a letter to the bank's president telling him why you're doing so. Be specific about the problems you encountered, including the names of employees who treated you inappropriately.

Too many people, especially older people, have a misguided sense of loyalty when it comes to their banks. But ultimately, banking is nothing more than a business relationship. If you can get an identical or better rate of interest at another bank, and be treated with the courtesy you have the right to expect, there's no good reason to stay with a bank just because you've been a customer there for years.

SAVINGS ACCOUNTS AND CERTIFICATES OF DEPOSIT

Generally, banks offer four different kinds of accounts. Savings accounts allow you to deposit and withdraw money at any time, although you usually can't write checks against the account. One exception to this rule is what's referred to as a money market account, which usually permits you to write a limited number of checks each month.

Most savings accounts pay interest, but not all of them do. For example, a Christmas Club account is a kind of savings account still offered by some banks. With a Christmas Club account, you deposit a fixed amount of money each week so that you will have sufficient funds to do your holiday shopping at the end of the year. While some banks pay interest on Christmas Club accounts, not all of them do, so be sure to check in advance to determine what your bank's policy is on these accounts. You may be better off with a regular passbook savings account.

When savings accounts do pay interest, it's usually at a lower rate than the bank would pay for a Certificate of Deposit, or CD. That's because a regular savings account allows you to withdraw money at any time, while a CD requires you to keep the money on deposit for a specified period of time. The longer the term of the CD, the higher the interest you'll be paid. If you need to take the money out before the CD's term is up, you have to pay a penalty, such as one quarter's interest, and you may be paid interest at the passbook rate on the amount you have left to withdraw after the penalty is subtracted. With most CDs, you can either choose to have the interest you earn added to the certificate, or have it sent to you in the form of a check each month or quarter, or have it transferred into another account, such as checking or savings.

When your CD matures, you can choose to let the CD roll over, in which case the bank reinvests the money in another CD for the same length of time, although usually at a different interest rate, depending on market conditions. Or you can cash it in and get a check, have it deposited in a different kind of account, or buy another CD with a different term.

In most cases, if you don't instruct the bank about what to do, it will simply "roll" the amount into a new CD. If it does, you can't withdraw the money without paying a penalty until the end of the CD's new term. By law, your bank must notify you at least 20 days before your CD expires so that you can tell it which option you prefer. Still, it's important to keep accurate records about when a CD you own is set to expire. That way, you aren't at the mercy of the bank's notification system if you want to get the money out of the CD and into a different investment.

CHECKING ACCOUNTS

Most of us pay our bills by check, and most of us are paid by our employers with a check. In the 1990s, more than $30 trillion each year changes hands in the form of checks. But many consumers take very little time to understand how checking works, or to find the best checking account for their purposes. Here's an overview.

Although there are a number of subtle variations in checking accounts, most of which are designed to entice you into giving your business to the advertising bank or brokerage, essentially there are only five kinds of checking accounts available to consumers. A regular checking account lets you write as many checks as you want provided you have funds in your account to cover them. Typically, a regular checking account pays no interest, and you pay a small charge to the bank for each check you write as well as a monthly service charge. At some banks, if you keep a minimum balance in your regular checking account, monthly fees and transaction charges may be waived.

Interest bearing checking accounts came into fashion in the 1970s and 1980s, when savings and loans were permitted to offer NOW accounts (NOW stands for Negotiable Order of Withdrawal). Today, just about every bank, savings and loan and credit union offers some kind of interest bearing checking account. With one of these accounts, you receive a specified rate of return when your balance meets or exceeds the bank's minimum balance requirements. Usually, this interest rate is a fraction below the rate you'd receive on a passbook savings account at the same institution. Provided you keep a minimum balance on deposit, there's usually no service charge on one of these accounts, although if you fall below the monthly minimum, service charges are often higher than what would be imposed on a regular checking account.

Money market accounts are offered by banks, and earn interest at a rate that changes with market conditions. If interest rates in general go up, so does the interest paid on your money market account. When interest rates go down, as they did during the early 1990s, the rate of return on a money market account drops as well. Generally, the minimum balance requirement for a money market account is higher than for other kinds of checking accounts, and some banks strictly limit the number of deposits you can make and the number of checks you can write each month before it begins to charge transaction fees to your account. As a result, a money market account isn't a very good choice if you plan on writing a lot of relatively small checks to pay your everyday bills.

A kind of checking account that's offered not by banks but by stock brokers and mutual funds is what's known as a money market fund account. Usually these accounts have some significant advantages over the money market accounts offered by banks and savings and loans. The interest rate on a money market fund account is usually a little higher than what a bank will offer, and few brokerages charge fees on these accounts. On the down side, you usually can't write checks for less than a minimum amount, such as $500. And since brokerage firms don't have to credit deposits as quickly as banks do, you may have to wait ten days or more before you can write a check against a recent deposit.

Stock brokerages also offer what are known as asset management accounts. To open one of these accounts, you usually have to deposit anywhere from $1,000 to as much as $25,000, depending on the brokerage. In addition, you'll usually pay an annual fee for the privilege of having one of these accounts, although you can generally write as many checks as you want each month without incurring a service charge.

Asset management accounts are one way to make dividends and interest from your investments easily accessible, since your brokerage can "sweep" them into the account, where they begin to earn interest immediately. If you wait for the brokerage to mail you a check, you can lose at least several days of interest payments; with an asset management account, you begin earning interest as soon as the money is moved from an investment into the account at the brokerage. Accounts at major brokerage firms aren't protected by FDIC coverage. Instead, they are covered by the SIPC. SIPC stands for the Securities Investors Protection Corporation, which protects brokerage accounts up to $500,000, including up to $100,000 in cash. If you are thinking about using a checking account offered by a brokerage firm, be sure that the company has SIPC coverage.

No matter what kind of checking account you open, the process of writing a check is the same. When you write a check in payment for goods or services, the person to whom you write the check usually presents it to his bank for payment. The bank then sends it to your bank, which debits (subtracts) the money from your checking account.

Until 1988, the time that could elapse between when you presented a check for payment and when your account would be credited varied from bank to bank. Since then, regulations established by the Federal Reserve Board have standardized this time period. For example, under Federal Reserve rules, if you deposit a check for $1,000 which you received from a government agency, or which was drawn on the same bank as the one where you are making the deposit, the full amount must be available to you on the next business day. If the check was drawn on an out of town bank, $100 of the total must be made available to you for withdrawal on the next business day; the bank may wait until the fifth business day after the deposit to make the remaining $900 available. Rules for other kinds of checks vary; your bank must tell you how much of the amount of any check you deposit will be available on the next business day, as well as how long you must wait before you have access to any remaining amount.

If you write a check when you don't have enough money to cover it, (what banks call "nonsufficient" or "insufficient" funds) your check can bounce. If it does, your bank can charge you a fee for the trouble it incurs in refusing to honor the check. In addition, the person to whom you wrote the check will probably be charged a fee by his bank, which he's entitled to collect from you.

Bounced checks can end up costing you big money, and if you write more than one your credit rating can be seriously damaged. And if you knew that your account didn't contain enough money to cover a check you wrote, you could be charged with criminal fraud. Depending on the size of the check and the laws in your state, you could end up facing either misdemeanor or felony charges. On top of that, many states allow someone who receives a check that bounces to collect two or even three times the amount of the check as civil damages, along with court costs and attorney fees.

Just about anyone who has ever had a checking account has inadvertently bounced a check from time to time. In order to protect their customers against the hassles associated with a bounced check, many banks now offer what's known as over-draft protection. In essence, overdraft protection is a loan pro-vided by the bank to cover a check written against an account with insufficient funds. Like other loans banks make, you'll be charged interest on the overdraft coverage your bank extends. Unlike some other loans, this protection can be extremely ex-pensive, depending on the overdraft coverage provisions offered by your bank.

For example, suppose you have $80 in your account when you write a check for $85. The bank covers the $5 overdraft by advancing $100 into your account. You then have to repay the full $100, usually at a much higher interest rate than what the bank offers for other kinds of consumer loans. The bank may try to reassure you by only subtracting a low minimum pay-ment from your account each month, but it may ultimately take you as long as several years to repay the loan, and that's provided that you never use the overdraft protection again. Be-fore signing up for overdraft protection, be sure you under-stand the interest rate and how long it will take you to pay off the advance if you make only the minimum payments your bank requires. In some cases, it may actually be cheaper to take a cash advance against your credit card and deposit it into your checking account to cover an insufficient funds check.

SPECIAL CHECKS

In addition to the checks most of us write and receive every day, there are several other kinds of checks that have some ad-ditional guarantees of payment built in.

A certified check is a check drawn on a person's or business' account which the bank guarantees to honor. These checks are often used when large amounts of money are involved, or when the party accepting the check has reason to believe that you might try to stop payment. To obtain a certified check, you must go to your bank. You write a check on your account, and a bank officer stamps the word "certified" across its face. At the same time, the bank freezes an amount in your account that equals the amount of the check. Once the check is delivered to the person named as the payee, you cannot stop payment on it.

A cashier's check offers a guarantee of payment because it's drawn on the bank's own account. To obtain a cashier's check, you give the bank the money to cover the check, or let it withdraw the money from your account. The bank then issues the check made out to the person you designate. Cashier's checks are often used to pay the closing costs associated with buying real estate. Like certified checks, you cannot stop payment on a cashier's check once it is given to the person named as the payee.

Travelers' checks can be useful when you are away from home and you want to purchase goods or services from someone who would be reluctant to take your personal check. Travelers' checks are guaranteed by the bank or company that issues them, and they can be replaced if they are lost or stolen. You may pay a fee to obtain travelers' checks based on the dollar value of the checks you buy, although some banks that sell travelers' checks will waive these fees for customers with relatively large accounts.

Although travelers' checks remain popular, they've become less attractive as more and more consumers switch to using bank credit cards to pay for travel expenses. The advantage of using a credit card becomes even greater when you are travelling overseas, since transactions using a credit card are posted at the most favorable exchange rate which is generally reserved for transactions of $1 million. Travelers' check transactions don't receive this favorable treatment, so using them will usually cost more than using a credit card.

Money orders are the "poor man's checking account," and they can work pretty well if you don't need to use them very often, and the amounts you need them for are relatively small. To obtain a money order, you take cash to a bank, currency exchange or even to the post office. In return for the cash plus an additional fee (generally from 50 cents to a few dollars) the clerk issues you a money order imprinted with the amount to be paid. You fill out the blanks and send it or give it to the person to whom you are making payment. Like certified and cashier's checks, you can't stop payment on a money order once you've delivered it to the person named as the payee. Unlike certified and cashier's checks, the maximum amount of a money order is limited to anywhere from $250 to around $700, depending on where you buy it. So if the bill you want to pay exceeds this amount, you have to buy more than one money order and pay an additional fee for each one.

ELECTRONIC BANKING AND AUTOMATED TELLERS

Since the 1980s, banks have been issuing an increasing number of ATM cards that give you instant access to money in your checking or savings account (ATM stands for Automated Teller Machine). In technical terms, an ATM card is a debit card — when you use it to obtain cash, your bank debits, or withdraws, money from your account. If you use it to make a purchase, the money is withdrawn from your account and electronically credited to the account of the merchant. In most cases, cash withdrawals are limited to a maximum amount that you can withdraw during any one day, typically anywhere from $200 to $500, depending on the terms of your ATM agreement with your bank.

While ATM cards can be convenient, there can be costs attached to using them. First, many banks charge a fee each time you use your ATM card, and in the past few years these fees have increased substantially. Second, you lose the "float" on your money that you get when you pay for something by check. The float is the time between the time you write your check and the time the check is credited to the payee's account.

A special federal law, the Electronic Funds Transfer Act, regulates ATM card use, and provides specific procedures you must follow if your card is lost or stolen, or if you note an error in your bank statement. If you lose your card or if it's stolen, you must report the loss to the bank that issued the card as soon as possible. If you discover an unauthorized withdrawal on your account, your liability is limited to $50 if you report it to the bank within two business days. If you report within three to 60 business days to report the unauthorized withdrawal, your potential liability is limited to $500. But if you wait more than 60 days to report an unauthorized withdrawal, you could lose everything in your account.

Today, most banks that issue ATM cards belong to one or more major networks that give you access to your account from just about anywhere in the world. In the U.S., the two biggest ATM networks are Cirrus and Plus Systems.

To get cash at an ATM, you either insert or swipe your card through a reader that decodes information imprinted on the magnetic strip on the back of your ATM card. The ATM then asks you to enter your PIN, or personal identification number. You enter this number by punching the corresponding buttons on the ATM control panel. If you enter the wrong number, you usually get one more chance to enter it correctly. If you make a mistake the second time around, the ATM will refuse to complete the transaction. And if you've inserted the card into the machine it may refuse to return it, since the assumption is that a person legally entitled to use the card would know the correct PIN.

If you enter the correct PIN, the ATM's video screen will give you a choice of transactions. Some machines only allow you to make withdrawals or check your account balance, but other machines will let you make deposits into your account, transfer money from one account to another, or even pay a credit card bill.

At the conclusion of the transaction, you get your card back and a printed receipt for your transaction. Be sure to keep this slip until you have a chance to check it against your monthly statement. Never leave your receipt at the ATM. According to some bank experts, criminals have been known to use video cameras and binoculars to watch and record customers as they enter their PINs into an ATM machine. They then collect the customers' discarded receipt and use the information it contains along with the PIN to get access to the customers' account.

For the same reason, never write your PIN on your ATM card, since doing so will give a thief instant access to your account. And for your own safety, avoid using ATM machines at secluded locations after dark, since you could fall prey to a robber intent on getting you to withdraw money from your account. If you must use an ATM at night, see if you can find one at an all night grocery or in some other well lighted location where the presence of other people might discourage a robbery attempt.

TRUTH IN SAVINGS

Since June of 1993, the federal Truth in Savings Act has required banks to provide standardized information about their checking and savings accounts. By requiring all banks to use the same terms to describe interest rates and service charges, the government hopes to make it easier for consumers to pick the account that best suits their individual needs.

For example, before the Truth in Savings Act went into effect, many banks advertised "free" checking accounts. But instead of being truly free, many of these accounts were free for only a limited time, or carried minimum balance requirements and charged transaction fees that the consumer often didn't know about until after the account was opened.

Today, if a bank advertises a free account, the account must be exactly that. If the account is free for only a limited time, the bank must tell you exactly what time limit applies. If there are charges for writing a check or using an automated teller machine, they must be disclosed at the time you open the account. However, even on free accounts, banks still may impose charges for bounced checks or stop payment orders, the cost of printing checks, and for services such as cashier's checks which are unrelated to the account, but you must be told what these fees will be when you apply for an account.

Another important part of the Truth in Savings Act is the law's requirement that banks express the interest they pay on an account as its Annual Percentage Yield, or APY. The APY is what you will earn on an account if you allow all the interest earned during a year to remain in the account and continue to compound. For example, if you purchase a one year certificate of deposit for $1,000 with an APY of 4.1 percent and you leave the interest in the account, at the end of the year you'll have $1,041.

One reason that the APY requirement was included in the Truth in Savings Act was to protect consumers from banks that advertised high initial interest rates in order to get deposits, then lowered the rate after a brief period of time. For example, a few years ago some banks offered one year CDs with an initial interest rate of 10 percent for the first thirty days, but then dropped the rate to 2 percent. Before Truth in Savings was enacted, it was often left up to the depositors to figure out what their money would be worth at the end of the year. Under Truth in Savings, banks can still offer a higher initial rate, but they must disclose the APY when both the beginning rate and the lower subsequent rate are combined.

Under the Truth in Savings Act, a consumer who doesn't receive all the information required has one year from the date of the alleged violation of the Act in which to file a lawsuit. Lawsuits can be filed in either state or federal court. If found guilty of violating the Truth in Savings Act, a bank can be held liable for any actual damages the consumer suffers, and an additional penalty of anywhere from $100 to $1,000 per violation. The law also authorizes class action lawsuits by groups of similarly affected consumers. If a class action suit proved successful, the financial institution could face a penalty of not less than $500,000 or 1 percent of its net worth.

FINANCIAL PLANNERS

In the past decade, the number of "financial planners" has skyrocketed. But because there's almost no regulation of the financial planning field, just about anyone can set himself up as a financial planning consultant. In fact, many insurance agents with little training in anything other than convincing you to buy an insurance policy you may or may not need today call themselves financial planners.

These "planners" are salespeople, and like other salespeople they earn their money from the commissions on the products they sell you. For these financial planners, there's a built in conflict of interest. In order to increase their own incomes, they have to sell customers on purchasing investments that pay higher commissions (usually the most risky investments) or they have to convince their customers to invest larger chunks of their money than they may feel comfortable in doing.

Some planners will charge an hourly fee to the customer for setting up a financial plan, but they then deduct any commissions they earn on the products they sell from the fee they charge the customer. This may give their customers the illusion that the planner is working for them; but he isn't. In fact, all he's doing is covering himself against the possibility that you won't accept his recommendations.If you don't, he still bills you for the time he spent in preparing your plan, often at a rate of $75 per hour or more.

If you are going to use a financial planner, the only ones to consider are "fee-only" planners, those who charge a fee for their services but receive no compensation from the companies whose products they recommend. In addition, you should only consider using a planner who has been certified either as a Chartered Financial Consultant (ChFC) or as a Certified Financial Planner (CFP). To obtain either one of these designations, a financial planner must have completed courses in areas such as estate planning, investments, and taxes. However, keep in mind that the organizations that grant these designations have no enforcement powers if the planner fails to perform up to your expectations. And be aware that many commission based financial planners also have these designations after their names.

Some financial planners advertise that they are registered with the federal Securities and Exchange Commission as Registered Investment Advisors, or RIAs. But there aren't any requirements for becoming an RIA other than completing a registration form and sending in the required $150 fee to the SEC. Don't be fooled into thinking that the RIA designation means the financial planner's qualifications are better than someone who hasn't registered with the SEC.

The best way to judge a financial planner is to talk to his previous clients who have finances similar to yours and find out how happy they are with the services he's provided. If you're young, don't rely on the positive reviews given by a couple approaching retirement age, since the advice that would best serve them would probably not work best for you. And don't let a financial planner try to tell you that he can't give you the names of his other clients due to confidentiality requirements. All he has to do is get their permission for you to talk to them. If they've been pleased with his work, they shouldn't be at all reluctant to give him a recommendation.

BROKERS AND BROKERAGE FIRMS

In most cases, if you want to buy stocks, bonds, or other

securities, you'll need a stockbroker to handle the transaction on your behalf. (There are some stocks you can buy without a broker's help, as we'll see later.)

Brokerage firms generally fall into one of two categories. A full-service brokerage sells a full range of financial products, maintains a large research staff to track the stocks that are hot and the ones that are falling in value, and provide advice to investors about where they should invest their money. To pay for all this service, investors pay high commissions on each transaction, and may even be charged a fee if they don't use their accounts to trade securities on a regular basis.

A discount brokerage doesn't provide any advice about how you should invest your money, but merely buys and sells securities according to your instructions. Since the discount brokerage doesn't have to pay the salaries of economists and other research personnel, it charges a substantially lower commission than the full-service brokerage. Depending on which discount brokerage firm you use and the size and type of transaction involved, you can save more than half of what a full-service brokerage would charge.

No matter which kind of brokerage firm you use, make sure that you're the one who does the picking and not the other way around. Some brokers looking for business will "cold call" names they obtain from a mailing list company. If you've ever owned an insurance policy or responded to a sales pitch for an investment letter, chances are you are on one of these lists. You want to select your own broker, and to do so you will need to do some research.

In most cases, experts suggest that you use brokers who work for firms that belong to the New York Stock Exchange. The broker himself should have at least several years of experience, and he should be willing to give you the names of several clients who have been satisfied with his work during that time.

You should also check with your state's office of securities regulation to find out if any of the broker's customers have filed complaints about the way he handled their accounts, as well as how those complaints were resolved. Thanks to an arrangement with the National Association of Securities Dealers, your state's securities regulators can provide you with a ten year history of the broker's employment record, including previous firms for which he worked, and tell you if the broker has ever been charged with fraud, claimed bankruptcy, or had court judgments assessed against him. You don't have to pay anything to take advantage of this service, and it could help you avoid a broker with a checkered past. And you can find out about the history of the brokerage firm for which he works at the same time.

If you decide to use a full-service brokerage, remember that your broker is essentially a salesperson whose livelihood depends on the commissions he generates. To improve his own financial status, he has to convince you to buy securities (on which he will collect a commission) or sell securities (on which he also gets a commission). In some cases, his brokerage firm may give him special incentives, like cars, golf clubs, or even vacation trips in order to convince you to buy certain stocks or other investments that bring additional profits to the brokerage. In fact, some brokerages penalize brokers who don't steer you into certain investments.

For example, suppose you want to buy shares in the LMN mutual fund. Your brokerage administers a similar fund, the NOP fund. If the broker convinces you to buy NOP instead of LMN, he may get a bonus, since the brokerage firm will collect the administrative fees for handling your account. If he can't convince you to buy NOP, he could find himself losing clerical and secretarial support, and a number of such failures could even cost him his job.

Additionally, brokers earn the highest commissions when they sell you high risk investments. If you are a conservative investor interested in preserving your assets, you don't want to put your money into options trading or new mutual funds that have no established history. But those are exactly the kinds of investments that earn brokers the highest commissions.

By law, brokers are supposed to explain the risks involved in making a particular investment, and they are only supposed to recommend investments that meet your own goals for your money. If your broker doesn't provide this information, or makes promises that the investment doesn't deliver on, you may be able to recover some of your losses through arbitration. In order to minimize the number of lawsuits filed against brokers for bad advice, most brokerage agreements now require you to submit any claim you have to arbitration. Depending on your agreement, the arbitration may be conducted by an independent organization such as the American Arbitration Association, or it may be run by the New York or American Stock Exchange, or the National Association of Securities Dealers.

At an arbitration hearing, you can represent yourself. If your case is clearly documented with notes you made during conversations with your broker and any correspondence, sales materials or other documents the broker provided to you, you may not need a lawyer to represent you. In fact, if the amount you're trying to recover is relatively small, you may not be able to find a lawyer to represent you even if you do want one. However, you can probably get at least an initial meeting with a lawyer who will give you some idea of just how strong your case is, and he may be able to provide you with some worthwhile advice about how to present your case in advance of the arbitration hearing.

Although procedures may vary in some small details, arbitration hearings are typically conducted by a panel of three arbitrators that you and the brokerage firm agree on before the hearing. Both sides present whatever evidence they have to support their arguments. In most cases, the full hearing is conducted in one day, but in some cases it may take longer.

After the arbitrators hear the evidence and examine the documentation each side provides, it usually takes from four to six weeks or so before you receive notification of their decision. You generally won't receive any information about how the arbitrators arrived at their decision. In most cases, neither side can appeal an arbitration panel's decision, unless you can show that the arbitrators' failed to follow their own rules in conducting the hearing or examining evidence. But unless your evidence that the arbitrators acted improperly is strong, the cost of filing an appeal will usually make doing so a waste of time.

STOCKS AND BONDS

When you buy stock, you are buying a share of ownership in the corporation that issued it. The corporation issues the stock as a way to help finance its operations. If the company does well, the price of the stock goes up. When the company doesn't do well, the price of the stock goes down.

Shares of stock in most large companies are publicly traded, either on a stock exchange, such as the New York Stock Exchange or the American Stock Exchange, or in what's known as the "over-the-counter" market, where stocks are bought and sold not by making trades on the exchange floor but by telephone calls made from one brokerage to another. Some small companies don't offer their shares for sale to the general public, but raise money by selling shares to the friends and family members of the company's founder. This kind of corporation is known as a closed corporation. One advantage to a closed corporation is that the sale of its stock to friends and family is not as strictly regulated as when shares are offered to the public at large. When a company offers its stock to anyone who wants to buy it, it must comply with a variety of state and federal laws before it can sell a single share. The company must issue a prospectus, listing all of the potential risks involved in its operations as well as its profit potential.

If the shares are to be offered in more than one state, this prospectus must be reviewed by the federal Securities and Exchange Commission, or SEC, which can require the company to provide additional warnings if it feels the prospectus is overly optimistic about the company's chances of success. Even after the prospectus is approved by the SEC, however, that doesn't mean the SEC endorses the stock offering. All it means is that the prospectus has made the disclosures required under federal law. Similar requirements are imposed by state laws when the stock is being offered for sale to the public in only a single state.

Stocks fall into one of two categories. Common stock, is, as its name suggests, the type of stock most commonly issued by a corporation. If the company profits, its management may decide to pay out what's known as a dividend, a share of the profits. Or it may decide not to pay dividends, and instead reinvest the profits in expanding the business. When you own common stock, you have no specific right to receive dividends unless and until the board of directors votes to issue them. And even if you are receiving dividends on shares of common stock, the board can decide to terminate them if it feels the money you are receiving could be put to better use elsewhere.

With preferred stock, you are usually promised a specified dividend which you receive quarterly. On the down side, however, the price of preferred stocks usually doesn't rise as quickly as the price of common stock in the same company. If the company suffers hard times you may find your dividend payment suspended, although you have a "dividend preference" which means you get to catch up on unpaid dividends when (and if) times improve before the company can make dividend payments to the owners of common stock. And most preferred stocks can be "called" by the company, which means they can buy them back from you, or exchange them for shares of common stock if the company feels dividend payments are too high.

Although in most cases you must buy shares of publicly traded stock through a stock brokerage firm, there are some companies that will help you avoid a broker's commission charges on additional purchases of stock. These companies offer what are known as DRIPs, or Dividend Reinvestment Plans. After you make your initial purchase, any dividends you earn on them are automatically reinvested in new shares for your account, purchased at the current market value. Some DRIPs even let you invest cash to buy additional shares. A word of warning about DRIPs — it usually takes much longer to buy or sell stocks through one of these plans than through a broker, so if the timing of your transactions is important, these plans may not be for you. To find out if a company you're interested in has a DRIP, write to it at its corporate offices, directing your inquiry to the Investor Relations Department.

Unlike what happens when you buy a stock, when you buy a bond you don't get any ownership of the company that issued it. Instead, you become one of the company's creditors. In essence, a bond is simply a loan agreement under which the company agrees to pay you a specified rate of interest for a specified period of time until the bond matures. In some cases, bonds, like preferred stocks, may also be called or paid off before they mature. This is most likely to happen when interest rates fall and it's cheaper for the company to pay off old high interest dates by borrowing at a lower rate in the current market.

Corporations aren't the only entities that issue bonds. The federal, state, and local governments also issue bonds as a way to raise money, and some quasi-governmental bodies, like water and sewer districts may also issue them to pay for expansion and improvements in the services they provide. Bonds issued by the federal government are known as treasury bonds; those issued by state and local governments and agencies are known as municipal bonds.

Interest you earn on a treasury bond is taxed by the federal government, but not by state or local governments. Interest you earn on municipal bonds usually isn't taxed by the federal government, or by the state and local tax departments in the states that issue them. Interest on corporate bonds is taxed by everybody.

Although you can buy individual bonds, you may also invest in what's known as a bond mutual fund. These funds diversify your investment by buying the bonds of a variety of bond issuers, which minimizes the risk you face if one or more of them goes broke. Most financial experts suggest that small investors use one of these funds to invest in the corporate or municipal bond market, but they suggest that you invest directly in treasury bonds, since the only way these bonds can fail is if the U.S. government decides to stop paying its bills, a highly unlikely scenario.

Another way that the federal government raises money is through the sale of U.S. Savings bonds. These bonds can be especially attractive to those who want a safe investment at a relatively low cost. You can invest up to $15,000 per year in Series EE savings bonds, and for as little as $25. If you hold the bond for at least five years, you get a guaranteed rate of return which is usually a little higher than what you would get on a CD. (To obtain information about current interest rates, which are adjusted periodically, call 1-800-US-BONDS toll-free.)

You can cash savings bonds after you've held them for six months without incurring any penalty. You don't have to pay a commission to buy a savings bond, there's no state or local income tax imposed on the interest they earn, and federal income taxes are deferred until you redeem the bond (cash it in). And if you use them to finance a child's college education, you may not have to pay any federal income tax at all if your family income falls below a certain level.

LIFE INSURANCE

Life insurance, like other kinds of insurance, is a kind of gambling proposition. You bet that something bad will happen to you, while the insurance company bets that it won't, at least not until it's made enough money to cover its losses if you win your bet. Of course, with life insurance, if you do win, you're not around to collect on your wager. The proceeds of your policy will be given to whomever you name in the policy as your beneficiary.

Life insurance comes in a bewildering array of variations. There's whole life insurance, variable life insurance, and universal life insurance, all of which are collectively known as cash value life insurance policies. With these policies, a portion of the premium you pay goes to purchase insurance coverage, while another portion is used as an investment. Taxes on the investment portion of the policy are generally deferred until you collect the proceeds.

Insurance companies love to sell cash value policies, since the amount they pay you on the investment portion of the policy is always less than what they expect to make on the investment of your money, and their salespeople will almost always try to convince you that a cash value policy is the best way for you to insure your life. But no matter how persuasive they may be in this regard, it's important to remember that insurance salespeople rarely have your best interests as their sole motivating factor. They are paid a commission on the policies they sell, and they receive their highest commissions when they sell you a cash value policy.

To defray the costs of those commissions, the insurer simply builds higher costs into the premium you pay, or credits you with less interest during the early years of the policy. With some whole life policies, for example, you don't get any of the investment portion of the premiums returned if you cancel the policy during the first two or three years of ownership. And even after ten years of paying premiums, the accumulated cash value of your policy will be just about the same as the total of your premium payments.

Of course, you will have had life insurance coverage for the entire period of time. But there's another way to get good life insurance coverage to protect your loved ones at a much lower cost, one that leaves you with plenty of money to invest in higher yielding investments than a cash value policy.

For a premium that's about one-eighth to one-tenth of what you'll pay for a cash value policy, you can purchase what's known as term life insurance. In fact, because the premiums are so low, you can afford a term policy with a much larger death benefit than what a cash value policy offers. Most term insurance premiums rise a bit each year you own your policy, but the increase is usually minimal, and since your income will most likely have risen as well you probably won't even feel the increased premium.

In some cases, you can buy what's known as 5 or 10 year level premium term life. Since the premiums don't rise every year, you pay somewhat more in premiums at the beginning, but you may end up paying less at the end of the term than you would if you had purchased an annual term policy.

Although term life insurance policies are generally a much better buy than cash value policies, there are some kinds of term insurance coverage you should try to avoid. One such policy is mortgage-life insurance. A mortgage-life policy pays off the mortgage on your home. But your beneficiaries may have enough income to meet the mortgage payments and would be better served if they could put the proceeds of the policy to some other use, such as paying for educational or medical expenses, for investments, or merely to help pay everyday living expenses. With a mortgage-life policy, they get no say in how the proceeds are spent.

On top of that, consider the fact that most mortgage-life policies are what's known as "decreasing" term insurance. This means that as the balance you owe on your home decreases, so does the amount of insurance coverage you have. For the same amount of money or less, you could buy a regular term insurance policy and know that if you died while covered the policy would pay a specific amount to your loved ones.

For the same reasons, buying credit-life insurance to pay off a car, a boat, or some other personal debt if you die before you make the last payment is usually a mistake. You can get cheaper insurance coverage elsewhere without limiting how your survivors can spend it.

You should also avoid life insurance policies sold by companies through television advertisements that prey on the elderly by suggesting that they won't be able to afford a decent funeral for themselves or their spouse without some extra coverage. These policies cost much more than policies bought elsewhere, and they pay very limited benefits for the first several years of coverage — usually, all you get is the refund of premiums paid.

There's no hard and fast rule about how much life insurance coverage you need. An adequate policy is one that will allow your surviving spouse and other dependents to keep up the lifestyle they have now. If your spouse works outside the home, you may need to purchase less coverage than if he or she has no independent source of income.

In fact, some people don't need to buy any life insurance at all. If you are young and single with no dependents, there's no need for you to own a life insurance policy. If you're retired, your children are on their own, and your pension, investments and Social Security benefits will adequately provide for your spouse, you probably don't need life insurance either, unless you have so much money that the policy would be used to pay off your estate taxes. And don't forget that your employer may provide group term coverage at no cost to you as an employee benefit. If the amount of this coverage is adequate, there's no need to buy additional life insurance.

If you have life insurance, in most cases you won't be around when it comes time to pay off. However, some insurance companies have begun to offer policies that allow you to collect at least some of the death benefit on the policy before you die, but when you're faced with an expensive terminal illness, such as full-blown AIDS.

Otherwise, it will be up to your beneficiaries to collect the death benefit on your policy. Of course, it will be much harder for them to do so if they don't know where your policy is, so be sure to let your spouse or the person you designate as the executor of your will know where to find it.

To file a claim, the beneficiary will need to notify the insurance company's claims department. The claims department then sends a form for the beneficiary to complete and return to the claims department along with a certified copy of the insured's death certificate and the policy itself. Always remember to keep a copy of the policy, and mail everything to the insurer by certified mail, return receipt requested.

Always be sure to name a beneficiary on your life insurance policies. When you do, the money passes to the beneficiary free of any probate delays or expenses. If you don't name a beneficiary, or if the beneficiary died before you did, the policy's proceeds are considered part of your probate estate, and it could be months before they are distributed. It's another good reason to take a day every year in order to review your affairs and make sure that everything is up to date.

In most cases, your beneficiary will receive a check in the mail for the lump sum amount of the death benefit, unless he's indicated that he wants the money converted into an annuity which pays a specified sum every year. However, some companies make a point of having a company representative deliver the check in person. While insurers claim that this is evidence of how much they care about their customers, in fact it's just one more way for the insurer to try to convince you to buy one of its products.

As the beneficiary of a life insurance policy, you don't have to accept a visit from a salesman in order to get the death benefit paid to you. When the salesman calls to schedule an appointment, thank him politely for his concern and interest and then tell him to mail the check. If you want to buy something from him later, fine, but you shouldn't make any financial decisions while you're under the stress of a recent death, or feeling obligated to the insurance company for its "generosity."

Although most life insurance claims are paid without much fuss on the part of the insurer, there are times when a claim may be delayed or even denied. The most common problem occurs when the insured person dies within what's known as the "contestability period," typically the first two years that the policy is in force. During this period, if the person named in the policy dies, the company has the right to investigate the cause of death to be sure that the person insured didn't misrepresent his health in order to obtain the policy. For example, suppose you died of cancer within eight months of buying your policy. You knew you had the disease at the time you bought the policy, but you lied about your health on the policy application. Your beneficiary wouldn't be able to collect on the policy because of your failure to disclose the disease, which amounted to using fraud to get the coverage.

Unfortunately, some insurance companies use the contestability period to deny payment of death benefits when they have only the slightest evidence (or even no real evidence at all) of a misrepresentation by the insured. They may refuse to pay, hoping that the beneficiary will simply not pursue the claim, or they may agree to settle the claim for a smaller amount by suggesting that a court battle to make them pay the full amount will take years. If the beneficiary needs the money, he may decide to settle and take the smaller amount just to meet mounting expenses.

An insurance company that refuses to pay a legitimate claim is acting in bad faith, and it can be liable not only for paying the benefit but also for punitive damages for its intentional failure to honor its contract. For a more thorough discussion of what constitutes bad faith, you should read the next chapter, where we discuss insurance companies in more detail.

Like other kinds of insurance companies, most life insurance companies are regulated only on the state level. If you have a question or complaint about the tactics used by a life insurance salesman, or if you have a problem with the way a life insurer handles your claim, you should contact your state department of insurance.

You'll find the addresses and telephone numbers of the departments for all fifty states and the District of Columbia at the end of the next chapter. But be aware that many state insurance departments are less than zealous in guarding the rights of consumers. You may have to file a lawsuit to collect on a life insurance claim that was denied for no legitimate reason.

CHAPTER TEN
YOUR INSURANCE

Just about everybody owns at least one insurance policy, and just about everyone who has purchased insurance has some kind of horror story to tell about the upward spiral of insurance premiums, the difficulty in dealing with claims adjusters, and the indifference of insurance agents in helping you design an insurance policy that provides the maximum amount of protection at the lowest possible price.

You can find information about specific kinds of insurance policies in other chapters of this book. For example, homeowner's insurance is discussed in "Your Home," health and disability insurance is discussed in "Your Health," life insurance is discussed in "Your Money and Investments," and automobile insurance is discussed in "Your Car." In this chapter, we will take an overview of the insurance industry in general, look at how insurers are regulated, examine the tactics insurance agents use to sell policies and insurance adjusters use to settle claims, and tell you how to fight back when your insurer raises rates or tries to settle a claim for less than it's worth.

HOW INSURANCE WORKS

Essentially, insurance is a risk spreading arrangement in which a large number of people buy policies by paying a relatively small amount of money into a pool. When one of the losses covered by the policy is experienced by a policy owner, he files a claim with the insurance company, which reimburses him for the loss according to the terms of the policy. The insurance company, the holder of the pooled money of the policy owners, charges an administrative fee and adds on a margin of profit to the premium paid by each policy owner.

Sounds simple, doesn't it? In reality, however, insurance has become a far more complicated matter than it sounds. Today, there are nearly 6,000 companies writing a variety of insurance policies covering everything from life and health to property damage and business coverage. The three largest life insurance companies alone have assets in excess of $200 billion dollars. According to some studies, every man, woman and child in the United States pays more than $1,300 in insurance premiums per year.

Of course, most of that money is returned to policy owners when they file claims on their policies, right? Wrong. According to a recent study reported in *Consumer Reports*, the average American family spent a total of nearly $9,000 just for automobile insurance during the 1980s. But the average family filed only one claim for the same period, which on average totaled $600. So where did all the rest of the money paid in premiums go?

Much of it went to pay insurance company executives and employees their salaries, to pay commissions to insurance company salespeople, to buy giant office buildings and furnish those offices with fine art and expensive furniture. Another big chunk went to lawyers who defended insurance companies from lawsuits filed by their own policy holders after their claims were denied. Some of it was paid as a dividend to the owners of the insurance companies. And some of it went to investments in speculative stocks and junk bonds that fell in value. In fact, of all the money paid in insurance premiums, only about half of it went to pay the claims of insurance company policy holders.

Insurance companies argue that the chief cause of high rates is the increasing number of lawsuits that are filed each year in the United States. What they don't tell you is that many of these suits are filed because some insurance companies do their very best to find a reason not to pay claims, even legitimate ones. In fact, if it wasn't for the explosion in the sale of insurance, especially liability insurance, there might not have been a corresponding explosion in litigation at all.

Think about it for a moment; in the early years of this nation, before there were so many homeowner insurance policies sold, if your neighbor or a relative slipped on the stairs in front of your home, chances are he'd pick himself up, dust himself off, go on with his business and make nothing more of it. But today, the first thing most people think of when they fall on their neighbor's property is making a claim against the homeowner, even when the accident is the result of the person's own negligence. After all, he's insured, isn't he? And since we all know insurance companies have lots of money, what's wrong with getting a share of it by claiming medical expenses, lost wages and damages for pain and suffering?

There are plenty of lawyers who are willing to handle these very speculative cases for a contingency fee, a percentage of any settlement they receive, but who wouldn't go near a personal injury case if there wasn't a big pot of money shimmering in the distance.

A large portion of the responsibility for high insurance rates also lies with individual consumers, who have been indoctrinated to believe that they are entitled to compensation for every injury, no matter how slight. Recently, a business man who lives in New York City slipped and fell on a street in midtown Manhattan. There was no one around him at the time he fell, no cars that he was trying to dodge, and no injury other than a slight tear in the knee of his pants. And yet he felt compelled to call an attorney to find out if there was some way he could sue the city for his injury.

"I figured I should check it out with a lawyer," he said. "Besides, my friends all tell me that since the city has insurance it ought to be liable, and I ought to get something out of this."

Of course, one of the ways consumers are indoctrinated in this belief is through the advertising and sales pitches utilized by insurers and insurance agents and brokers. We are convinced to buy insurance out of fear that someone will file a claim against us that we won't be able to pay out of our own resources. Insurance agents love to tell prospective clients all sorts of horror stories about the multi-million dollar judgments handed out by courts against businesses and individuals who didn't have adequate insurance coverage. In these stories, the injury suffered by the successful claimant hardly seemed significant, but was ultimately ruinous for the unwise, unwary and uninsured plaintiff.

Having said all of this, it's a simple fact of life that in modern day America you really can't afford to be without adequate insurance coverage. But before you buy, there are some important facts you need to know.

HOW INSURANCE COMPANIES ARE REGULATED

For the most part, insurance company regulation is left to the individual states as the result of the federal McCarran-Ferguson Act. The McCarran-Ferguson Act was passed at the urging of insurance companies after the U.S. Supreme Court ruled that insurance companies were subject to federal antitrust and price fixing laws. By passing McCarran-Ferguson, Congress effectively overruled the Supreme Court's decision, and exempted insurance companies from federal regulation.

But while state insurance departments have the responsibility of overseeing insurance companies who sell policies in their state, the way in which these departments meet this responsibility raises questions about just who they are in business to protect — the insurance companies' customers, or the insurers themselves. Suspicions about where the loyalty of the insurance regulators' lies is raised even further when you realize that many state insurance commissioners who manage these insurance departments are themselves former insurance company executives. And in some cases, insurance department regulators who leave government service soon find themselves employed by the very companies they had authority over only weeks or months before.

Under state laws, insurance departments are responsible for setting the licensing requirements for insurance companies, as well as setting standards for insurance brokers and agents. They also have the authority to investigate complaints and impose fines and other punishments, including suspending or revoking authorization to do business in the state, on insurance companies that break the law or fail to abide by department regulations.

State insurance departments vary pretty widely in just how effectively they protect consumers from the abuses practiced by insurers. In some states, such as California and New York, insurance regulators are generally quite diligent about investigating complaints against insurers. Other states do very little. Virtually all state insurance departments are understaffed and overburdened when it comes to dealing with the complaints of insurance companies' policy holders.

Still, if you ever feel that you've been unfairly denied payment of a legitimate claim, or if you believe that an insurance salesman has misrepresented a policy to you, you should file a complaint with the state insurance department. Doing so puts the insurer on notice that you will not stand for being treated unjustly. And in some states, it may even lead to a public inquiry about the insurance company's business practices.

INSURANCE AGENTS AND BROKERS

Insurance agents and brokers both earn their living by selling insurance policies and receiving a commission. Agents work for one company, while brokers may work with a number of companies. In the end, however, their standard of living is based on getting consumers to buy as much insurance as possible, at the highest price possible. The insurance agent who volunteers information about ways to lower insurance premiums is a rare creature indeed.

This is understandable. Insurance agents and brokers aren't recruited by the big insurance companies through appeals based on serving the best interest of consumers. Insurance company recruitment ads appeal to potential salespeople by promising high incomes. And insurance salespeople who don't sell enough insurance or don't sell enough of the right kinds of insurance don't stay employed for long.

There's nothing wrong with making money, of course, and so there's no real objection to be made about insurance salespeople earning large incomes. What is objectionable, however, is the representation made by insurance companies that their salespeople are your pals, and that you can trust them to work for you and sell you the policies that provide the best coverage you need. Always remember that these salespeople work for insurance companies, or for themselves, but they don't work for you.

When you want to buy insurance, the salesperson's warm personality and interest in your golf game or your children's dance recitals may be absolutely genuine, but it has nothing to do with whether or not to buy a policy from him. Your only concern should be getting the best coverage at the lowest possible price. If you've been using an agent whose company now wants more money for coverage that you can obtain elsewhere for less, either give the salesperson an opportunity to get his company to lower your premium or take your business to the new company.

Look at it this way: would your friendly insurance salesperson pay for your losses out of his own pocket if the company he represents refused to pay your claim? Of course not. Neither should you be required to pay more than you need to pay for insurance coverage just because the salesperson has a personality you like. Insurance is a business, but too many people pay too much for coverage because of a misguided sense of loyalty to their insurance agent.

In fact, some insurance agents are less than completely honest about the way they describe their policies. They make statements about how you'll be covered for this problem or that problem, when they may not know exactly what their company's policy will actually cover, or when they know for a fact that the policy won't provide the coverage you need. The most important fact to remember about insurance is that the only coverage you have is what is stated in the policy.

Unfortunately, it's hard to find out exactly what coverage you have until after you purchase your policy. That's because in most cases you won't receive the policy until after you've paid your initial premium, filled out your application, and had it accepted by the insurance company's underwriters (the only people with the authority to bind the insurance company).

It's true that in some cases the salesperson can issue what's known as a binder, which provides you with some immediate coverage, but if the underwriters reject your application you won't receive any permanent coverage. And even with a binder, all you have is the insurer's promise to provide temporary coverage under the terms of a policy you haven't seen.

One important piece of information you must know before you buy a policy is what the policy excludes from coverage. For example, suppose you want to buy an insurance policy from a salesperson to provide liability coverage for your small business. You need to know the exclusions in the policy you are considering before you buy it. While it's true that state laws require insurance companies to give you a brief period in which to review the policy and receive a refund if you decide not to keep it, this may be a case of too little, too late. Experience shows that very few people take advantage of this so-called "free look," most likely due to the fact that getting insurance is a time consuming and essentially unenjoyable task. It's more likely that once you get a policy, you're going to keep it.

You should refuse to do business with any insurance salesperson who suggests that you misrepresent or omit requested information about your health or background on the insurance application. This is what's known in the insurance industry as "clean-sheeting," the practice of leaving out information on your application in order to obtain the policy and allow the salesperson to obtain his commission. If you go along with this request, you can be denied payment of a claim if the insurer discovers your deception. And claiming that you made the statement at the salesperson's urging or direction is a poor defense, since it's going to be your word against his. If you run into a salesperson who suggests this tactic as a way to get better coverage at a lower price, run, don't walk, to the state department of insurance with your complaint.

Finally, take statements that the insurance salesperson "will go to bat for you if you file a claim and have it denied" with a large grain of salt. Claims adjusters generally don't pay any attention to salespeople when they make their decisions about your claim. They only look at what the policy says they have to pay. And insurance salespeople who have high claims to sales ratios may find themselves out of a job, since the insurance companies make their money by insuring people who rarely make claims, not by paying out lots of claims on a regular basis. Ultimately, the terms of the policy and your own persistence are all that you can rely on when it comes to getting your claims paid.

INSURANCE POLICIES TO AVOID

Insurance companies will insure just about anything, provided that they can make money doing so. However, there are some kinds of insurance policies that you should avoid like the plague, either because they pay benefits only under very limited conditions, or because they cost too much in relation to the coverage you get, or both. Never buy any of the following kinds of insurance policies:

- *Credit life insurance policies offered by a bank or other lender.* These policies are what are known as decreasing term life insurance policies. The total amount the policy will pay decreases along with the balance you owe. If you die with only one payment left to make, that's all the policy pays. You can almost always get level term life insurance, which will pay a specified benefit amount if you die, for far less than what a credit life policy costs.

- *Accidental death and dismemberment policies offered by credit card issuers and department stores.* The advertisements for these policies promise to pay big benefits to your loved ones if you die in an accident on a common carrier, such as an airline, bus, or train. But the circumstances under which you can collect are pretty limited (commercial air travel is the safest possible way to get from one place to another) and the cost of the coverage is relatively high, especially when you can obtain coverage at no additional cost by charging your plane, bus or train ticket to some MasterCard and Visa cards. Check your cardholder agreement to see if you have such coverage, or call the customer service number shown on your monthly statement. Similarly, never buy an accidental death policy from one of those machines you see at the airport. It's simply not worth the cost.

- *"Dread disease" policies, which cover you only if you suffer from a specified disease such as cancer, should also be avoided.* Again, the benefits you'll receive are far too little in relationship to the premium you'll be asked to pay. And if you come down with a disease other than the one named in the policy, you won't get any benefits from the policy.

- *Hospital expense policies that pay a specified amount of money when you are hospitalized.* These policies are essentially a very limited form of disability insurance, and cost much more than the coverage is worth when compared to standard health and disability insurance policies.

•*Mail order life insurance policies advertised on television and aimed at the elderly or those who can't obtain coverage elsewhere.* You've seen the commercials — an elderly woman tells her friend about how the cost of her husband's funeral nearly bankrupted her. "If it hadn't been for that insurance policy John bought a few years ago," she says, "I don't know what I would have done." By playing on the fears of the elderly that they'll be driven to the brink of financial ruin by the high cost of burying a spouse, these companies make big profits while providing little coverage. And if you buy one of these policies and die during the first two years you own it, your beneficiary gets "limited benefits," which may amount to little more than the return of the premiums you paid for the coverage.

DEALING WITH CLAIMS ADJUSTERS

No matter how much insurance companies advertise their willingness to pay claims, the fact of the matter is that insurance claims adjusters make a name for themselves in the company not by paying claims, but by denying them, or settling them for less than what the insurer is contractually obligated to pay. In fact, a claims adjuster's career is in jeopardy if he doesn't settle claims for as little as possible.

When you have a claim on any kind of insurance policy, you will have to file a claim form. On this form, you are required to provide the insurance company with information that it will use in order to decide how much to pay on a claim. But that's not all you agree to provide under most insurance policies. For example, here's language from one homeowners insurance policy about the additional requirements you must meet in order to have your claim paid:

"The insured shall give immediate written notice to the company of any loss, protect the property from further damage, forthwith separate the damaged and undamaged personal property, put it in the best possible order, furnish a complete inventory of the destroyed, damaged and undamaged property, showing in detail quantities, cost, actual cash value and amount of loss claimed; and within sixty days after the loss, unless such time is extended in writing by the company, the insured shall render to the company a proof of loss signed and sworn to by the insured stating the knowledge and belief of the insured as to the following:

The time and nature of the loss, the interest of the insured and of all others in the property, the actual cash value of each item thereof and the amount of loss thereto, all encumbrances thereon, all other contracts of insurance, whether valid or not, covering any of said property, any changes in the title, use, occupation, location, possession or exposure of said property since the issuing of this policy, by whom and for what purpose any building herein described and the several parts thereof where occupied at the time of loss and whether or not it then stood on leased ground, and shall furnish a copy of all the descriptions and schedules in all policies and, if required, verified plans and specifications of any buildings, fixtures, or machines destroyed or damaged.

The insured shall, as often as may be reasonably required, exhibit to any person designated by the company, all that remains of any property herein described, and submit to examinations under oath by any person named by the company, and subscribe the same; and, as often as may be reasonably required, shall produce for examination all books of accounts, bills, invoices, and other vouchers, or certified copies thereof if originals be lost at such reasonable time and place as may be designated by this company or its representatives and shall permit extracts and copies thereof to be made."

Needless to say, any company that feels obligated to include this kind of language in an insurance policy is not going to go out of its way to pay you the full value of your claim without a fight.

The best way to minimize hassles when you have an insurance claim is to have as much documentation as possible of the value of the covered items. If you have a homeowner's claim, you should have receipts of all the items for which you are seeking reimbursement, as well as photographs or videotapes of the items which you've insured. If possible, use a camera that places a date on the image; some insurers may claim that the photo is out of date, or represents things you bought after the claimed loss as a method of delaying or denying payment. The more documentation you have of your loss, the less chance the adjuster has of contesting a legitimate claim.

Like it or not, when you have a loss which you believe is covered under the terms of an insurance policy you have purchased, your first step in obtaining reimbursement will be to file a claim with your insurer. Once you do, you will be contacted by the insurance company's claims department.

Your first contact will probably be with a telephone adjuster, especially if the claim you file is relatively small. Telephone adjusters are the low man on the totem pole in the world of claims adjusting. They are usually new to the insurance claims field, and may have only a few weeks of training before they begin to handle claims. In most cases, they are only empowered to conduct an initial investigation, although in some cases they may be authorized by their supervisor to settle small claims up to a specified amount.

Field adjusters (also referred to as outside adjusters) travel to the site of a claim and investigate it on behalf of their employer, the insurance company. Their job is to get you to settle for the smallest amount possible. In order to advance with the company, they must not be seen by their superiors as being too generous with "the company's money."

As with telephone adjusters, outside adjusters are usually empowered to settle a claim only up to a specified amount. If you can prove and they believe that the claim is worth more than what they are authorized to pay, your claim is then referred to a senior adjuster, and if it's beyond the senior adjuster's preauthorized limits, to a regional claims manager. If he can't approve your claim, then the national claims manager is called in to handle the matter. Insurance companies also use independent adjusters, financial consultants and other professionals, all for the purpose of reducing, delaying or denying payment of your claim.

No matter what level of adjuster you are dealing with, no matter how friendly or helpful the adjuster seems to be, remember that the adjuster's role is to delay settling your claim as long as possible, settle your claim for the smallest amount possible, or deny your claim entirely if there's any way to justify doing so.

Whenever you deal with your insurance company's claims department, be sure to get the name and title of anyone you speak to, his direct telephone number or extension, and the name of his immediate supervisor. Keep a log of the dates and times of any conversations you have about your claim; the adjuster is doing the very same thing. In fact, many adjusters will tape record their conversations with you as a way of protecting themselves and the company. If an insurance adjuster asks for your permission to tape your conversation, tell him you want a copy of the tape, or better yet, tape the conversation yourself for your own records.

If a claims adjuster tells you that the company has decided to deny your claim, or offers to pay you less than the amount you believe is fair compensation, ask to speak to the adjuster's supervisor. In some cases, you may get the initial decision overturned or modified in your favor. But if you still aren't satisfied, write to your state insurance department immediately. Outline your problem with the company, enclose a copy (not the original) of your policy, and copies of any correspondence you've exchanged with the company or its representatives. Keep all your originals in a safe place, along with a copy of your letter to the insurance department.

Never deposit or cash a check from an insurance company until you are absolutely sure it is what you expect. If your house is damaged or destroyed, your homeowners' policy will often provide for payment for temporary living expenses. If you get a check for these expenses from an adjuster, make sure that accepting it does not require you to relinquish your rights to other payments you may have coming to you. There should be a notation on the check indicating what is being paid.

Never sign a check which contains a restrictive endorsement, a statement on the back of the check which states that by signing the check you are waiving all other claims that you may have under your policy, unless you are absolutely sure you won't need any more money from your insurer. And never sign a release offered to you by an adjuster until you are absolutely certain you have received everything you are entitled to under the terms of your policy.

Insurance companies have batteries of lawyers at their disposal whose job it is to figure out how to minimize the claims the company pays. In a serious dispute with an insurance company, you probably will need the assistance of a good trial lawyer who is willing to take your case on a contingency fee basis. You'll learn more about how to find a lawyer in Chapter Seventeen, "When You Need A Lawyer."

HOW TO PICK THE RIGHT INSURANCE COMPANY FOR YOU

Insurance companies pay millions of dollars each year to promote themselves on television and radio and in magazines and newspapers. The advertising slogans used by these companies have become a part of the American vocabulary.

"Get Met. It Pays."
"You're In Good Hands With Allstate."
"Like a Good Neighbor, State Farm is There."

The purpose of all this advertising is to convince you that if you buy insurance from them, your life will be better, your worries will be over, and you'll be dealing with folks just like you who only want what's in your best interest.

Don't believe it for a second, and whatever you do, never pick an insurance company solely on the basis of its advertising. There's only one consideration that should guide you in deciding which insurance company to give your business to, and that is whether or not the company pays legitimate claims quickly and fairly.

Obviously, you don't want to rely on the assurances of the salesperson about this most important consideration. No insurance salesperson will ever tell you his company does a lousy job with claims. To learn the truth about a company's reputation when it comes to claims paying, talk to the people to whom it makes those payments. If you're buying an automobile policy, call local repair shops and ask them what they think of the company's claims paying policy. If you're purchasing health insurance, call local hospitals (especially the one where your doctor has admitting privileges) and ask the people in the accounting department what they think about the way the company pays its claims, and ask your doctor's office manager what he or she thinks about the company's claims handling.

Some experts suggest you look at ratings of insurance companies, such as those issued by A.M. Best or Standard and Poor's. These ratings are supposed to tell you about the financial stability of a particular company. It won't hurt to look at these ratings, but don't put too much faith in them. In 1990, Executive Life Insurance of New York and California was given the highest rating possible by both services; in 1991, the company went insolvent, and thousands of policy holders waited and worried for months while regulators tried to figure out how to put together a plan to pay at least some of the promised benefits. Although both Best and Standard and Poor's claim to have tightened their standards since the Executive Life failure, it remains to be seen just how much more effective the new ratings systems are.

WHEN YOUR INSURANCE COMPANY ACTS IN BAD FAITH

In some cases, insurance companies have been known to refuse to pay claims that they knew they were obligated to pay. When an insurance company engages in this kind of behavior, it is said to be acting "in bad faith."

Insurance is a contract between you and the insurer. In return for your premium, the insurer agrees to pay you the benefit it promised when you have a legitimate claim. When it refuses to do so, it violates the assumption implied by the law that people who make contracts will do what they promise.

Some insurance companies have refused to pay legitimate claims, counting on the fact that the consumers whose claims are denied won't have the time or the inclination to fight back. However, in some cases even relatively small claims which were refused have led to lawsuits that ended with the insurance company being held liable for thousands of dollars (and in some cases, millions) in punitive damages, monetary awards designed to punish insurers who refuse to live up to the terms of their own policies.

If you have a legitimate claim and your insurance company refuses to pay it, doing nothing is the worst thing you can do. You need to get in touch with a lawyer who specializes in prosecuting bad faith cases against insurance companies. As with other kinds of trial lawyers, these attorneys take worthwhile cases on a contingency fee basis, which means they are only paid when they collect money for their clients, either as a settlement or as damages awarded in a lawsuit.

You don't have to be threatened, intimidated or bullied by an insurance company that refuses to pay an honest claim. The law is on your side, and the more consumers who raise their objections to insurance companies' unethical claims practices, the sooner everyone will benefit.

STATE INSURANCE DEPARTMENTS

The following list provides you with the addresses and telephone numbers of the state department of insurance for all 50 states and the District of Columbia. Although the list was accurate at the time this book was printed, insurance department offices do occasionally move. If you can't reach the insurance department at the address or phone number provided here, call directory assistance for your state capital.

Alabama
Insurance Department
135 South Union Street
Montgomery, AL 36130
(205) 269-3550

Alaska
Commerce and Economic Development Department
Insurance Division
P.O. Box D
Juneau, AK 99811
(907) 465-2515

Arizona
Insurance Department
3030 North 3rd Street
Suite 1100
Phoenix, AZ 85012
(602) 255-5400

Arkansas
Insurance Department
400 University Tower Building
Little Rock, AR 72204
(501) 686-2900

California
Commissioner of Insurance
770 L Street
Sacramento, CA 95814
(916) 445-5544

Colorado
Regulatory Agencies
Insurance Division
1560 Broadway
Denver, CO 80204
(303) 894-7499

Connecticut
Insurance Department
165 Capitol Avenue
Hartford, CT 06106
(203) 297-3800

Delaware
Insurance Department
841 Silver Lake Boulevard
Dover, DE 19901
(302) 736-4251

District of Columbia
Superintendent of Insurance
613 G Street, N.W.
Washington, DC 20001
(202) 727-7424

Florida
Insurance and Treasurer Department
The Capitol Plaza, Level Eleven
Tallahassee, FL 32399-0300
(904) 488-3440

Georgia
Insurance Department
2 Martin Luther King Jr. Drive
716 West Tower Street
Atlanta, GA 30334
(404) 656-2056

Hawaii
Commerce and Consumer Affairs Department
Insurance Division
1010 Richards Street, Box 3614
Honolulu, HI 96811
(808) 548-6522

Idaho
Insurance Department
500 South 10th Street
Boise, ID 83610
(208) 334-2250

Illinois
Insurance Department
320 West Washington Street, 4th Floor
Springfield, IL 62767
(217) 782-4515

Indiana
Insurance Department
311 West Washington Street, Suite 300
Indianapolis, IN 46204
(317) 232-2385

Iowa
Commerce Department
Insurance Division
Lucas State Office Building
Des Moines, IA 50319
(515) 281-5523

Kansas
Insurance Department
420 S.W. 9th Street
Topeka, KS 66612
(913) 296-7801

Kentucky
Public Protection and Regulation Cabinet
Insurance Department
229 West Maine
Frankfort, KY 40601
(502) 564-3630

Louisiana
Insurance Department
P.O. Box 94214
Baton Rouge, LA 70804-9214
(504) 342-5900

Maine
Superintendent of Insurance
State House Station 148
Augusta, ME 04333
(207) 289-1090

Maryland
Insurance Department
501 Saint Paul Place
Baltimore, MD 21201
(410) 333-2520

Massachusetts
Consumer Affairs and Business Regulation Executive Office
Insurance Division
280 Friend Street
Boston, MA 02114
(617) 727-7189

Michigan
Licensing and Regulations Department
Insurance Bureau
P.O. Box 30220
Lansing, MI 48909
(517) 373-9273

Minnesota
Labor and Industry Department
443 Lafayette Road
St. Paul, MN 55155
(612) 296-2342

Mississippi
Insurance Department
P.O. Box 79
Jackson, MS 39205
(601) 359-3569

Missouri
Economic Development Department
Insurance Division
P.O. Box 690
Jefferson City, MO 65102
(314) 751-2451

Montana
Commissioner of Insurance
126 North Sanders
Helena, MT 59601
(406) 444-2040

Nebraska
Insurance Department
941 O Street, Suite 400
Lincoln, NE 68508
(402) 471-2201

Nevada
Commissioner of Insurance
1665 Hot Springs Road
Carson City, NV 89710
(702) 687-4270

New Hampshire
Insurance Department
169 Manchester Street
Concord, NH 03301
(603) 271-2261

New Jersey
Insurance Department
20 West State Street
Trenton, NJ 08625
(609) 292-5360

New Mexico
Superintendent of Insurance
P.O. Box 1269
Santa Fe, NM 87509-1269
(505) 827-4500

New York
Insurance Department
Agency Building 1
Empire State Plaza
Albany, NY 12257
(518) 474-4550

North Carolina
Insurance Department
Box 26387
Raleigh, NC 27611
(919) 733-7343

North Dakota
Insurance Department
600 East Boulevard Avenue
Bismarck, ND 58505
(701) 224-2440

Ohio
Insurance Department
2100 Stella Court
Columbus, OH 43266-0566
(614) 644-2651

Oklahoma
Insurance Department
P.O. Box 53408
Oklahoma City, OK 73152-3408
(405) 521-2828

Oregon
Insurance and Finance Department
21 Labor and Industries Building
Salem, OR 97310
(503) 378-4100

Pennsylvania
Insurance Department
1326 Strawberry Square
Harrisburg, PA 17120
(717) 787-5173

Rhode Island
Business Regulations Department
233 Richmond Street
Providence, RI 02903
(401) 277-2246

South Carolina
Insurance Department
P.O. Box 100105
Columbia, SC 29202-3105
(803) 737-6117

South Dakota
Department of Insurance
910 East Sioux Avenue
Pierre, SD 57501
(605) 773-3563

Tennessee
Commerce and Insurance Department
500 James Robertson Parkway
Nashville, TN 37243
(615) 741-2241

Texas
Insurance Board
1110 San Jacinto
Austin, TX 78701-1998
(512) 463-9979

Utah
Insurance Department
P.O. Box 45803
Salt Lake City, UT 84145
(801) 538-3800

Vermont
Insurance Department
89 Main Street, 2nd Floor
Montpelier, VT 05602
(802) 828-3301

Virginia
Insurance Commissioner
1220 Bank Street
Richmond, VA 23219
(804) 786-7694

Washington
Insurance Commissioner
Insurance Building
MSAQ-21
Olympia, WA 98504-0321
(206) 753-7301

West Virginia
Insurance Commission
Capitol Complex
Charleston, WV 35305
(304) 348-3394

Wisconsin
Insurance Commission
P.O. Box 7873
Madison, WI 53707-7873
(608) 266-3585

Wyoming
Insurance Department
122 West 25th Street
Cheyenne, WY 82002-0440
(307) 777-7401

CHAPTER ELEVEN
HEALTH CARE AND THE LAW

Medical technology has advanced rapidly in the past several decades, in some cases so rapidly that the law has had to struggle to deal with a multitude of health care issues that didn't exist even thirty years ago. Machines can keep a person's heart beating and lungs taking in air even though the person has no hope of ever recovering to lead a normal productive life. Life spans continue to increase, resulting in a proliferation of nursing homes, retirement centers, and other living arrangements for the elderly. At the same time, those with incurable diseases challenge government attempts to deprive them of the right to end their own lives. Fertility treatments and surrogate parenting make it possible for those who could not have children on their own to now have a biological family. Experimental treatments for cancer and other diseases are available at great expense, but health insurance rarely pays for these treatments. Promising new drugs and treatments are withheld from the public for years while government mandated testing takes place at great expense to the drug manufacturer. Non-traditional therapies such as chiropractic, nutritional therapy and other holistic healing practices are under fire from the medical establishment and the government agencies they dominate. Hospital bills continue to soar, and in many cases contain charges for services that were never even delivered.

In this chapter, we will look at these and other issues surrounding you and your right to receive and reject medical treatment, as well as how the law affects your ability to determine the best course of treatment for your own family. We'll take a look at the government's role in deciding what's best for you, and how you can help keep health care costs down and fight back when faced with unnecessary treatment, excessive charges for medical services and medical malpractice.

YOUR RIGHTS AS A PATIENT

For years, most Americans have held medical professionals in high esteem, treating them with the reverence and awe older cultures reserved for priests and wise men. Medical doctors have done little to discourage this worshipful attitude. They prescribed treatments and performed operations with little concern for obtaining the patient's input beforehand. When they succeeded, the success was all theirs; when they failed, the problem was fate.

Today, the sense that physicians are miracle workers has eroded somewhat, but most of us are still overwhelmed and intimidated by health care and those who provide it. We schedule appointments with doctors who then keep us waiting for hours past the original appointment time. Before we even see the doctor, we fill out reams of forms and answer endless questions from receptionists, medical assistants and office nurses, only to have the doctor finally appear, glance at our chart and ask "So what seems to be the problem?" We submit to tests without any real explanation of what they are intended to reveal, pay big laboratory bills, and in some cases never even learn what, if anything, those tests revealed.

You don't have to take it. As a patient, you have clearly defined legal rights which give you the power to deal with physicians not as a passive supplicant subject to those who provide medical treatment but as an equal partner in managing, maintaining, and improving your health. Let's take a look at those rights and how they help you.

First, you have the right to be fully informed about any medical condition you have and to receive a full and clear explanation of any treatment or surgical procedure your doctor proposes and give your consent before it takes place. This is the legal doctrine known as "informed consent."

Under this doctrine, you must be told what condition you are suffering from, the treatment or procedure that the doctor proposes, the benefits you can reasonably expect if you agree to the treatment, as well as the potential risks involved. You also have the right to know about alternative treatments that may be available, and have an explanation from the doctor as to why he believes that the treatment he recommends is better. Finally, you have the right to know what the probability of success is if you decide to follow the doctor's recommendations.

All of this must be explained to you in as plain a manner as possible, describing all the details of the treatment as specifically as possible, and the doctor must answer any and all questions you have before he obtains your consent. If he fails to do so, he can be charged with battery, or sued for negligence.

Unfortunately, many doctors still resent being questioned by their patient about a proposed course of treatment. They may try to shrug away your concerns about possible complications or your desire for information about alternative forms of treatment. Some doctors even become quite indignant and try to intimidate the patient into "following doctor's orders." Don't let this happen to you. If you don't understand the doctor's diagnosis, ask him to explain it again. If you don't understand why he proposes a particular course of treatment and discourages your consideration of some other procedure, ask him to explain it again. If he tells you that the risks are very small, ask him to be more specific about just how small they are. And don't feel pressured into giving your consent until you've had an opportunity to consider everything you've learned and make a rational decision.

If necessary, take the time to talk with family members, or to get a second opinion. In fact, many health insurers now will pay for a second opinion in order to avoid paying for surgery that the second doctor deems unnecessary. While taking the time to get a second opinion won't be possible in an emergency (for example, your appendix has ruptured and immediate surgery is required), emergencies make up only a small part of the medical treatment most of us receive. Remember, you have the legal right to be fully informed before giving consent to any treatment or procedure your doctor suggests.

Of course, a doctor has the right to refuse to treat a patient (unless he is an emergency room physician), provided that his refusal isn't due to an illegal act of discrimination. If you disagree with your doctor about the manner in which he wants to treat your medical condition, he can legally refuse to provide you with any more services, but only after you have found another doctor, or when enough time has passed in which you could have found one.

In general, anyone over the age of 18 is considered capable of giving consent for his or her own medical treatment, unless mentally incompetent and unable to understand the consequences of giving consent, or when under the influence of drugs or alcohol. For persons under 18, the parent or legal guardian must give consent for treatment before it can take place. In some cases, however, such as treatment for drug or alcohol problems, pregnancy or sexually transmitted diseases, or for purposes of obtaining contraceptives, state laws often permit minors to obtain medical treatment without parental consent.

This leads to one of the more curious situations in modern America. If your 12 year old daughter falls on the playground at school and skins her knee, you'll probably be called to school to give your consent before she can be bandaged by the school nurse, because the law considers her incapable of giving informed consent to her own treatment. But if the same child wants to obtain birth control pills, you will never know about it from the school officials or physicians who prescribe and supply them to her, because the law prohibits them from telling you.

YOUR RIGHTS IN THE HOSPITAL

Federal law protects you from being turned away from a hospital emergency room, and most states have similar laws. So if you go to an emergency room, even for non-emergency treatment, you must at least be examined by a doctor on duty. You can't be refused an examination, even if you are without health insurance coverage.

However, once you've been examined in the emergency room, the hospital is not required to admit you if your condition is stable and you can be sent home or transferred elsewhere. The only time the hospital must provide treatment and keep you in the hospital is in the event of an actual emergency, or if you are a woman in active labor.

If you've ever been in an emergency room, especially in a big city hospital, you know that it's not a pretty place. Doctors and nurses spend the bulk of their time treating rape victims, shooting victims, drug addicts who have taken an overdose, and accident victims. As a result, although you cannot be turned away from an emergency room, you may spend hours waiting to see a doctor, especially if your complaint is a relatively minor one. In addition, using the emergency room as a substitute for a family physician drives up medical costs for everyone, since the bills of those who can't pay are spread out among the hospital's paying patients in the form of higher rates for everyone. Many cities and towns have low-cost family health centers which can provide at least basic services to the poor. If you can't afford insurance, contact your county health department to find out what services may be available in your area.

If you are admitted to a hospital, you have certain rights which are designed to protect your health, your dignity, and your right to choose the treatment you will receive. The American Hospital Association has established the "Patient's Bill of Rights," which a number of states have enacted into law, and which describes your rights as a hospital patient. Among other rights, hospital patients have a right to receive considerate and respectful care. You don't have to tolerate hospital staff who call you names like "Sweetie," "Honey" or "Gramps." You are entitled to complete, understandable information about your condition, the treatment prescribed, and your prognosis. You are entitled to sufficient information from your doctor to allow you to give informed consent to any treatment, as well as an explanation of the consequences you may suffer by refusing such treatment. The Patients' Bill of Rights also guarantees confidential treatment of your hospital records and privacy in the administration of your medical care.

Finally, the Patients' Bill of Rights gives you the right to receive a fully itemized bill from the hospital, as well as an explanation of the charges. Do not be afraid to exercise this very important right. One recent study of hospital bills found that more than 95 percent of them contained errors, the vast majority of which favored the hospital, not the patient. And another study put the average overcharge in hospital bills at more than $1,200.

You are not required to pay a hospital bill at the time you are discharged, and you should take a few days to review the bill before you make payment. The hospital should give you the opportunity to speak with a representative who can explain the charges and how they are calculated. If you are billed for care, medication, or equipment which you did not receive, you have no obligation to pay for them.

In most cases, the hospital's representative may have the power to delete these charges after investigating them. But if he can't, or won't, and you still believe the charges are mistaken, be sure to notify your health insurance company's claims department of your concerns as soon as possible. If you don't have insurance, or even if you do, you can also contact your county health department or medical board and ask it to investigate. It may be able to have the charges removed or reduced. But if you are still unhappy with the bill, you can either refuse to pay the disputed portion and wait for the hospital to try to collect it, or you can get an attorney to assist you in fighting the charges. If you refuse to pay the amount in dispute, be sure to notify the hospital in writing of the reason for your refusal. It may report you to a credit bureau as delinquent, but it will have to note that your refusal to pay is because you dispute the amount in question.

YOUR RIGHT TO REFUSE MEDICAL TREATMENT

In addition to the rights listed above, the federal Patient Self-Determination Act requires hospitals to provide information to patients about living wills and your right to refuse life-prolonging medical treatment which does not improve the quality of life.

In 1990, the United States Supreme Court ruled that states may require clear and compelling evidence of a person's desire to have medical procedures withheld or withdrawn when they can prolong life without providing any hope for recovery. Implicit in that decision was the constitutionally guaranteed right of every person to decide for himself when to have those procedures terminated.

As medical technology advances, persons who in the past would have died a so-called "natural" death, can now be kept breathing, and their hearts kept beating, through the use of this advanced technology. However, for most people the concept of "life" involves much more than being kept alive by machines and being fed through gastric tubes that funnel food and water into an often unconscious body.

In order to guarantee that no one will interfere if you decide that you do not want to have your life prolonged through artificial means when there is no hope of recovery, there are several legal documents you should create. The first of these is the well-known Living Will.

Currently, 47 states and the District of Columbia have enacted Living Will statutes that set out the requirements for making a valid directive to your physicians which states your wishes in the event you suffer from a terminal condition. Generally, a Living Will is a document that directs your doctors to withhold or withdraw life sustaining measures when you suffer from an illness or injury from which you are not expected to recover. This document must be signed by you in the presence of two or more witnesses, none of whom should be a health care provider or a person who would stand to receive a share of your property in the event of your death, such as your spouse, a child, or someone you named as a beneficiary of a life insurance policy.

The exact form for creating a Living Will varies from state to state, and while it's likely that a Living Will executed in one state would be honored in another, most experts recommend that you execute a new Living Will if you move permanently from one state to another. Obtaining the appropriate Living Will form is easy, and you don't have to pay the $30 or more some lawyers charge; the forms themselves are contained in the state statute authorizing the creation of a Living Will. You can also obtain the form for use in your state from a doctor, hospital or medical clinic, or by writing to:

The Society for the Right to Die
250 West 57th Street
New York, NY 10107

The Society for the Right to Die will send you one set of advance medical directives, including a Living Will, at no charge, if you send them your name, address, and a self-addressed, stamped business size envelope.

In addition to a Living Will, the Society for the Right to Die also recommends that you complete a document known as a Durable Power of Attorney for Health Care. With this document, you appoint someone you trust to make decisions about your health care on your behalf in the event you cannot make them for yourself.

You may wonder why you would need a Durable Power of Attorney for Health Care if you already have a valid Living Will. Living Will statutes don't always cover every possible contingency you might face in a health care crisis that renders you unconscious or incapacitated. Some doctors, when faced with a situation that they believe falls outside the scope of your Living Will declaration, might refuse to honor the wishes you have expressed. By using a Durable Power of Attorney for Health Care, the person you appoint to speak for you (known as your attorney-in-fact) can make decisions about your health care as you would make them for yourself if you were able.

Like the laws authorizing Living Wills, legislation authorizing the Durable Power of Attorney for Health Care vary from one state to another, and it's important to use the correct form for the state in which you reside. You can find the correct form in your state's statutes at the public library or in the law library at your county courthouse. Or write to the Society for the Right to Die at the address above to receive a free copy of the appropriate form for use in your state.

If you create a Living Will, a Durable Power of Attorney for Health Care, or both, you should provide copies to your family doctor, who will make it a part of your medical record. In addition, it's a good idea to provide copies to your spouse, family members, or others who may be in a position to provide this information to a physician in case of a medical emergency.

As with other legal documents, you have the right to revoke a Living Will and a Durable Power of Attorney for Health Care at any time. To do so, you can simply tear the document up, give written notice of the revocation to your doctor and others who have copies, or merely tell them that you are revoking the documents. To be sure that there are no misunderstandings, written revocation is probably the best course to follow. But courts have held that an oral revocation of these documents is valid; in fact, if you can communicate your intention to revoke these documents in any way (such as by grunting, nodding, or blinking), courts have held that the revocation would be valid.

YOUR MEDICAL RECORDS AND RIGHT TO PRIVACY

Conversations you have with your doctor as well as your medical records are protected by what's known as the "doctor-patient" privilege. This means that, in most cases, they cannot be divulged or released to anyone without your consent. But as with most laws that protect our individual rights, there are exceptions when this information can be released without your consent and even over your objections.

For example, if your doctor treats you for a stab wound or gunshot wound, state laws require him to report the treatment, either to the police or to the state health department. Similarly, a doctor who treats a child for suspected child abuse must report his suspicions to the appropriate authorities. If your doctor treats you for one of a variety of contagious diseases, such as tuberculosis, AIDS, or measles, he may be required to report this to the state health department as well. If you tell your doctor that you plan to physically harm someone else, the laws in most states would allow the doctor to notify your intended victim. And if you sue your doctor for malpractice, your records will be used as evidence in the lawsuit.

Other than in the examples above, your medical records are closely guarded, and the details of your illnesses (both physical and mental) are known to no one but you and your doctor, right?

Wrong. In fact, dozens of people have access to your medical records, or can easily get access to them. That's because every time you apply for insurance, or file a health insurance claim, you sign a waiver, or release, which authorizes the insurer to inspect your medical records. In addition, this release authorizes the insurer to share any information it finds in your records with other insurers all around the country. If you refuse to sign the release, the insurance company has the right to reject your application for a policy or refuse to pay your claim.

In practical terms, signing this release means that your doctor will provide your records to a company called the Medical Insurance Bureau (MIB). The MIB, located in Boston, Massachusetts, is run as a kind of cooperative by most of the nation's insurance companies, who obtain your records by showing that you've either applied for an insurance policy or made a claim on an existing one. In fact, it's easier for an insurance company clerk to get access to the materials in the MIB computer than it is for you to get it yourself. That's because the MIB won't release the information it has about you directly to you; instead, it will only send them to a doctor you designate to receive your file.

Similarly, in nearly half the states, a patient has no legal right to see the records about him contained in his doctor's files. In these states, medical records are considered the property of the doctor, not the patient.

Even in those states that have laws which allow a patient access to his medical records, there are restrictions placed on just how much access the patient can have. In some states, you have to make a written request to the doctor; in others, hospitals must give you access to your records, but private physicians don't have to do so. And in most of these states, you still can't get access to your records if your doctor thinks it would not be in the best interests of your health to give them to you.

Once you've cleared all these hurdles, you still aren't home free. Your doctor or hospital will charge you a copying fee for the materials in your file, and in some states they can tack on an extra charge to cover their administrative costs in providing your records to you. When you consider that a stay of only a few days in the hospital can result in hundreds of pages of medical records, the cost to obtain copies can add up pretty quickly.

And once again, you'll find that it's often easier and less expensive for someone other than yourself to get access to these records. For example, although you will be charged for copies and administrative time, many hospitals will provide your records to a doctor who requests them without charging the doctor anything at all.

While more and more states seem to be moving toward providing patient's with easier access to their own medical records, there's still a long way to go. And penalties for violating the confidentiality of these records need to be stiffened. Unfortunately, current laws still seem designed to favor the doctors and insurance companies who lobby diligently in the state legislatures for laws that protect them from liability, or at least limit their liability as much as possible without raising an outcry from the public.

You can find out what rights you have in regard to your medical records by checking your state's statutes, which you can find at most public libraries and in the library at your county courthouse, or by contacting your state's department of health. You'll find the address and telephone number for the department of health in your state listed at the end of this chapter. Your state representative's office is the place to contact if you are dissatisfied with current state laws on access to medical records.

CONTRACEPTION AND ABORTION RIGHTS

In today's atmosphere, it's hard to believe that up until the early 1960s state laws still prohibited doctors from prescribing birth control devices, and that the people who used them, even when married to one another, could be found guilty of committing a crime by doing so. It wasn't until 1965 that the U.S. Supreme Court ruled that the right to advertise, distribute, and use contraceptives was guaranteed by the right to privacy in the U. S. Constitution. Similarly, as an adult you have the right to consent to sterilization procedures which render you permanently incapable of reproduction.

As with any medical procedure or treatment, contraception and sterilization carry certain known risks. One of the most significant risks is that the procedure won't work, and you find yourself or your partner facing an unwanted pregnancy. In most cases, if the use of a contraceptive device results in a pregnancy, there is little you can do legally to make the manufacturer of the contraceptive or the doctor who prescribed it responsible for your predicament. Birth control pills, diaphragms, prophylactics (rubbers) or other devices come loaded with warnings about the possibility that they won't work. Unless you can show that you were unaware of these warnings, a prospect which is very unlikely, you won't succeed with a lawsuit based on contraceptive failure.

Another risk associated with contraceptives involves the health of the person using the device. Studies have shown that some women who use birth control pills have experienced higher incidences of breast cancer, high blood pressure, strokes, and other health problems. As a result, the FDA now requires the manufacturers of birth control pills to provide extensive information to consumers about those risks in each package. This differs from FDA rules about other kinds of prescription medications, which only require the manufacturer to provide information about possible side effects and complications to physicians.

Because of the vast amount of information that the manufacturers of birth control pills are required to supply directly to the users of their products, it's increasingly difficult for women who suffer from known side effects to successfully sue these manufacturers.

When a sterilization procedure fails, it's somewhat more likely that a lawsuit against the doctor who performed the procedure will succeed, although there isn't any guarantee of success in every case. Some judges still believe that the birth of a child is something to be viewed with joy, not dismay. However, every state now permits lawsuits for "wrongful pregnancy" which is a type of medical malpractice. Success depends on proof that the reason for the pregnancy was because the doctor failed to perform the procedure properly. In some cases, tubes that have been cut properly can reconnect on their own; in these cases, the doctor would not be liable for the unwanted pregnancy.

Even in a successful wrongful pregnancy suit, the damages which can be awarded are usually limited to the costs incurred during the pregnancy and delivery for health care, and for related items such as wages lost because of the pregnancy. But if the pregnancy results in a healthy child, the view that a child is a blessing still prevails, and you cannot receive compensation for the costs of raising the child to adulthood.

Just as the right to contraception and voluntary sterilization is guaranteed by the U.S. Supreme Court's interpretation of the Constitution, the right to abortion is similarly protected. However, while a woman has the right to obtain an abortion, the Court has also recognized that state laws may impose reasonable restrictions on that right. Under the famous *Roe v. Wade* decision and subsequent pronouncements from the Supreme Court, states can require women in the middle stages of pregnancy to have their abortions performed in a hospital or clinic rather than in a doctor's office, and can even ban abortions in the later stages of pregnancy, except for those necessary to save the life or protect the health of the expectant mother.

States can also impose brief waiting periods between the time a woman first seeks an abortion and the time she obtains it. And states can require that minors who want an abortion notify at least one parent before she can obtain it, although they must also give the minor the opportunity to authorize the abortion without parental notification. States cannot, however, require minors to obtain parental consent to an abortion, nor can they require that a pregnant woman of any age obtain the consent of the father before obtaining an abortion.

REPRODUCTIVE RIGHTS

For many couples, having children is a high priority, so high that they are willing to invest months and years of their time and tens of thousands of dollars in infertility treatments. In some cases, these couples have been victimized by clinics that advertise high success rates in overcoming fertility problems and make promises about the chances of a successful pregnancy that are unsupported by statistics.

Every year, nearly 200,000 women in America utilize artificial insemination as one method of increasing their chances for having a baby. Of these women, about one-third actually become pregnant. In some cases, the woman is inseminated with her husband's sperm. In others, the sperm of an anonymous donor is used.

Artificial insemination is legal throughout the country, but there is very little legal regulation of the clinics that perform artificial insemination procedures. As a result, some serious legal problems have occurred which you need to be aware of and avoid to the best of your ability.

One of these problems has to do with the health history of an anonymous sperm donor. In this age of AIDS and other sexually transmitted diseases, it is essential that you only use a sperm bank which tests the semen of its donors, freezes the semen and then retests the donor six months later for evidence of HIV or other sexually transmitted diseases.

Another problem occurs when a sperm bank maintains inadequate records about the donor of sperm being used in an insemination procedure. In one case, a white woman was supposed to be inseminated by her husband's sperm. Her husband was also white, but when the baby was born, she was black. She filed suit against the sperm bank and eventually received a substantial financial settlement.

It's also probably safer to use a sperm bank and clinic rather than a private physician. In a recent case, a doctor who ran a sperm bank served as its principal donor as well, and hundreds of his patients may in fact have given birth to the doctor's own children. If these children should meet and mate, there's an increased likelihood of genetic problems in the children that they may bear. While the chance may seem remote, many of the women who underwent artificial insemination at this doctor's clinic live in the same city, so the possibility of such a union between half-brother and half-sister does exist.

Another procedure that many couples have resorted to is that of "in vitro" fertilization. In this procedure, a woman's eggs are extracted from her ovaries and placed in a petri dish, where they are mixed with sperm. If any of the eggs are fertilized, one or more are replanted in the woman's uterus, and the rest are frozen for future use.

While some pregnancies do result from in vitro fertilization, many do not. As a result, many couples repeat the procedure at least several times before a pregnancy results, and in some cases in vitro fertilization simply doesn't work at all. With an average cost per procedure of as much as $10,000, the bill for several attempts can skyrocket pretty quickly. In most cases, in vitro fertilization procedures aren't covered by insurance, although at least ten states now require insurers to include coverage for in vitro fertilization in group insurance plans they offer to employers.

In vitro fertilization clinics are, for the most part, unregulated by either the state or federal government. If you are considering the use of in vitro fertilization, be wary about clinics that claim high success rates and minimize the chances of failure. You should receive very specific information about the number of procedures the clinic has performed, how many they've performed on women with fertility problems similar to yours, and how many of those women carried their babies to term and gave birth to a healthy child. Don't settle for information that only relates to successful fertilizations, since many fertilizations end in miscarriages.

You also need to consider what steps you need to take in regard to the disposition of any frozen embryos in case your marriage breaks up or if you decide to abandon efforts to become pregnant through in vitro fertilization. In a Tennessee case that received national publicity during the early 1990s, a couple that had frozen seven embryos became embroiled in a custody dispute over the fate of the embryos; the wife wanted to continue trying to become pregnant, while the husband argued that they should be destroyed. After nearly four years and thousands of dollars in legal fees, the Tennessee Supreme Court held that the embryos could be destroyed, and in 1993 they were. But this decision applies only to Tennessee, and other states might decide the issue differently. By making the decision before you begin in vitro fertilization procedures, you can include a written agreement about their disposal in your contract with the clinic.

Surrogate parenting is yet another way in which couples have attempted to defeat their infertility problems. In surrogate parenting, a couple enters into an agreement with another woman, who agrees to be inseminated with the man's sperm and carry a resulting fetus to term. Although these agreements vary somewhat in their exact terms, they generally provide that the surrogate mother's living expenses and medical bills during the pregnancy will be paid by the couple. When the child is born, the woman relinquishes any rights she has to the child, and the couple takes their new baby home.

The legality of surrogacy contracts is still in question. In some states, such contracts are legal if properly drawn and in conformity with requirements set out by state law. Other states make them illegal, and consider surrogacy arrangements to be nothing more than the buying and selling of human life. And other states give the surrogate mother a window during which she may change her mind and decide to keep the baby.

Because these laws vary so widely and are changing so rapidly, if you are considering entering into a surrogacy contract, you should meet with an attorney before you sign an agreement with a surrogacy clinic or a surrogate mother. Don't rely on the statements made by a lawyer who is trying to get you to become a surrogate mother or who represents a woman offering her services as a surrogate mother without getting independent legal advice. The typical surrogacy agreement can cost a couple more than $20,000. In this case, a lawyer's fees may be a worthwhile added expense to prevent problems now and in the future.

MEDICAL MALPRACTICE

In legal terms, medical malpractice consists of any professional misconduct or unreasonable lack of skill by a physician in the performance of his professional duties. A physician may be guilty of malpractice when he fails to perform a procedure with the level of skill which would be expected of what the law calls "an ordinary physician." Depending on the state, the performance of a doctor charged with malpractice may be compared to doctors in the same geographic area, or who practice in the same medical specialty, or who practice anywhere in the United States.

Illegal or immoral conduct by a physician, such as pressuring a patient into having sexual relations, also constitutes malpractice. And failing to obtain your informed consent before treating a patient is another form of medical malpractice.

Hospitals may also be charged with malpractice when they fail to provide the care that it should be reasonably expected to provide when compared to other hospitals.

Rising malpractice claims and the subsequent increases in malpractice insurance premiums have led many physicians to proceed with excessive caution before suggesting or implementing any medical procedure. Batteries of expensive tests may be ordered, many of which are unnecessary, and all of which ultimately increase the cost of medical care to everyone. In addition, some areas of medicine, such as obstetrics and gyne-cology, have become so burdened by malpractice claims that many practitioners have chosen to abandon these fields of prac-tice entirely. This also results in higher medical costs to con-sumers, since those doctors who continue to practice in these fields face less competition. And when competition decreases, prices invariably increase.

To help understand what medical malpractice is, it's helpful to understand what kinds of actions do not constitute malprac-tice.

First, the fact that medical treatment or a surgical proce-dure doesn't cure an illness or improve your condition doesn't necessarily mean that the physician is guilty of malpractice. Many medical conditions defy treatment in spite of a doctor's best efforts. For example, doctors tend to treat cases of hyperten-sion, or high blood pressure, with prescription medication and recommended changes in the patient's diet. But some cases of hypertension don't respond to these standard treatments. Pro-vided that your doctor used accepted medical procedures and used the level of skill in providing them that an ordinary physi-cian would be expected to use, no malpractice has been com-mitted.

Second, even if a treatment makes you feel worse than you did before it was administered, your doctor may not be guilty of malpractice. Every patient who undergoes surgery faces risks of complications, infection, or even death. Every patient who takes a prescribed medicine runs the risk of serious side effects. But as long as the doctor explained the risks and the patient gave informed consent to the treatment, no malpractice has occurred.

So what does constitute medical malpractice? Here are some examples:

- Prescribing drug dosages in excess of those recommended by the manufacturer for the condition being treated.
- Prescribing drugs or utilizing equipment which has not been approved by the federal Food & Drug Administra-tion (FDA).
- Misdiagnosis that occurs because of the doctor's failure to follow standard procedures. For example, a doctor failed to diagnose a skull fracture in a patient who had suffered

a serious fall from a bicycle when he sent the patient home without first ordering x-rays. The patient's condition deteriorated, and he died several days later. Because the doctor did not follow standard medical procedures by ordering x-rays, he was guilty of malpractice.

•The failure of hospital nursing staff to follow the doctor's prescribed course of treatment. If the nurse on duty fails to give prescribed medication according to the doctor's orders, or fails to change surgical dressings as required, the nurse, the nurse's supervisor and the hospital may all be charged with malpractice.

Not all medical treatments, no matter how skillfully performed, will be successful. Patients may have waited too long to seek medical attention, or they may not respond as would be expected under normal circumstances. No doctor can guarantee that he or she can return a patient to good health. But the failure to restore a patient's health is not in itself evidence of malpractice.

If you believe your doctor or the hospital where you were treated is guilty of malpractice, you don't need to rush off to a lawyer right away. Instead, get in touch with your state's Board of Medical Examiners (you can get the telephone number from directory assistance in your state capital, or from the capital's telephone directory) and ask it for information about how to file a complaint about the treatment you received. The Board will forward you the appropriate forms to fill out, or put you in touch with the agency that investigates such complaints.

After you fill out and return your complaint form, it will be investigated by a "peer review board" consisting of other doctors. A hearing may be held at which you and your doctor may be given the opportunity to be heard. If the board's investigation indicates that your doctor failed to observe the standards of an ordinary physician, you have a good chance of winning a malpractice case.

Unfortunately, because these boards are made up of other doctors, questions have been raised about just how thoroughly they investigate complaints brought before them, and how often they let doctors get away with improper behavior. If you aren't satisfied with the results of a review board investigation, you can still consider filing a malpractice lawsuit. This is one of those instances when you really can't do-it-yourself, and you will probably need to meet with an attorney who specializes in medical malpractice cases. Initial consultations with these attorneys are usually free, which means that you can receive a pretty good idea of how valid your complaint is at no cost. And attorneys who handle medical malpractice cases take them on a contingent fee basis, which means that they receive a portion of any settlement or judgment they obtain on your behalf, but receive no fees otherwise. (However, you are responsible for court costs and expenses related to your lawsuit.) You'll find more information about how to hire a lawyer in Chapter Seventeen.

HEALTH INSURANCE

Trying to make sense of the current state of health insurance in America is a test of any lawyer's skill. President Clinton had promised during his election campaign to drastically restructure the way in which Americans obtain health insurance coverage, and in September of 1993, his proposals for universal health care coverage were made public.

Under these proposals, extensive coverage of medical and surgical procedures, diagnostic testing, and hospitalization and hospice care would be made available to all U.S. citizens and legal residents. Employers would generally be required to pay 80 percent of the cost of coverage, while employees would pay the rest, as well as an annual $400 deductible. No family would be required to pay more than $3,000 per year for covered medical services. However, the self-employed would pay 100 percent of the cost of their own coverage, although they would also be allowed a tax deduction.

Although the Clinton Administration's plan has now been made public, it will undoubtedly be subject to a great deal of debate and many revisions. Months of Congressional hearings will follow before a final plan is devised, voted on and signed into law. And many more months will follow before the legislation actually takes effect; the Clinton plan would not begin to be implemented until 1995 or 1996.

Our discussion here is based on the law as of the end of 1993; if and when President Clinton's plan is enacted into law, significant changes will occur. To learn about these changes, you may want to subscribe to The ProSe Letter, our quarterly newsletter about the law. You can find information about how to subscribe at the beginning of this book.

Most of us obtain our health insurance coverage through a group plan, usually through our employer. Under a group health insurance plan, coverage is provided under what's known as the master policy, a contract between the insurance company and the employer. Individuals within the covered group are typically provided with insurance certificates and plan summaries, which provide detailed information about the health plan.

For those who cannot obtain health insurance through their employer or other group, another option is an individual policy. Premiums for these policies are higher, in part because of the added cost of administering the individual health plan. Comparison shopping is essential when buying health insurance on an individual basis, and you will need to carefully review the terms of several proposed contracts in order to determine which policy offers the best protection at the most reasonable rate.

One important advantage of group health plans is that coverage of individual members of the group; the insurance company can only cancel the policy for the entire group. An individual's group coverage can be discontinued, however, when the individual is no longer a member of the group. However, if you receive group through your employer, and your employer has 20 or more employees, a federal law (known as COBRA) requires your employer to offer you the option of continuing your group health coverage for up to 18 months following termination, unless you were fired for gross misconduct. However, you become responsible for the full cost of the premiums for this coverage, and you will also be charged a 2 percent administrative fee by the insurer. When the 18 month period ends, you then have the option of converting to an individual health policy. Some states have laws similar to COBRA which extend protection to those employees not covered by federal law.

WHAT DOES HEALTH INSURANCE COVER?

At present, there is no standardized health insurance available across the entire country. For the most part, the regulation of insurance companies is left to the individual states, although the federal government regulates some kinds of employer sponsored health insurance plans through the Employee Retirement Income Security Act (ERISA).

The basic protection offered by health insurance is payment of fees charged by doctors, surgeons and other medical specialists, as well as the laboratory and diagnostic tests they order for the patient. Both in-patient and out-patient services are generally covered under this type of health insurance. In some instances, the insurance plan also covers the cost of prescription drugs.

Health insurance generally doesn't pay the entire cost charged for these medical services. Through various formulas, the insurance companies compute what they consider to be a reasonable fee for these services. Even if the doctor charges more than this fee, the company will not pay more than what's known as the usual and customary charge. And before it pays anything, you'll almost always be required to pay an annual deductible, such as $250, $500, or even $1,000 for medical expenses before the insurer begins to pick up these costs.

Another common feature of health insurance is coverage for hospitalization. With hospitalization coverage, the agrees to pay a daily rate for a hospital room (typically, this coverage applies only to semi-private rooms), although the insured has the option of paying the difference if he wants a private room.

In addition to the limit on the daily rate paid for a hospital room, the health insurance policy may also set a limit on the number of days for which coverage will last, which is based on the type of illness which resulted in the need for hospitalization. For example, a hospital stay to undergo a hemorrhoidectomy may only be covered for three days, while a stay for brain surgery will almost certainly be covered for a much longer period.

In addition to the cost of the hospital room, hospitalization insurance usually will cover other expenses incurred during the hospital stay, such as medications, therapy and tests ordered by your doctor.

In some instances the coverage provided under hospitalization and health plans can be exhausted if a long-term illness, expensive surgery or other costly treatment is required. To protect against these high medical expenses health insurers provide what's known as major medical coverage, either as a separate policy or in combination with the medical and hospitalization provisions outlined above.

The costs covered under the major medical provisions are usually limited to a certain percentage of the total bill up to a specified dollar limit, and after a deductible has been paid by the insured. Once the deductible is paid and the dollar limit is reached the insurer then picks up the rest of the cost, up to the limits of your policy. Let's see how this would work in real life.

Suppose a hospital stay results in a $60,000 bill. Your policy carries a $1,000 deductible, covers 75 percent of major medical expenses up to $5,000 (called the co-payment) and then pays 100 percent of recognized expenses. Your total out-of-pocket expenses for the hospital stay under this policy would equal $2,250, or your deductible plus $1,250, which represents your 25 percent co-payment. The insurer would pick up the rest.

WHAT HEALTH INSURANCE DOESN'T COVER

Not all medical procedures are covered under standard health insurance policies. Most policies exclude coverage for what insurers consider preventive care, such as routine physicals, contraception and cancer screening. Policies often exclude coverage blood tests and x-rays unless they occur immediately before you are admitted to a hospital. Payments for eye exams, chiropractic or acupuncture treatment, and non-prescription medications or vitamin supplements are also typically excluded from many policies, although they may be available if an additional premium is paid.

Most health insurance policies will contain some provision about pre-existing conditions. Each policy has its own definition of a "pre-existing condition" but generally it's defined as a health problem that existed before the insurance coverage was purchased. The contract designates a particular length of time, such as the year before the policy was purchased, as the relevant time period. Any illnesses or injuries that occur after the policy was purchased which can be traced back to a condition occurring within this time period will be excluded from coverage.

In many cases, however, this exclusion is only temporary. For example, a "12/12" pre-existing condition clause means that the policy will exclude coverage of an illness or injury that occurred within 12 months of purchasing the policy for the first 12 months that the policy is in effect. After that, the policy pays for treatment of the pre-existing condition just as it would for any other covered medical problem.

One controversial exclusion contained in the majority of health insurance policies bans insurance company payments for experimental treatments. In some cases, incurable diseases such as bone and liver cancer may only be treatable with experimental procedures. Several court battles have been waged by those suffering from incurable diseases against insurers, seeking a court order requiring the insurance company to pay for these treatments. The results of these suits has been mixed. However, some health insurance companies now allow members to pay an additional premium for coverage of experimental cancer treatments and transplant procedures. While this insurance may cover 80 percent to 100 percent of the cost of these procedures, "stop-loss" provisions in the policy may limit the total amount of the insurer's liability to a specified amount, such as $500,000 or $1 million.

OTHER LIMITATIONS

The amount of coverage provided by your health insurance may be affected by other insurance that covers the same condition. For example, if you are injured in an automobile accident, your employer's group medical plan, an individual health plan, and the medical insurance portion of your auto insurance coverage may all provide similar benefits. In order to avoid paying you more than once for the same injury, health insurance policies include a provision that limits each insurer's liability to a percentage of the total cost.

Another clause routinely found in health insurance policies deals with subrogation. Under a subrogation clause, you give the insurer the right to recover any amounts you might be entitled to from someone who caused your illness or injury. For example, if you are injured in an accident because of someone else's negligence, he may be held liable for your medical expenses; but by the time a settlement or lawsuit determines the amount of that liability, your insurance company will probably already have paid the medical expenses. A subrogation provision entitles the insurance company to recover the amount it paid to you from this settlement or judgment. Any excess, however, is yours.

CANCELING YOUR COVERAGE

An insurance company may cancel insurance coverage for a variety of reasons, such as failing to pay premiums and false representations about the medical condition of the insured on the insurance application. Some policies contain a guaranteed renewability provision, under which you may be given the opportunity to continue health protection to a particular age (such as 65). However, your premiums will be adjusted periodically, and most such policies give the insurer the right to cancel you as long as it cancels everyone in the state where you live. So guaranteed renewability isn't necessarily guaranteed at all.

GOVERNMENT SPONSORED HEALTH INSURANCE

Since 1965, government-sponsored health insurance plans have been available to certain segments of the population. Medicare is the federal health insurance program designed to provide care to the elderly population. The Medicaid program provides health care for the poor. You'll find more information about both of these programs in Chapter Thirteen, "Your Government Benefits," beginning on page 307.

MANAGED HEALTH CARE PROGRAMS

The rising costs of medical care have prompted the insurance industry and the medical profession to reevaluate the way health care is delivered and how it is paid for by insurers. Traditionally, medical care has been provided on what's referred to as a "fee-for-service" basis. Under this standard, every time a person has a doctor's appointment, or undergoes laboratory work or any other medical procedure, a bill is prepared for that service. As a result, many people forego routine examinations or delay seeking medical care until an injury or illness becomes serious because they fear the cost associated with receiving medical care.

In the 1970s, some new ways of providing health care coverage were developed as alternatives to the traditional fee-for-service method of obtaining medical care. Health maintenance organizations, or HMOs, place an emphasis on early detection and health promotion. Rather than pay for each service and then seek reimbursement from an insurer, members of an HMO pay a fixed monthly premium in advance for access to a variety of health care services.

Medical costs are controlled under an HMO plan because the contractual relationship between everyone involved specifies how much will be paid for services rendered. The person enrolling in the HMO knows that he must pay a fixed monthly premium in order to obtain medical care. The doctors and hospitals affiliated with the HMO know that they will be paid a fixed price for their services, no matter how often they treat a patient and how many diagnostic tests they order. As a result, they have an incentive to contain costs by emphasizing preventive medicine and keeping patients healthy rather than treating them only when a crisis has occurred. Members of an HMO may be educated and counseled about diet, exercise and general health issues in order to have healthier lifestyles. Unnecessary tests or other diagnostic services are eliminated and hospital stays are minimized in order to cut health care expenses.

In 1973, Congress enacted the Health Maintenance Organization Act to help encourage the development of HMOs. This legislation authorizes the use of federal grants and loans to develop HMOs, and requires businesses with more than 25 employees to offer HMOs as an alternative health care plan. Several states have enacted similar laws that require employers not covered by the federal law to offer HMOs as an alternative health care option.

Although the organization and structure of HMOs are continually being re-evaluated, there are essentially three types of HMOs. Under the staff model, HMOs directly employ the physicians who will work for them. These doctors work as a team to provide medical care. The HMO member then chooses a primary care physician from that group. While the team of HMO doctors provides both general and specialized care, it may also contract with outside specialists for specific services.

In a group model HMO, the physicians are not directly employed by the HMO. Instead, they work as an independent group to provide health care to the HMO members. These groups may provide services to several HMOs, as well as to the general public. Members of the HMO may not be able to tell the difference between the staff model and group model, since the distinction comes from the terms of the contract signed by the physicians.

An HMO which operates as an individual practice association, or IPA, can be more easily distinguished from the other two types of HMOs. In an IPA, individual physicians sign a contract with an HMO to provide health care to HMO members on a prepaid basis. A list of these physicians is provided to HMO members, who then select the doctor they want as their primary care physician.

The most important advantage for members of an HMO is that they know with reasonable certainty how much their medical care will cost each year. A predetermined annual premium is paid to the HMO in exchange for access to health care services, although for some services there may be a small co-payment required. And if the HMO is offered by an employer, all or some of the premium may be paid as an employee benefit.

As an HMO member, you don't have to worry about choosing physicians with particular specialties or deciding which hospital to pick if surgery is needed. All treatment is obtained through physicians and hospitals that have contracted with the HMO, and you must obtain treatment within the HMO system for services to be covered. And while a participant in a traditional health insurance plan has to file claim forms, there is usually no claim filing involved in an HMO.

On the other hand, there can be disadvantages to an HMO. HMOs operate as self-contained units, and all of a patient's needs are handled by doctors, diagnostic personnel and hospital staff that are associated with that HMO. If a specialist is needed, you are limited to those on the HMO's list. Some HMOs prohibit members from going to an emergency room without prior approval unless a life threatening emergency exists. Some people chafe at the limited freedom of choice involved in selecting the doctors who will treat them.

There can be other problems as well. In order to contain costs and increase profitability, some of the treatment received at the HMO may be provided by nurses or physician's assistants rather than by doctors. Some people are simply not comfortable with this method of providing medical care.

Health care costs are also controlled by eliminating tests or services the doctor considers non-essential. A criticism of HMOs is that they may be reluctant to provide services that the patient wants and which may even be medically necessary, in order to cut corners and increase profit margins.

Another alternative to traditional health insurance is what is known as a preferred provider organization program, or PPO. Essentially, a PPO is a network of doctors that have agreed to provide lower cost medical services in return for becoming the exclusive network of health care providers for one or more insurance companies.

When you join a PPO through your health insurer, you can go to any doctor listed on the PPO's list of approved doctors to obtain health care services. Your insurer then pays the pre-negotiated price of your visit to the doctor. If you use a doctor who isn't part of the PPO network, you receive only partial reimbursement from your insurer, or perhaps none at all, depending on the terms of your policy.

Insurers like PPOs because they help keep costs down and allow the insurer to predict its costs more accurately, since the PPOs doctors have all agreed to a reduced fee schedule, and the insurer can anticipate the number of visits patients will make through actuarial studies.

Some PPO networks are quite extensive, so you won't find your choice of physicians as restricted as it might be in an HMO. In fact, you should ask the PPO's sponsor to provide you with a list of the doctors that are authorized to provide PPO services before you sign up. You may find that your current primary care physician is already on the PPO's list of authorized doctors.

Doctors like PPOs because they assure them a relatively steady stream of patients and fees, without limiting their ability to take on members of the general public as patients.

There are some precautions you should take before joining a PPO. Most importantly, you should know what criteria the insurer or PPO sponsor uses to evaluate a doctor's credentials. For some PPOs, the main consideration is the reduced charges the doctor is willing to offer. Length of practice, certification as a specialist and commitment to providing services promptly and in a caring manner may not be considered, or considered only briefly, before admitting the doctor to the PPO panel.

Be sure to read and understand your PPO policy's provisions for obtaining emergency treatment or the services of a specialist. Some plans require your primary care physician to obtain permission from the PPO administrator before admitting you to the hospital or referring you to a specialist. If you don't, you may have your benefits reduced, or have your claim refused entirely.

Most PPOs are sponsored by insurance companies, which are regulated by your state insurance department. The insurance department can tell you how long the insurer and the PPO have been authorized to operate in your state and if either has been the subject of any serious complaints or investigations. You can find the address and telephone number of the department's office listed at the end of Chapter Ten, "Your Insurance," beginning on page 227.

DISABILITY INSURANCE

Disability insurance is supposed to provide you with financial protection when you are severely injured or seriously ill and unable to work, by replacing at least some of your wages. While it's possible to buy disability policies that will replace all of your lost wages, insurers don't like to offer them because they believe such policies discourage workers from trying to recover and get back to work.

Disability insurance is sometimes offered as a fringe benefit by employers, or you can purchase an individual policy. If you think you need to buy a disability policy, there are some things you need to look for to make sure you are getting the best possible coverage in return for your premium payment.

The most important consideration in buying a disability policy is the way the policy defines disability. Some policies only pay if you are rendered incapable of performing any kind of work at all. Suppose you are a construction worker making $40,000 per year and you become disabled to the extent that you can no longer perform the duties associated with being a construction worker. Your disability policy may not pay anything if the insurance company doctor says you are capable of working at a fast food restaurant and earning minimum wage. A policy like this is of little value.

Some disability policies pay only if you are unable to perform any occupation for which you are qualified by education or training. With one of these policies, if you are a construction worker whose disability keeps you off the high steel, but whose training would qualify you to serve as a trade school instructor in the construction field, your policy wouldn't pay off, even if you couldn't find a job as an instructor.

The disability policy you want to buy will agree to make payments based on your inability to work in your usual occupation. Under one of these policies, a construction worker who can't perform the usual and customary duties of his normal employment is considered disabled.

Some disability policies pay benefits based on a percentage of your regular income, while other policies pay a fixed monthly benefit, such as $2,000 per month. In either case, you'll probably be faced with a waiting period before the company will begin paying benefits. The longer the waiting period, the lower the premium. One important aspect of the waiting period which you need to consider is how it is calculated if you are disabled, return to work, and then suffer a recurrence of the same problem. Some policies make you start the waiting period all over again; better policies waive the waiting period if the problem reappears within a stated period of time, such as six months or a year.

You'll also need to know how long your coverage will last. Some policies will pay benefits up until normal retirement age, while others will pay benefits for only a specified period of time, such as five or ten years. If you are young and have a family to support, the longer the benefits will come, the more protection you are providing for your family.

You also need to find out if the amount of coverage will be automatically adjusted for inflation, and if you'll be able to purchase additional coverage later if your income increases substantially. Check to see if the policy you are considering reduces your benefits if you also receive Social Security disability payments or workers compensation. Look for a policy that includes what's known as a "waiver of premium," which means you don't have to pay the policy's premiums while you are disabled.

Finally, be sure you understand what the policy says about pre-existing conditions. Most policies exclude payments for conditions that existed before you bought the policy, either for a specified period of time or in some cases, forever.

For more information about how to buy insurance, file claims, and other issues related to insurance companies, be sure to read Chapter Ten, "Your Insurance," beginning on page 227.

STATE DEPARTMENTS OF HEALTH

Alabama
Department of Public Health
434 Monroe Street
Montgomery, AL 36130-1701
(205) 242-5095

Alaska
Division of Public Health
P.O. Box H
Juneau, AK 99811-0601
(907) 465-3030

Arizona
Department of Health Services
1740 W. Adams Street
Phoenix, AZ 85007
(602) 542-1000

Arkansas
Department of Health
4815 W. Markham Street
Little Rock, AR 72205
(501) 661-2111

California
Department of Health Services
714 P Street
Sacramento, CA 94234-7320
(916) 445-4171

Colorado
Department of Health
4210 E. 11th Avenue
Denver, CO 80220
(303) 320-8333

Connecticut
Department of Health Services
150 Washington Street
Hartford, CT 06106
(203) 566-4800

Delaware
Division of Public Health
P.O. Box 637
Federal Street
Dover, DE 19901
(302) 739-4726

District of Columbia
Department of Public Health
1660 L Street, NW
Washington, DC 20036
(202) 673-7700

Florida
Department of Health and Rehabilitative Services
1317 Winewood Boulevard
Tallahassee, FL 32399-0700
(904) 488-6294

Georgia
Division of Public Health
Department of Human Resources
878 Peachtree Street, NE
Atlanta, GA 30309
(404) 894-7505

Hawaii
Department of Health
P.O. Box 3378
Honolulu, HI 96813
(808) 586-4400

Idaho
Department of Health and Welfare
450 W. State Street
Boise, ID 83720-5450
(208) 334-5500

Illinois
Department of Public Health
535 W. Jefferson Street
Springfield, IL 62761
(217) 782-4977

Indiana
State Board of Health
1330 W. Michigan Street
P.O. Box 1964
Indianapolis, IN 46206-1964
(317) 633-0100

Iowa
Department of Public Health
Lucas State Office Building
East 12th and Walnut Streets
Des Moines, IA 50319-0075
(515) 281-5787

Kansas
Department of Health and Environment
Landon State Office Building
Topeka, KS 66612-1290
(913) 296-1500

Kentucky
Department of Health Services
Cabinet for Human Resources
275 E. Main Street
Frankfort, KY 40621-0001
(502) 564-7736

Louisiana
Office of Public Health
P.O. Box 60630
New Orleans, LA 70160-0629
(504) 568-5050

Maine
Bureau of Health
State House, Station 11
August, ME 04333
(207) 289-3201

Maryland
Department of Health and Mental Hygiene
201 W. Preston Street
Baltimore, MD 21201
(301) 225-6860

Massachusetts
Department of Public Health
150 Tremont Street
Boston, MA 02111
(617) 727-0201

Michigan
Department of Public Health
P.O. Box 30195
Lansing, MI 48909
(517) 335-8000

Minnesota
Department of Health
717 Delaware Street, S.E.
Minneapolis, MN 55440
(612) 623-5000

Mississippi
State Health Department
2423 N. State Street
P.O. Box 1700
Jackson, MS 39215-1700
(601) 960-7400

Missouri
Department of Health
P.O. Box 570
Jefferson City, MO 65102
(314) 751-6400

Montana
Department of Health and Environmental Services
Cogswell Building
Helena, MT 59620
(406) 444-2544

Nebraska
Department of Health
301 Centennial Mall, South
P.O. Box 95007
Lincoln, NE 68509
(402) 471-2133

Nevada
Department of Health
505 E. King Street
Carson City, NV 89710
(702) 687-4740

New Hampshire
Department of Health and Human Services
6 Hazen Drive
Concord, NH 03301
(603) 271-4685

New Jersey
Department of Health
CN 360
Trenton, NJ 08625-0360
(609) 292-7837

New Mexico
Department of Health
1190 St. Francis Drive
P.O. Box 26110
Santa Fe, NM 87502-6110
(505) 827-0020

New York
New York State Health Department
Corning Tower II, Empire State Plaza
Albany, NY 12237-0001
(518) 474-2121

North Carolina
Division of Health Services
Department of Environmental Health and Natural Resources
1330 St. Mary Street
Raleigh, NC 27605
(919) 733-7081

North Dakota
Department of Health
State Capital
600 E. Boulevard Avenue
Bismarck, ND 58505-0200
(701) 224-2370

Ohio
Department of Health
246 N. High Street
P.O. Box 118
Columbus, OH 43266-0118
(614) 466-3543

Oklahoma
Department of Health
1000 N.E. 10th Street
P.O. Box 53551
Oklahoma City, OK 73152
(405) 271-4200

Oregon
Health Division
Department of Human Resources
1400 Southwest Fifth Avenue
P.O. Box 231
Portland, OR 97201
(503) 378-3033

Pennsylvania
Department of Health
Health and Welfare Building
P.O. Box 90
Harrisburg, PA 17108
(717) 787-5901

Rhode Island
Department of Health
3 Capitol Hill
Providence, RI 02908-5097
(401) 277-2231

South Carolina
Department of Health and Environmental Control
2600 Bull Street
Columbia, SC 29201
(803) 734-4880

South Dakota
Department of Health
445 East Capitol Avenue
Pierre, SD 57501-3185
(605) 773-3361

Tennessee
Department of Public Health
344 Cordell Hull Building
Nashville, TN 37247-0101
(615) 741-3111

Texas
Texas Department of Health
1100 W. 49th Street
Austin, TX 78756-3199
(512) 458-7111

Utah
Department of Health
288 North 1460 West
Salt Lake City, UT 84116
(801) 538-6101

Vermont
State Health Department
60 Main Street
Burlington, VT 05401
(802) 863-7200

Virginia
State Health Department
Main Street Station
1500 East Main Street
Richmond, VA 23219
(804) 786-3561

Washington
Department of Health
MS ET-21
Olympia, WA 98504
(206) 586-5846

West Virginia
Department of Health
1800 Washington Street
Charleston, WV 25305
(304) 348-0045

Wisconsin
Division of Health Services
P.O. Box 7850
Madison, WI 53707
(608) 266-3681

Wyoming
Department of Health and Human Services
117 Hathaway Building
Cheyenne, WY 82002-0710
(307) 777-7656

CHAPTER TWELVE
YOUR RETIREMENT

If you're nearing retirement age, congratulations! After a lifetime of work, it's nice to think about taking some time for yourself, to relax, to travel, to do what you want to do with the rest of your life. And for most retirees, there's plenty of life left to look forward to; according to statistics, if you've made it to age 65, on average you can expect to live another 15 years if you are a man, and another 19 if you are a woman. And one in 10 retirees can be expected to live into his or her nineties.

If you're still years away from being ready to retire, you should be doing some serious financial planning to ensure that you'll have enough money to support yourself in your retirement years. According to most financial experts, you will need annual funds equal to between 70 and 80 percent of your present income in order to maintain a comfortable lifestyle when you retire. If you're like many older Americans, you are probably counting on Social Security to provide the a major portion of your income after retirement.

But Social Security alone isn't enough to provide an acceptable retirement lifestyle for most people, nor was it ever intended to do so. At its inception during the Depression, Social Security was designed to serve as a safety net, not as the primary source of income for those who had left the work force.

Happily, Congress has recognized the value of allowing workers to plan for their retirement by enacting a number of laws that actually encourage both employers and employees to set aside additional retirement funds. In many cases, these funds are allowed to accumulate tax-free, and in some cases even your contribution to a retirement program is deductible from current income taxes. For the middle class, some of these retirement plans are among the last tax shelters available.

In this chapter, we'll look at some of these retirement programs. Our goal isn't to advise you about how to invest the money you plan to use in your retirement, but to instruct you about the way the law allows you to plan for a secure future when your working days are done.

We'll also look at the cost of nursing home care, and ways in which you can plan to meet those costs if you or a loved one ever needs to spend time in a nursing home facility. However, we don't discuss the criteria to use in choosing a nursing home in this chapter; for that information, you'll need to turn to Chapter Two, where choosing a nursing home is discussed in detail. And for a complete discussion of Social Security and Medicare, turn to Chapter 13, "Your Government Benefits."

YOUR PENSION

More than 50 million American workers belong to pension plans regulated by the Employee Retirement Income Security Act of 1974. This law, along with the Retirement Equity Act of 1984 and the Tax Reform Act of 1986, sets the minimum standards for pension plans in private industry. These federal laws provide that age and service requirements for pension plan eligibility must not be unreasonable, and that employees who work for a specified minimum period for an employer who provides a pension plan will receive at least some pension benefits when they retire.

In general, a plan must allow an employee to participate if the employee is at least age 21 and has completed one year of service for the employer. However, if the pension plan provides for full and immediate vesting, two years of service may be required.

Although plans are permitted to use the "elapsed time" method to compute service requirements, under which the total period of time worked from the date of employment to the date of termination is considered, under most plans a year of service is usually considered to be a 12 month period during which the employee performed at least 1,000 hours of service. Hours of service are defined as hours for which the employee was paid or was entitled to be paid (including pay for vacation time and sick leave) as well as hours for which back pay is awarded.

Generally, pension plans offered by private employers fall into one of two categories. Defined benefit plans pay participants a monthly income from the date of retirement until death. The amount paid out to participants depends primarily on how long you worked for your employer, and how much you earned during your employment there. For example, your defined benefit plan may provide that you will receive a monthly payment of $50 per month for every year of service you had with your employer.

Once an employee becomes a participant in a defined benefit pension plan, retirement benefits begin to accrue. When those benefits become "vested," the employee obtains a permanent right to receive them at retirement age, even if he stops working for or is terminated by the employer before then.

Contributions an employee makes are always fully vested, which means that if you leave your job you are entitled to receive the funds you paid into the retirement plan, plus interest. Your employers' contributions may become vested according to one of two schedules.

Under what's known as "cliff vesting" you must be fully vested not later than after five years of service if your plan is administered for a single employer. If the plan is a multi-employer pension plan (a collectively bargained plan to which more than one employer makes contributions) then full vesting must take place after no more than 10 years of service. You have no vested rights until you complete the appropriate term of service.

If your plan has what's known as "graded vesting" you must be at least 20 percent vested after three years of service, and receive an additional 20 percent in each of the next four years, so that you are fully vested at the end of seven years of service.

The Pension Benefit Guaranty Corporation (PBGC), an agency of the federal government, insures defined benefit pension plans of businesses that run into financial trouble, but this insurance won't necessarily replace all of the benefits you would lose if your employer went out of business. For example, in 1994 the maximum amount a single 65 year old pensioner would receive annually from the PBGC would be approximately $28,000 per year. Married pensioners, or those who retired earlier than age 65, would receive less. And PBGC coverage doesn't extend to defined contribution plans, or to other benefits retirees may have been receiving, such as health or life insurance.

Under a defined contribution plan, such as a 401(k) plan, profit-sharing or money purchase plan, you, your employer, or both contribute a sum of money into your retirement fund every year. The money you contribute is exempt from income tax, and the earnings also accumulate tax-free until you begin to make withdrawals at retirement.

The money contributed to a 401(k) or other defined contribution plan is usually invested in one of several mutual funds. For the most part, how your contributions are invested in the mutual funds offered by your pension plan is left up to you. If the investments you make are wise, you will retire with a large pension fund, which you can either take as a lump sum distribution or turn into a monthly payment. On the other hand, if the investments aren't very good, you may end up with a fairly small sum when you retire.

Keep in mind that while federal laws set minimum standards for pension plans, employers are not legally required to provide any pension benefits at all. Nor do these laws require that pensions pay any specified amount of benefits to recipients. And while federal law protects some retired workers when their pension plans are terminated, at present there is no similar protection when an employer decides to terminate retirees' health care benefits.

In fact, a number of large companies have begun to cut back or eliminate entirely the health benefits they offer to retired workers, and many more anticipate doing so in the future. Retired workers are also seeing increases in the amounts of deductibles and co-payments they must make out of their own pockets. And some companies are now asking retired workers to pay at least a portion of the cost of health care coverage which had previously been provided by the employer at no cost to the retiree.

If you retire at age 65, Medicare coverage will pay for most of your hospital and medical expenses, and a Medigap policy can be purchased to cover the rest. But until there's a national health insurance plan enacted by the federal government, workers who retire before age 65 may find themselves scrambling to obtain health insurance coverage when companies cut back benefits.

KEEPING TABS ON YOUR PENSION PLAN

ERISA requires employers that provide pension plans to give covered employees written information about the details of their pension plan. As a plan participant, you should automatically receive a summary plan description. This is a document that includes information on how your pension plan operates; when you are eligible to receive pension benefits; how to calculate the amount of benefits you will receive; and information about how to file a claim.

Under federal law, you must receive a summary plan description within 90 days after you become a participant in the pension plan. The summary plan description must be written in easily understandable language, but what kind of language suffices to meet this requirement is open to debate. Some summary plan descriptions are written more clearly than others, so if you have questions, you'll need to ask your plan's administrator for additional clarification.

In addition to the summary plan description, under federal law you are also entitled to receive the following information automatically:

- Summaries of any changes in the summary plan description within 210 days of the end of the plan year in which the change took place
- An updated summary plan description at least every ten years (five if there were changes in the plan)
- A summary of the annual report of the plan
- A statement of the nature, form and amount of deferred vested benefits after your employment has ended, and
- Information on pension plan survivor coverage

You also have the right to receive an Individual Benefit Statement, which will tell you the dollar amount of any benefits you have earned under the pension plan and whether you have become vested in the plan. Although your plan's administrator may provide this information voluntarily, it isn't required to do so automatically. Some plans do not, and by law you must request an Individual Benefit Statement in writing if you want to receive one. Under federal law, the plan administrator need honor only one such request annually from each plan participant.

The best way to determine what your annual pension benefits will be when you retire is to examine the summary of your plan's annual report. In it, you will find such information as the amount your pension benefit is reduced if you are married (since your spouse may outlive you and continue to receive pension payments, most employers generally pay a smaller benefit to married employees), and what will happen to your benefits if you take a leave of absence from your job but return to it later. ERISA has established rules that prevent workers from losing all their pension benefits for a break in service, but these rules are very complicated and depend to a large extent on when the break in service takes place and how long it lasts. Your pension plan documents will describe the exact terms that apply to your plan.

You also will need to know if your pension benefits are reduced by part of your Social Security benefit. Some pension plans "integrate" the payments retired workers receive with the amount of benefits Social Security provides. You can find information about integration of benefits in your pension's summary plan description, but you may need to ask your plan administrator for help in figuring out just how much your payments may be reduced.

Some experts suggest that employees who are worried about the financial stability of their pension plan obtain a copy of its annual federal tax return. A copy of this return, made on Form 5500, can be obtained by writing to the PWBA Disclosure Office, U.S. Department of Labor, Washington, D.C. 20210. This form requires the employer to notify the IRS of the pension fund's assets and liabilities, show how the plan's money is invested, and whether the company is current on its payments into the pension fund. Most importantly, it also requires your employer to tell the IRS if it is considering terminating the plan.

PAYMENT OF PENSION BENEFITS

Your summary plan description contains information about when you may retire and begin to receive benefits, as well as how those benefits will be paid. Generally, pension plans pay benefits either in equal monthly payments, or as a lump sum. However, some plans may require that you take a lump-sum distribution if you leave your job before retirement and the total value of your benefits is $3,500 or less. And if the value of your benefits is greater than $3,500, you may be given the choice between an immediate lump sum payment or monthly payments that begin at the retirement age set out in the plan.

By taking a lump sum payment, you have the opportunity to invest your pension funds as you wish. However, unless you put the funds into an IRA, the full amount you receive is taxable in the year in which you receive it unless you use what is known as "forward income averaging". But forward income averaging is only available if you receive your pension funds after you reach age 59½.

If you decide to deposit your retirement funds into an IRA, you need to know about new laws that change the way these funds must be transferred, or "rolled over." Until 1993, you were allowed to take up to 60 days to transfer retirement funds into an IRA without incurring any taxes or penalties. Now, however, your funds must be transferred directly to the trustee for your IRA from your pension plan administrator. If the money is delivered to you, the pension plan administrator must withhold 20 percent of your pension funds and forward that amount to the IRS.

You, however, must come up with the full 100 percent to deposit in your IRA or pay a penalty of 10 percent of the amount withheld. That means tapping your other savings in order to avoid paying the penalty. So unless you need the money and are willing to pay the penalty on an early withdrawal, your best bet is to be sure that your employer's pension plan transfers your benefits directly into your IRA.

PENSION RIGHTS FOR SURVIVING SPOUSES

Under federal law, a pension plan that provides retirement benefits in the form of monthly payments must provide survivor benefits. This means that once an employee becomes partially or fully vested in a pension plan, his or her spouse will automatically be entitled to receive survivor benefits when the covered worker dies.

Survivor benefits must be paid to your spouse if you die before retirement. However, this doesn't mean that benefit payments will begin immediately following your death. Nor will your surviving spouse receive all that you would be entitled to upon retiring.

Instead, payments to your spouse may begin when you would have first become eligible for benefits had you lived. For example, if your pension plan would allow you to begin receiving retirement benefits at age 55, and you die at age 53, your spouse may have to wait two years before benefit payments begin. And generally, the amount of the benefit will be half of what you would have received if you had taken retirement at that age.

If you die after retirement, your surviving spouse is entitled to receive half of what you were receiving as a pension benefit, and payments must continue until the spouse's death. This is what's known as a joint-and-survivor benefit.

In either case, your spouse is permitted to waive these rights to receive pension benefits from your employer. If he or she does, you will get a larger pension benefit during your lifetime. But if your spouse waives this right and you die, no further pension benefits will be paid to your spouse after your death. Unless there's adequate income to maintain your spouse's standard of living without your pension payments, or unless your spouse is suffering from a terminal illness and will die before you do, waiving survivors' rights in order to increase your monthly pension is not a good idea.

INDIVIDUAL RETIREMENT ARRANGEMENTS

An Individual Retirement Arrangement, or IRA, is one method of saving money for retirement. An IRA can be used by anyone who receives earned income. IRAs were created by the

Employee Retirement Income Security Act (ERISA) of 1974. Money that is put into an IRA and any interest or profits that accumulate on these funds may not be subject to taxation until these funds are withdrawn after retirement, depending on the taxpayer's filing status and total adjusted gross income. This results in a double tax savings.

The first tax savings usually occurs when the money is put into an IRA. A full or partial income tax deduction may be allowed each year on an account holder's tax return. If a taxpayer is covered by a retirement plan at work, fully deductible contributions are allowed for couples filing jointly whose adjusted gross income is less than $40,000, and single people or heads of households with adjusted gross incomes under $25,000. Partial tax deductions are allowed for some higher income taxpayers.

For taxpayers who aren't covered by retirement plans at work, a full tax deduction is allowed for single taxpayers and heads of households. Couples filing jointly get a full deduction if their adjusted gross income is not more than $40,000, and a partial deduction if their incomes do not exceed $50,000.

The second tax savings associated with an IRA occurs because the interest earned on the IRA funds also accumulates tax-free. Only after the taxpayer begins to take withdrawals are taxes assessed, and (at least in theory) the taxes owed will be lower, since the retiree will be in a lower tax bracket after retirement than before.

IRAs can be established at various institutions, including banks, insurance companies and savings and loan associations. The money placed in an IRA will be invested in certificates of deposit, stocks, bonds, flexible annuity contracts or similar investment opportunities.

Anyone who has "earned" income qualifies to have an IRA. Earned income includes wages, salaries, commissions or any other income acquired through personal efforts. Income received through dividends, interest, pensions and other types of "unearned" income does not qualify for IRA treatment. Since 1985, however, alimony has been considered earned income for determining IRA eligibility.

Each individual IRA owner decides how much money will be put into his or her account each year, up to the limits set by law. The maximum amount contributed annually to an IRA cannot exceed $2,000 or 100 percent of earned income, whichever is less. This limit applies each year, and a participant cannot put $1,500 into the IRA one year and then make a $2,500 contribution the next year in order to make up the difference.

Married couples may establish separate IRAs if each of them is employed. This means that up to $4,000 ($2,000 in each IRA) may be contributed annually. Even if only one spouse works or has earned income, an IRA account can be set up for the benefit of the non-working spouse. The total annual contribution in this situation is limited to $2,250, which can be divided between the working and non-working spouse's accounts as the couple wishes, provided that no more than $2,000 goes into either account.

Contributions can be made as soon as the IRA is established. While there's no law that establishes a minimum amount which must be deposited to open an IRA, most financial institutions set their own minimum requirements. In most cases, this amount is relatively low, often as little as $25 or $50 at banks and savings and loans.

There is no lower age limit for making contributions to an IRA, but there is an upper age limit. Once a participant reaches the age of 70½, money can no longer be put into the IRA.

Funds generally cannot be withdrawn from the IRA without a penalty until the participant reaches the age of 59½. If money is withdrawn prior to reaching age 59½, there is a 10 percent penalty imposed on the withdrawal, in addition to the normal income tax that must be paid on these funds. However, if the participant dies before reaching age 59½, the estate or heirs will not be penalized with the additional 10 percent tax when the funds are withdrawn. The 10 percent penalty is also inapplicable if the participant has become totally and permanently disabled and withdraws funds before age 59½.

Between the ages of 59½ and 70½, withdrawals can be made whenever the participant wants. Once the age of 70½ is reached, however, withdrawals must begin by April 1 of the following year. The amount of these withdrawals must be at least a minimum amount set by the IRS and based on your remaining life expectancy. For example, if the IRS' life expectancy tables shows that a person of your age can expect to live 14 more years, you must take an amount equal to one-fourteenth of your funds from your IRA in the first year. Amounts are adjusted annually as your life expectancy changes.

Although there are many advantages to opening an IRA, a few disadvantages also exist. One drawback is the limit on the amount of the annual contribution. The $2,000 maximum is relatively low and does not compare favorably to amounts that can be placed in other retirement plans. The 10 percent penalty for early withdrawal is another disadvantage of IRAs.

RETIREMENT PLANS FOR THE SELF-EMPLOYED

Self-employed individuals have been able to set up tax-deferred retirement plans since 1962, when the Self-Employed Individuals Tax Retirement Act, or "Keogh" Act, was passed by Congress. Over the last thirty years the contribution limits have gradually increased from a $2,500 per year limit to a $30,000 per year limit for some plans. Although there are a number of similarities between Keogh plans and Individual Retirement Arrangements (IRAs), there are also some important differences.

Any individual who is self-employed may set up a Keogh account for money earned from self-employment. Doctors, lawyers, shop owners, or anyone who moonlights in order to earn extra money can all be Keogh participants.

In some instances, a Keogh plan is set up by someone who has full-time employees working for him. Federal law requires that these employees be included in the retirement plan when they meet certain eligibility requirements.

The federal government has not set any minimum balance which must be deposited when a Keogh plan is established. However, banks, brokerage houses, insurance companies, mutual fund companies and other institutions which can assist in setting up Keogh plans will often set minimum opening balances for Keogh plans.

In order to take advantage of the tax benefits of a Keogh plan, the account must be established by December 31 of the year for which tax benefits are being claimed. For example, if you want to obtain the benefit of your Keogh on your 1994 taxes, it must be set up no later than December 31, 1994.

This is different from the requirement for IRAs, which can be set up until April 15 of the following year. However, contributions to both Keogh plans and IRAs can be made until April 15 of the next year.

There are three major types of Keogh plans: (1) profit-sharing plans; (2) money purchase pension plans; and (3) defined benefit pension plans.

The profit-sharing plan is the most popular Keogh plan because of its simplicity. Annual contributions of up to 13.04 percent of self-employed earnings or $30,000 (whichever is less) can be made to the retirement plan. A participant can change this percentage from year to year and even opt to make no contribution at all during a given year.

The money purchase pension plan allows you to contribute a higher percentage of your earnings to your Keogh account, but that percentage cannot be changed from year to year. This feature of money purchase pension plans can be an important one, since if other employees are included in the plan you are still obligated to make the designated contribution to their accounts, even in years when your business loses money. Contributions up to the lesser of 25 percent of self-employment earnings or $30,000 can be made to a money purchase plan.

In the first two types of Keogh plans the focus is on how much money will be put into the plan on an annual basis. For this reason they are classified as defined contribution plans. Under the third type of Keogh plan, the defined benefit plan, just the opposite is considered. A participant decides how much money he wants to receive during retirement, and an actuary or Keogh specialist helps him calculate how much money must be contributed each year to meet that goal.

Under the defined benefit plan, a limit is placed on the annual income that can be received each year from the plan. The maximum annual income is the lower of the average income from the participant's three consecutive highest earning years, or a specified dollar figure which is adjusted annually for inflation. In 1993, that figure was approximately $112,000. Based on the goal set by the Keogh participant and the age at which contributions begin, it is possible that 100 percent of self-employment income may be put into the Keogh plan.

Funds from a Keogh plan cannot be withdrawn without penalty until the participant is 59½ years of age. A 10 percent penalty is imposed for early withdrawals. Between the ages of 59½ and 70½ the participant has the option of tapping these retirement funds or letting them continue to accumulate. But once a Keogh participant reaches the age of 70½, he has until April 1 of the following year to begin withdrawing retirement funds, either in a lump sum or in installments.

You may also want to consider opening what's known as a Simplified Employee Pension-Individual Retirement Arrangement (SEP-IRA). A SEP-IRA is much like a Keogh profit sharing plan, and its contribution limits are the same. With a SEP-IRA, you can contribute up to 13.04 percent of self-employment earnings, up to an annual maximum contribution of $30,000. But the SEP-IRA is far easier to administer than most Keogh plans, since it's handled like other IRAs.

You can set up a SEP-IRA at the same financial institutions that offer Keogh plans. Like other kinds of IRAs, you may begin to take withdrawals from your SEP-IRA when you reach age 59½, and you must begin to withdraw funds when you reach age 70½.

FOR MORE INFORMATION

For more information about the federal laws regulating pensions, the U.S. Department of Labor's booklet entitled "What You Should Know About the Pension Law" is available free of charge. You can obtain a copy of this booklet by requesting it in writing from the U.S. Department of Labor, Pension and Welfare Benefits Administration, Washington, D.C. 20210. For information about PBGC insurance, you can write to the Pension Benefit Guaranty Corporation, 2020 K Street, N.W., Washington D.C. 20006.

Another helpful publication *Staying Independent: Planning for Financial Independence in Later Life* is available from the federal government's Consumer Information Center. The booklet costs 50 cents, and can be obtained by writing to:

Consumer Information Center
P.O. Box 100
Pueblo, Colorado 81002

NURSING HOMES

If there's anything that can strike fear in the heart of a person approaching retirement, it's the thought of an expensive stay in a nursing home. And nursing homes are expensive, with annual costs averaging between $30,000 and $40,000 annually. (Keep in mind that this is the average; some nursing homes cost less, while others cost much, much more.)

There are ways to finance a nursing home stay, however, and it's not always necessary to spend every penny you have to do so. But first, let's define some terms.

Generally, nursing homes fall into one of three categories. A skilled nursing facility, or SNF, is one in which nursing care is available 24 hours a day for residents who have serious health care needs. An SNF may also provide rehabilitative therapy.

An intermediate care facility, or ICF, provides less extensive health care than does an SNF, and generally does not provide round the clock nursing care. ICFs are populated primarily by residents who need minimal medical assistance, but who can no longer live on their own and require help with their personal care.

A residential care facility, or RCF, is one which provides housing and help with personal care, such as assistance in getting dressed, eating, and grooming. But a RCF doesn't provide medical or skilled nursing services.

It's the last two of these that causes the greatest number of financial problems for retirees. While Medicare will help pay for care in a SNF after hospitalization, (and provided other conditions are met) it does not pay for intermediate or residential care.

To pay for these services, retirees have several choices. The first is to use their own savings. The second is to rely on their children and other family members to bear the cost of long term nursing home care. For wealthy retirees, the first option is certainly plausible; but for most retirees, the second one is not. Generally, the law doesn't require children to pay for nursing home care for their parents, and most of us would be reluctant at best to even ask our children to do so.

NURSING HOME INSURANCE

A third choice is to purchase nursing home insurance, sometimes called long term care insurance. Dozens of insurance companies now sell nursing home insurance policies, with more than a million such policies now in effect.

Under most nursing home insurance policies, you receive a fixed amount of money for each day you are in a nursing home facility, up to the limits of your coverage. The amount you receive will depend on the exact terms of your policy. For example, in some cases, you may receive a daily benefit of $50, while other policies may simply agree to pay the full daily amount charged by the nursing home.

When you are considering purchasing a nursing home insurance policy, there are some provisions to which you must pay particularly close attention. You'll want to get the answers to these questions before purchasing any nursing home insurance policy.

- *What is the policy's "triggering event" for paying benefits?* Many policies begin payment when your nursing home stay is due to your inability to perform the functions of everyday living, such as eating, dressing, and bathing. Others require a doctor's certification that nursing home care is medically necessary. No policies pay benefits if you simply decide you are tired of living at home, or if you enter a nursing home only for the convenience of your family members.

- *What is the benefit period of the policy?* Some plans will let you pay premiums for twenty years or more, but then only provide coverage for a nursing home stay of two, three, or five years. While statistics show that most long term nursing home stays last less than five years, the best policy to consider is one that will pay benefits for as long as you are alive and in a nursing home.

- *What is the "elimination" period of the policy?* The elimination period is the number of days you must live in a nursing home before policy benefit payments begin. Some policies have no elimination period and will begin paying benefits from the day your nursing home stay begins. But the shorter the elimination period, the higher your premiums will be. If you have other resources you can tap to pay for at least some of your nursing home costs, you can reduce your premium by choosing a longer elimination period.

• *What types of nursing home care are covered?* Some policies will pay only for care in a skilled nursing facility, while others will provide benefits for all levels of nursing home care.

• *What are the policy's provisions regarding preexisting conditions, and what are its exclusions from coverage?* For example, many nursing home insurance policies will not pay benefits when a nursing home stay is due to mental illness. And some policies will not pay benefits if your nursing home stay is the result of a medical condition that existed before the policy was purchased, or may only begin coverage after the policy has been in force for a specified period of time, such as one year.

• *Does the policy give you protection against inflation?* Some policies automatically adjust benefits and premiums annually to account for inflation, while others allow you to buy additional coverage each year.

• *Does the policy require hospitalization before entering the nursing home?* A number of nursing home policies require policyholders to be hospitalized for a specified period of time before going into the nursing home and receiving benefits. Many older individuals enter nursing homes without hospitalization, however, so it pays to find a policy without this requirement.

• *Will the policy pay benefits for home health care?* Although home health care is usually less expensive than that provided in a nursing home, many policies will not pay for home health care, and those that do usually require a higher premium.

The cost of a good nursing home insurance policy can vary pretty widely, depending on a number of factors. The younger you are and the better your health is at the time you purchase your policy, the lower your premiums will be. And you can reduce premiums even further by lengthening the elimination period, or by reducing the amount of the daily benefit you receive.

In general, if you're age 55, you can expect to pay between $1,000 and $2,000 annually for nursing home insurance. At age 65, premiums will run between $2,500 and $4,000, and twice that if you are 75 or older. And if you are older than 75, you may not be able to purchase nursing home coverage at any price.

Remember that unless your policy contains what's known as a waiver of premium, you will have to continue making premium payments while residing in a nursing home, or lose your coverage. Many policies do contain premium waivers, however, and you should be sure one is included in any policy you are considering.

MEDICAID

The fourth and final way to pay for nursing home care is to have the government bear the cost. In fact, nearly half of all nursing home residents have their bills paid by Medicaid.

To be eligible for Medicaid, you must be considered medically needy and in need of assistance. In general, this means that your income and assets must fall below certain levels established by the government. These levels are very low, and so in most cases older Americans in the middle class don't automatically qualify for Medicaid. To obtain Medicaid benefits, they must "spend down" their assets until they are poor enough to be eligible. In a few states, however, no matter how much spending down of assets you do, you will remain ineligible if your income exceeds a specified level.

Medicaid considers the assets and income of both spouses when one or the other seeks nursing home benefit payments. All of the couple's "countable assets" are combined and divided equally between them. Countable assets include stocks, bonds, bank accounts and certificates of deposit, as well as investment property, vacation homes and second vehicles. Non-countable assets include your primary residence, a car, household effects and personal jewelry and clothing, as well as a prepaid funeral or burial account. Life insurance policies may be either countable or non-countable, depending on whether or not you have a cash value policy (countable above a certain value) or a term policy (non-countable). Other kinds of assets may be either countable or non-countable, depending upon how your state has categorized them. Your state Medicaid office can provide the exact list it uses to categorize assets.

The spouse who is not entering the nursing home (called the "community spouse") is allowed to keep all of his or her own income, and half of all joint income, up to a maximum amount established each year. If the amount falls below the poverty line for a family of two, then the community spouse may receive additional allowances from the income of the other spouse (called the "institutionalized spouse). And if housing costs for the community spouse are very high, or if other dependents of the institutionalized spouse live with the community spouse, some additional allowances may also be made.

While in many cases potential Medicaid recipients spend down their assets by paying for nursing home care out of their own pockets, there are some strategies that can be followed to protect your children's inheritance. These strategies allow you to transfer assets to family members, or create a trust, and still qualify for Medicaid.

Transferring assets to your spouse doesn't really help, since as we've already seen Medicaid takes the assets of both spouses into account when determining eligibility. You must transfer your assets to others, such as your children, in order to remove them from consideration by Medicaid. And you cannot simply transfer them one day and enter a nursing home the next at Medicaid's expense.

Under federal law, you must be denied eligibility for Medicaid if you give your assets away or sell them for less than their fair market value within 36 months of applying for Medicaid. You will remain ineligible for Medicaid benefits for 36 months or a period of time equal to the value of the assets divided by the average monthly cost of nursing home care in your state, whichever is shorter.

For example, suppose you gave your vacation condominium worth $60,000 to your daughter and then applied for Medicaid. In your state, the average monthly cost of nursing home care is $3,000. As a result, you would be ineligible for Medicaid for 20 months (60,000 divided by 3,000).

In addition, if you transfer assets to your spouse, and your spouse then transfers those assets to a third person, the ineligibility period applies to those transfers as well.

Some kinds of transfers are exempted from the 36 month ineligibility rules. For example, you may transfer your home to children who have helped care for you in the home during the two years prior to applying for Medicaid.

Another way to transfer assets and remove them from consideration when determining your eligibility for Medicaid benefits is to create a so-called "Medicaid Qualifying Trust." For example, you and your spouse may create an irrevocable trust, naming a third person as trustee and yourselves as the beneficiaries. In this trust, you give the trustee the power to provide you with income generated by the trust assets, but not to return any of the assets to you. Since the trustee cannot make the assets included in the trust available to you, they are not included in the assets considered by Medicaid in determining your eligibility.

Another irrevocable trust that you may want to consider names a trustee and a third party, such as a child or friend, as beneficiary. You are also named as a beneficiary. The trustee is authorized to pay out both income and assets as he sees fit to the third party beneficiary, but does not authorize him to give any of the assets to you. In this way, the assets are protected if you go into a nursing home, since the trustee has no power to give them to you. And the third party beneficiary can obtain assets and give them back to you if necessary, although this person must be someone you can absolutely count on to do so. Otherwise, he can take the assets he receives from the trust and do with them as he pleases.

You cannot use a revocable trust to keep your assets from being counted by Medicaid, since Medicaid assumes that you would revoke the trust and use those assets to pay your nursing home expenses. And you cannot create an irrevocable trust that gives the trustee the power to give you any or all of the assets it contains, since Medicaid assumes that the trustee would make them available to the beneficiary for nursing home expenses.

Creating a Medicaid Qualifying Trust is tricky, and probably not a good do-it-yourself project. A lawyer who is well versed in state Medicaid law should be able to assist you in creating one of these trusts for a relatively modest fee.

CHAPTER THIRTEEN
YOUR GOVERNMENT BENEFITS

Over the past sixty years, the U.S. government and the states have devoted an increasing portion of their budgets to a variety of social programs designed to provide financial security and assistance for the poor, the sick, and the elderly. Beginning with the Social Security Act of 1935, and continuing with such programs as Medicare, Medicaid, Food Stamps, and others, the government has consistently increased the number and types of welfare benefits available to the public.

In this chapter, we will examine the most common government benefit programs, discuss the rules for eligibility and tell you how to apply for these benefits. We will also look at some of the benefits provided to America's military veterans by the government.

SOCIAL SECURITY

Although most Americans think of Social Security in regard to the retirement benefits it provides, in actuality Social Security is an entire system of insurance benefits. In addition to retirement, Social Security also provides disability and health benefits to those who are eligible, as well as providing survivor benefits to the dependents of a worker who dies. In a recent year, 41 million individuals received some kind of Social Security benefits. Of these, 29 million were retired workers and more than seven million were the survivors of a deceased worker, while nearly five million were recipients of disability benefits.

Although most people believe that workers receiving benefits from Social Security are merely being repaid out of their earlier contributions, this belief is a mistaken one. In fact, these benefits are financed by the Social Security taxes paid by those who are currently in the work force.

Currently, employees are taxed at the rate of 6.2 percent of their earnings for their contributions to Social Security's Old Age, Survivors, and Disability Insurance (OASDI). This tax is imposed on earnings up to a maximum amount set by law, and adjusted every year for inflation. In 1993, the maximum amount this tax was imposed on was $57,600.

In addition, workers are taxed at the rate of 1.45 percent for Medicare, the health insurance coverage provided by the federal government. In 1993, the maximum amount of earnings this tax applied to was $135,000; however, with the passage of President Clinton's budget, this maximum was removed, and now all earnings are subject to this tax.

If you work for another, your taxes are matched by your employer, but if you are self-employed you pay double the percentages stated above. However, you are also entitled to take a deduction of some of this amount on your tax return, so the burden on the self-employed is lessened to some extent.

Just about every worker in the U.S. is covered by Social Security, although there are a few exceptions. For example, railroad employees are covered under the Railroad Retirement System, and some federal workers hired before 1984 are covered by a separate Civil Service Retirement System. Some state and local government workers are covered by their own retirement programs, and employees who don't earn enough in wages may not be covered, although they may be eligible for benefits on a spouse's record.

WHO IS ELIGIBLE FOR SOCIAL SECURITY BENEFITS?

In order to qualify for Social Security benefits for themselves and their dependents, workers must earn a specified number of work credits. A work credit is earned when your wages for the year reach a specified amount, which is adjusted periodically. In 1993, workers earned one credit for each $590 they earned. However, no matter how much money you earn, you cannot earn more than four work credits in any one year.

In general, in order to receive retirement benefits from Social Security, you will need to have worked for at least ten years and have earned 40 work credits. The number of credits you need to have earned in order to receive disability benefits varies, depending on the year in which you were born and the year in which you became disabled. For example, a worker who was born in 1929 and became disabled in 1989 needed 9½ years or 37 credits to be eligible for disability benefits. But a worker born in 1965 who became disabled in 1990 needed credit for having worked half the time between age 21 and the time he became disabled. And other variations apply to determine dependents' eligibility for survivors' benefits.

In addition to having earned enough work credits, other criteria must also be met before you become eligible for Social Security benefits. To receive retirement benefits, you must be 62 years of age or older. To receive benefits as the dependent spouse of a retired worker, in most cases you must also be at least 62 years of age, although there are exceptions. And children of retired, disabled, or deceased workers are entitled to benefits as well, provided they meet Social Security's eligibility requirements. Your local Social Security office has the most current information on eligibility requirements.

RETIREMENT BENEFITS

Social Security retirement benefit payments are not automatic, so you must apply for them. Current Social Security Administration rules allow you to apply for benefits as many as three months before the month in which you want to begin receiving them. So if you are planning to retire in May, you can actually apply for benefits in February. In most cases, it's a good idea to apply in advance, since completing the application process can take some time. You are generally not eligible for benefits covering any period before the month in which you apply or in which you become eligible for benefits, whichever is later. However, if you retire at age 65 or older, you can apply for benefits at any time after you turn 65 and receive back payments of up to six months of benefits before the month in which you make your application.

Traditionally, age 65 has been the age for retirement, although many people choose to retire earlier and some choose to retire later. In any case, you become eligible for full retirement benefits under Social Security when you reach age 65. If you decide to retire before age 65, you are eligible to receive a reduced amount of Social Security benefits when you reach age 62. If you retire at age 62, the reduction in your benefit is 20 percent; if you retire at age 63, it's 13$^1/_3$ percent; and if you retire at age 64, the reduction is 6$^2/_3$ percent. This reduction in benefits is permanent, and you will always receive a lower monthly payment than you would have received if you had waited to retire until you turned 65.

On the other hand, your retirement benefits will be higher if you postpone your retirement past age 65, at least for the next several years. For example, in 1993, a worker who delayed retiring until he turned 66 received a 4 percent increase in the benefit he received. However, beginning in the year 2000, the age at which full retirement benefits will be paid will be gradually increased, so that by the year 2027 you will have to be at least 67 years old to obtain full benefits.

Deciding when to retire depends to some extent on considerations other than the amount of Social Security benefits you will receive. Your health, your other sources of retirement income, and your interest and ability in continuing to work all must be taken into account. Even so, knowing how much you can expect to receive each month from Social Security can help you reach your decision.

Beginning in the year 2000, Social Security will provide an annual earnings and benefit statement to every participant in the system. Until then, you can obtain an estimate of how much you will receive when you retire by completing Social Security Form 7004, "Request for Earnings and Benefit Estimate Statement." You can obtain this form from your local Social Security office, or by calling the Social Security Administration's toll-free telephone number, 1-800-772-1213. By calculating your past and present annual earnings along with your own estimate of the money you will earn each year until you stop working, the Social Security Administration can tell you approximately how much you will be eligible to receive upon retirement.

Form 7004 is also used to request the record of your annual earnings as reported to Social Security. It's important to review this information periodically and to report any mistakes you discover in your record. Mistakes can occur if you have changed jobs, worked for more than one employer at the same time, or for any number of other reasons, including simple clerical errors in reporting your correct Social Security number.

In some cases, fraud may also be the reason for an error in your record of earnings. For example, a record that shows income higher than what you've actually earned could mean that your number is being used by someone else, such as an illegal alien. According to some studies, as many as four million individuals are currently using false Social Security numbers — one of these individuals may be using yours. And if the record shows earnings much lower than what you actually earned, it may mean that an employer isn't paying into the system as required, even though he may be withholding the required amount from your paychecks.

Most experts suggest that you check your earnings record at least once every three years, since the statute of limitations on appealing an error in your record is three years, three months, and three days. However, you may request your earnings record at any time and without limitation on the number of requests you make, so you might want to consider making requests more often if you have any reason to be concerned about the potential for errors.

You aren't required to actually stop working in order to receive Social Security retirement benefits. But if you continue working, the benefits you receive from Social Security may be reduced if your wages exceed a specified amount, which changes each year. For example, if you were receiving retirement benefits in 1993 and were under age 65, you could earn no more than $7,680 in wages before having your Social Security benefits reduced. The reduction in benefits would equal $1 for each $2 you earned in excess of this amount.

If you were between the ages of 65 and 70, you could earn up to $10,560 without experiencing a reduction in your retirement benefits.If you earned more than this amount, your benefits would have been reduced by $1 for each $3 you earned in excess of the maximum. However, if you were 70 or older, you could work and earn as much as you wanted without having any reduction in your monthly retirement check.

Since 1983, some Social Security retirement benefits have been taxable. Under the 1983 tax reform law, benefit recipients paid taxes on as much as 50 percent of their Social Security retirement payments, if they were single and their total annual income (including Social Security) exceeded $25,000, or if they were married and their income exceeded $32,000.

Beginning in 1994, an additional income tier was added by the Clinton Administration's 1993 tax bill. Single Social Security recipients are required to pay taxes on up to 50 percent of benefits if their income is between $25,000 and $33,999 and on 85 percent of their benefits if they earn more than $34,000. Married couples are subject to taxes on half their Social Security benefits when their income is between $32,000 and $43,999 and taxes on up to 85 percent of their benefits if their total income exceeds $44,000.

SURVIVORS' BENEFITS

If you earned enough credits to be covered by Social Security, your spouse and your dependents may be entitled to receive benefits when you die. One of the benefits your survivors may be eligible for is a one-time lump sum death benefit payment of $255. In some cases, when the surviving spouse is covered by the deceased worker's benefit record in the month before death, this benefit is paid automatically when a worker dies, and the surviving spouse need not apply to the Social Security Administration to obtain it. In other cases, however, the benefit must be applied for by the survivor within two years of the worker's death. (In this context, "worker" may also mean "retiree.")

The Social Security Administration has established the priority rights to this death benefit payment. First priority goes to a spouse who lived in the same household as the worker when the worker died. Second priority goes to a spouse who was not living with the worker at the time of death, provided that the surviving spouse was entitled to or eligible for benefits based on the deceased spouse's record for the month in which the death occurred. Third priority goes to a child or the children of the deceased worker who were eligible for benefits in the month the worker died (such as minor children, or older children who are disabled).

Dependents who are the survivors of a deceased worker may also be eligible for a monthly benefit payment if they meet one of the following criteria:

- They are the surviving spouse and are age 60 or older
- They are the surviving spouse of any age and are caring for the deceased worker's child under 16, (or a disabled child) who is getting a benefit based on the deceased worker's earnings
- They are the surviving spouse, age 50 or older, and they become disabled no more than seven years after the worker's death or after becoming entitled to benefits based on the deceased worker's earnings
- They are the parents of the deceased worker, are at least 62 years of age, and depended on the deceased worker's support
- They are the unmarried children of the deceased worker and are under 18 years of age (19 if they are full-time high school students)
- They are the deceased worker's unmarried children 18 years of age or older, who became severely disabled before they became age 22, and who remain disabled

In determining survivor benefit payments, the Social Security Administration will check a surviving spouse's earnings record to determine if he or she is eligible to receive benefits on his or her own record. If that payment would be larger than the payment due from the deceased worker's record, the larger payment will be made.

DISABILITY BENEFITS

When a worker covered by Social Security becomes disabled or blind, he may be entitled to receive disability benefits. In addition, certain family members may qualify for benefits based on the disabled worker's earnings record. These relatives would include:

- Your unmarried children (and in some cases, a grandchild) under age 18, or under age 19 if attending high school full-time

•Your unmarried child 18 years of age or older, when that child was disabled before reaching age 22

•Your spouse age 62 or older

•Your spouse of any age who is caring for a child of yours under age 16, or who is disabled and also receiving disability checks

In addition, certain relatives may qualify for disability benefits if you should die. This would include your disabled surviving spouse age 50 or older, when he or she became disabled before you died, or within seven years of your death. And a disabled ex-spouse who is 50 or older may also be entitled to disability benefits based on your record, if your marriage lasted at least 10 years.

The criteria for determining eligibility for Social Security disability benefits are extremely strict. While private disability insurance may pay for short-term disability or partial disability, or provide benefits when you can't work at your regular job, Social Security does not. Under Social Security's eligibility rules, you must be completely unable to do any kind of substantial gainful work for which you are suited, and the disability must be expected to last for at least a year or result in death. To qualify for disability payments on the basis of blindness, your vision must not be correctable to better than 20/200 in your better eye, or your visual field must be 20 degrees or less even when using a corrective lens.

In addition, you must also have worked long enough and recently enough at a job covered by Social Security in order to be eligible for benefits. The exact number of work credits you need will depend on your age when you become disabled. If you become disabled before you reach age 24, you will need to have earned six work credits in the three years immediately before becoming disabled. Between ages 24 and 31, you need to have earned credits for at least half the time between age 21 and the time you become disabled. For example, if you became disabled at age 29, you would need 16 credits, which equal credit for four years out of eight.

And for workers older than age 31, you must generally have the same number of credits as you would need for retirement, and have earned at least 20 credits in the last ten years.

If you have earned sufficient work credits to qualify for disability benefits, your application is reviewed by a physician and a disability evaluation specialist at the Disability Determination Services (DDS) office in your state, which will decide if you are entitled to receive benefit payments.

This evaluation team will review reports submitted by your physician about your disability. Your physician will be asked for information about the nature of your condition and when it began, the medical tests that have been conducted, and the treatment you have received. Your doctor will also be asked about how your condition limits your everyday activities and your ability to perform work related tasks such as walking, sitting, lifting, and carrying.

In some cases, a determination can't be made by the DDS team without further information, and you may be required to take another medical examination. In most cases, your own doctor will be asked to administer this examination. The Social Security Administration pays for the cost of this examination and any other medical tests it may need, and may even pay for your travel expenses related to the examination.

In determining whether or not you are disabled under Social Security's rules, the Social Security Administration considers five questions.

- *Are you working?* If you are and your earnings average more than $500 per month, you cannot generally be considered disabled.

- *Is your condition so severe that it interferes with basic work related activities?*

- *Is your condition found on the Social Security Administration's list of "disabling impairments?"* If so, you are automatically considered disabled. If not, Social Security compares your disability to those on the list to determine if it is of equal severity to a listed condition. If it is, then your claim is approved; if not, the process goes on to the next question.

- *Can you continue to do the work you did during the last 15 years?* If the answer is yes, your claim is rejected. If the answer is no, the evaluation process goes on to ask the final question.

•*Can you do any other type of work, when your age, educa-tion, past work experience and transferable work skills are taken into account?* If you can, no benefits are awarded. But if you can't, you will be entitled to receive disability payments.

If your disability claim is approved, you will receive a writ-ten notice from the Social Security Administration, showing the amount of the monthly benefit you will receive and the date on which payments will start. In general, you will receive your first Social Security disability check in the sixth full month after you became disabled. Along with your check, you will also get a copy of a booklet describing your responsibilities as a disabil-ity payment beneficiary. Among these responsibilities are pro-viding notice to the Social Security Administration if your condition improves enough to allow you to perform substan-tial gainful work.

If your claim is denied, or if you disagree with any decision made by the Social Security Administration in handling your claim, you have the right to appeal the decision, and the Social Security office will even help you complete the paperwork for filing an appeal. Initially, your appeal will lead to reconsidera-tion of your file by persons within the Social Security Adminis-tration other than those who made the decision you are appealing. If you are still dissatisfied, you may then appeal for a hearing before an administrative law judge. If the judge fails to address your concerns, you may then appeal to the Appeals Council, and if you still are dissatisfied, you may file an appeal in the U.S. District Court.

You should apply for Social Security disability benefits as soon as you become disabled, either by visiting, writing to or telephoning your local Social Security office. Since the Social Security Administration must obtain medical information to evaluate your ability to work, it usually takes from 60 to 90 days to process a Social Security disability claim. To help speed your application through the evaluation process, be sure to pro-vide the following documents to the Social Security Adminis-tration:

•Your Social Security number and the numbers of your spouse and children, if they are applying for benefits, and proof of each applicant's age

- The name, address, and telephone number of any doctor, clinic, hospital, or other health care institution that treated you for the disability and the dates on which you received those treatments
- A summary of your employment history during the past 15 years, including where you worked and the kind of work you did
- A copy of your most recent W-2 form from your employer, or a copy of your most recent tax return if you are self-employed
- If your spouse is applying for benefits, the date of any prior marriage

MEDICARE

Medicare is our national health insurance program, providing benefits for people 65 years of age and older, certain disabled people who are under age 65, and people of any age who suffer from permanent kidney failure.

Medicare provides two kinds of insurance protection. Part A Medicare provides hospital insurance coverage; Part B Medicare is a voluntary enrollment program of medical insurance. Part A is financed by payroll deductions of 1.45 percent from each employee's pay, and matching contributions made by employers. Part B coverage is financed by monthly premiums paid by those who choose to enroll in the program.

MEDICARE PART A COVERAGE

Most Americans age 65 or older are eligible for Medicare Part A coverage. You are eligible for Part A benefits at age 65 when you are receiving Social Security retirement benefits, or if you have not yet begun to receive such benefits but are eligible to receive them, or if you would be entitled to benefits based on your spouse's work record and your spouse is at least 62 years old, or if you have worked for a federal, state, or local government which does not participate in Social Security long enough to be eligible for Medicare coverage.

You are eligible for Medicare Part A coverage before you reach age 65 if you have been receiving Social Security disability benefits for 24 months, or you have worked for a federal, state, or local government and meet the requirements of the Social Security disability program. If you receive a disability annuity from the Railroad Retirement Board, you are also eligible for Medicare Part A coverage, although a waiting period must be served before you begin to receive benefits.

Special eligibility rules apply to people who have permanent kidney failure. If you receive maintenance kidney dialysis or receive a kidney transplant, you are entitled to Medicare coverage at any age, provided you are insured or getting monthly benefits from Social Security or the Railroad Retirement Board, or you have worked for federal, state, or local government long enough to be insured by Medicare.

Part A coverage will help pay for inpatient care in a hospital or skilled nursing facility, home health care, and hospice care. If you need care in a hospital, Medicare helps pay for up to 90 days in any Medicare participating facility during each benefit period. A benefit period starts the day you enter the hospital, and ends when you have been out of the hospital or a skilled nursing care facility for 60 consecutive days. If you are out of the hospital for at least sixty consecutive days and then go back in, you start a new benefit period.

In each benefit period, Medicare hospital insurance will pay for all covered services for the first 60 days, except for a deductible. This deductible increases annually; in 1993, it was $652. For days 61 through 90, Medicare pays for all covered services except for a daily coinsurance amount. This amount, which also increases annually, was $163.

If you need to remain in the hospital for longer than 90 days, you can choose to use some or all of the 60 lifetime "reserve days" of coverage Medicare provides. However, once your 60 reserve days are used up, they are gone forever.

When you are in the hospital, Medicare Part A pays for a semi-private room and meals; regular nursing services; operating and recovery room expenses; coronary care and intensive care; drugs, laboratory tests, and x-rays; medical supplies and appliances; physical therapy and other rehabilitative services; and services required to prepare your for kidney transplant surgery.

If you need to remain in a skilled nursing facility after your hospital stay, Part A may also help pay for up to 100 days in each benefit period. The first 20 days are completely covered, but you must make a coinsurance payment for days 21 through

100. In some cases, Medicare Part A will also help pay for home health care after you have been released from the hospital. And if you suffer from a terminal illness, Part A will sometimes help pay for hospice care that provides pain relief and other support services during your final illness.

MEDICARE PART B COVERAGE

To obtain Medicare Part B medical insurance coverage, you must meet eligibility requirements and pay a monthly premium (in 1993, $36.60). When you apply for Medicare Part A coverage, you will have the option of rejecting Part B coverage. If you decide not to enroll at the same time you become eligible for Medicare hospital insurance, you can enroll later, but only during the annual general enrollment period which runs from January 1 through March 31 each year. However, your coverage won't start until July of the year in which you enroll, and your premium will be 10 percent higher for each year that you could have been enrolled in Part B coverage, but weren't. (Special rules may apply if you are covered by your employer's group health insurance policy; your local Social Security office can tell you if these rules might apply to you.)

Once you are enrolled in Medicare Part B medical insurance, you must pay an annual deductible before Medicare will pay for any covered services. Currently, this deductible is $100. After you meet the deductible, Medicare will generally pay 80 percent of the "approved charges" for covered services during the rest of the year. You must pay at least the 20 percent of approved charges which Medicare does not cover. And in some cases, because Medicare's approved charges are lower than what your doctor actually charges, you must also pay any charges in excess of what Medicare approves.

For example, suppose your doctor charges $200 for a service that Medicare approves at $150. If you've already met your deductible, Medicare will pay 80 percent of $150, or $120. You must pay $30 (representing your 20 percent co-payment) and an additional $50 (the amount in excess of what Medicare approves for the procedure).

The list of services covered under Medicare is fairly extensive. However, some services are not covered, including most nursing home care, and other types of custodial care (care which doesn't require any particular skilled medical training). Medical care you get outside the U.S. is excluded in most cases, although in some limited situations care you receive in Mexico or Canada might be covered. Dental care and dentures, routine checkups, immunizations, prescriptions, routine foot care, eye and hearing tests, eyeglasses and hearing aids, and personal comfort items are all excluded from Medicare coverage.

In order to protect yourself against some of the costs which Medicare does not cover, you may want to consider purchasing a so-called Medigap policy. Typically, one of these policies will pay part or all of Medicare's deductible and coinsurance amounts, and most such policies also pay for at least some health services not covered by Medicare.

In order to put an end to the confusion caused by what had been a multitude of Medigap policies, Congress enacted legislation which limited insurers to offering one of ten approved Medigap plans. However, not every Medigap insurer offers each of these plans in every state. Your state's department of insurance can provide information about the plans available where you live. You'll find a list of these offices at the end of Chapter Ten, "Your Insurance."

As you would for any kind of insurance purchase, do some comparison shopping before settling on a Medigap insurance provider. In some cases, annual premiums for identical coverage can vary by several hundred dollars from one company to another.

Under federal law, it is illegal for an insurance company or agent to sell you a policy that duplicates Medicare coverage or a Medigap policy which you already own. This law was passed to protect older Americans from being conned into buying insurance that they don't need, a practice that was relatively common during the 1970s and 1980s.

Another common scam was for an insurance salesperson to claim that the Medigap policy he was offering was authorized by the federal government, and this scam continues even today. If you are ever approached by an insurance salesperson using this tactic, call the U.S. Department of Health and Human Services at 1-800-638-6833 to make a complaint.

If you are covered by your employer's group health plan, your coverage can sometimes be continued or converted to a policy that supplements Medicare coverage when you reach age 65. Your company's employee benefits coordinator can give you information about the specific provisions of your plan.

Finally, the Qualified Medicare Beneficiary (QMB) program is available to help low income individuals qualify for both Part A and Part B Medicare coverage. Under this program, state Medicaid programs are required to pay deductibles, premiums and co-payments for certain elderly and disabled individuals with very low income and extremely limited assets. In 1993, this coverage was expanded to additional individuals through the Specified Low Income Medicare Beneficiary (SLMB) program. You can find out more about the requirements for participating in these programs by calling the federal Health Care Financing Administration toll-free at 1-800-638-6833.

MEDICAID

Because Medicare and Medicaid are often mentioned together when the media discusses government health care programs, many people believe that the two programs are the same. In fact, Medicaid is a program administered by the states in order to help with little or no income or other resources obtain medical care, no matter what their age.

While some of the funding for Medicaid comes from the federal government, other funding comes from state budgets, and each state sets its own rules about Medicaid eligibility and the services provided to Medicaid recipients, although these rules must be in accordance with federally established guidelines. Under these guidelines, all state Medicaid programs must cover at least the following services:

- inpatient and outpatient hospital services
- laboratory, x-ray, and family planning services and supplies
- physician and nurse-midwife services
- rural health clinic services
- periodic screening, diagnosis and treatment for those under 21, and skilled nursing facilities and home health services for those 21 and over.

Most Medicaid programs also pay for other kinds of services, such as long term psychiatric care, dental care, prescriptions, and nursing home care for the elderly.

In general, Medicaid is available to any person over age 65 who are blind or disabled, or who is a member of a family with children which is deprived of the support of at least one parent, and whose income and other resources are very low. Just how low varies from state to state, and each state may adjust this figure from time to time. In addition, other eligibility requirements vary among the states. As a result, it's virtually impossible to discuss each state's requirements in detail here.

To find out if you are eligible for Medicaid in your state and to apply for assistance, you should contact your state's Medicaid office. Depending on the state in which you live, the Medicaid program may be administered by the Public Welfare Department, the Department of Welfare, or the Office of Social Services. You can find out exactly where to go for more information by contacting your state representative, or by calling the general information number for your state government, located in your state's capital city.

FOOD STAMPS

Originally enacted into federal law in 1964, the Food Stamp program today helps more than 1 out of every 10 Americans purchase food at a low cost. Eligible applicants receive food stamps in an amount based on factors such as their incomes and the number of persons in their households. Food stamps are accepted as if they were cash at grocery stores authorized by the government to participate in the Food Stamp program. These stores then deposit the stamps with their banks, which return them to the government for credit.

Food stamps are intended by the government to be used for the purchase of nutritious food. By law, they cannot be used to buy items such as alcoholic beverages, cigarettes or tobacco, cleaning supplies, paper products, or to purchase hot ready-to-eat foods or food that will be eaten in the store. However, some stores do accept food stamps for such purchases, in violation of the law. And in some communities there is a thriving "black market" for food stamps, where food stamps are bought for less than their face value. Anyone who is caught and convicted of defrauding the Food Stamp program is subject to federal criminal penalties, including fines, imprisonment, or both.

All U.S. citizens and aliens with permanent resident status are eligible to participate in the Food Stamp program, and some other legally admitted aliens are also eligible. Eligibility is determined solely on the basis of financial need, as determined by the government. While the eligibility requirements change each year, in general you cannot have household assets in excess of $2,000 ($3,000 if at least one household member is age 60 or older). Countable assets include bank accounts, stocks and bonds; your home and the surrounding lot, household goods, personal belongings and life insurance policies are generally not counted in determining your eligibility for food stamps.

In addition, your income must fall below a certain figure determined annually. For example, in 1993 a household with two individuals under age 60 could have no more than $996 in gross monthly income and no more than $766 in net income in order to qualify for the program. A similar sized household which contained at least one person age 60 or older, or which contained a disabled person could have no more than $766 in net income, but did not have to meet the gross income requirement. For purposes of the Food Stamp program, gross income includes money from just about any source, including work, pensions, child support, public assistance, and veterans' benefits, while net income is what remains after allowable deductions are taken.

To apply for food stamps, you will need to visit your state's Office of Public Assistance or Department of Welfare. You will need to bring documents with you to help establish your eligibility, so be sure to call first to find out exactly what documentation you will have to provide. If your application is approved, you should receive your first supply of food stamps within 30 days of applying for them, although in an emergency you may receive them within five days of making your application. Once you are approved for the program, you will receive a notice telling you the amount of food stamp assistance you will receive, as well as a date when you will be required to reapply to continue receiving benefits.

SUPPLEMENTAL SECURITY INCOME (SSI)

The federal Supplemental Security Income (SSI) program was enacted into law by Congress in the early 1970s. The SSI program is designed to ensure that low income individuals who are disabled, blind, or elderly receive a guaranteed minimum monthly income. Although essential funding for the SSI program is provided by the federal government, the benefits available to SSI beneficiaries vary from state to state, since each state is free to add to the base amount paid out of federal funds. Currently, nearly 6 million Americans receive SSI benefits.

Approval for SSI benefits is based on your physical condition, financial status, and living situation. In general, to be eligible to receive SSI benefits, you must reside either in the U.S. or in the Northern Mariana Islands. You must be a citizen of the U.S., or a legally admitted alien, or an alien living in the U.S. and in the process of receiving permission from the Immigration and Naturalization Service (INS) to stay in the country.

In addition, you must have limited resources and income, and be at least 65 years of age, or be blind, or disabled. The standards for measuring blindness and disability are those used by the Social Security Administration to determine eligibility for disability payments, and are discussed in detail in this chapter's section on Disability Benefits.

To apply for SSI benefits, you should visit your local Social Security Office. To help Social Security process your application as quickly as possible, be sure to bring along the following information and supporting documents:

- Your Social Security card
- Your original birth certificate, or a certified copy, or other proof of your age;
- Information about your income and resources, such as bank books, paycheck stubs or federal income tax returns.

If you believe you are eligible for SSI because you are disabled or blind, you will also have to provide medical records, and the names and addresses of the doctors and health care facilities at which you have been treated.

VETERANS' BENEFITS

Since the 1930s, the Veterans' Administration and its successor, the Department of Veterans' Affairs (VA) has provided a wide variety of health care, disability, educational, financial and other benefits to millions of America's military veterans and their dependents.

If you served in a branch of the military and received any kind of discharge other than dishonorable, chances are you are eligible for VA benefits. However, if you enlisted in the military after September 7, 1980, or if you were commissioned or entered active duty as an officer after October 16, 1981, you must have completed two years of active duty or the full period of your initial service obligation in order to be eligible, unless you have a service-connected disability or were discharged for disability or hadrship late in your enlistment.

In addition, if you served in any of a number of civilian support groups during World War I or World War II, you may also be eligible for these benefits. In order to learn which of these groups have been certified as eligible to receive VA benefits, contact your local VA office, which can also provide you with information about how to obtain the discharge papers necessary for obtaining benefits.

The wide range of benefits available through the VA is too extensive to discuss in detail here, especially since not all veterans qualify for all the programs offered by the VA. You can obtain detailed information about benefits and your eligibility from the Department of Veterans' Affairs office in your area. To help the VA determine your eligibility for benefits, you will need a copy of your discharge form DD214. If you do not have this form, you will need to provide your name at the time of service, branch of service, dates of service and military identification number to the VA office.

CHAPTER FOURTEEN
YOUR TAXES

In the previous chapter, we looked at some of the many benefits provided by the government to those who live in the United States. In this chapter, our focus is on the taxes we pay to fund many of these programs and to finance other government functions.

There are dozens of good books and magazines devoted to telling you ways to legally reduce your taxes and instructing you about how to complete your income tax returns, so we won't discuss those topics here. Our purpose in this chapter is to talk about the laws surrounding income tax preparation, tax filing, and the penalties that can be imposed if you file late or not at all. We will also discuss some of the other kinds of taxes that government imposes, as well as changes in the federal income tax rates mandated by the Clinton Administration's 1993 deficit reduction plan.

We don't discuss property taxes on real estate in this chapter; instead, you'll find a discussion of that topic in Chapter Four, "Your Home." Similarly, you will find a discussion of estate and inheritance taxes in Chapter 15, "Your Estate."

INCOME TAXES

It seems as if some Americans can never quite get used to the idea of paying income taxes. In fact, just about every year another self-proclaimed expert comes forward to claim that the federal income tax is unconstitutional. And just about every year, the federal government puts this so-called "expert" behind bars and imposes penalties and interests on the unpaid taxes he owes to the IRS.

No matter how we may feel about it personally, the legality of the income tax is well established. The passage of the 16th Amendment to the Constitution in 1913 gave Congress the power to levy an income tax, and that power has been consistently upheld by the federal courts.

The Internal Revenue Service (IRS) is the federal government's tax collecting agency. In addition to collecting taxes, it publishes all the federal government's official tax forms and schedules. The IRS also interprets and enforces the tax laws enacted by Congress. Needless to say, those interpretations are designed to maximize the amount of revenue the federal government receives, not to minimize the tax burden placed on individuals and companies.

Not so long ago, the IRS offered taxpayers few opportunities to complain about the treatment they suffered when taxes were collected, or penalties imposed. Many observers felt that the IRS simply was not held accountable for its actions in the same way other government agencies were.

In 1988, Congress enacted the "Taxpayer's Bill of Rights," which imposed new limits on the IRS and required it to inform taxpayers about their rights when the IRS investigated their returns. Under the Taxpayer's Bill of Rights:

- You have the right to professional representation in any IRS hearing
- You have the right to record interviews conducted by IRS agents
- You have the right to end an interview and seek a tax professional's assistance
- You have the right to propose installment payments on taxes you owe
- You have the right to appeal tax auditor's decisions and tax liens
- You have the right to get help from a Problem Resolution Officer (PRO) to prevent the IRS from seizing property or garnishing wages, or forcing you into bankruptcy.

One of the most important provisions of the Taxpayer's Bill of Rights is your right to have a Problem Resolution Officer's assistance. If you have a complaint about an overdue refund, or the imposition of additional taxes, or any complaint about the way you have been treated by an IRS employee, you should contact the Problem Resolution Officer (PRO) at the IRS Service Center for your area. These specially trained personnel then have five days in which to attempt to resolve your problem. If they cannot do so, then you must be advised of the status of the problem and provided with the name and telephone number of the person who is responsible for handling it.

PREPARING AND FILING YOUR TAX RETURN

In response to complaints from taxpayers and Congress, the IRS has spent a great deal of time and money trying to design forms that will simplify the process of paying your federal income taxes. Yet many Americans still find themselves bewildered about which forms to use and how to complete them.

Even with simplification, completing anything more complicated than a Form 1040-EZ (the simplest tax form) can take hours of compiling records, reading instructions, and filling out the appropriate forms and schedules. By its own estimates, the IRS figures it will take the average taxpayer 3 hours and 23 minutes to complete Form 1040, and another hour and a half to complete both Schedule A (Itemized Deductions) and Schedule B (Interest and Dividend Income). That's in addition to the more than 5½ hours you'll spend gathering the necessary documentation and reading instructions on filling out the forms.

As a result, about half of all taxpayers seek outside help in preparing their tax returns, and many others rely on the wide variety of tax preparation guides and software published each year.

There are several kinds of professional help available to assist you in preparing your tax return. If your income is relatively modest and your return isn't too complicated, you may want to consider the use of a tax preparation firm such as H & R Block, which charges set fees for preparing your tax forms. These fees vary with the complexity of your return, but they tend to range from around $50 to $100 for most relatively simple returns. If your return is more complex, or if you need tax planning assistance, you can have your returns prepared by an accountant or CPA. Accountants hourly fees for preparing tax returns generally run around $75 per hour, and having your return prepared by an accountant or CPA will generally cost several hundred dollars or more.

You may also want to consider using one of the nation's approximately 30,000 "enrolled agents" to prepare your tax return. Enrolled agents have been certified by the IRS after taking an examination administered by the Treasury Department regarding tax laws. They must also spend at least 72 hours every three years attending refresher courses in order to maintain their enrolled status. And enrolled agents who belong to the National Association of Enrolled Agents are required to take at least 30 hours of tax course annually. Generally, having an enrolled agent prepare your return will cost you somewhere between what you would pay at a tax preparation service and the fee a CPA would charge.

If you are over 65, another form of tax preparation assistance may be available. In most parts of the country, college students majoring in accounting or law will help prepare simple income tax returns for senior citizens, often at no cost to the individual. You can find out about programs of this type in your area by looking for announcements in your local newspaper beginning each January. If your community has a council on aging, or department of senior citizen affairs, it should also be able to provide you with information about the availability of these or other volunteer tax preparation programs in your area.

Remember that no matter who actually prepares your return, you remain responsible for its accuracy, and any misstatement of income or deductions can lead to the IRS assessing back taxes, interest and penalties. For that reason, it's important that you have your tax preparer take the time to explain how he or she arrived at your tax liability figures.

If you don't understand the preparer's explanation, it may be worthwhile to have the forms reviewed by another, independent tax preparer. However, just because two tax preparers disagree about the way to prepare your return doesn't mean that either of them is necessarily lax or negligent. Remember that interpretations of the tax laws can vary, and a more aggressive tax preparer may feel that you are entitled to credits and deductions that a more conservative one would not. To some extent, you will need to rely on your own judgment and the comfort level you feel about filing an aggressive return with the IRS.

You can also call the IRS for advice about particular aspects of your tax return, but be forewarned that some studies have shown that IRS telephone advice is incorrect as often as 40 percent of the time. And even if you rely on the IRS for information in preparing your return, you may not be able to avoid additional taxes and interest simply because the IRS operator you spoke with gave you the wrong advice. The only advice from the IRS that protects you later from attempts to impose additional taxes and penalties is advice you get in writing — and the IRS doesn't give written advice freely.

Remember to keep copies of any records you provide to your tax preparer. The U.S. Tax Court has ruled that you are responsible for substantiating the deductions you claim on your tax return. The fact that your tax preparer lost the records supporting your return does not excuse you from this obligation.

You are also responsible for ensuring that your return is sent to the IRS on time, or that any necessary extensions for filing are sent before the April 15th deadline.

While April 15th has become the most dreaded day on many taxpayers' calendars, it is possible to receive an automatic four-month extension for filing your income tax return. To do so, you'll need to file IRS form 4868 by April 15th. By filing this form, you will be able to delay filing your tax return until August 15th. If you need even more time and you can show a good reason for needing another extension, the IRS may grant an additional filing extension until October 15th.

Keep in mind that while you can receive an extension of time for filing your return, you won't receive an extension for paying taxes, which are still due on April 15th. By that date, you will have to make an estimated payment of what you owe. If your estimate is too low, you will be faced with a 1/2 percent per month penalty as well as interest on the balance you owe when you complete your return. Of course, if you overestimate your tax liability, you will receive a refund of the amount you overpaid.

What happens if your tax return contains an error? Of course, you'll be required to pay any additional tax you owe, along with any interest or penalties that may have accrued. However, some tax preparers will agree to pay the interest and penalties if the error was their fault. Find out your tax preparer's policy in advance and get it in writing, since penalties and interest can be hefty additions to your tax bill.

If you discover an error after you've filed your return, you may be able to sidestep any penalties if you file an amended return listing the additional income. And similarly, if you discover that you failed to take a legitimate deduction or credit on your return, you can file an amended return and ask for a refund of the amount overpaid.

GETTING A TAX REFUND

One of the few pleasures many of us experience in regard to paying income taxes is getting a refund each year from the IRS. In fact, however, getting a big refund check means that you either had too much withheld from your paycheck, or you overpaid your estimated taxes during the previous year. In essence, getting a refund from the IRS means that you've given the government what amounts to an interest free loan of your money.

To reduce the size of your refund, you should ask your employer for a new Form W-4. You can take additional allowances on this form to reduce the amount of tax withheld from each paycheck. Just be sure that the amount of tax withheld from your check equals the amount of tax you actually owed during the previous year, or at least 90 percent of the amount you will owe this year.

If you are self-employed you can reduce the amount of your estimated tax payments, but again you need to exercise caution and avoid reducing them too much, or you could be subject to penalties for underpayment.

There are other good reasons for avoiding putting too much of your money into the hands of the IRS by having too much withheld from your check. Under federal law, the IRS can withhold all or part of your annual income tax refund for a variety of reasons. If you owe back child support, defaulted on a federally guaranteed student loan, Veterans' Administration loan or Small Business Administration loan, or if you owe back taxes, penalties or interest on a previous year's taxes, your entire refund may be withheld to satisfy your outstanding debt.

Many a divorced spouse has been surprised to have an anticipated income tax refund withheld to pay back taxes owed from a joint return filed while she was still married. While it may be possible to get this money released by claiming that she filed her return as an "innocent spouse" who did not have actual knowledge of what the joint return she signed contained, getting an innocent spouse ruling is time consuming and may not even be successful. All in all, it's best to let the IRS have no more of your money than it needs to meet your current tax obligation.

Under federal law, if you file your return by the April 15th deadline and you don't receive your refund by June 1st, you are entitled to receive interest on the refund, unless it's being held back for one of the reasons stated above. The earlier you file your return in the tax season, the less time you'll have to wait to receive your refund, since IRS workers have fewer returns to handle early in the year. If you will be entitled to a refund from the IRS, you should probably file your return as soon as possible in order to receive your refund quickly. It may take as few as three or four weeks to receive a refund if you file in January, but if you wait until April, eight to ten weeks could pass before you get your refund check.

If you haven't received your tax refund from the IRS within ten weeks of filing your return, you can check on its status by calling the IRS' special Automated Refund Information (ARI) telephone number. You'll find this number listed in the instructions for preparing your tax return. When you call this number, you will need to provide your Social Security number, your filing status, and the amount of the refund you are expecting to receive. The IRS can then give you an estimated time for the delivery of your refund check.

If you don't receive your refund in the promised time limit, your next step is to contact the IRS Center where you mailed your return. Include your name, address, Social Security number and an explanation of your problem. Send your letter by certified mail, return receipt requested, and keep a copy of your correspondence for your files.

If you still don't get your refund, or if you are dissatisfied with the response you receive, contact the Problem Resolution Officer at the IRS Service Center where you mailed your return. The PRO will look into the matter and report back to you within five working days. If your refund is being withheld because of overdue child support or an unpaid government loan, the PRO will provide you with information about the steps you will need to take to contest the withholding.

WHEN YOU OWE ADDITIONAL TAXES

If you will receive a refund from the IRS, the earlier you file your return, the more quickly you will get your refund check. On the other hand, if you will owe money to the IRS, there's really no good reason to file your return before the April 15th deadline.

Even if you have money withheld from your paycheck, you may still owe additional taxes if you have not had enough withheld, or if you have income from investments, capital gains, and bank account interest. To determine the best time for you to file, you should do at least an estimate of your total tax liability and the amount you have already paid to the IRS early in the year.

If you will owe more than $500 when you file your income tax return, you should either change the amount of your withholding or file estimated tax payments. Together, these payments should equal the amount of your annual tax liability.

Generally, estimated tax payments are made by filing Form 1040-ES on a quarterly basis, along with 25 percent of what you expect to owe at the end of the year. If your income varies widely, you are permitted to make estimated tax payments as income is earned (you can also pay the full amount at the beginning of the year, but there's generally no good reason to do so). For more information about estimated taxes, you can visit your local IRS office, or contact the IRS at the number listed in the back of the instruction book accompanying your Form 1040.

If you owe more than you expected to when April 15th rolls around and can't pay the full amount, file your return and send in as much of what you owe as possible. Failing to file a return or pay taxes can subject you to some very stiff financial penalties, including a fine of up to 25 percent of the total amount of taxes you owe, ½ percent per month as a penalty for late payment, and interest charges of seven percent annually.

If you don't have the money on hand and there's no good way to raise it, you should inform the IRS as soon as possible of your predicament. If your inability to pay is due to long-term unemployment or other hardship, you can file Form 1127, "Request for Extension to Pay Taxes." You can receive an extension to pay your tax bill until June 15th by filing this form. Or you can file Form 9465, requesting an installment plan, along with your tax return and a payment for as much as you can afford.

If you simply file your return without making the required payments (a practice we don't recommend), the IRS will contact you by mail with a demand for payment within about two weeks after you file. If you still don't have the money, call the IRS at the number listed on the demand to see if it's possible to work out a payment schedule. But don't be surprised if the IRS takes a tough stand and demands payment. The IRS can and will seize bank accounts and real estate and garnish your paycheck if you owe taxes and ignore its demands for payment.

STATE INCOME TAXES

In addition to the federal income tax, every state except Alaska, Florida, Nevada, South Dakota, Texas, Washington and Wyoming also imposes an income tax on those who live within the state's borders, or who live elsewhere but earn income within the state. Many cities now impose an income tax as well. These taxes are generally based on the adjusted gross income a taxpayer reports to the federal government, with additional modifications for taxes paid to another state, additional deductions for interest earned on bonds issued by the state or cities in the state, and sometimes with income added back in. For example, Alabama and New Jersey allow taxpayers to deduct more for medical expenses than the federal government permits, but Colorado, Illinois, and other states require you to add your federal deduction for state income taxes back into your taxable income.

Like the IRS, state revenue departments look with great disfavor upon those who fail to file their tax returns on time or fail to pay the taxes they owe, and many of the remedies used by the IRS will be used at the state level as well. Because state income tax laws vary so widely and change so frequently, it's important to get personal advice from an accountant or another tax professional for any questions you may have about the specific laws in your state.

INCOME TAX AUDITS

Few occurrences strike as much terror in the human heart as an audit notice from the Internal Revenue Service. Although only about 1 percent of all tax returns are audited in any one year, the chance still remains that one day you may be faced with an audit of your income taxes. Over time, about half of all taxpayers will be audited at least once, and the odds increase along with the amount of income you report.

If you do receive correspondence from the IRS in the mail, don't panic. In some cases, what you receive may not be an audit notice at all, but an "automated adjustment notice," telling you that you owe additional tax. You're most likely to receive one of these because of an error you made in computing your income or taxes, or because you failed to report some income to the IRS which was reported to it on a 1099 form, such as dividends or interest.

Just because you receive an automated adjustment notice (also called a CP2000) doesn't mean that you must pay the amount assessed without question. In many cases, the IRS itself has made a miscalculation of the taxes you owe, or entered data about your income incorrectly. Under federal law, you have the right to appeal an automated adjustment notice in writing within 60 days. Even when an actual audit is conducted, you may not need to actually meet in person with an IRS agent. Some audits (called "correspondence audits") are conducted entirely by mail. In a correspondence audit, you're asked to justify some part of your return by providing additional documents through the mail.

If you are asked to send supporting documents to the IRS through the mail, never send originals, since they may go astray. Always send photocopies, and mail any correspondence by certified mail, return receipt requested, so you will have proof that you mailed your response by the deadline the IRS gave you for responding to its inquiry. (Receipts provided by private delivery services such as Federal Express may not be accepted by the IRS or the Tax Court).

While the correspondence audit notice you receive will often include a telephone number for you to call, doing so is generally a waste of time. The IRS employee who takes your call will not have your file available, and that means you will end up having to handle the matter by mail anyway. If you do call, however, be sure to keep a detailed log of the date and time of your call, as well as the name and title of any IRS employee with whom you speak.

No matter what, never ignore a letter or other inquiry from the IRS about your taxes. Doing so may subject you to additional negligence penalties, and could lead to a full-blown audit that might otherwise have been unnecessary.

When the IRS first contacts you about an audit, it will send you a copy of its publication entitled "Your Rights as a Taxpayer." In this booklet, you will find an explanation of the Taxpayers' Bill of Rights enacted by Congress, as well as a description of how the IRS conducts audits and collects unpaid taxes.

If an audit must be conducted in person, it will either take the form of an office audit where you visit the auditor at his or her office, or a field audit (the auditor comes to your home or business). Most IRS audits are office audits, and an office audit is always preferable, since it prevents the auditor from going on a fishing expedition in the records at your place of business.

Even if the IRS requests a field audit, you can keep the auditor away from your business or home by providing all of your financial records to your tax adviser and asking that the audit be conducted at his place of business. While this should be enough by itself to stop an audit from being conducted in your home, you may also have to show that a field audit would be disruptive to your business to keep the auditor away from your office.

Generally, you will have at least several weeks to prepare for an IRS audit, so you should have plenty of time to put together the documents you will need to support your return, such as canceled checks, receipts, brokerage statements and bank records. If you need extra time, however, you may request a change from the original appointment time set by the IRS.

Since the IRS generally has three years from the date you filed your return or its due date (whichever is later) to begin an audit, you need to keep your tax records and supporting documents for at least that long. This three-year limit doesn't apply, however, if you understated your income by more than 25 percent, in which case the IRS then has six years in which to assess additional taxes, and if you filed a fraudulent return, there is no time limit at all. As a result, it's best to keep your tax records on file for at least six years. And some records, such as those relating to your IRA or other retirement benefit plans, should be kept indefinitely.

In some cases, the IRS may not be able to complete an audit within the three year time limit expires, and may ask you to agree to a voluntary extension of this time limit. While you don't have to agree to such an extension, the usual IRS response to a refusal is to disallow every questionable item on the return being audited. A better strategy is to negotiate an extension with a definite expiration date, and to limit the extension to only those items which are in question at the time the extension is granted. In this way, you can keep the IRS from expanding its inquiry into other areas of your return during the extension period.

Most experts recommend that you have the person who prepared your taxes appear at the audit with you to explain how your return was done. In fact, if your tax return was prepared by an attorney, a CPA, or an "enrolled agent," he or she can appear in your place, and you don't even have to attend the audit. (Any other kind of tax preparer may accompany you to an audit, but can't represent you.) Many tax advisers even suggest that it's better for the taxpayer to stay away, since the professional representing you doesn't have the same emotional involvement in the outcome of the audit, and so isn't as likely to say or do something that raises the suspicion or the ire of the auditor.

In the event that you decide to appear at the audit, it may be tempting to take a tough attitude with an IRS auditor, but it's always a bad idea to give in to the temptation. Being rude to the auditor won't help your case any, and may actually prompt a more penetrating examination of your records than would have occurred otherwise.

The most important tip we can give you if you are ever called for an audit by the IRS is this: Never give an IRS auditor any more information than what was requested. Unless you are one of the 50,000 unlucky souls called in for what's called a Tax Compliance Measurement Audit, which looks at every single item on your tax return, your audit will be limited to certain areas of your return, which you will know about in advance. Limit your responses to any questions the auditor asks to these areas. If the auditor starts off on a fishing expedition into other areas of your return, tell him that you do not wish to discuss them until he makes a formal request to audit that portion of the return.

Never respond to an auditor's rejection of a deduction or tax credit by saying something like "Well, we've always taken that deduction in the past." The auditor doesn't care, except to use that information to question previous returns you have filed. And remember that if the auditor is rude or unpleasant, you are legally entitled to request the assignment of another auditor.

When the audit is concluded, you will receive a copy of the auditor's report. If you disagree with the auditor's conclusion that extra tax is due, you can make an immediate appeal to the auditor's supervisor. If the auditor's supervisor agrees with the report's conclusion that you owe more money to the IRS, you have the right to file an additional appeal within 30 days to the IRS Appeals Division.

If you pursue your appeal to this step, chances are you may be able to settle your case for an amount that's less than what the auditor originally imposed as an additional tax. That's because Appeals Division officers can consider the cost of litigation and the risk that the IRS might lose a court appeal in evaluating your claim. According to statistics, approximately 9 out of 10 cases heard by the Appeals Division are settled.

If you still aren't satisfied, you can take your appeal to Tax Court. And if the amount in question is less than $10,000, you can use the Tax Court's Small Claims Division, which uses simplified procedures, although you may want to have an attorney or other tax professional's assistance in presenting your appeal. Eventually, you can even appeal to the U.S. Supreme Court, but remember that the Supreme Court hears only a handful of the many petitions brought before it in any session. Unless your tax issue is one that will have a far-reaching effect, it's unlikely that the Supreme Court will hear your case.

Of course, the best way to avoid trouble with the IRS is to minimize the possibility that your income tax return will raise a question when you send it to the IRS. That means you should be sure to file all the required forms and answer all the questions asked on your return, even if they don't seem to apply to your situation. You will also want to be sure to double check the accuracy of your W-2 and any 1099 forms you receive, and be careful to report all the income on these forms to the IRS.

RECENT CHANGES IN FEDERAL TAX LAWS

In 1993, Congress approved a number of changes in the federal tax laws designed to increase revenue and decrease the federal deficit. While some of these changes affect a relatively small number of taxpayers, others will have a more far reaching effect. Some of the more significant changes include:

- Increasing the number of tax brackets from three to five. Under the old tax laws, the top tax rate was 31 percent.Under the new law, a 36 percent top tax rate is imposed on singles earning over $115,000, and married couples who file jointly and earn more than $140,000. And for anyone earning more than $250,000 (whether single or filing jointly) the top rate increases to 39.6 percent.

- Increasing federal taxes on most gasoline and diesel fuel purchases by 4.3 cents per gallon, and extending a previous 2.5 cent per gallon increase that was due to expire in 1995 for an additional four years.

- Reducing the number of allowable deductions related to job-related moving expenses. Under the old tax laws most direct and indirect expenses connected with a job-related move were deductible if the taxpayer's new job was at least 35 miles farther from the old home than was his old job. Now, the distance requirement is 50 miles, and expenses for househunting trips and meals en route from the old home to the new one are no longer deductible.

- Increasing the amount of tax on affluent Social Security recipients. Under the previous law, the maximum amount of Social Security subject to tax was 50 percent. Under the new law, a single person receiving Social Security and having a total income of $34,000 or more, and a couple with income in excess of $44,000 will pay taxes on as much as 85 percent of their Social Security benefits. Singles earning between $25,000 and $33,999, and couples with incomes between $32,000 and $43,999 will still pay taxes on up to half their Social Security benefits.

- Removing the cap on the Medicare tax. Under the old law, wages and income from self-employment up to $135,000 were subject to Medicare taxes (employees pay 1.45 percent, which is matched by their employer, while the self-employed pay 2.9 percent). Under the new law, the cap is removed, and Medicare tax is owed on every dollar earned during the tax year. More than 1 million Americans will pay additional taxes as a result of this change.

- Cutting the deduction for business meals and entertainment expenses from the previous level of 80 percent to 50 percent, and eliminating the deduction permitted for club dues when membership was primarily for business purposes.

In some cases, the deficit reduction bill actually lowered taxes and expanded tax credits. For example, under the old law working families with children could qualify for an earned income credit of up to about $2,400 if their income fell below $23,000. Under the new law, the maximum credit is raised to more than $2,500, the income requirement for families is raised to $25,300, and childless workers between age 25 and 64 with incomes below $9,000 would be eligible for up to $306 in earned income credit. It's estimated that more than 22 million households will qualify for at least some earned income credit under these new eligibility rules.

OTHER TAXES THAT GOVERNMENTS COLLECT

While the federal government and many states get much of their funding through income taxes on individuals and corporations, there are many other kinds of taxes assessed on Americans.

One of the most common of these is the sales tax. Currently, 46 states and the District of Columbia impose sales taxes on at least some purchases, and many cities and towns also impose a sales tax. Depending on where you make your purchase, you may pay as much as 10 percent in local and state sales taxes.

Unlike income taxes, which are "progressive" (that is, the more you earn, the more you pay) sales taxes are considered "regressive" taxes, since they are assessed at the same rate on everyone, regardless of income. A person who makes $10,000 per year must pay the same sales tax rate on his or her purchases as the person making $1 million or more.

States can only charge sales taxes on items actually purchased within their boundaries; however, they may also impose a use tax on items bought elsewhere for use inside the state. Collecting these taxes has posed something of a problem, however, since state revenue departments can't guard checkpoints and roadblocks to find out what you've purchased outside the state (although most would probably like to do so). However, some states have become more aggressive about collecting use taxes in recent years, even going so far as to post auditors at major airports and other points of entry to collect data about goods brought home from foreign countries.

A tax that's similar to a sales tax is an excise tax. An excise tax is money the government collects in return for letting you pursue a certain occupation, or buy certain kinds of items, such as alcohol or tobacco products (so-called "sin taxes" on these items are actually excise taxes). Duties on foreign goods brought into the U.S. collected by the Customs Service are another kind of excise tax.

There are almost as many kinds of excise taxes as there are stars in the sky. Bought a ticket to a concert or a sporting event? You've probably paid a state or city excise tax on it.

Rented a car on a business trip? There's an excise tax on that, too, as well as on the cost of the hotel room you stayed in.

In some larger cities, these excise taxes on services used by business visitors and tourists can be substantial. For example, rent a car at O'Hare International Airport in Chicago and you'll be charged a tax of 18 percent for the privilege. Tax rates on tourists visiting New York, Philadelphia, Los Angeles and other big cities are comparable.

Federal estate taxes and state inheritance taxes assessed on the money you leave your loved ones provide funds to the government even after you've died. For a discussion of these taxes and ways in which you can minimize them, be sure to read Chapter Fifteen, "Your Estate."

CHAPTER FIFTEEN
YOUR ESTATE

In this chapter, we'll look at one of the most important legal documents a person can have, a valid Last Will and Testament. We'll also talk about establishing a support trust for your children, and discuss some of the estate planning tools you can use to minimize probate costs and estate taxes. Finally, we'll examine the estate planning craze of the 1990s, the living trust, and show you why having one may not be necessary, or even desirable.

Before we begin, however, it's important for you to know that the whole field of estate planning is extremely complex. Federal and state estate and inheritance tax laws are a jumble for even experienced lawyers, and interpretations of these laws vary widely. In addition, as the federal and state governments look for more ways to get their hands on your money, the likelihood that the current laws will be revised in ways that will cost you and your loved ones a bigger share of the wealth you have accumulated over the years increases almost every day.

If your estate is large, it's probably a good idea to get some professional, up-to-the minute advice about planning your estate. You may also want to consider subscribing to ProSe Associates' quarterly newsletter for details about the latest developments in this field. You'll find information about how to subscribe elsewhere in this book.

YOUR ESTATE
Your estate is made up of all the property you own, or in which you have some ownership interest at the time of your death. Under federal estate tax law, your estate consists of your

individual property, your share in jointly owned property, life insurance, pension benefits, death benefits, property you transferred to another while you were still living, but which you maintained control of, and anything else you own when you die, such as your right to the repayment of debts that are owed to you. Debts and taxes that you owe to others are also considered a part of your estate, and must be paid out of your assets after you die.

The federal government imposes no estate taxes on any property you leave to your surviving spouse. In 1993, you could transfer up to $600,000 to persons other than your spouse without incurring federal estate taxes, but this amount may change in the future, as Congress has considered lowering the exemption to only $200,000.

Some states charge inheritance taxes, which are payable not by the estate but by the beneficiary. However, most provide relatively large exemptions for spouses and surviving children. When you leave property to more distant relatives, or to someone unrelated to you, the amount of the inheritance tax assessed in some states can be fairly large. In some states, the amount of inheritance tax charged to an unrelated beneficiary can be 17 percent or even more.

YOUR LAST WILL AND TESTAMENT

Every adult should write and execute a valid last will and testament. Without one, you give up the right to decide how your property will be distributed when you die. And although there are other ways to distribute what you own, such as joint tenancy with right of survivorship, living trusts, and tenancy by the entirety, experience shows us that none of these methods ever covers all of a person's property.

For example, suppose you are killed in an airplane accident. You've put your bank accounts in joint tenancy with right of survivorship, your house and car are titled the same way, and your life insurance policy names a beneficiary. However, when you charged your airplane ticket to your credit card, you automatically received $100,000 in accidental death coverage. The proceeds of that insurance protection belong to your estate, since you didn't have the opportunity to name a beneficiary on the policy. That money will be distributed according to state law, and it may not be done in the way you would have preferred.

The popular belief is that if you have a spouse but no children and you die without a will, your spouse will get everything you leave behind. Unfortunately, that's not necessarily true. Every state has its own laws (called laws of intestate succession) about how to distribute the property of a person who dies without a will. Your spouse may end up with only one-half of your property, or even less. If you have parents who are living, they may be entitled to a portion of your estate.

If you don't have a spouse or children, the state may give some of the money to your parents and some to your surviving brothers and sisters. They may not need the money as badly as someone else you know and care for. Having a will is the only way to make sure money and property you may not even know you have goes to the people you want to receive it.

Another reason a will is so important is that it allows a parent to make decisions about who will take care of surviving children, and who will manage the money and property left to them until they are old enough to manage it themselves. In most cases, you would probably expect your surviving spouse or the child's other parent to handle this responsibility. But it's possible that you and your spouse could die simultaneously, or very soon after one another.

Without a will, a court will have to make the decision about who to name as your child's guardian for you. Courts try very hard to make good decisions about these issues, but a court may not make the same decision you would have made. Having a valid last will and testament is the only way to make sure your children go to the people who you believe are most likely to raise them the way you would have raised them yourself.

Finally, if you're living in a non-traditional relationship, a valid last will and testament is essential if you want to provide for the surviving partner. State laws recognize the rights of a legal spouse to share in your estate, but they don't extend those rights to a live-in partner. To make sure that someone you aren't legally married to is entitled to receive a share of your estate, you have to provide for that person in your will.

HOW TO WRITE YOUR WILL

The basic requirements for making a valid will are relatively uncomplicated. The person making the will, called "the testator," must be legally competent. To be legally competent, the testator must be over the minimum age set by state law (18 in most states), and of sound mind. A person is considered of sound mind when he understands the nature and extent of the property he owns, and recognizes what lawyers refer to as the "natural objects of his bounty." Generally, that means the testator knows who his family members are, although it doesn't mean the testator actually has to leave them any of his property. The testator also has to know that by making a will he is deciding how his property will be distributed when he dies.

Although the exact form for writing a will can vary, most simple wills follow a similar pattern. The will begins with a title at the top of the first page, such as "Last Will and Testament of John Jones." In the first paragraph, the person making the will states his name, place of residence, and declares that what follows is his last will and testament, and that it revokes any and all previous wills and codicils. This paragraph may also include a statement that the testator is of sound mind and under no duress, but adding such a clause doesn't mean that the will can't be challenged if someone believes you were incompetent or under the undue influence of another when you made the will.

The next paragraph usually describes the testator's marital status, the name of the spouse (if any) and the names of the testator's children.

In the next paragraph, the testator names an executor to manage the details of probate, and authorizes him to hire any professional assistance he needs, such as accountants or lawyers, and to pay for these out of the estate. It can also be used to direct the executor about how any taxes should be paid.

The next paragraphs will make any gifts of specific property to specific beneficiaries. For example, if you want to leave your antique dueling pistols to your nephew Claude, this is the place to do it. If you're leaving your house, car, and boat to your daughter Amie, you'll make that gift in one of these paragraphs.

After you've made specific gifts, you'll make a gift of your residuary estate. Your residuary estate is everything that's left over after you've made all your specific gifts.

After you've made a distribution of all your property, your will must be executed correctly in order to be legally enforceable. In general, this means it must be signed at the end, and in front of the legally required number of witnesses. Most states require two witnesses, while a few others require three. Having more witnesses than required isn't a problem, but having too few witnesses can invalidate your will. Witnesses have to be of legal age, and no one named in the will to receive property (known as a beneficiary) should serve as a witness, since that may also invalidate the will, at least in regard to the property left to that beneficiary.

When you sign your will, most states require that you "publish" it. That means you must tell your witnesses that the document you're signing is your last will and testament, and that you're asking them to sign it as witnesses. The witnesses don't have to know what your will says, but they do have to know that it is your will.

Sign only the original of your will, so that if you decide to change or revoke it later, you'll have to destroy only the original. Signed copies could turn up later and make for a confusing and expensive situation as the court tries to decide which will is the valid one.

In some states, you can create an additional document known as a self-proving affidavit, which you and your witnesses sign in front of a notary public. This affidavit states that you signed your will, the witnesses saw you sign it and signed it themselves as witnesses, and that they believed you were of sound mind and memory at the time of the signing.

A self-proving affidavit can speed up the probate process in the states where they are allowed, since your executor won't have to locate the witnesses and bring them into probate court to testify as to the authenticity of your will.

Once your will is properly signed and executed, you should keep it in a safe place, such as a fireproof box in your home. Don't put your will in a bank safe deposit box, since there can be delays if your state tax authority or the Internal Revenue Service decides to seal the box until an inventory can take place.

While you can pay a lawyer to draw up a simple will, there are some very good software packages that can help you create your own will without a lawyer's help. One such package is OverDrive System's "Home Lawyer," which can help you create a valid will, including a support trust for minor children.

You may also want to consider using one of the many "will kits" available at book and stationery stores. While it's possible to create a valid will using one of these kits, you must be very careful to observe all the formalities required by your state's laws when you execute the will. However, if the kit doesn't seem to meet your specific needs, or if you don't understand how to use it, you will be better off visiting an attorney for assistance. In most parts of the country, you can have a lawyer write your will, provide the witnesses and supervise the signing for less than $100. Of course, the more complicated your will is, the more a lawyer's assistance will cost.

NAMING AN EXECUTOR

Your executor, or personal representative, is the person who will be responsible for administering your estate. You should choose this person carefully. The responsibilities of an executor are serious, and you'll want someone who will take them seriously. Because your executor will need to be available to sign legal documents and appear in court proceedings, it's a good idea to appoint someone who lives in the area, or at least in the same state you live in. If you appoint someone from out of state, the probate court may appoint an additional executor who lives in state, which may mean extra fees charged against your estate.

You should ask the person you want to serve as your executor in advance, so he will know that you've named him and can begin the probate process. To be on the safe side, many people choose to name an alternate executor, just in case their first choice is unable to serve. You don't have to name an alternate, but if you don't and for some reason your first choice can't serve, the court will appoint someone to do the job, and that person may not be someone you would have chosen.

Unlike the witnesses to a will, it's permissible to have one of your beneficiaries serve as executor. In fact, most married people name their spouse as their executor. However, you should remember that being an executor is more than just an honorary position, and that the executor's responsibilities are serious ones. If you don't think your spouse is up to the task, you'll do him or her a favor by naming someone else.

Because most people choose someone they trust as executor, they usually don't require that the executor be bonded. A bond is only required when there's some concern that the executor will misuse his or her authority and diminish the value of your estate. But the cost of obtaining a bond is an expense of your estate, and that in itself can reduce its value (the bigger your estate, the more expensive the bond will be).

NAMING YOUR HEIRS

Technically, a person you name in your will as a recipient of some or all of your property is called a beneficiary, while an heir is someone who has a legal right to the property of a person who dies without leaving a will. However, in popular usage "heir" has also come to refer to anyone who receives property through a last will and testament, and that's the way we'll use it in our discussion here.

When you write your will, you can leave your property to anyone you want, including organizations such as charities or foundations. When you make a gift of property to someone, you need to identify the recipient with enough clarity so that the court can tell whom you intended the recipient to be. For example, if you want to leave $10,000 to your friend, Ed Smith, that's the way to identify him in your will. ("I give the sum of $10,000 to my friend, Ed Smith".) And if there's any chance of confusion between the Ed Smith you want to receive the money and someone else with the same name, state the address of the Ed Smith you're giving the gift to.

Occasionally, you may read about people who try to leave their estate to a pet dog or cat. Doing so is a mistake; despite the efforts of animal rights activists, a pet is still legally considered to be an item of personal property, and you can't leave property to property. You can, however, leave your pet to someone you know will take care of it, and make a gift of money to that person to use in paying for the pet's care.

Generally, you don't have to leave anything to anyone you don't want to receive your property, even if they are the "natural object of your bounty," with one important exception. Every state either has a law that automatically gives your spouse one-half of all your marital property (called "community property states") or that entitles your spouse to receive a portion of your estate, even if you specifically disinherit him or her (called "equitable distribution" states). In equitable distribution states, this legal right to receive a share of your estate is called the spouse's right to "elect against the will." Depending on the state you live in, the share your spouse is entitled to receive ranges from one-third to one-half of your estate.

The only way in which a surviving spouse can be legally excluded from receiving a share of your property when you die is if he or she waives the right to receive property in a valid written contract, such as a prenuptial agreement. For a further discussion of prenuptial agreements, you should read Chapter 2, "Marriage, Divorce, and Family Law" beginning on page 19.

NAMING A GUARDIAN

If you have children who are minors, you should name a guardian for them in your will. The guardian is the person you want to take responsibility for raising and caring for your children.

If you're married, your spouse will become the guardian for the children of your marriage. If you're divorced and your former spouse is still living, he or she will usually obtain full custody of your mutual children, unless he or she has been found unfit and had parental rights terminated. Even so, your will should name an alternate guardian who will serve if your spouse or ex-spouse dies at the same time you do, or shortly thereafter.

The person you choose to serve as guardian may also be the person you want to serve as trustee for your children's support trust. By giving the same person control over your children's physical custody and management responsibility for their property, you can eliminate the possibility of a conflict in the decisions made about your children's education, health and well-being.

On the other hand, if you are concerned about the way an ex-spouse might handle the property and money you leave for your children, it may be best to name someone else to serve as trustee. In this way, you protect the value of your estate and help ensure that it goes to the children and not into the pocket of your ex-spouse. While your children could challenge a parent's mishandling of the trust, it may not be worthwhile for them to do so if the money's gone and there are no other assets from which they can collect any losses.

Whomever you choose to serve as guardian will be subject to approval by the court. Generally, a person will be qualified to serve as guardian if he or she is a legal adult and has the ability and willingness to care for your children.

Most people choose close friends or family members who already have a relationship with the children to serve as guardians. Some people name the children's grandparents to serve as guardian, but if you are considering doing so, remember that your children will need care for years to come; if the grandparents are already fairly old, they may not want to take on the responsibility of raising their grandchildren during the remaining years of their lives.

If your children are old enough to understand the concept, you may want to consider their wishes as well in naming a guardian. In any case, you'll want to obtain the advance permission of anyone you want to name as guardian.

WHAT NOT TO PUT IN YOUR WILL

Your will is not the place to include instructions about your funeral, burial, cremation, or organ donation. Nor is it the place to inform family members about the prepaid funeral arrangements or cemetery lot you purchased. In the days immediately following your death, it may not occur to anyone to look at your will for these instructions. By the time anyone does, it may be too late to follow the wishes you expressed.

If you want to donate your body to a medical school for research, or donate specific organs for transplant, you should make those arrangements in advance and be sure that someone close to you is aware of them, so there's no delay in complying with your wishes. Similarly, make sure that your minister, family members or your executor know about any special requests you have about how your funeral or memorial services should be conducted. And if you have already purchased a burial plot or vault, don't keep that information to yourself. Many families have incurred added expenses by purchasing a new burial site only to discover after the fact that arrangements had already been made by the deceased.

Finally, while plays, movies and television programs often depict wills that make unflattering comments about an heir ("I leave nothing to my sister, Bunny, because she treated me so cruelly when we were young") I don't recommend including provisions like this in your will. If you don't want to leave property to someone, you don't have to give a reason for the omission.

TESTAMENTARY TRUSTS

If you have minor children, or if you are concerned about your survivors' ability to manage the property you leave to them, you can create a testamentary trust for them in your will. The property you want them to receive will be managed for them by the trustee you name until they are old enough to have full control of it. You can authorize your trustee to use assets of the trust for your loved one's living expenses, medical expenses, and the cost of their education.

Just as your executor should be someone you trust, so should your trustee. You can choose whether or not to have your trustee bonded, but keep in mind that the cost of the bond will be an expense of your estate. You can choose a bank or other financial organization to serve as trustee. However, most banks charge fairly significant fees for serving as trustees, and unless the trust is a large one, a bank may pool its assets with other small trusts and manage them as one unit.

You may also name an alternate trustee if your first choice is unable or unwilling to serve. If you don't name an alternate, the court will name one for you if your first choice is unavailable.

CHANGING YOUR WILL

The law allows you to change your will in one of two ways. You can amend your will by creating a document called a codicil. A codicil is a separate document which you attach to your will that changes one or more of its provisions. To be valid, a codicil must be executed the same way your will is executed, that is, you have to sign it in front of the required number of witnesses, and they have to know that the document is a codicil to your will. I don't recommend using a codicil to change your will. Codicils can get lost or separated from the will to which they are attached, and they may unintentionally contradict some other term of your will in a way that will lead to disputes and delays in the distribution of your estate.

The other way to change your will is to write a new one, including the statement that it revokes all your previous wills. If you choose this method, it's still a good idea to destroy the signed original of your previous will, as well as any unsigned copies, to further ensure that there won't be any confusion about which will is the one you want to take effect.

Never try to change a will by making erasures or lining through provisions. Doing so may invalidate your entire will, which means your estate will pass according to the laws of intestate succession in your state.

When should you change your will? The answer depends chiefly on your own circumstances, but in general you may want to consider changing your will in any of the following circumstances:

- •When a beneficiary you've named dies before you do
- •When the financial circumstances of a beneficiary change significantly (such as when someone you've named to receive a large amount of property receives a financial windfall from another source that makes your gift unnecessary)
- •When your own financial circumstances change, or when you dispose of property that you intended to leave to another in your will
- •When you marry
- •When you divorce
- •When you move from one state to another.

CONTESTING A WILL

Although it happens more frequently (and more dramatically) in movies and television, wills sometimes are challenged, or contested. Your will can only be contested by someone who claims a valid and legal interest in your estate. This could include family members who would inherit under your state's laws of intestate succession, or beneficiaries you named in a previous will but left out of the one being offered for probate.

There are several grounds for contesting a will. The one most often used for contesting a will is that the testator was not competent. Another ground is that the formalities for executing the will were not fully met, and so the will is invalid. Wills may also be challenged on the grounds of fraud or mistake, or that the document was never intended to serve as a will in the first place. That's why it's important to state early on in the document that you intend for it to be your will.

One of your executor's responsibilities is to defend your will's validity if it is contested. If your will is successfully contested, the law of intestate succession will be used to distribute your estate. The best way to minimize the chances of a successful challenge to your will is by being sure to carefully follow all the required steps in executing it, including telling the witnesses that the document is your will and having the witnesses sign it correctly.

You can also include what's called a "no-contest" clause, a provision in your will that entirely disinherits any one who challenges it. However, some courts won't honor this provision if the person bringing the challenge can show a reasonable basis for making it, even if the challenge proves unsuccessful. And if someone brings a successful challenge, the provision won't be enforced anyway. Still, if you are concerned that someone without a reasonable claim might challenge your will's provisions, it may be worthwhile to include a no-contest clause.

DYING WITHOUT A WILL

As we've already mentioned, every state has laws that will distribute your property if you die without a will. These are called the laws of intestate succession, or descent and distribution. They're the state's way of trying to decide what you probably would have done with your property if you had made a will. In essence, intestate succession is the state's way of writing your will for you.

Unfortunately, these laws cannot take into account the many differences people experience in their feelings toward the "natural objects of their bounty." The laws of intestate succession assume you love your children equally, and so each of them gets an equal share in your estate. They don't distinguish between the child who gives you respect and lives in a way that makes you proud to be his parent and the child that's ignored you, been disrespectful to you, or failed to live up to your expectations. The laws of intestate succession don't know about the next door neighbor who has helped you paint your house, fed and cared for your children when you were sick, listened to your problems, and who is closer to you than your own brother or sister. So no matter how fair these laws try to be, they can never be as fair as you can be yourself. By taking the time to write your own will, you'll have the peace of mind of knowing that things will be handled as you want them to be.

PROBATE FACTS AND FALLACIES

After the death of a person who has left behind a will, a court proceeding must usually be held to determine that the will is valid. This is the much dreaded process called probate.

Your executor is the person responsible for settling your estate. The executor asks the probate court to recognize your will and authorize him or her to administer your estate according to its terms. With the court's approval and under its supervision, your executor will pay all the bills, taxes and legitimate claims made against your estate, while challenging claims which are not valid. The executor then distributes the remaining assets to the heirs you've named in accordance with your instructions. After performing these duties, the executor will be released by the court from any further duties, and your estate will be closed.

When your will is probated, your witnesses will be called to court to testify that the signatures on the will are yours and theirs. In most states, this procedure can be eliminated by executing a self-proving affidavit at the same time you execute your will. This affidavit takes the place of a court appearance by the witnesses. To make a self-proving affidavit valid, it must be signed and witnessed by a notary public or some other person authorized under state law to administer oaths.

Lately, there's been a great deal of controversy about the expense and time involved in probating a will. Probate can take anywhere from several months to more than a year, and costs can be as much as 5 percent of the value of your estate. In response to the concerns raised about this process, many states have taken steps to simplify probate procedures. If your estate is very small, you may be able to avoid probate entirely. There are also a variety of methods that people use to transfer ownership of their property to avoid probate.

There are several ways to transfer property at the time of your death that avoid the probate process. Probably the most commonly used method is joint tenancy with right of survivorship. When one of the owners of property held in this manner dies, the property automatically belongs to the surviving joint owner.

While this method can be an effective way to pass along property ownership, it can have its drawbacks. While you're alive, you can lose your property to the creditors of your joint tenant. And giving someone a joint tenancy in property you previously owned by yourself can cause gift taxes to be incurred.

Another way to transfer property to another while you are alive is by making gifts. Under federal law, you can give as much as $10,000 annually to any one you choose without incurring any tax liability, and if you're married, your spouse may do so as well. So, for example, a married couple can give as much as $40,000 to their son and his wife in a single year without incurring any taxes. However, making an outright gift means there's no way to control the property once it's been given, so if you are concerned about the recipient's ability to handle money, this tactic may not be right for you.

You can pass the proceeds of life insurance policies, pension and IRA benefits by naming a specific beneficiary, which avoids the probate process for these assets. You may even want to name a contingent beneficiary, so this property won't go into your probate estate if the first beneficiary dies when you do, or within a short period of time after your death.

You can also escape estate taxes on the proceeds of life insurance policies by transferring ownership of the policies to the beneficiary, or by creating a life insurance trust. However, even in these arrangements, you may be faced with the prospect of paying gift taxes if you continue making the premium payments, even when the amount of the premiums falls below the normal $10,000 annual exclusion. And in some cases the IRS has included life insurance policies as part of the deceased's estate even when he tried to give the policy to the beneficiary, but when he retained what are called "incidences of ownership," such as the right to change premium payments or borrow against the policy.

Another very simple way to avoid probate is to open a kind of bank account known as a Totten Trust. With a Totten Trust, you open a bank account in your own name, but as trustee for the person you want to receive the money when you die. These accounts, also known as P.O.D. accounts (for "Pay On Death"), differ from other kinds of trusts because you get to keep total control over the money in the account while you are alive. You can add money, make withdrawals, or even close the account without having to worry about the beneficiary making a claim that you breached your duty as trustee. Your bank's new account representative can provide more information about how to set up a Totten Trust account in your state.

THE LIVING TRUST

In the past several years, living trusts have become one of the hottest tools for estate planning, and for lawyers, banks, and insurance companies, one of the most lucrative. Hundreds of seminars on the horrors of probate and the advantages of creating a living trust are conducted each week in cities and towns all across the country.

Essentially, a trust is a legal arrangement by which one person or persons (the "trustee") takes title to property, which is then held and managed for the benefit of another (the "beneficiary"). A living trust (in legalese, an "inter vivos" trust) allows you to decide who will manage your property, for how long, and how and when the assets in the trust will ultimately be distributed. Depending on the way the trust is written, you may be able to make changes in the uses to which the trust is put, and you could even decide to revoke it and put the ownership of trust property back into your own name. As a result, a living trust gives you somewhat greater flexibility than other estate planning tools.

Living trusts fall into one of two categories. An irrevocable living trust cannot be changed or revoked once it is in place. A revocable living trust can be modified or canceled as long as the person who creates it (called the "settlor" or "grantor") is alive and competent. In most cases, an irrevocable living trust has the advantage of being exempt from taxation as part of your estate, but once it's made, you can't get out of it. And if you retain any ownership interest or try to exercise control over any property in the trust, you lose the tax advantage, so you shouldn't name yourself as trustee or as beneficiary of an irrevocable living trust.

Assets in a revocable living trust are calculated as part of your estate when it comes time to figure estate taxes, since by its very terms you continue to maintain control over how the property will be used. Both irrevocable and revocable trusts pass ownership of the property to the persons you name as beneficiaries outside of probate. As a result, the transfer usually takes place much more quickly than one that comes about through a will. A trust adds an element of privacy as well, since a will admitted to probate becomes a public record, while a trust does not.

The most popular form of living trust in use today is the revocable trust. To create this kind of trust, you take all or a portion of your property and transfer it into a trust. You then name yourself as the trustee. You name a successor trustee who will take over upon your death and also name the beneficiaries of the trust who will receive the property when you die. Under the terms of the trust, you can still do all the things with your property that you did previously, including selling it, exchanging it for other property, or just using it for yourself.

Any property you forget to transfer to the trust, which you decide not to transfer, or which you later acquire in your own name, such as an inheritance or a court judgment, remains outside the trust and is subject to probate, unless you take the time to make the necessary transfer of ownership.

In some cases, that may not even be possible. For example, if you are killed in an accident, your estate may receive a settlement from an insurance company. That property won't go into the living trust you created, and so it will become a part of your probate estate.

One of the reasons lawyers like to promote living trusts as an estate planning tool is that the fees for creating a trust document are generally much higher than for writing a simple will. For example, an attorney who charges $100 to write your will may charge five or ten times more than that for creating a living trust. In addition to legal fees, you also have to pay the cost of transferring title and registering title documents with the county recorder of deeds and secretary of state's office. If you name a bank or some other institution to serve as a co-trustee, you'll pay a fee for that service as well, which is why banks like to promote seminars about living trusts. Life insurance companies like to promote living trusts as a way to reduce probate expenses and estate taxes, but they use the seminar approach to convince you to buy extra life insurance to cover any probate fees and estate taxes that still may need to be paid on property outside the trust.

In some cases, the cost of these services could easily exceed the cost of probate, especially if your estate is relatively small. As we've already seen, for some small estates probate procedures are now so simple that there's no delay and virtually no cost to the process.

In a number of cases, elderly people in the middle and lower-income brackets, most of whom are poor candidates for a living trust, report being pressured by door-to-door sales people to purchase living trust "kits." The kits generally consist of some preprinted forms and a few pages of largely inadequate instructions. In return for the kit, some companies have collected as much as several thousand dollars, mostly by overemphasizing the difficulties of probate, and by playing on fears that probate expenses and taxes will deplete the person's estate and leave nothing for a spouse, children, or other loved ones.

Unfortunately, many of these people ended up spending money they should have used for their daily living expenses in the hope of providing a larger estate to their heirs, who may have been better equipped to handle the financial burden of probate.

If you decide you want to create a living trust, you may be able to do-it-yourself, and at a far lower cost than the huge fees these con artists are collecting. If you have a computer, there are several good software programs available to help you design and create a valid living trust. If you prefer to do things the old fashioned way, "Plan Your Estate With A Living Trust," written by Denis Clifford and published by Nolo Press is a good source of information, and includes tear-out forms which you can use to create your own living trust.

CHAPTER SIXTEEN
YOUR DAY IN COURT

Although the main purpose of this book is to help you avoid legal problems by understanding your legal rights and responsibilities, the day will almost certainly come when you will be required to participate in a legal proceeding in some capacity, whether as a plaintiff, a defendant, a witness, or as a jury member.

In this chapter, we will take a look at the judicial system, explore some alternatives to litigation, and follow the steps involved in a civil lawsuit. We'll also examine the role of a witness, and discuss what happens when you are called for jury duty. Finally, we will review small claims court procedures and the way to make small claims court work for you.

In this chapter, our emphasis is on the procedures involved in non-criminal or civil matters. For a discussion of criminal court proceedings, you should turn to Chapter Seventeen, "Crime and Punishment."

THE AMERICAN JUDICIAL SYSTEM

The United States has both a federal and state court system. Federal courts include district courts which try cases involving federal crimes, as well as civil cases between citizens of different states which involve more than $10,000, or when a federal law gives them jurisdiction.

Federal courts also include the bankruptcy courts and Tax Court, which hears disputes between the Internal Revenue Service and taxpayers. Federal courts also include the Courts of Appeals, which hear appeals from the decisions of lower courts and from federal agencies, the Court of Customs and Patent

Appeals, which reviews decisions of the patent and trade office, and the Supreme Court of the United States.

State courts follow a similar structure. At the bottom level are local courts which hear minor criminal charges, cases involving zoning violations, and small claims; juvenile courts which deal with offenses committed by minors; probate courts which hear cases involving wills, estates, adoptions, and similar matters; trial courts which hear criminal and civil cases; appellate courts which review appeals from the lower courts, and state supreme courts which supervise all the courts below them and hear final appeals constitute the state system.

The decision as to which court has jurisdiction over a particular matter depends on a number of factors. These factors include the amount of money or property in dispute, whether the matter is criminal or civil in nature, and the county and state you live in as well as the residence of the opposing party.

BEFORE YOU FILE A LAWSUIT

With the increasing amount of litigation in our society, it's important to give some consideration to alternative ways of dealing with disputes other than in the courtroom.

More and more, lawyers are recommending that their clients consider pursuing methods other than lawsuits as a way to settle disputes. These so-called "alternative dispute resolution" or ADR methods include a number of techniques. Some of these methods, such as conducting a trial in a private court system, tend to be fairly expensive, and lend themselves more to disputes between businesses than to disputes between individuals, or between an individual and a business. However, a couple of alternative dispute resolution techniques can sometimes be used by individuals at a substantial savings in time and money.

One increasingly popular method of alternative dispute resolution is mediation. In mediation, the parties to the dispute select an impartial person trained in negotiation techniques to help them arrive at a mutually satisfactory settlement of their problem. The mediator's role isn't to impose a solution, but to help the parties find areas of mutual agreement, and to help each of them understand the other side's position. In addition, a good mediator helps each side determine what it really wants to receive in order to come away satisfied with the settlement, rather than seeking the most it may be legally entitled to receive.

Mediation is conducted in a very informal matter, and the procedures mediators use vary. Some mediators like to have both parties in the same room, while some shuttle back and forth between the parties in an attempt to keep personality conflicts to a minimum. Mediation is a voluntary process, and generally either party may decide to end its participation in mediation at any time. In many parts of the country, courts now require couples involved in certain kinds of disputes, such as those concerning child custody and visitation privileges, to attempt to resolve their differences through mediation before bringing their dispute into the courtroom.

If you decide to try mediation as a means of resolving a dispute, be sure to find a well-trained and qualified mediator to assist you. Although a number of lawyers, former judges, and social workers have established firms offering mediation services, there are no licensing standards in place for mediators, and so just about anyone can claim to be a mediator. You and your opponent in the dispute should interview several mediators before settling on the one to assist you.

Another, somewhat different method of alternate dispute resolution is arbitration. In arbitration, your dispute is heard by one or more arbitrators selected by mutual agreement of you and your opponent in the dispute. Although the procedures still aren't as formal as those used in the courtroom, they are much more formal than those used in mediation. Witnesses are sworn in and examined and cross-examined as they would be during a trial. Each side gets to make opening and closing statements, and the party whose complaint led to arbitration gets to rebut the defendant's claims.

After all the evidence is heard, the arbitrators take the case under consideration, and in most cases issue their decision within a few weeks of the hearing. In most cases, the arbitrator's decision is final, and the only basis for an appeal is that the arbitrator somehow violated the rules of arbitration in reaching his decision. However, since arbitrators don't issue explanations of their rulings, establishing a basis for an appeal is a difficult and daunting task.

In a growing number of contracts, such as the one you have with your stock brokerage and the warranty you receive when you purchase a new car or a major appliance, an arbitration provision is often included. Under this provision, if you and the other party cannot arrive at an acceptable resolution of a problem, you must take your claim to arbitration rather than filing a lawsuit. In many of these contracts, however, the decision of the arbitrator is binding only on the company. If you are unhappy with the outcome, you may still pursue your claim in court. Be sure you understand the terms of the arbitration clause in any consumer contract you enter, however, since some clauses do require both parties to abide by the arbitrator's decision.

You can obtain more information about arbitration from the American Arbitration Association, which has regional offices in major cities across the country. Or you can write to the AAA's national headquarters at 140 West 51st Street, New York, NY 10020.

THE LAW OF TORTS

Many lawsuits are based on breach of contract, the failure of one party to live up to his part of an agreement. In most civil lawsuits, however, your claim will be based on the law of torts.

A tort is the action (or in some cases, inaction) of another which injures you or damages your property, and which was the result of the negligence or the intentional misconduct of the person who committed it. A tort of negligence occurs when the person who causes you to suffer a loss fails to exercise a reasonable amount of care under the circumstances. For example, suppose you are driving home from work one day when a car fails to stop for a stop sign and strikes your vehicle broadside. The driver of the other car didn't see the stop sign because he was busy tuning the car radio to his favorite talk show. In doing so, he committed a tort of negligence, and you can file suit for the damages you suffered because of that negligence.

In determining whether a person is guilty of a tort of negligence, the court asks whether or not the person accused of the tort acted as a "reasonably prudent person" would act in the same situation.

By a reasonably prudent person, the law generally means an adult of average age and experience who suffers from no physical or mental disability. However, when judging the conduct of someone who is physically disabled, the law compares that person's conduct to what would be reasonably expected of a person with the same disability.

While the law makes this concession in judging the actions of the physically disabled, it doesn't make a similar concession for those who suffer from a mental disability. So, for example, a person who would be considered mentally incompetent and unable to face criminal charges could still be sued for damages in a civil lawsuit.

An intentional tort occurs when someone deliberately takes some action (or fails to act) in a way that causes you harm. Some of the more common kinds of intentional torts include assault (putting you in fear of an imminent attack) and battery (actually touching you in an offensive matter). Fraud, conversion (stealing your property) and false imprisonment (confining you against your will) are other intentional torts, as are libel and slander (defaming you or damaging your reputation).

Another kind of intentional tort occurs when someone causes you emotional anguish through outrageous conduct. For example, suppose you break up with a person you dated for a few weeks. Instead of merely going away and getting on with his life, this person begins to send you sexually explicit and threatening letters and leaves bouquets of dead flowers on your doorstep. He begins to call you hundreds of times a day, hanging up as soon as you answer the phone. As a result, you are afraid to go out in public. You have nightmares, become physically ill, and are unable to go to work for days and weeks at a time.

This tort is known as the intentional infliction of emotional distress, and a person who engages in this kind of outrageous behavior can be liable for damages in a civil lawsuit, in addition to the criminal charges he might face for his conduct.

In some states, and in some cases, it isn't necessary to show either negligence or intentional misconduct in order to bring a successful civil suit. Under the legal doctrine of strict liability, you may be able to recover for injuries you suffer as the result of another's activities without having to prove that they did anything other than engaging in the activities.

For example, suppose you buy a paint sprayer which runs off an air compressor. When you use it according to the instructions provided by the manufacturer, the paint jar of the sprayer explodes, cutting your hand and lodging a shard of plastic in your eye.

Under the doctrine of strict liability, you can receive compensation for your damages without showing that the manufacturer of the sprayer did anything other than market a product that was unreasonably dangerous. You don't have to show how the product's defect came into being; you only have to show that the product was defective, that the manufacturer offered the product for sale (in legal terms, "allowed it to enter the stream of commerce") and that your injury resulted from using the defective product.

Not every state has recognized the doctrine of strict liability, however, and in the states that have not you must still show that the manufacturer was negligent in allowing the defective product to reach the public.

WHEN YOU FILE A LAWSUIT

Court proceedings generally begin with the filing of a complaint and the issuance of a summons. The complaint sets forth the grounds for the lawsuit, called the "cause of action." It states the injury or damage you've suffered, the names of the persons you believe are responsible, and the type of remedy you are asking the court to impose. It also makes a statement regarding why this particular court has jurisdiction, the authority to hear the case.

The summons is a legal notice issued by the clerk of the court telling the person or persons you've named as defendants that legal action has been commenced against them. It directs the defendant to file an answer with the court by a specified date. A summons must be formally served, or delivered to the defendant. In most cases, this "service of process" is done in person, perhaps by the sheriff or another law enforcement officer. More often, the summons is served by a professional process server, or some other disinterested party. In some cases, service may be made by sending a copy of the summons and complaint through the mail.

The defendant has a specified period of time in which to respond to the summons and complaint with what's known as an "answer." The answer may be used to deny the plaintiff's charges entirely, or to assert an "affirmative defense" to the plaintiff's claim. An affirmative defense in a personal injury case, for example, might be that you were injured through your own negligence, not the alleged negligence of the defendant.

Another common answer to a complaint is one which contains a motion asking the court to dismiss the charges for failing to state a cause of action. Suppose the complaint states that the plaintiff purchased a ladder from your hardware store, and that the ladder subsequently broke, causing the plaintiff to be injured.

A claim like this would probably be dismissed for failing to state a cause of action, since the plaintiff hasn't alleged that you did anything wrong that would make you responsible for the injuries. However, most courts will allow a plaintiff to amend his complaint to state a cause of action, so any sense of relief you may get as the result of obtaining a motion to dismiss under these circumstances may only be temporary.

Along with the answer, the defendant may also file a counterclaim. A counterclaim may state that, rather than the defendant being liable for damages, in fact the plaintiff took some action which resulted in damages to the defendant. Suppose the original complaint charged the defendant with negligence in operating his motorcycle, which resulted in an accident with the plaintiff's automobile. A counterclaim might state that the plaintiff was actually negligent in the way he drove his car, and that this negligence was in fact the cause of the accident and the losses suffered by the defendant.

A person who receives a summons in a civil lawsuit may choose whether or not to respond to the court. However, failing to respond will most likely result in a default judgment being entered against the defendant.

Once the defendant's answer and any counterclaim is received by the court, a trial date will be set and what's known as "discovery" will begin. Discovery procedures are used to obtain evidence that will strengthen each party's case, and also to prevent either side from being surprised by undisclosed facts or unknown witnesses. (Unlike the way trials are often represented in movies and television programs, "surprise" witnesses don't often appear in real life trials.)

Discovery techniques include depositions, the oral questioning of the parties to the lawsuit as well as witnesses, and interrogatories, which are written questions that must be answered in writing. Depositions and interrogatories are both given under oath, and you could be charged with and convicted of perjury if you give answers that are untruthful.

While depositions and interrogatories are the best known forms of discovery, there are others as well. A "request for admissions" takes place when one side asks the other to admit to some important fact, or to attest to the authenticity of some document to be used as evidence. For example, the plaintiff's attorney may make a request for admission asking the defendant to agree to the fact that a specific document is a contract signed by both parties. If this fact is true, the defendant will admit to it. If it's not, or if there's some doubt on the defendant's part about the document's authenticity, he can deny the admission, or state that he has insufficient facts to support an admission.

A "request for production and inspection" is a form of discovery often used in business disputes. When a request for production and inspection is delivered, the party receiving it is asked to produce any and all books and documents in its possession that are pertinent to the lawsuit, or physical evidence that the party making the request cannot obtain through other means. If the party receiving the request refuses to do so, it must provide its reasons for denying the request. The party making the request can then ask the court to compel the production and inspection of the evidence. However, any request for business documents and other evidence must be fairly specific in stating what exactly is being sought, since otherwise the party making the request could simply go fishing through all of a company's files in search of evidence supporting its case.

Another form of discovery, one which is often used in personal injury cases, is the physical examination of the plaintiff. In cases brought to determine whether or not a person is competent, or to decide the fitness of a parent to have custody, mental and psychological examinations of the parties may also be sought.

Either side in the case may choose to file certain motions with the court. These motions are requests that are made to the court regarding some issue in the case, and asking the court to make a decision. Among the most common types of motions are those that ask the court to allow a plaintiff to amend a complaint, which ask the court to order the opposing party to comply with discovery requests, and which ask the court to dismiss the charges against a particular defendant.

Pretrial conferences may be called in order to allow both parties to discuss the issues in the case. Pretrial conferences are intended to minimize delays in trial proceedings, and in many cases these conferences will lead to an out of court settlement so that a trial will not need to take place at all. However, if a settlement can't be reached before the trial date set by the court, the next step in the litigation process is the trial itself.

Once the case is called to trial, a jury will usually be selected to hear the case, unless the parties have agreed to have the case tried by the judge. We'll say more about juries a little later on.

Each side then gets to make it's opening statement. These statements are summaries of what each party will try to establish during the length of the trial. In some cases, the attorney for the defendant may decide to wait to make his opening statement until later in the proceedings, after the plaintiff has completed presenting his case.

Because the plaintiff has the burden of proof and has to prove its case, the plaintiff gets to go first in presenting his case. That means calling witnesses and presenting evidence in support of the claim made against the defendant. After the plaintiff's attorney finishes questioning a witness (called "direct examination,") the lawyer for the defendant gets the chance to cross-examine the witness, to point up contradictions in the witness' testimony, to show that the witness is unreliable, or to show that the witness has an interest in having the outcome of the case decided in favor of the plaintiff.

After all of the plaintiff's witnesses have been called and all the evidence in support of the plaintiff's case has been presented, the plaintiff "rests his case." At this point, the lawyer for the defendant will ask the court to dismiss the case for lack of proof. If the plaintiff hasn't been able to set out enough evidence to support his claim, a motion to dismiss may be granted. More likely, however, the motion will be denied, and the defendant then gets to present his case. If he's reserved the right to make his opening statement to the jury, this is the time when he'll do so. Otherwise, the defendant begins by calling witnesses and presenting evidence designed to refute the plaintiff's claims.

Just as the defense gets to cross-examine the plaintiff's witnesses, the plaintiff can cross-examine the witnesses testifying on the defendant's behalf. After all of the defense witnesses have been called and the defense rests its case, the plaintiff gets the opportunity to present what's known as "rebuttal evidence." This rebuttal evidence is additional testimony from witnesses or other evidence that explains away some of the defense's case, or which contradicts it outright.

Each side then gets to make a closing statement, which summarizes its arguments and case and asks the court or the jury to provide a favorable judgment. Just as the plaintiff gets the chance to present rebuttal evidence after the defense presents its case, the plaintiff also gets the chance to speak after the defense makes its closing statement, in a final attempt to convince the court to find in the plaintiff's favor.

If a jury trial has been conducted, the jury will then be given instructions by the judge. These instructions include the law that governs the case, the way the jury must apply the law to the facts, and the burden of proof that must be met in order for the plaintiff to win. In most civil cases, the plaintiff must prove its case by a standard known as "a preponderance of the evidence." Basically, this means that the jury must believe that it's more likely than not that the defendant is liable for the damages the plaintiff claims.

The jury is then sent off to a room in the courthouse where it will deliberate until it reaches its decision, or until it becomes clear that the jury is deadlocked and cannot reach a decision. Deadlocked, or "hung" juries don't occur as often in civil cases as they do in criminal trials. Unlike criminal cases, which almost always require the jury to reach a unanimous decision, civil cases can often be decided by a decision of a simple majority of the jurors, or in some cases when two-thirds of them reach agreement.

Once the jury reaches its decision, it returns to the courtroom, where the verdict is announced. At this point, the lawyer for the losing side will almost always ask for what's known as a "judgment notwithstanding the verdict." This motion asks the court to disregard the jury verdict and find in favor of the losing side instead. Courts will not grant this motion unless the verdict is clearly outrageous in light of the evidence presented during the trial. In most cases, a final judgment reflecting the jury's decision is entered by the court. At this point, the losing side in the trial must decide whether or not to appeal the trial court ruling.

Generally, an appeal can only be filed when the losing side can make the argument that the court erred in some courtroom procedure or in its interpretation of the law governing the case. The party filing the appeal, called the "appellant" usually can't re-argue the facts of the case to the appeals court. However, in some cases an appeals court can "remand," or return the case to the trial court for further consideration of the facts in light of the appeals court's instructions on how they should be interpreted under the law.

While the steps above provide a general outline of the procedures followed in most civil courts, remember that state court rules and procedures do vary somewhat from place to place. If you are involved in a lawsuit, your attorney can give you more information about the exact procedures that will be followed in the court hearing your case.

You may also be surprised to learn that most trials contain little of the drama associated with the courtroom dramas portrayed in films and plays. In many cases, the lawyers will conduct a lot of business up at the judge's bench, trying to settle procedural issues out of earshot of the jury. And the judge may order the jury out of the courtroom during certain parts of the trial as he attempts to determine whether or not evidence can be admitted for the jury's consideration.

The lawyers won't often have the certainty of a Perry Mason or an Arnie Becker, but then again they don't have the luxury of a script to follow and a director who can yell "Cut" and reshoot the scene when a line is flubbed. Nor will they be likely to wander around the courtroom or approach the witnesses to look them in the eyes and elicit some surprising admission. In most courtrooms, lawyers are required to remain standing at a podium several feet from where the witness sits, and may only approach the witness with the permission of the judge. In general, a lawyer who conducted himself the way most television and film lawyers do would find himself faced with contempt of court charges on a regular basis.

And even after the trial has been completed and while the jury is deliberating, the case may be settled, so the tension and excitement associated with the jury's return to the courtroom may never even be experienced. All in all, real life trials contain little of the electricity most of us are familiar with from their fictional counterparts.

BEING A WITNESS

A witness is a person who provides oral evidence in a legal proceeding concerning some event or fact of which he has knowledge and which is crucial to the outcome of the proceeding. A witness may be asked to appear in court and many do so voluntarily, especially when they are friends or family members of one of the parties to the lawsuit.

In other cases, witnesses may be subpoenaed. A subpoena is an order from the court which commands a person to appear and testify. The person who receives the subpoena is legally obligated to obey it. Witnesses who fail to appear and testify after being subpoenaed may be subject to charges of contempt of court. In addition, a witness who appears but refuses to answer questions when under examination can also be held liable for contempt of court. It's true that under our Constitution, no witness can be forced to testify if the testimony would be self-incriminating. But that only means that the witness can refuse to answer questions that might lead to criminal charges. Questions that might expose the witness to civil liability are permissible, and must be answered.

When you are called to testify at a deposition, you will probably meet at the offices of the lawyer who called you to testify. The attorney or attorneys for the other side will also be present, and a court reporter will also be present to record the questions and your answers. As the questioning proceeds, you will undoubtedly find that one side or the other will raise objections to the questions being asked. These are objections "for the record," and their merits will be decided later on by the judge. Once the objection has been made, you will be required to answer the question. If the objection is later upheld by the court, that question and your answer to it will be inadmissable for consideration in deciding the outcome of the case.

Witnesses are generally entitled by statute to receive compensation for their travel expenses and to certain minimal fees set up by state laws. A special class of witnesses are so-called "expert" witnesses, whose testimony includes information that requires special professional knowledge. These expert witnesses are generally allowed to receive extra compensation from the party that calls them to testify, in addition to the statutory witness fee. As a result, many expert witnesses are often attacked as "hired guns" willing to testify on behalf of anyone willing and able to pay their fees. In some cases, this criticism is well-justified. A jury generally has the right to know who is paying the fees of an expert witness, and to take that into consideration when evaluating the witness' testimony.

When a witness is called to court to testify, he or she will be required to swear that the answers he gives to the questions asked will be truthful. Witnesses who fail to testify truthfully can be prosecuted for perjury, a crime punishable in some states by up to ten years in prison.

The witness will first be examined by the attorneys for the party who called him to testify, and then cross-examined by the attorney for the opposing party. During cross-examination, the opposing party's attorney will attempt to impeach the witness, or question his or her truthfulness. Impeachment can include the introduction of evidence which shows that the witness should not be believed, including evidence about the character or reputation of the witness. For example, if the witness has previously been convicted of income tax evasion, the attorney cross-examining the witness may call this to the attention of the jury in his questioning, as a way to show that the witness has been less than truthful in the past. Or if your testimony contradicts something you said in an earlier deposition, the lawyer will draw this out in order to question your truthfulness, your memory, or both.

If you are ever called to appear as a witness at a deposition or in a trial, you will probably have a discussion with the lawyer calling you in advance of your appearance. During this meeting, the lawyer will review your testimony, give you advice about what to wear to court and how to conduct yourself during the examination and cross-examination, and tell you what questions he will ask and what questions to expect from the opposing attorney. As long as the lawyer doesn't try to influence you to change your answers or to avoid telling the truth, there's nothing illegal or unethical about this practice.

Most likely, the lawyer will give you the following advice about how to conduct yourself. You should speak clearly and distinctly in response to questions you are asked, but you should not offer additional information beyond that sought by the questioning attorney. Don't nod or shake your head as a response, since your answers must be recorded by the court reporter.

In addition, you should not try to anticipate an attorney's questions, but wait until he has finished asking it before you begin your answer. After the attorney finishes the question, it is a good idea to hesitate for a moment before answering so that opposing counsel may have the opportunity to raise any objections, such as that the question is irrelevant, or hearsay.

When each side has completed its questions, you should wait until the judge tells you that you are excused before you get up from the jury box. By being a courteous witness, you can improve the credibility of your testimony in the eyes of the court, and that can be of great help to the party on whose behalf you are testifying.

SERVING AS A JUROR

A jury is a group of citizens empowered by the law to pass judgment on the behavior of others. A jury examines the evidence presented in court, determines the facts of the case based upon that evidence, and decides whether to deny or grant a civil claim or (in criminal cases) whether to convict an accused criminal or acquit him.

Potential jurors are selected in a variety of ways, depending on the particular jurisdiction. In most cases, the names of jurors are drawn from a list of persons registered to vote, or who have valid driver's licenses. From this list, the names of potential jurors are drawn, and they are then issued a summons to appear at the courthouse for jury duty.

In some states, statutes automatically exempt certain people from serving as jurors. Government officials, convicted criminals, and judges are often exempted from serving as jurors by these statutes. And every jurisdiction allows other persons called for jury duty to apply for an exemption. Exemptions from jury duty are based on cause, such as illness, important family obligations, or because the person called to jury duty performs an important public function, such as by serving as a firefighter or police officer. However, exemptions from jury duty are not granted lightly, and the person who is not excused but who simply fails to appear for jury duty as scheduled can be charged with criminal contempt of court. If the person is found guilty, a fine, imprisonment, or both can be imposed as punishment.

Much of your time as a juror will be spent in a jury room, where you will wait with other potential jurors to be called to serve on a jury panel for a specific trial. A jury panel is generally chosen at random from the larger group of jurors in the jury room. The jurors who will hear a particular trial are picked from the jury panel. Those who are not chosen to serve may be asked to return to the pool to be considered for inclusion on another jury panel, or they may be excused from further duty until the next time they are summoned.

To select the specific jurors who will hear evidence and render a verdict in a trial, an oral examination by the judge and the attorneys for both parties is conducted. This examination is called the "voir dire," an old French term meaning "to speak the truth. This examination is used to decide if there are any reasons why you should not be permitted to hear the case to be tried. This is referred to as being "excused for cause."

For example, you may be excused from serving if you know one of the parties in the proceeding, or if you have seen or read news accounts of the matter that would affect your ability to act impartially in considering the evidence. And in addition to being excluded for cause, each side has a number of what are called "peremptory challenges," which they can use to exclude jurors without giving any reason for doing so.

The voir dire process continues until a full jury has been "empaneled," or selected to hear the case. Although by statute many states still require the empaneling of 12 jurors to hear any trial by jury, other states empanel juries consisting of six to eight members.

Once you are selected to serve on a jury, you will be seated in the jury box in the courtroom. As a juror, it is your task to listen closely to the testimony presented in the courtroom. You will be warned by the judge not to discuss the case until the trial is over, even with other jurors. This rule is essential in order to prevent jurors from evaluating evidence before the case is completely presented and all the parties have had a chance to tell their version of the events to the court.

You will also be advised not to read newspaper articles, listen to radio programs or watch television newscasts that deal with the trial in which you are serving as a juror. You are to consider only the evidence presented in the courtroom, without regard for any information that could be obtained from other sources.

After you have heard all of the evidence and been instructed by the judge regarding the law in the case at hand, you and your fellow jurors will retire to a room where you will attempt to reach a verdict. A jury foreman will be selected to preside over the jury's deliberations. In some jurisdictions, jurors elect the person who serves as foreman, while in others the judge may appoint the foreman, or the task falls to the first juror selected.

As a juror, you should listen openly to the views of the other jurors about the facts of the case as they understand them. You should not hesitate to express your own opinions about what you have heard in the courtroom. If you have a question about some testimony, or if you need to see certain evidence, you can ask the bailiff assigned to guard you from outside interference to send a request to the judge. Whether or not you will receive the material you request will depend on what you are asking for and the law in the jurisdiction.

In some cases, jurors have little trouble reaching a decision in a short period of time. In other cases, significant differences of opinion may exist. When there are differences among the jurors, it is important to remember that it is the first responsibility of you and your fellow jurors to try to come to a fair decision.

In most criminal cases, the jury must unanimously agree to a verdict before returning it to the court. However, in many jurisdictions, civil cases may be decided by a majority vote of the jurors, so the prospect of a hung jury is unlikely.

Once the jury has reached its decision, it will return to the court and announce its verdict. Once the verdict is announced, the jurors will be thanked by the court and excused. In most states, jurors who have completed hearing a case will be allowed to return to their everyday lives. In a few states, however, jurors may be empaneled on more than one jury during the period for which they have been called.

Many people view the prospect of being called for jury duty with just about the same level of enthusiasm they reserve for dental surgery conducted without benefit of anesthesia. Others fear that their employers will refuse to let them serve, or fire them if they do.

Regarding the first concern, there isn't much that can be said to convince people otherwise when they believe that jury duty is anything less than a tiresome burden, to be avoided if at all possible. In many instances, these people are right. Being called for jury duty can disrupt your life for days, weeks, or even months, and many of the cases juries hear are less than fascinating.

On the other hand, it might be a good idea to look at jury duty from a somewhat different point of view, by putting yourself in the shoes of the parties to a lawsuit or a person accused of a crime. In that situation, you would want your case heard by interested and attentive jurors who recognize the importance of what they're doing in deciding your fate.

As for the concern that an employer will fire you for responding to a summons to jury duty, the laws in nearly every state specifically prohibit this practice. And many employers, recognizing the important work a jury does, will even continue to pay employees during the time they are serving on a jury, although they usually subtract the amount the worker receives from the court for jury service.

SMALL CLAIMS COURT

Small claims courts hear disputes involving claims for relatively small amounts of money, usually less than $2,000. Because of the small amounts involved, small claims courts use simplified procedures which generally allow the parties to appear in court without benefit of counsel. Unlike regular civil trials in which months or even years may pass before a trial date arrives, most small claims cases are scheduled to be heard within several weeks after the plaintiff files suit. And while other trials may take days, weeks, or even months to complete, the actual court hearing of a small claims case rarely takes more than a few minutes.

Many small claims courts hear cases after normal working hours so that the parties involved in the suit don't have to take a day off from work in order to appear in court. And while small claims cases are usually heard by a judge, in some jurisdictions they may also be heard by a referee, someone who may or may not be trained as an attorney.

While small claims court procedures vary from state to state, they do share some basic similarities. A person who wants to file a small claims suit should go to the local courthouse. In some locations, you must complete a form provided by the court for your complaint, but other jurisdictions aren't so strict, and as long as the complaint is stated clearly enough so that the defendant will know what claim you are bringing, it will be attached to a summons to be served to the defendant. A clerk of the court will help you complete the paperwork necessary to serve a summons on the defending party.

You will have to pay a filing fee, usually less than $20, and you may have to pay an extra fee for delivery of the summons to the defendant. In some jurisdictions, however, process can be served by any adult who's not a party to the suit, or by certified mail, so you may be able to have a friend serve the summons at no charge, or have it delivered by the post office at a minimal cost. If a friend acts as your process server, be sure to have him complete and sign the Proof of Service form and return it to the court. Otherwise, the defendant may later deny ever receiving notice of the summons, and that can delay you in collecting any default judgment awarded by the court.

When the defendant receives the summons, he may be required to file an answer to the complaint, but in many small claims courts all he must do to contest the claim is appear in court on the day of the trial to present the other side of the story. In many cases, being served with a summons to appear in small claims court will prompt a settlement offer that may be acceptable to both parties, and so the case can be dismissed before the trial.

If you and the defendant are unable to settle the matter before the date set for the court hearing, you should appear in the courtroom in advance of the time your trial is scheduled. In fact, many experts suggest attending a small claims court session a few days before your own trial is scheduled, so you can familiarize yourself with the court procedures and the judge's methods of handling cases. For example, some judges take very active roles in questioning the parties and their witnesses, while others pretty much let each party make their own case without a lot of questioning.

Before you go to court, it's a good idea to practice your presentation a few times. Small claims court dockets are usually crowded, and the judge may have to hear dozens of cases in a single session. You want to present your case as succinctly as possible, without going into issues that don't really concern the court. For example, if you have a breach of warranty case, it doesn't really matter to the judge that the customer service clerk you spoke to was rude or unfriendly, or that you weren't allowed to speak to the manager because he was out to lunch when you called. All that matters in a case like this is:

- You purchased an item with a warranty
- The item had a defect that was covered by the warranty
- The warranty was still in force when you brought it in for repairs
- The merchant or manufacturer refused to honor the warranty,
- You were damaged by the refusal, since you lost the value of the merchandise and incurred additional expense getting it repaired or replaced.

In addition, you will want to present yourself as a reasonable person seeking a reasonable solution. To that end, it's a good idea to be neatly dressed when you appear in small claims court, although you don't have to get out your best suit or dress for the occasion. Always be courteous to the judge, to your opponent, and to the opponent's witnesses. Shouting, using profanity, or interrupting the judge or other witnesses is a sure way to damage your case, and could even lead to a citation for contempt of court.

When your case is called, as the plaintiff you will have the opportunity to present your evidence to the judge first. If you have witnesses who will be appearing on your behalf, they will be given a chance to testify as to their knowledge about the matter in dispute. You should also have copies of any photographs, papers, invoices, or other correspondence which may help to bolster your case.

Once the court has heard your side of the case, the defendant will be given an opportunity to present his version of the dispute. In most small claims courts, the plaintiff will then get a chance to speak last and rebut any statements made by the defendant. Once the judge has gathered all of the information from both sides, he will render a decision, usually within a few days of the trial. If the court decides the case in favor of the plaintiff, the defendant will be ordered to pay some or all of the amount you have claimed, and may be required to reimburse you for court costs and filing fees in addition to the damages you claimed. But if the judgment is in favor of the defendant, you will not be entitled to receive any payment.

In most cases, you should expect to receive payment of any judgment for at least a week or two after the court issues its ruling. But if you don't have your money at the end of this period, there are some steps you can do to get the judgment paid.

First, you should send a copy of the judgment to the defendant along with a letter demanding payment. If the amount in question is a substantial one, you may be willing to let him pay the judgment in installments. If you agree to this arrangement, however, be sure to put the agreement in writing, and have the defendant sign it.

If the defendant refuses to pay, you may return to court and request a court order of execution, which commands the county sheriff or other law enforcement official to attach property belonging to the defendant, or to garnish wages. You can often find out where the defendant works and the locations of property such as bank and brokerage accounts, because the defendant will be required by the court to fill out a form listing his assets at the time the judgment is entered against him, and return it to you within a specified period of time. A losing defendant who refuses to complete this form can be guilty of contempt of court, unless he pays you the full amount of the judgment before the time period for returning the form expires.

If you are the loser in a small claims court case, you should be sure to obtain a form known as a "Satisfaction of Judgment" from the clerk of the small claims court. When you pay the amount you owe to the plaintiff, be sure that the plaintiff signs this form. You will then make a copy of the form for your records and file the original with the court, so there is a record of the payment in the event of a later dispute.

CHAPTER SEVENTEEN
CRIME AND PUNISHMENT

Even if you live your entire life without ever being arrested or charged with a crime, even if you are never the victim of a crime, crime in America has a significant impact on your life. Crime costs everyone, whether it's in the increased cost of purchasing an insurance policy to protect your home or business, the higher prices you pay for goods and services charged by businesses in order to help them recover some of the losses they experience through theft and employee dishonesty, or the increased taxes you pay to cover the costs of larger police forces and more jails and prisons.

In this chapter, we will discuss the way the law categorizes crimes and the punishment that the law provides for those convicted of committing a crime. We will explore the legal rights guaranteed to those who are suspected of a crime, as well as the rights of those who are charged and convicted of violating criminal laws. And we'll also examine the growing number of laws at both the state and federal level designed to help the victims of crimes.

First, however, a word of warning. If there's any area of the law where "doing-it-yourself" is the wrong strategy to follow, it's the area of criminal law and procedure. While you have a constitutional right to represent yourself in a criminal proceeding when you are charged with a crime, trying to do so is extremely foolish. The area of criminal law is extremely complex, and it's essential to obtain the assistance of the best legal counsel you can afford when you are suspected of or charged with a crime.

If a lack of money is the issue, you have the right to have a court-appointed attorney made available to you at no cost to yourself when you are charged with a crime. While in some cases these court-appointed attorneys are not the most experienced in the area of criminal law, they can at least help you protect yourself from doing or saying something that increases your chance of being convicted of a crime.

Whatever decision you make, remember that federal and state criminal laws and procedures vary, and so the advice contained here can only be regarded as general in nature. If you are facing potential criminal charges, do yourself a favor and get the help of an attorney as soon as possible.

WHAT IS A CRIME?

A crime is committed when someone takes an action (or fails to take some action) in violation of a statute enacted by a state legislature, or by Congress. Crimes involving prohibited actions include those prohibiting murder, assault, battery, burglary, robbery, theft, arson, and rape, as well as the other activities most of us are likely to think of as crimes. Crimes involving prohibited inaction include, for example, failing to notify state welfare authorities of suspected child abuse, when a statute requires you to do so because you hold a special position of trust, such as that of a doctor, nurse, or teacher.

Crimes are prosecuted by the state, and not by individuals. However, a crime may also be a tort, or civil wrong. For example, if you are raped, the state may prosecute the person who committed the rape under criminal statutes. And as the victim of the rape, you can bring a civil lawsuit against your assailant in order to recover for the injuries you suffered as a result of the rape, including medical expenses, lost wages, and damages for pain and suffering and the intentional infliction of emotional distress.

Your right to sue in civil court is not dependent upon the state's obtaining a criminal conviction, since the burden of proof in a civil lawsuit is lower than that in a criminal trial. We'll discuss the burden of proof which the prosecutor must meet in order to obtain a conviction in more detail later in this chapter. A discussion of the burden of proof that must be met in a civil lawsuit can be found in Chapter Sixteen, "Your Day in Court."

Because some violations of the law pose a more serious threat to order and public safety than others, the law divides crimes into several different categories. A "petty offense," which may also be called a "violation," is the kind of crime that poses the least risk to society. Petty offenses include such acts as illegal parking, running a stop sign and other traffic offenses, and other acts such as littering or burning leaves in violation of a state law or local ordinance.

In most cases, when you are charged with a petty offense, you will not be placed under arrest, but will instead be issued a citation, a kind of summons that orders you to either pay a fine or appear in court to defend yourself against the charge at a specified date. But if you are wanted for a more serious crime, or if you have previously ignored citations issued to you, you may be placed under arrest and taken into custody.

That's because the law in most jurisdictions makes ignoring citations a misdemeanor, the next category of crimes. Acts classified as misdemeanors are considered to present a greater threat to the public safety than petty offenses. Some of the crimes typically classified as misdemeanors include assault (you threaten to punch your neighbor in the nose) and battery (you actually punch him). Shoplifting of inexpensive items, writing insufficient funds checks for small amounts, and committing acts of vandalism are other crimes usually considered misdemeanors.

While the penalty for committing a petty offense is generally only a fine, in most states the penalty for committing a misdemeanor may include a fine, a prison term of less than one year, or both. Depending on state law, you may or may not be entitled to a trial by jury when you are charged with a misdemeanor, since the U.S. Constitution does not require jury trials when misdemeanor charges are involved.

You are entitled to a trial by jury when you are charged with a felony, the most serious kind of crime. Typical felonies include murder, manslaughter, rape, arson, and robbery. And some crimes which might otherwise be classified as misdemeanors can be considered felonies depending on the manner in which they are committed. For example, assault and battery are usually misdemeanors, but when committed with a gun or other dangerous weapon, or when they are committed in an especially violent or brutal way, are considered aggravated assault and battery, crimes categorized as felonies. Similarly, while shoplifting an item that costs a few dollars is usually a misdemeanor, shoplifting an item above a value specified by state law (such as $200) may be classified as a felony.

The penalties for committing a felony are the most severe allowed by law. For example, while a misdemeanor may be punishable by up to a year of imprisonment, a felony is usually punishable by at least a year in prison. A fine may also be imposed against a convicted felon. And for some very heinous felonies, such as premeditated murder, the majority of states allow the prosecution to seek the death penalty, while others may provide for a life sentence without the possibility of parole.

WHAT THE POLICE CAN (AND CANNOT) DO

Being a police officer in the United States is a demanding and often thankless job. In addition to the element of physical danger that many law enforcement officers face on an almost daily basis, today's police officer is required to have an extensive knowledge of state and federal statutes and court decisions that regulate the way in which he conducts himself when investigating a crime or making an arrest. And because these laws are constantly changing to reflect the beliefs and needs of society, what was permissible yesterday may be prohibited today, and vice versa.

As we've already seen, the Bill of Rights is the source of many of our individual rights, and as such it's also the source of many of the restrictions placed on law enforcement authorities. The Bill of Rights was created to limit the government's authority over the individual citizen, and as such one of its chief concerns was protecting the average person from being subjected to random investigations and "fishing expeditions" by the police.

The Fourth Amendment contains some of the most important safeguards afforded to private citizens in this regard. The Fourth Amendment's core protection is contained in the clause which prohibits "unreasonable searches and seizures."

As interpreted by the courts, this means that, except in extraordinary circumstance, the police may not search your home, your office, your car, your garage, or anyplace else in which you have a "reasonable expectation of privacy" without first obtaining a warrant that describes the place to be searched and the items or persons being sought. Nor may you be arrested without probable cause, the presence of enough facts to convince a reasonable person that crime has been committed, and that you are the person who committed it. In many cases, the police must obtain a warrant outlining the nature of the crime and their reasons for naming you as the suspect before you can be arrested. But if you commit a crime and are caught in the act by the officer, or if the officer has reason to believe that you committed a serious crime and will flee before a warrant can be obtained, you can generally be arrested without a warrant.

At the time our Bill of Rights was created, searches and seizures were a much less complicated issue than they are today. In the eighteenth century, there were no electronic listening devices, no telephones to wiretap, and no cellular telephones and two-way radios to listen in on. Court decisions over the past half-century have expanded the definition of what constitutes a search to consider these technological developments. As a result, government officials must obtain a warrant in order to electronically "bug" a home or office and eavesdrop on conversations held there, and they must also obtain a warrant to wiretap your telephone.

The situation is somewhat murkier, however, when law enforcement authorities listen in on conversations you conduct on a cordless or cellular telephone, or over a two-way radio. Some courts have held that your expectation of privacy in these communications is not as great as when you use a regular telephone, since these devices transmit your conversation over the air and thus are susceptible to being overheard by anyone else who has a similar device. Other courts, however, have held that the police have no greater latitude in listening to these communications than they do in tapping your telephone, and that evidence obtained by listening in without a warrant is not admissible in court.

At one time, if you were conducting activities outside your home but within the confines of a fence erected on your property, the police would have been required to obtain a warrant to enter and search for evidence of criminal activity. Today, however, most courts have held that no warrant is needed for police officers to fly over your property and make observations that lead to an arrest warrant. These courts have reasoned that your expectation of privacy on the grounds outside your home is lower than it was in the past, due to the fact that anyone in an airplane or helicopter can see what's happening on the ground below.

Court decisions have also defined what constitutes an arrest, a "seizure" of the individual. In general, courts have held that an arrest occurs when a person is taken into actual physical custody by a law enforcement officer.

For example, suppose you are driving down the highway when you see the flashing lights of a patrol car in the road ahead. As you approach, an officer signals for you to stop. You pull your car over out of traffic, and the police officer inquires about where you are coming from and where you are going. He asks you if you have had any alcoholic beverages to drink, and if your answer is affirmative, when you had your last drink. He then thanks you for your time and sends you on your way.

In this situation, you have not been arrested. Because of the need to keep drunk drivers off the road, the police in many states have set up so-called "sobriety checkpoints" at which they stop drivers and question them briefly to determine whether or not they are intoxicated. Such checkpoints are considered permissible under the U.S. Constitution, although some state courts have held that they violate state constitutional provisions.

However, suppose you are walking down the street when a police officer stops you to inquire about your business in the area and to ask for identification. He tells you that there has just been a burglary in the area, and that you match the description given by witnesses of one of the burglars. He then asks you to get into his patrol car, and takes you to the police station, where you are detained for several hours. In this case, a court might conclude that you had been arrested illegally, since the police officer detained you for more than a brief period of time and transported you to the police station, an act that would lead a reasonable person to believe that he was not free to leave of his own accord.

Whether an arrest is lawful or unlawful is a decision for a court to make. In no case should you ever resist a law enforcement officer who is placing you under arrest, no matter how unfair you believe that arrest to be. Not only are police officers allowed to use force to make an arrest, you may be charged with the separate crime of resisting arrest. If you are, you may be tried for and convicted of resisting arrest even if you are acquitted of the other charges that led to the arrest.

CRIMINAL PROCEDURE

As we've already seen, in the United States we have two systems of courts. Similarly, we have two systems of criminal justice as well. At the federal level, you may be charged with a crime when you do something prohibited by a federal statute, and your trial on federal charges will be conducted in a federal district court. If you are found guilty and sentenced to serve a prison sentence, that sentence will be served in a federal prison.

If you commit a crime prohibited by state law, your trial will be conducted in a state criminal court, and any prison sentence imposed will be served in a state institution. In either case, however, your rights when accused of a crime are guaranteed by the U.S. Constitution. And if you are charged with a crime under state law and the state's constitution grants criminal defendants greater rights than those contained in the federal Constitution, those safeguards will apply as well.

The most essential protections granted to individuals suspected of or accused of a crime are those contained in the Bill of Rights. And of these, the most important are those guaranteed by the Fifth Amendment.

As it has been interpreted by the U.S Supreme Court, the Fifth Amendment requires the government to take certain steps in order to ensure that you are not deprived of "life, liberty, or property, without due process of law." If you are arrested, the police must inform you of your right to remain silent and to have the assistance of a lawyer, as well as the right to a court-appointed lawyer if you cannot afford to hire one on your own.

In addition, you must be warned that anything you say may be used against you in court. This is the famous Miranda warning, named for the man whose appeal led to the Supreme Court's decision that the failure of the police to provide notice of these rights was unconstitutional.

It's not enough to tell you what your rights are, however. The police must give you the opportunity to exercise those rights, by letting you call a family member, friend, or an attorney. Holding an arrested suspect in isolation and refusing to let a lawyer or family member visit is also a violation of the suspect's constitutional rights. And once you indicate that you want to speak to a lawyer, the police must halt all questioning unless a lawyer is present. However, if you change your mind and initiate further conversations with the police, any statements you make may be used by the government in prosecuting you.

You have a right to know the nature of the crime you have been charged with, and to appear before a judge within a reasonable period of time in order to enter your plea to the charges. If you are not released from jail on your own recognizance (your written promise to appear for trial) you have the right to have reasonable bail set.

Bail is money which is posted with the court to guarantee that you will show up for your trial and other court proceedings related to the charges brought against you. What constitutes "reasonable" bail depends on a number of factors, including the nature of the crime with which you are charged, your previous criminal record, and your ties to the community. If you are charged with a relatively minor crime, have no past convictions, and have family and a job in the community, your bail may be relatively low.

But if you've been charged with a serious crime, have been convicted of other crimes in the past, and have nothing to keep you in the community, bail may be quite high. And in some cases, "reasonable" bail may be no bail at all, requiring you to remain in jail during the course of the criminal proceedings against you.

The most common kind of arrangement for paying pail is a bail bond. A bail bond is a promise by a licensed bonding agency that it will pay the court the full amount of your bail in the event you fail to appear in court as required. Generally, you'll be required to pay at least a percentage of the total bail to the bonding company (called a bail bondsman) as a nonrefundable fee for its services. And you will often have to offer property you own, such as your car or home, as collateral, which the bondsman can tap in the event you fail to make your court appearances.

After a bail hearing, the next procedural step in many states is a preliminary hearing, which may take place several days or weeks after your arrest. At this hearing, the state will make a presentation of the evidence it has against you in order to show the court that a crime had been committed and that it had probable cause to arrest you for committing it. Your attorney will have the opportunity to cross-examine witnesses called by the state, and you may be able to call witnesses to testify on your behalf.

After hearing the state's case against you, the presiding judge will decide whether or not there is sufficient evidence to proceed. Depending on the state in which the charges have been brought, the next step is to set a date for trial, or send the case to the grand jury. (In some states, charges are presented to the grand jury without the need for a preliminary hearing — you can see why it's so important to have specific legal advice about the laws in your state.)

In states where a grand jury indictment is required, the state gets to present all the evidence it has in support of your arrest. You are not entitled to appear before the grand jury to defend yourself against the charges, nor may your attorney represent you at the proceedings. On the other hand, you need not appear before a grand jury if you are asked to do so, and depending on the nature of the crime and the evidence the state has collected against you, it may be unwise to do so, since your attorney won't be allowed to assist or advise you during the proceedings.

If the grand jury believes that there is enough evidence to make a trial worthwhile, it will return a "true bill of indictment" against you. You will then be arraigned before a criminal court judge, at which time you will enter a plea to the charges against you.

In criminal cases, you generally have three kinds of plea to choose from. You may plead "guilty," "not guilty," or "no contest" sometimes referred to as a plea of nolo contendere. By pleading guilty, you avoid the necessity of a trial, but you also subject yourself to whatever punishment the court deems appropriate.

If you plead guilty, in serious cases you won't be sentenced immediately. Instead, the judge will send your case file to the state board of probation, where a probation officer will review the charges, any previous criminal record which you have, and your current family and job situation. After completing this review, the probation officer will send a recommendation to the court as to the sentence you should receive. While this report is influential, it is not binding, and unless the crime you committed carries a mandatory sentence imposed by statute, the judge may be able to modify your sentence by making it more or less severe.

Pleading "no contest" has essentially the same effect as pleading guilty, but with one very important difference. A guilty plea may be considered as evidence in a civil suit brought by the victim of your crime, while a no contest plea cannot be used against you.

If your plea is "not guilty," the next step is the scheduling of a criminal trial. Under the Sixth Amendment, you have a right to "a speedy and public trial, by an impartial jury. . .," when charged with a serious crime. State law usually defines the time limit within which your trial must begin. If the prosecution does not bring you to trial within this time, you can petition the court to have the charges against you dismissed. However, if the delay in beginning the trial is caused by you or your lawyer, these statutes do not apply.

While most of us think of a jury in a criminal case as consisting of twelve people, not every state requires so large a jury. In some states, six people may be enough to constitute a valid jury in some criminal trials, while others may require eight jurors. However, the U.S. Supreme Court has ruled that six is the minimum number of jurors required in a criminal trial, and a conviction by a jury smaller than six in number is invalid. And if you are charged with a petty offense or a misdemeanor, in some states you aren't even entitled to a trial by jury.

Much of the procedure for selecting a jury is similar to that used in selecting a jury in a civil lawsuit, and is discussed in detail in Chapter Sixteen, "Your Day in Court." Potential jurors are examined by both the prosecution and defense attorneys to determine if there is any reason that the potential juror could not render a fair and impartial decision. A juror may be challenged "for cause" and excluded from the jury if either side believes that he would be unable to be fair. Additionally, each side may exclude a certain number of potential jurors without giving a reason for doing so, by exercising what are known as "peremptory challenges."

Once the jury is selected and sworn in, the trial begins. The prosecuting attorney will make an opening statement, in which he will describe the charges against you and how he hopes to prove those charges, and your attorney then gets to follow with his own opening statement.

The prosecutor then gets to present his case, calling witnesses and presenting evidence which is intended to prove to the jury that a crime was committed and that you are the person guilty of committing it. Your attorney may try to prevent the introduction of certain evidence by making what's known as a motion to suppress before your trial begins.

Generally, a motion to suppress is granted only when the evidence was illegally obtained, such as when it was discovered during an invalid search and seizure, or when the police failed to give you the required Miranda warnings at the time of your arrest. Otherwise, the evidence will probably be allowed, although your attorney may object again at the time the prosecutor introduces it.

Your attorney can also cross-examine the witnesses who the prosecutor calls on to testify against you. Cross-examination is intended to cast doubt on the truthfulness of a witness, to question his memory about the events to which he testifies, or to otherwise discredit the witness's testimony. Your attorney is not required to cross-examine witnesses, however, and may not do so for a variety of tactical reasons. In some cases, a witness's testimony on direct examination is of so little consequence that to cross-examine him may give the evidence more weight than it deserves in the mind of the jury. In other cases, the prosecutor's own examination of the witness may have been inadequate, and cross-examination may bring out facts that could damage your case by revealing something that the jury didn't learn during direct testimony.

After the prosecution rests its case against you, your attorney will probably ask the court to dismiss the charges against you. However, as long as the prosecution has made at least a prima facie case against you, the trial will probably be allowed to continue. Your own lawyer will then present evidence designed to cast doubt on the prosecution's case. He may call witnesses to testify on your behalf, such as by providing you with an alibi for the time at which the crime was committed. The prosecution may cross-examine any witnesses called to testify for the defense.

Your lawyer may or may not allow you to testify on your own behalf, depending on whether he believes your appearance will do more harm than good. While the Fifth Amendment prevents the government from compelling you to testify against yourself, if you take the witness stand voluntarily, you may be placed in the awkward position of doing so during cross-examination by the prosecuting attorney. For this reason, your lawyer will need to consider carefully how much harm your testimony may cause your defense, and weigh that against any potential benefit. If you do not take the stand, the jury will be instructed not to infer anything about your guilt by your failure to testify on your own behalf.

After the defense rests its case, closing arguments are made by each side. In some jurisdictions, the defense goes first, then the prosecutor. In others, the prosecutor goes first, the defense follows, and then the prosecutor gets to make a rebuttal statement. At this point, the judge will instruct the jury about the law it must apply in deciding the case. The jury will then retire to the jury room, where it will vote as to whether or not the prosecution proved its case beyond a reasonable doubt, the burden of proof that must be met in order to obtain a criminal conviction. In some cases, the jury may become deadlocked, failing to reach a decision after deliberating for a long period of time. If the deadlock cannot be broken, a mistrial is declared, and the state then has to decide whether or not to retry the case or dismiss the charges against you.

In most cases, however, the jury will be able to return a verdict. If the verdict is guilty, you may be ordered to jail until you are sentenced by the court, a procedure which will take place some weeks after your conviction. However, depending on the circumstances, you may be allowed to remain free on bail during this period. If the verdict is not guilty, you are generally free to return to your daily life. The state may not prosecute you again for the same crime, since to do so would violate the Fifth Amendment's prohibition against double jeopardy.

But while the prohibition against double jeopardy protects defendants from being tried twice by the same government for the same crime, the Supreme Court has held that it does not apply when a defendant is charged with crimes under both state and federal law. The same crime may result in trial, conviction and punishment at both the state and federal levels without subjecting the defendant to double jeopardy. A recent example of this occurred when the police officers accused of beating motorist Rodney King in Los Angeles were acquitted of assault charges in state court, but were then indicted and convicted in federal court for violating King's civil rights.

Double jeopardy also doesn't apply when you appeal your conviction and the appeals court overturns your conviction. In this case, the state may decide to prosecute you again. And in most cases, a mistrial does not prevent the prosecution from bringing you to trial again on the same charges.

If you are convicted by the jury, your lawyer will probably ask the trial judge to set aside the jury's verdict and declare you not guilty. But instances in which jury verdicts are set aside are rare, and so your next step will be to file an appeal to a higher court asking that the verdict be overturned. Appeals must be based on the fact that the trial court erred during the trial in a way that prejudiced the jury's decision.

For example, suppose the judge allowed the prosecution to present evidence that you had previously been convicted on similar charges. By doing so, the judge may have allowed the jury to become prejudiced against you in a way that's prohibited by the law. A jury is only supposed to concern itself with the evidence in the case at hand, rather than the defendant's previous criminal record. As a result of allowing this evidence to be presented to the jury, the judge has committed what's known as a reversible error. Your conviction would be overturned, and a new trial granted.

HOW CRIMES ARE PUNISHED

After your trial, the court will impose its sentence on you for the crime you committed. The Eighth Amendment to the U.S. Constitution prohibits the court from subjecting you to "cruel and unusual punishment." Among other things, this means that the punishment must fit the crime. But deciding what punishment is permissible in light of the Eighth Amendment can be a difficult task.

While it's fairly obvious that imposing the death penalty on someone convicted of a first time burglary is almost certainly cruel and unusual punishment, the courts have allowed persons with multiple convictions for non-violent crimes such as writing bad checks to be sentenced to life in prison without parole as habitual offenders. In other cases, persons sentenced to lengthy prison terms for the possession of small amounts of marijuana have also been upheld when challenged on Eighth Amendment grounds. On the other hand, physical abuse, such as beatings and torture, have consistently been held to constitute the kind of cruel and unusual punishment prohibited by the Eighth Amendment.

In addition to fines and imprisonment, the federal government and an increasing number of states have begun to seek the forfeiture of property used in the commission of a crime, or gained through criminal activity. In a number of cases, courts have even allowed the government to seize the property of persons who were not charged with any crimes themselves. For example, in one case a restaurant was forfeited by its owners after a bartender was charged with selling drugs on the premises, despite the fact that the owners of the restaurant had no knowledge of the bartender's criminal activities.

With our nation's prisons filling up more quickly than ever, criminal courts have turned to other kinds of sentences as an alternative to imprisonment. One of the more traditional alternatives is probation. Probation allows the person convicted of a crime to remain free, subject to restrictions imposed by the court. For example, a convict on probation may be required to check in with a probation officer on a regular basis, and may be prohibited from leaving the state without the court's permission. If the convict violates these or any other reasonable terms imposed by the court, he can be imprisoned. Not every person convicted of a crime is eligible for probation; the court considers such factors as the severity of the crime, the previous history of the convicted criminal, and the potential for rehabilitation of the convict.

Another alternative form of punishment is community service. Community service is most often used in misdemeanor cases, or occasionally when the criminal has been convicted of a non-violent felony, such as embezzlement. Community service can take a variety of forms, including everything from cleaning up roadside parks to presenting speeches and seminars on the evils of crime. Community service is sometimes granted when the convict has a high level of visibility to the public. For example, celebrities such as rock musicians and movie actors may be given sentences of community service because the court believes that more good can be done for society through the celebrity's service than through his imprisonment.

Although probation is sometimes confused with parole, and while there are similarities, they are not the same. Probation is granted at the time a convict is sentenced, while parole is granted later, after the convict has served a portion of his prison sentence. As with probation, not every convicted criminal is eligible for parole; those convicted of first degree or capital murder (the worst types of killing), and those who are found to be habitual criminals are commonly ineligible for parole.

Another similarity to probation is that parole is usually based on the convict's obeying certain conditions set forth by the parole board. A convict who violates the terms of his parole may be returned to prison to finish the rest of his sentence.

WHEN JUVENILES BREAK THE LAW

In most cases, when a minor is accused of breaking the law, he will not be tried for his crime in the regular criminal court. Instead, his case will be heard in a juvenile court. The law and society have long believed that most young people below a certain age are incapable of knowing the consequences of their actions to the same extent as an adult does.

In some cases, however, when the crime committed is particularly serious, or when the juvenile has had a history of other offenses, he may be charged in criminal court rather than in juvenile court. As more and more young people become involved in gang activities, drive-by shootings, drug dealing and murder, an increasing number of cases which once would have been tried in juvenile court are now being heard in regular criminal court. A juvenile who is tried in criminal court is subject to the same punishment as an adult, including life in prison without parole, although some states have held that juveniles cannot be sentenced to death.

Juvenile court proceedings are very similar to those conducted in criminal court, although there are a few important differences. First, in most cases juvenile court records are not available to the public, in order to avoid marking a youth as a criminal for his entire life. Second, trials in juvenile court are not decided by a jury. The juvenile court judge hears the evidence and makes the decision about the minor's guilt or innocence.

Otherwise, a youth accused of breaking the law has all the same rights as an adult criminal defendant, including the right to remain silent and to have an attorney's assistance. If your child is ever accused of breaking the law, you should be sure to get a lawyer's assistance as soon as possible.

VICTIM'S RIGHTS

While a criminal defendant has a wide variety of constitutional rights, until very recently the law said little about the rights of those who are the victims of crimes. Today, that situation has changed with the enactment of a number of laws on both the state and federal level designed to insure that the victims of crime are not forgotten in the criminal justice system.

Many states, such as Nebraska, Rhode Island, Oklahoma, Washington and Wisconsin have enacted legislation under the general heading of the Victim's Bill of Rights. Some states have gone even further, enacting amendments to their constitutions regarding victim's rights.

For example, the state of Florida has such an amendment, stating in part that victims of crime have the right "to be informed, to be present, and to be heard when relevant, at all crucial stages of criminal proceedings." California, Michigan and Rhode Island have also added victim's rights amendments to their constitutions.

The Federal Victim and Witness Protection Act provides that the presentence report, used by the judge in federal cases to determine the sentence of the defendant, contain information regarding the impact of the particular crime on the victim (or his or her family). This report must address the financial losses suffered by the victim, as well as the medical, social and psychological impact of the crime on the victim. Victim impact statements are also required in the District of Columbia and the majority of state courts.

For several years, a United States Supreme Court ruling barred the use of victim impact statements in cases where the death penalty might be imposed, but this prohibition was later overruled by a later Supreme Court case. Now victim impact statements may be used in any type of case, if allowed by state law.

Under the Federal Victim and Witness Protection Act of 1982, the federal courts, in sentencing a defendant who has been convicted of a crime, may require that the offender make restitution to his or her victims, or the estate of a victim who was killed or has died prior to sentencing.

Restitution, in which the convicted defendant pays the victim of the crime directly to compensate the victim for his or her losses, serves two important functions. It compensates the victim for the harm done and (in theory, at least) it helps to rehabilitate the criminal as well.

Restitution can include reimbursement for the victim's lost wages, medical and funeral expenses, and personal property damages suffered as a result of the crime. The convicted defendant may also be ordered to pay the cost of therapy undertaken by the victim in connection with the crime.

Under the federal law, if the judge decides not to order restitution, it must state its reasons, on the record, at the time of sentencing. And most states now have similar laws allowing their courts to order restitution by defendants convicted of state crimes or explain why they have not done so.

In many cases, unfortunately, an order of restitution from the convicted defendant is of no help to the victim of a crime, because the convict is in prison and unable to work and has no assets with which to pay restitution. The Federal Victims of Crime Act of 1984 made grants available to the individual states to help fund victim compensation and victim assistance programs. Money collected as fines in federal cases, as well as money collected under the federal version of the "Son of Sam" law, provides the funding for this program. These victim compensation programs provide direct financial aid to the victims of crime.

Some victim's compensation programs exclude victims who are members of the same household as the perpetrator of the crime, on the theory that aid to those persons would aid the criminal. However, many programs with such prohibitions are rethinking them, as this would deny assistance to battered women and the victims of child abuse in many cases.

While victim's compensation funds represent a step in the right direction, most of these funds are inadequate to fully compensate every crime victim. In cases of violent crime, these funds may never actually reach the victim directly, but are paid to hospitals and doctors to help compensate them for the services they rendered. While it's certainly worthwhile to apply for these funds if you have been the victim of a crime, remember that you can also file a civil lawsuit against a person who causes you injury or damages. In some cases, your only real hope of receiving anything close to adequate repayment for the losses you suffer may be through a civil suit.

Additional legal protections are sometimes extended to children who are victims of physical or sexual abuse, or other crimes. Children who are the victims of crime are often traumatized a second time when required to come face to face in court with the person who harmed them. Many states have enacted laws that allow the child to give his or her testimony without actually seeing the defendant. The U. S. Supreme Court has found that in certain cases, a child testifying as the victim of crime or as a witness may give testimony by closed circuit television without violating the defendant's right to confront his accuser. Some states have also extended the statute of limitations in child abuse cases, allowing criminal prosecution even after several years have passed, because some young victims of abuse are unable to report the crime until they are older.

To find out more about the availability of victim protection and compensation programs in your community, contact your local prosecuting attorney's office.

CHAPTER EIGHTEEN
WHEN YOU NEED A LAWYER

With more than 800,000 lawyers in the United States, you would think that finding a well-qualified and caring lawyer to help you with a legal problem would be a relatively easy task. You would be wrong. First, many lawyers work for government agencies or large corporations, so they aren't available to help the general public. Of the remainder, many will work in very specialized areas of the law that simply don't touch the life of the average person. (In fact, many of these lawyers will work as "outside counsel" to governments and large corporations that also employ their own "in-house" lawyers.)

Of the rest, some work at large law firms and charge fees that are out of the average person's range, some don't practice actively, some are barely competent, and some aren't competent at all. So the number of affordable, capable and caring lawyers from which you can choose, while still substantial, is much smaller than the 800,000 figure the press loves to quote.

Contrary to what the profession would like you to believe, becoming a lawyer is a relatively easy task. In some states, more than 80 percent of those who graduate from law school and take the bar exam are admitted on their first try.

Becoming a good lawyer, however, is much harder. Law schools don't spend much time on subjects such as client communications, billing practices and caring about the problems people face. And when they do, the focus of these classes is often centered on doing the bare minimum to keep the lawyer from having a complaint filed with the state Supreme Court or Attorney Disciplinary Committee.

Although the primary purpose of this book is to help you recognize, understand and even deal with legal problems without the need for a lawyer's help, there are times in just about everyone's life when a lawyer's assistance is going to be necessary. You should consider hiring a lawyer when:

- You are charged with Driving Under the Influence (DUI) or a similar offense that could result in the loss of driving privileges or imprisonment
- You are charged with any criminal violation or served with a civil lawsuit
- The state notifies you that it wants to take your home or other real estate you own under its condemnation powers
- You are asked to sign any document you do not fully understand or with which you do not agree, especially in regard to settling an insurance claim
- Your insurance company refuses to pay what you believe is a legitimate claim

FINDING THE RIGHT LAWYER

Understandably, the best time to find a lawyer is when you don't have an immediate need for one. By taking your time and interviewing several attorneys, you have a much better chance of finding one with expertise in the areas of law that affect your life most often, as well as one who with whom you will feel comfortable discussing your personal legal matters. A lawyer chosen at the last minute may turn out to be extremely competent and completely capable of helping you with your legal problems. On the other hand, he or she may lack the experience you need and the personality traits you prefer.

In some cases, such as if you are charged with a crime or jailed for a serious traffic offense, such as driving under the influence, you won't have the luxury of shopping around for a lawyer, at least not initially. In this case, it's probably best to find the first lawyer who can get you out of jail as soon as possible and protect you from doing or saying anything self-incriminating that might be used against you. (If you don't have the money to hire a lawyer on your own in one of these situations, you are entitled to have a lawyer appointed at no charge to you.) Once you're out of jail, you will have some time to select a lawyer who can help you.

One of the best ways to find an attorney is through a personal reference from your relatives or friends, provided that the attorney is one they actually used for a problem that's similar to the one you have. A referral to your next door neighbor's nephew Clarence isn't going to be much good if he's only been practicing for six weeks and you've got a serious criminal charge or civil suit facing you. You may also want to consult with your accountant, insurance agent, or some other professional whose judgment you respect for a referral, especially if you need help with a business transaction, financial planning, or a tax problem.

Your state and local bar association operates a lawyer referral service that can direct you to an attorney that practices in the area of law where you need assistance. A list of state bar association referral services is included at the end of this chapter.

If you decide to use a bar-sponsored referral service, you can expect to pay a small fee, usually $25 or so, for an initial consultation with an attorney. The quality of attorneys who participate in these referral programs can vary, and referrals are usually spread out among all those who participate in the program. Most if not all states require attorneys who participate in their referral programs to carry malpractice insurance, and will remove an attorney who is the subject of client complaints or who is disciplined by the state's highest court. But they usually don't require any extensive experience or expertise, so you still need to exercise caution before you hire one of these attorneys; being on the referral service's list of available attorneys is no guarantee of quality.

If you look in the Yellow Pages under "Attorney Referral Services," you will find at least several numbers to call. Most of these referral services are less than totally independent; they receive their financing from the attorneys who pay to be placed on the service's referral panel. For these services, that's all the qualification the lawyer needs to get a referral. The service doesn't investigate the lawyer's competence, although as with the state bar referral service it may require the attorney to carry malpractice insurance. Again, it's essential to talk to more than one lawyer before you make a decision on which one to hire.

Many people select their attorney based on advertisements on television, radio, and in newspapers and telephone directories. Before the 1970s, state bar associations and disciplinary authorities kept a pretty tight rein on lawyer advertising. About all you could tell from lawyer ads in those days was the firm's name, its telephone number, and the areas in which it concentrated its practice.

In the past twenty years, however, restrictions on lawyer advertising have been lifted, although the state is still permitted to regulate these advertisements to some extent. Within the profession, there's still a great deal of debate about lawyer advertising. Some lawyers feel that many lawyers' ads are tacky and a disgrace to the profession; others defend advertising as a way for potential clients to learn about their legal rights and the availability of professional help.

As with most such debates, both sides are right to some extent. Many lawyers' advertisements, especially on television, are badly thought out and poorly produced, especially the ones utilized by some of the more aggressive personal injury firms. On the other hand, some people who have a sense that they need a lawyer's help but don't know where to go or how to proceed can benefit from information about the availability of legal services. However, just because a law firm produces a slick and sincere sounding advertisement doesn't mean that the lawyers who will serve you are going to do a better job, or do it for less, than a lawyer who doesn't advertise.

One source of information about lawyers that is often overlooked by the general public is the Martindale-Hubbell Law Directory. This directory is available at most larger public libraries and every law school or courthouse library.

Arranged by state and city, it lists most of the practicing lawyers in the United States, where they went to law school, when they were admitted to practice, and the areas of law in which they concentrate. More importantly, it also gives evaluations of a lawyer's skills and reputation as measured by other lawyers in the community where he practices. A lawyer rated "a v," for example, has the highest possible rating from his peers in the legal community.

Finally, a growing number of employers now offer prepaid legal service plans as a fringe benefit for their employees. Members in prepaid legal services plans are generally entitled to receive a variety of legal benefits, including advice and consultation, at little or no cost. Many of these plans also provide for a no-cost review of legal documents. Check with your employer's personnel manager or benefits administrator to find out if a prepaid legal service plan is offered as a benefit where you work.

You can also join a prepaid legal service that enrolls individual members. Generally, you'll pay anywhere from $75 to $300 or more, depending on which plan you enroll in and the number of services provided. To find out more about prepaid legal service plans that enroll individual members, contact the National Resource Center for Consumers of Legal Services, P.O. Box 340, Gloucester, Virginia 23061.

MEETING WITH A LAWYER

Before your first meeting with a lawyer you are interviewing, take the time to prepare some specific questions to ask. Before you make an appointment, ask the attorney what he or she will charge for the consultation. Some lawyers, especially those who handle personal injury and worker compensation matters, offer a free first meeting. Others may charge a reduced fee for the first meeting, while still others charge at their usual hourly rate. Ask the attorney what materials you should bring to your first meeting, such as copies of contracts, letters, or a summons you received.

When you arrive at the lawyer's office for your first consultation, take a few minutes to size up the way the office looks and the attitude of the lawyer's support staff. Is the office neat or does it appear disorganized? Does the receptionist greet you pleasantly and courteously, or is the greeting surly or disinterested? Do the staff members dress professionally? While some law offices are plush, with oriental carpets and marble counters, others are much less grand. Keep in mind that the lawyers at either kind of office may be equally competent, and remember that the cost of any glitz and grandeur comes from one place, and that's the fees the law firm charges its clients.

When you finally sit down to talk with the lawyer, give the lawyer a brief description of the nature of your problem. Don't fall into the trap of trying to sound like Perry Mason, using legal jargon you may have picked up from television and books; the lawyer's unlikely to be impressed. Just tell your story in plain English.

Answer any questions the lawyer asks as honestly as you can, and don't try to hide information that you think puts you in an unflattering light or weakens your case. If your lawyer is going to help you, he has to know the whole story; few things make a lawyer more angry than to have a client withhold information that's pertinent to the problem.

You don't have to worry about the lawyer revealing what you tell him. Unless you are telling him about a crime you intend to commit, your statements are considered "privileged," which means they can't be disclosed by the lawyer without your permission, even if you decide not to hire him. However, if you take another person into the office with you, this privilege may not apply, since by discussing your problem in the presence of another person you have already treated it as being less than confidential between you and the attorney. You should leave your mother, your child, or any friends who accompanied you to the lawyer's office in the waiting room. If the lawyer needs to talk to any of these people, he'll let you know.

After you outline your problem to the attorney, ask him if he's successfully handled similar cases in the past. Ask him how many cases he's settled, as well as how many cases he has taken to trial and won.

Ask about the strategy he will follow if you hire him to represent you. If you want to negotiate a friendly settlement with your spouse in advance of a divorce, for example, you don't want to hire an attorney whose chief strategy is to be as confrontational and unpleasant as possible. Don't be afraid to ask questions if the lawyer uses terms you don't understand. A good lawyer will take the time to explain things patiently and clearly.

One important area that needs to be discussed is that of client communications. Some attorneys will provide their clients with virtually every piece of correspondence in regard to a particular matter, as well as copies of all the papers filed with the court. Other lawyers communicate very minimally with their clients. Getting some of these lawyers to do something as simple as returning a phone call can be torturous.

If you want to be completely informed about the progress of your case, be sure to tell the lawyer you are interviewing about your desire for ongoing communication at your first meeting. If the attorney seems reluctant to comply, or tries to tell you "that's just not the way we do things," you may want to consider looking elsewhere for a lawyer who is more willing to meet your expectations. Remember that the lawyer you hire works for you; you would be surprised how many lawyers seem to have forgotten this basic principle.

That doesn't mean your lawyer won't have other clients, and there may be times when for one reason or another (such as when the lawyer is in court or attending a settlement conference), he or she won't be immediately available to answer a phone call or explain the latest motion filed by your opponent. But it does mean that you should be able to expect a courteous and patient answer to your questions as soon as possible, and you should have telephone calls returned promptly.

LEGAL FEES AND EXPENSES

As the final step in selecting a lawyer to represent you, you will want to know the financial details of your relationship and have them put in writing. Legal fees vary widely and depend on a number of factors, including the location in which the lawyer practices, the size of the firm, and the lawyer's expertise and experience. A lawyer working as a sole practitioner in a rural part of a state like Kansas or Oklahoma might charge as little as $60 or $70 per hour for his services, while a senior partner at a 200-plus attorney firm in downtown Los Angeles might charge $400 an hour for doing essentially the same kind of work.

Any lawyer you hire should provide you with a written fee agreement which states either an hourly rate, a flat fee for services rendered, or a contingency fee arrangement. If your legal matter is complicated, the attorney may be able to offer no more than an estimate of what the total fee may be (although if he has experience in the area the estimate should be pretty close to the final bill).

Some lawyers charge what's known as a retainer, an up front payment from the client that the lawyer uses to get started on the matter at hand. Your fee agreement with the lawyer should provide that the lawyer will return any unused portion of the retainer, if, for example, he reaches a favorable settlement far sooner than he had anticipated.

If your arrangement involves a contingency fee, you will want a written description of what percentage the lawyer will take of any settlement or judgment you receive, as well as how the attorney's percentage of the amount collected will be calculated. Typically, lawyers who work on a contingency fee basis use a sliding scale to determine their slice of the pie. For example, your lawyer might agree to take 33 percent of a settlement received before going to trial, 40 percent of a settlement you accept after trial has begun, and 50 percent of anything you receive as a judgment at the end of trial. As with all legal fees, these percentages are negotiable, although most lawyers don't like to haggle over fees with their clients. Still, it never hurts to ask, especially if the chances of success and a substantial verdict in your favor are good.

One thing you should require is that expenses incurred by the lawyer on your behalf be deducted from a judgment or settlement before the lawyer takes his share. Otherwise, you'll come out with less money and the lawyer will get more. For example, suppose you accept a settlement of $100,000. Expenses were $4,000, and your lawyer's fee is 33 percent. If you deduct the $4,000 off the top, your lawyer will get $32,000 as his fee, and you will receive $64,000.

But if the lawyer takes his cut before expenses, he gets $33,333, or one-third of the total. You get $66,667, out of which you have to pay the $4,000 in expenses. That leaves you with $62,667, or more than $1,000 less than you would have received if expenses were deducted first. And the higher your expenses, the greater the difference in what you receive.

A number of states now require that all contingency fee agreements be put in writing, but even if your state doesn't have this requirement, do not proceed until you have a written agreement in place. And keep in mind that even in a contingency fee situation, as the client you bear the final responsibility for court costs and expenses incurred by the lawyer on your behalf.

In some cases, these expenses can really add up. That's because law firms have figured out that they can make a profit by charging high prices for services that don't cost them much to provide. For example, some law firms charge their clients as much as 30 cents or more per page for photocopies, when the same quality copies are available from the corner copy shop for five or six cents per copy. When you consider that lawsuits often require the making of hundreds or even thousands of copies, the bill can run up pretty quickly. Find out in advance what your lawyer's firm charges for these kinds of office expenses, and ask what you can do to lower them, such as providing documents to the lawyer in duplicate. Always insist that your lawyer provide you with an itemized statement and receipts for the expenses incurred on your case on a regular basis, at least quarterly, but preferably every month.

Lawyers are prohibited by the rules of ethics from taking some kinds of cases, such as divorces and criminal defense work, on a contingency fee basis.

Of course, there are some ways that you can help to minimize your attorney's fees, especially when you are being billed on an hourly basis. You should call or meet with your lawyer only when there is something specific that you want to discuss with him or her, and not merely to receive a progress report on your case. Lawyers who charge an hourly rate use what's known as a "minimum billing unit," such as one-tenth or one-quarter of an hour. Even if you spend less than a minute on the telephone with your attorney, you will be charged his minimum billing unit. If the lawyer's hourly rate is $150, for example, and he charges for a minimum one-tenth of an hour, your one minute phone call costs you $15!

Many legal matters can take months or even years to conclude, and there will be long periods when there will be no progress on your matter for your lawyer to report. Calling your attorney at these times will only add to the expenses you will ultimately need to pay.

WHEN YOU ARE DISSATISFIED WITH YOUR LAWYER'S PERFORMANCE

No matter how carefully you select your lawyer, it's still possible that you will be disappointed or unhappy with his performance, or concerned about his honesty, or just plain incompatible with him. Many clients don't express their concerns to the lawyer, suffering in silence, afraid that speaking up will make matters even worse.

Don't fall into this trap. If you have a problem with your lawyer, you owe it to yourself (and to him) to let him know about it. In some cases, doing so early on may actually rectify the problem in a way that makes everybody happy.

But if your lawyer seems unresponsive to your complaints, you may be forced to consider dismissing him and hiring another lawyer to take over your case. If you should decide that changing lawyers is necessary, you will need to start the interviewing process outlined earlier in this chapter all over again. One thing you don't want to do, however, is tell the new lawyer you are interviewing about your problems with your current lawyer until after he's evaluated your case and you are satisfied you want to hire him. Few things make a lawyer more uncomfortable than feeling that you are shopping for a second opinion.

Once you've decided on and hired the new lawyer to handle your case, you will need to get your files transferred from the original lawyer. To get them, you will need to pay any fees you still owe to the original lawyer. State laws give lawyers the right to what's known as a retaining lien on your files, which allows him to keep your documents and other property until his fee is paid. Even if you think the fee is unfair, your best bet is to pay it, get your documents back, and then file a complaint with your state's disciplinary authorities. Many state and local bar associations now run fee dispute arbitration services designed to help clients recover unreasonable legal fees. Your state bar association can tell you about the availability of one of these programs in your area.

UNETHICAL BEHAVIOR

Every state has a code of legal ethics designed to guide the behavior of lawyers. Enforcement of the rules of ethics is the responsibility of the Supreme Court of the state in which they are licensed to practice. In many states, the court delegates the initial responsibility for investigating complaints to a committee of practicing attorneys, although it retains the right to overrule the committee when it disagrees with a recommendation it makes to the Court.

Lawyers who violate the ethical rules in their state can be subjected to various forms of discipline, which include:

- An informal admonition from the disciplinary committee
- A private reprimand from the Supreme Court
- A public reprimand published in official court records
- Temporary suspension of the lawyer's license to practice
- Permanent removal of the lawyer's license (disbarment)

While the exact form of the code of ethics that governs lawyers' behavior varies somewhat from one state to another, they all have certain common characteristics. These rules require attorneys to represent their clients with competence and diligence, although that doesn't mean they have to be successful in representing you. Very few lawsuits end up without at least one loser.

Lawyers are obligated to avoid conflicts of interest when representing their clients. This means that if a lawyer's work for one client will materially interfere with his work for another client, he must notify them of the conflict and withdraw from representing one or the other. However, if both clients consent, in some cases the lawyer may be allowed to represent both parties. Situations where this is advisable are extremely limited, and we would strongly suggest that you avoid using an attorney who tries to represent you and another client when there's even the slightest hint of a conflict. You want your lawyer to represent your best interests without having to worry about his potential divided loyalty between you and another client.

The rules of ethics also prohibit your lawyer from accepting or rejecting settlement offers without your full knowledge and approval, require lawyers to charge only "reasonable" fees and keep clients "reasonably" informed about the progress of any matter. They also require lawyers who learn of unethical or improper behavior on the part of other lawyers to report it to the state attorney disciplinary authorities.

Unfortunately, while the intent of the rules of ethics is admirable, enforcement isn't always what it should be. Because the rules use terms like "reasonable" to guide a lawyer's behavior, there's a wide range of activities that may seem unreasonable to you but perfectly reasonable to other lawyers. Backlogs and delays in investigating complaints mean it may take months or even years before your complaint is heard. In most states, if you do file a complaint, you are sworn to secrecy, meaning you can't make your complaint public if the disciplinary committee refuses to sanction your attorney. Lawyers constitute the majority of members of attorney disciplinary committees, and in some states there are no non-lawyers on the committee.

Attorneys don't always report the unethical behavior of their colleagues, and when discipline is meted out, it is often far less than one might expect. Some lawyers who have stolen money from their clients, who neglected to file lawsuits before the statute of limitations ran out, and who lied to their clients about the progress being made on their cases have been allowed to continue practicing law, albeit after a suspension or other discipline. Attorneys are entitled to present "mitigating evidence" when they are charged with misconduct; for example, that they only stole their clients' money to pay for their drug habit. If the lawyer agrees to enter a rehabilitation program and make restitution, he may be allowed to resume his practice after a suspension of a year or so. To be sure, some attorneys are disbarred for serious misconduct, but many others escape the most serious punishment for one reason or another.

Because most attorney disciplinary committees won't provide information to the public about complaints they receive unless the complaint results in punishment, it's hard to find out ahead of time if a lawyer has had a history of complaints that resulted in no disciplinary action. You can find out more about the rules that regulate your lawyer's conduct by contacting your state bar association or the Supreme Court located in your state capital, or by looking them up in the state statutes available in the reference section of most larger public libraries.

If you believe that your lawyer has violated the ethical rules in your state, you should contact your local bar association or your state's Supreme Court for information about the procedure for filing a formal complaint. Most states now have forms which you will need to fill out, which will be sent to you along with a pamphlet containing instructions and outlining the disciplinary process.

Once you complete the forms and return them to the disciplinary committee, the committee staff will review your complaint to see if it states a violation of the state's rules of conduct for attorneys. If it doesn't, no further action will be taken by the committee. If it does, the committee will give your lawyer a chance to respond in writing, and if the committee decides his response is adequate, case closed.

If the committee doesn't receive a response from your lawyer, thinks the response is inadequate, or simply decides it needs more evidence, a hearing will be scheduled. On average, fewer than 1 in 10 complaints ever reach the hearing stage.

At the hearing, you may be called as a witness by the committee and asked to tell your story to the hearing panel, which usually consists of several practicing lawyers. Your lawyer will get a chance to respond to your accusations, and may be allowed to cross-examine you about your testimony. When the hearing is over, the panel will decide what, if any, discipline to recommend to the Supreme Court. The Court may then hear more evidence about the recommendation from the committee and from the attorney. Depending on the outcome of this hearing, the Court will then either accept the committee's recommendation, modify it, or reject it.

MALPRACTICE AND OTHER PROBLEMS

In the mid-1980s, a study conducted by the American Bar Association of 30,000 legal malpractice claims found that only a little more than 1 percent of those claims ever led to a successful malpractice lawsuit. Of that 1 percent, most "successful" plaintiffs ended up with less than $1,000 in compensation.

Generally, in order to win a malpractice suit against a lawyer who's botched his representation of you, you have to show that he failed to exercise the knowledge, diligence, and skill of an "ordinary" lawyer. Depending on the state in which you live, the "ordinary" lawyer against which your attorney will be measured may differ considerably. He may be compared to other lawyers in his community, or in the state in which he practices, or in the entire United States, or who practice in his field of the law.

Second, you have to show that because the lawyer failed to meet this standard, you suffered a loss which you would not have suffered otherwise, such as additional fees you had to pay to another lawyer to straighten out the first lawyer's mess, as well as damages the lawyer you are suing should have foreseen as a result of his malpractice.

While it may seem clear to you that your case meets the above standards, don't be surprised if you have a hard time convincing a lawyer to represent you in a malpractice case. First, many lawyers who seem eager to file suit against just about anyone don't like to take on legal malpractice cases, for the same reason they don't report violations of the disciplinary rules; the lawyer you want to sue is certainly a colleague, and may even be a personal friend of the lawyer you ask to handle your malpractice claim. In many parts of the country, there's still a sense that "it's us (lawyers) against them (the public)," and a lawyer who sides with the public may find himself ostracized by the rest of the local legal establishment. This problem isn't as severe in larger cities, where most lawyers know only a small proportion of the other lawyers in the community, but it can pose a real problem if you live in a smaller city, town, or in a rural area. You may have to go to a neighboring town or county to find a lawyer willing to help you.

The second reason it's hard to find lawyers to handle legal malpractice claims is that so many of them are unsuccessful. Lawyers don't like to take cases that are losers, or which end up in moral victories but little cash. As we noted earlier, just about 1 percent of legal malpractice lawsuits result in a verdict for the plaintiff, and the awards in these verdicts tend to be low. Even when cases are settled by the lawyer's malpractice insurance carrier, the figures are generally much lower than for other kinds of settlements. And if you are charging the lawyer with intentional misconduct, such as stealing money from a trust account, malpractice insurance coverage doesn't help, since it only covers negligent acts, not intentional ones. Almost every state now has what are called "client security funds" designed to help compensate the clients of a dishonest lawyer, but many of these programs (supported by assessments against lawyers licensed in the state) are underfunded and won't fully repay the clients' losses.

Still, if the evidence of malpractice is pretty clear, and the potential for a substantial jury award is great, you can find lawyers who are willing to handle legal malpractice claims, although you may have to look long and hard to find them. Even if you do, however, you can expect months or even years to pass before a settlement is reached or a verdict is handed down by a court. It takes a strong stomach to stand the stress of any kind of litigation; it takes a stomach of iron to file a legal malpractice suit.

IN DEFENSE OF LAWYERS

Although some of them don't like to acknowledge it, lawyers are people just like everyone else. The only difference is that they have special knowledge of the law. Lawyers aren't magicians or high priests, and they aren't infallible by any means.

In defense of lawyers, some clients have unrealistic expectations about just what a lawyer can do on their behalf. They ask the lawyer to bend the rules, impose unnecessary delays, use harassing tactics, and guarantee a favorable outcome. Some lawyers, unfortunately, fall prey to these demands, either because they don't want to turn down a paying client or because they can rationalize that they are fulfilling their responsibility to represent their clients with zeal.

Good lawyers, however, won't and don't give up their ethics in exchange for a paycheck, and they remember that their obligation to their clients is to represent them zealously "within the bounds of the law." They conform their behavior not just to the rules that govern attorney conduct (and which are mostly minimal standards) but go beyond the minimum to do what is right for the client, the court, and themselves. Lawyers like this are a priceless commodity, and if you are lucky enough to find one, you are very lucky indeed.

WHERE TO FILE ATTORNEY GRIEVANCES

Alabama
Attorney Grievance
General Counsel
Alabama State Bar
Center for Professional Responsibility
1019 South Perry Street
Montgomery, AL 36104
(205) 269-1515

Alaska
Attorney Grievance
Bar Counsel
Alaska Bar Association
P.O. Box 100279
Anchorage, AK 99510
(907) 272-7469

Arizona
Attorney Grievance
Chief Bar Counsel
State Bar of Arizona
363 North First Avenue
Phoenix, AZ 85003-1580
(602) 252-4804, ext. 225

Arkansas
Attorney Grievance
Supreme Court of Arkansas
Committee on Professional Conduct
364 Prospect Bldg.
1501 North University
Little Rock, AR 72207
(501) 664-8658

California
Attorney Grievance
Chief Trial Counsel
Intake/Legal Advice
State Bar of California
333 South Beaudry Avenue
9th Floor
Los Angeles, CA 90017
(213) 580-5000
(800) 843-9053 *(California residents only)*

Colorado
Attorney Grievance
Disciplinary Counsel
Supreme Court of Colorado
600 - 17th Street, Suite 510 South
Dominion Plaza Bldg.
Denver, CO 80202
(303) 893-8121

Connecticut
Attorney Grievance
Statewide Bar Counsel
P.O. Box 6888, Station A
Hartford, CT 06106
(203) 247-6264

Delaware
Attorney Grievance
Disciplinary Counsel
Board on Professional Responsibility of the
Supreme Court of Delaware
831 Tatnall Street
P.O. Box 1808
Wilmington, DE 19899
(302) 571-8703

District of Columbia
Attorney Grievance
Bar Counsel
District of Columbia Bar
515 - 5th Street, NW
Bldg. A, Room 127
Washington, DC 20001
(202) 638-1501

Florida
Attorney Grievance
Staff Counsel
Florida Bar
650 Apalachee Pkwy.
Tallahassee, FL 32399-2300
(800) 874-0005 *(out of state)*
(800) 342-8060 *(Florida residents only)*
(904) 561-5839

Georgia
Attorney Grievance
General Counsel
State Bar of Georgia
50 Hurt Plaza, Suite 800
Atlanta, GA 30303
(404) 527-8720

Hawaii
Attorney Grievance
Chief Disciplinary Counsel
Office of Disciplinary Counsel
Supreme Court of the State of Hawaii
1164 Bishop Street, Suite 600
Honolulu, HI 96813
(808) 521-4591

Idaho
Attorney Grievance
Bar Counsel
Idaho State Bar
P.O. Box 895
204 West State Street
Boise, ID 83701
(208) 342-8958

Illinois
Attorney Grievance
Attorney Registration and Disciplinary
Commission of the Supreme Court of Illinois
203 North Wabash Avenue
Suite 1900
Chicago, IL 60601-2474
(312) 346-0690
(800) 826-8625 *(Illinois residents only)*

Indiana
Attorney Grievance
Executive Secretary
Disciplinary Commission of the
Supreme Court of Indiana
150 W. Market St.
628 I.S.T.A. Building, Room 814
Indianapolis, IN 46204
(317) 232-1807

Iowa
Attorney Grievance
Ethics Administrator
Iowa State Bar Association
1101 Fleming Bldg.
Des Moines, IA 50309
(515) 243-3179

Kansas
Attorney Grievance
Disciplinary Administrator
Supreme Court of Kansas
301 West 10th Street
Kansas Judicial Center
Room 278
Topeka, KS 66612
(913) 296-2486

Kentucky
Attorney Grievance
Bar Counsel
Kentucky Bar Association
West Main at Kentucky River
Frankfort, KY 40601
(502) 564-3795

Louisiana
Attorney Grievance
Executive Counsel
Louisiana State Bar Association
601 St. Charles Avenue
New Orleans, LA 70130
(504) 566-1600

Maine
Attorney Grievance
Bar Counsel
Maine Board of Overseers of the Bar
P.O. Box 1820
Augusta, ME 04332-1820
(207) 623-1121

Maryland
Attorney Grievance
Bar Counsel
Attorney Grievance Commission of Maryland
580 Taylor Avenue
District Court Bldg., Room 404
Annapolis, MD 21401
(301) 974-2791

Massachusetts
Attorney Grievance
Bar Counsel
Massachusetts Board of Bar Overseers
11 Beacon Street
Boston, MA 02108
(617) 720-0700

Michigan
Attorney Grievance
Deputy Grievance Administrator
Michigan Attorney Grievance Commission
243 West Congress
Marquette Bldg., Suite 600
Detroit, MI 48226
(313) 965-6585

Minnesota
Attorney Grievance
Director
Office of Lawyers' Professional Responsibility
520 Lafayette Road, 1st Floor
St. Paul, MN 55155-4196
(612) 296-3952

Mississippi
Attorney Grievance
General Counsel
Mississippi State Bar
P.O. Box 2168
Jackson, MS 39225-2168
(601) 948-4471

Missouri
Attorney Grievance
General Chair
Missouri Bar Administration
P.O. Box 349
Sedalia, MO 65301
(816) 826-7890

Montana
Attorney Grievance
Administrative Secretary
Commission on Practice of the
Supreme Court of Montana
215 North Sanders
Justice Bldg., Room 315
Helena, MT 59620
(406) 444-2608

Nebraska
Attorney Grievance
Counsel for Discipline
Nebraska State Bar Association
P.O. Box 81809
Lincoln, NE 68501
(402) 475-7091

Nevada
Attorney Grievance
Bar Counsel
State Bar of Nevada
500 South 3rd Street, Suite 2
Las Vegas, NV 89101
(702) 382-0502

New Hampshire
Attorney Grievance
Administrator
New Hampshire Supreme Court
Professional Conduct Committee
18 North Main Street, Suite 205
Concord, NH 03301
(603) 224-5828

New Jersey
Attorney Grievance
Director, Office of Attorney Ethics
Supreme Court of New Jersey
Richard J. Hughes Justice Complex
CN-963
Trenton, NJ 08625
(609) 292-8750

New Mexico
Attorney Grievance
Chief Disciplinary Counsel
Disciplinary Board of the Supreme Court
of New Mexico
400 Gold SW, Suite 712
Albuquerque, NM 87102
(505) 842-5781

New York
Attorney Grievance
Chief Counsel
Departmental Disciplinary
Committee for the First Judicial Department
41 Madison Avenue, 39th Floor
New York, NY 10010
(212) 685-1000

North Carolina
Attorney Grievance
Counsel
North Carolina State Bar
208 Fayetteville Street Mall
P.O. Box 25908
Raleigh, NC 27611
(919) 828-4620

North Dakota
Attorney Grievance
Disciplinary Counsel
Disciplinary Board of the Supreme Court
P.O. Box 2297
Bismarck, ND 58502
(701) 224-3348

Ohio
Attorney Grievance
Disciplinary Counsel
Office of Disciplinary Counsel of
the Supreme Court of Ohio
175 South 3rd Street, Suite 280
Columbus, OH 43215
(614) 461-0256

Oklahoma
Attorney Grievance
General Counsel
Oklahoma Bar Center
1901 North Lincoln Blvd.
P.O. Box 53036
Oklahoma City, OK 73152
(405) 524-2365

Oregon
Attorney Grievance
Disciplinary Counsel
Oregon State Bar
P.O. Box 1689
Lake Oswego, OR 97035-0889
(503) 620-0222

Pennsylvania
Attorney Grievance
Chief Disciplinary Counsel
Disciplinary Board of the
Supreme Court of Pennsylvania
2100 North American Building
121 South Broad Street
Philadelphia, PA 19107
(215) 560-6296

Puerto Rico
Attorney Grievance
Presidente
Comision de Etica Profesional
Colegio de Abogados de Puerto Rico
Apartado 1900
San Juan, PR 00903
(809) 721-3358

Rhode Island
Attorney Grievance
Chief Disciplinary Counsel
Disciplinary Board of the Supreme Court of Rhode Island
Supreme Court Bldg.
250 Benefit Street
9th Floor
Providence, RI 02903
(501) 277-3270

South Carolina
Attorney Grievance
Administrative Assistant
Board of Commissioners on
Grievances and Discipline
P.O. Box 11330
Columbia, SC 29211
(803) 734-2038

South Dakota
Attorney Grievance
Investigator
Disciplinary Board of the
State Bar of South Dakota
P.O. Box 476
Tyndall, SD 57066
(605) 589-3333

Tennessee
Attorney Grievance
Chief Disciplinary Counsel
Board of Professional Responsibility
of the Supreme Court of Tennessee
1105 Kermit Drive, Suite 730
Nashville, TN 37217
(615) 361-7500

Texas
Attorney Grievance
General Counsel
State Bar of Texas
P.O. Box 12487
Capitol Station
Austin, TX 78711
(512) 463-1391

Utah
Attorney Grievance
Bar Counsel
Utah State Bar
645 South 200 East
Salt Lake City, UT 84111-3834
(801) 531-9110

Vermont
Attorney Grievance
Professional Conduct Board
16 High Street
P.O. Box 801
Brattleboro, VT 05301
(802) 254-2345

Virginia
Attorney Grievance
Bar Counsel
Virginia State Bar
801 East Main Street, 10th Floor
Richmond, VA 23219
(804) 786-3140

Virgin Islands
Attorney Grievance
Chair
Ethics and Grievance Committee
U.S. Virgin Islands Bar Association
P.O. Box 6520
St. Thomas, VI 00801
(809) 774-6490

Washington
Attorney Grievance
Chief Disciplinary Counsel
Washington State Bar Association
2001 - 6th Avenue
500 Westin Bldg.
Seattle, WA 98121-2599
(206) 448-0307

West Virginia
Attorney Grievance
Bar Counsel
West Virginia State Bar
State Capitol
2006 Canawha Blvd.
Charleston, WV 25301
(304) 348-2456

Wisconsin
Attorney Grievance
Administrator
Board of Attorneys Professional Responsibility
Supreme Court of Wisconsin
Tenney Building
110 East Main Street, Room 410
Madison, WI 53703
(608) 267-7274

Wyoming
Attorney Grievance
Bar Counsel
Wyoming State Bar
P.O. Box 109
Cheyenne, WY 82003-0109
(307) 632-9061

STATE BAR ASSOCIATIONS

Alabama
Alabama State Bar Association
P.O. Box 671
Montgomery, AL 36101
(205) 269-1515

Alaska
Alaska State Bar Association
P.O. Box 100279
Anchorage, AK 99510
(907) 272-7469

Arizona
State Bar of Arizona
363 North First Avenue
Phoenix, AZ 85003
(602) 252-4804

Arkansas
Arkansas State Bar Association
400 West Markham
Little Rock, AR 72201
(501) 375-4605

California
State Bar of California
555 Franklin Street
San Francisco, CA 94102
(415) 561-8200

Colorado
Colorado State Bar Association
1900 Grant Street
Suite 950
Denver, CO 80203
(303) 860-1112

Connecticut
Connecticut State Bar Association
61 Hungerford Street
Hartford, CT 06106
(203) 525-8106

Delaware
Delaware State Bar Association
708 Market Street Mall
P.O. Box 1709
Wilmington, DE 19899
(302) 658-5278

District of Columbia
District of Columbia Bar Association
Suite 600
1707 L Street, NW
Washington, DC 20036
(202) 331-3883

Florida
The Florida State Bar Association
650 Apalachee Parkway
Tallahassee, FL 32399-2300
(904) 561-5600

Georgia
State Bar of Georgia
800 The Hurt Building
50 Hurt Plaza
Atlanta, GA 30303
(404) 527-8700

Hawaii
Hawaii State Bar Association
P.O. Box 26
Honolulu, HI 96810
(808) 537-1868

Idaho
Idaho State Bar Association
P.O. Box 895
Boise, ID 83701
(208) 342-8958

Illinois
Illinois State Bar Association
424 South Second Street
Springfield, IL 62701
(217) 525-1760

Indiana
Indiana State Bar Association
230 East Ohio
Indianapolis, IN 46204
(317) 639-5465

Iowa
Iowa State Bar Association
1101 Fleming Bldg.
Des Moines, IA 50309
(515) 243-3179

Kansas
Kansas State Bar Association
1200 Harrison
P.O. Box 1037
Topeka, KS 66601-1037
(913) 234-5696

Kentucky
Kentucky State Bar Association
West Main at Kentucky River
Frankfort, KY 40601
(502) 564-3795

Louisiana
Louisiana State Bar Association
601 St. Charles Avenue
4th Floor
New Orleans, LA 70130
(504) 523-1414

Maine
Maine State Bar Association
124 State Street
P.O. Box 788
Augusta, ME 04332
(207) 622-7523

Maryland
Maryland State Bar Association
520 West Sayette Street
Baltimore, MD 21201
(301) 685-7878

Massachusetts
Massachusetts State Bar Association
20 West Street
Boston, MA 02111
(617) 542-9103

Michigan
State Bar of Michigan
306 Townsend Street
Lansing, MI 48933
(517) 372-9030

Minnesota
Minnesota State Bar Association
430 Marquette Avenue
Suite 403
Minneapolis, MN 55401
(612) 333-1183

Mississippi
Mississippi State Bar Association
643 North State Street
P.O. Box 2168
Jackson, MS 39225
(601) 948-4471

Missouri
The Missouri Bar Association
P.O. Box 119
Jefferson City, MO 65102
(314) 635-4128

Montana
State Bar of Montana
P.O. Box 577
Helena, MT 59624
(406) 442-7660

Nebraska
Nebraska State Bar Association
635 South 14th Street
Lincoln, NE 68508
(402) 475-7091

Nevada
Nevada State Bar Association
201 Las Vegas Blvd., South
Las Vegas, NV 84101
(702) 382-2200

New Hampshire
New Hampshire State Bar Association
112 Pleasant Street
Concord, NH 03301
(603) 224-6942

New Jersey
New Jersey State Bar Association
1 Constitution Square
New Brunswick, NJ 08901-1500
(201) 249-5000

New Mexico
State Bar of New Mexico
P.O. Box 25883
Albuquerque, NM 87125
(505) 842-6132

New York
New York State Bar Association
One Elk Street
Albany, NY 12207
(518) 463-3200

North Carolina
North Carolina State Bar Association
P.O. Box 25908
Raleigh, NC 27611
(919) 828-4620
North Dakota
State Bar Association of North Dakota
P.O. Box 2136
Bismarck, ND 58502
(701) 225-1404

Ohio
Ohio State Bar Association
1700 Lakeshore Drive
Columbus, OH 43216-0562
(614) 487-2025

Oklahoma
Oklahoma State Bar Association
P.O. Box 53036
Oklahoma City, OK 73152
(405) 524-2365

Oregon
Oregon State Bar Association
5200 SW Meadows Road
Lake Oswego, OR 97035
(503) 620-0222

Pennsylvania
Pennsylvania State Bar Association
100 South Street, P.O. Box 186
Harrisburg, PA 17108
(717) 238-6715

Rhode Island
Rhode Island State Bar Association
115 Cedar Street
Providence, RI 02903
(401) 421-5740

South Carolina
South Carolina State Bar Association
950 Taylor Street
Columbia, SC 29201
(803) 799-6653

South Dakota
State Bar of South Dakota
222 East Capitol
Pierre, SD 57501
(605) 224-7554

Tennessee
Tennessee State Bar Association
3622 West End Avenue
Nashville, TN 37205
(615) 383-7421

Texas
State Bar of Texas
P.O. Box 12487
Capital Station
Austin, TX 78711
(512) 463-1463

Utah
Utah State Bar Association
645 South 200 East
Salt Lake City, UT 84111
(801) 531-9077

Vermont
Vermont State Bar Association
P.O. Box 100
Montpelier, VT 05601
(802) 223-2020

Virginia
Virginia State Bar Association
801 East Main Street, Suite 1000
Richmond, VA 23219-2900
(804) 786-2061

Washington
Washington State Bar Association
2001 - 6th Avenue
500 Westin Building
Seattle, WA 98121
(206) 448-0441

West Virginia
West Virginia State Bar Association
State Capital Complex
Charleston, WV 25305
(304) 346-8414

Wisconsin
State Bar of Wisconsin
P.O. Box 7158
Madison, WI 53707
(608) 257-3838

Wyoming
Wyoming State Bar Association
P.O. Box 109
Cheyenne, WY 82003
(307) 632-9061

A

Abortion rights, 12-13, 260-61
Abuse, of the elderly, 41
Accidental death and dismemberment policies, 234
Adjustable rate mortgage, 75-76
Administrative law judge (ALJ), 140
Adoption, 25-27
  opening of records, 27
Adverse possession, 92
After market parts, 108
Age Discrimination in Employment Act, 126
Agents, insurance, 231-34
Aging, *See* Elderly
AIDs victims, and early collection of life insurance benefits, 222
Airbags, 109
Alcohol, driving under influence of, 114-15
Alcohol test for job applicant, 129
Alimony, 29, 30
Alternative dispute resolution, 364
Alzheimer's Disease, 37-38
American Arbitration Association (AAA), 104, 216, 366
American Automobile Association (AAA), 106
American Hospital Association Patient's Bill for Rights, 253
American judicial system. *See* Court system
American Stock Exchange, 217
Americans with Disabilities Act (ADA), 3, 128, 129, 137
Annual percentage yield (APY), 211
Answer, 369
Antenuptial agreements, 21-23
Anti-theft device, 109
Appeal, 373
Arbitration, 365-66
  in brokerage agreements, 216, 366
  for fee dispute, 414
Architectural drawings, 88
Arms, right to bear, 9-11

Artificial insemination, 261-62
Assault and battery, 387-88
Assembly, right of, 9
Asset management accounts, 205
Assignment, of lease, 59-60
Assisted living facility, 40
Attorney General, state offices of, 171-78
Attorney grievances, filing, 420-37
Attorney-in-fact, 38
Attractive nuisance doctrine, 83
Audit, income tax, 336-40
AutoCAP, 104
Automatic teller machines, 181, 209-11
Automobile. *See* Cars
Automobile insurance, 107
  collision and comprehensive, 108-9
  holding down insurance costs, 109-10
  no-fault insurance, 107-8
AUTOSOLVE, 104

B

Bail, 392
Bail bond, 392-93
Bail bondsman, 393
Bail hearing, 393
Bailment provision, 99
Bait and switch, 97
Bank credit cards, 181
Banking your money, 199-202
Bankruptcy, 195-98
  and corporate ownership, 118
  and sole proprietorship, 118
Bar-sponsored referral service, 407
Beneficiary, in life insurance, 223
Best, A. M., 240
Bill of Rights, 1-2, 388
Binder, 72
Blank work order, 107
Body, donation of, to medical school, 353-54
Bona fide occupational qualification or (BFOQ), 127
Bond mutual fund, 219

E

H

I

T

Taft-Hartley Act, 132-33
Tax Compliance Measurement Audit, 339
Taxes, 328. *See also* Income taxes
estate, 343, 346
excise, 342-43
property, 17, 83-87, 91
state inheritance, 343
Taxpayer's Bill of Rights, 328-29, 337
Tax Reform Act (1986), 288
Telemarketing sales, 158-61
Tenants. *See also* Landlord-tenant relationship
finding good, 52-54
tips in being smart, 57-59
Tenants rights organizations, 51
Term life insurance, 221
Testamentary trusts, 354
Testator, 348
Third Amendment, 12
Thirteenth Amendment, 2
Title insurance, 73-74, 78-79
Torts, 366-68
Totten trust, 359
Traffic tickets, 112-14
Travel, right to, 15-16
Travelers' check, 208
True bill of indictment, 393
Trust
irrevocable, 305, 360
life insurance, 359
living, 359-62
Medicaid qualifying, 305
revocable, 305, 360
testamentary, 354
Totten, 359
Truth-in-Lending Act, 185-87
Truth-in-Lending Statement, 77
Truth in Savings Act, 211-12
TRW, 186

U

Umbrella insurance policy, 85
Uncontested divorce, 28

Unemployment compensation, 125, 138-41
Uniform Limited Partnership Act, 120
Uniform Reciprocal Enforcement of Support Act, 32
Unions, 132-34
U.S. Savings bonds, 219

V

Variance, 81
Vehicle Identification Number, 98
Vesting, of pension benefits, 288-89
Veterans' benefits, 325
Veterans loan, guarantee, 77
Victim's Bill of Rights, 401
Victim impactment statements, 401
Victim's rights, 400-3
VOCAL (Victims of Child Abuse Laws), 34

W

Wage earner's plan, 196-97
Wage garnishment, 130-31
Walk-away lease, 103
Warranties
car, 101-2
contractors, 89
Implied
of habitability, 58-59
of merchantability, 100, 164
Warrants, 389-90
Will, 346-47
changing, 355
contesting, 356
dying without, 356-57
living trust, 359
naming guardian in, 352-53
naming executor for, 350-51
naming heirs in, 351-52
probating, 357-59
publishing, 349
storage of, 349-50
and testamentary trusts, 354